SYMBOLIZATION

SYMBOLIZATION
A Revised Psychoanalytic General Model of Mind

Anna Aragno, Ph.D.

IPBOOKS.net
International Psychoanalytic Books

International Psychoanalytic Books (IPBooks),
New York • http://www.IPBooks.net

ISBN: 978-0-9965481-8-2

1. Psychoanalysis. 2. Symbolism (Psychology).
3. Mind and body; Mind-Body Relations.

Library of Congress Control Number: 2015956750

Contents

Foreword to the New Edition

This book was written twenty-six years ago, originating in ideas proposed in my doctoral dissertation. I entered the field in the eighties, mid-stream in life, late, by most standards, from the arts, humanities, and languages, eager to learn, with a curious, already formed critical intellect and a passion for psychoanalysis. At the time debates were still simmering over the problems of metapsychology and whether it ought to be preserved and amended or killed outright. Early on in my training I discovered that my primary interests were not clinical but metatheoretical. I was instinctually drawn to the philosophy of science and language, neurobiology, sociobiology, and to question our theory of mind in relation to our methodology.

The extraordinary potential of our method and Freud's first *general* theory of mind, as heralded in the Dream book, (1900), I found, was obfuscated by acrimonious arguments between those *for* developing the natural science claims of Freudian metapsychology (1915) and those for debunking it altogether, a battle that ripped apart the core backbone and scientific aspirations of the Freudian framework. Subsequently the field split up into many 'schools' each under the banner of a small piece of the large discipline they inherited, splintering the whole. Where radical revision and updating was called for the field divided instead and so has remained: a community sidetracked, much of its prime data usurped and sub-divided between neuroscience and cognitive studies, a field stuck in a paradigm crisis.

Freudian metapsychology requires that our phenomena be accounted for along various dimensions—topographical, dynamic, economic, structural, and adaptive. But without the scaffolding of a central metatheory for the transformative action of its therapy according with principles underlying its general theory of mind, Freud's aspirations for a scientific metapsychology fell by the wayside, a term so rarely used nowadays as to have been forgotten. Integrating a broad interdisciplinary base of studies led me over and over again back to what Freud *specifically* pointed to in order to advance the scientific base of the field; "**What characterizes psycho-analysis as a science is not the material which it handles but the technique with which it works.** What it . . . achieves is nothing other than the uncovering of what is unconscious in mental life." (Freud, 1917, 389) The key question then to pose was: *how does it work*? Since its method is a "dialogue" (a "conversation" Freud called it) the place to look, in my opinion, was a developmental approach to the study of semiosis, language, and semantic reference in dialogues, with an eye to understanding the basic principles underlying *all* sign and symbol systems.

Freud's decoding of the language of the deep Ucs as a primary process form of cognition continues to be the entry point for the study of the development and evolution of the human mind while the implicit plasticity and epigenetic composition of Freud's topographical model continues to provide important inroads. A more fleshed out bio-semiotic developmental model of mind built on the skeletal outline of Freud's tripartite topography (Aragno,1997/2016), composed of micro-genetic steps towards symbolization in various semiotic systems, undergirds the evolution of mind, ontogenetic development, and the dialogical progressions in phases of psychoanalytic therapy that lead to the translation of the unconscious into conscious awareness.

Psychoanalytic phenomena are pluralistic, multi-perspectival, each dimension contributing its own facet of inquiry, revealing its own developmental line, according to its own operative principles. *Meta*-theoretical principles, however, are articulated at the highest levels of abstraction. I am not the first to consider semiosis as the natural soil of psychoanalysis. This book is a study of those functional progressions in semiotic forms as viewed from within the psychoanalytic process and method. As such it is an updated revision and expansion of Freud's topographical model of mind. Despite the complexity of different semiotic forms and particularly their multi-layered organization and concomitant interplay of usage, this is a simple model to understand, and could be expressed mathematically, by those so inclined.

Ultimately, however, a model is tested by its results: I believe I have demonstrated the value and usefulness of this model in presenting new theoretical insights in many papers on subjects as diverse as empathy and art. Most importantly its generativity lead me to a whole new work inspired by the as yet poorly charted terrain of supervision, 'Forms of Knowledge' a psychoanalytic study of human communication, where semiotic principles and unconscious processes are extended into triadic semantic-fields and group situations.

"Where Id was, there Ego shall be" refers to the effects of a *dialogue* in which interpretive activities lead to the 'working-through' of many personal experiences, past, present, and contextual, generating 'insight' along many trajectories. This implies that this dialogue's semantic and referential perspectives touch on and linguistically engage a multitude of interrelated mental functions generating neurobiological shifts that, among many other things, impact on a reorganization of the nervous system. And all of this depends on symbolization. Language, our most expedient and efficient sign system, is our medium and instrument. It stands to reason, then, that practicing psychoanalysis without a profound understanding of the principles underlying the nuances and changing forms in semiotic processes would be like a surgeon holding a scalpel with little knowledge of anatomy.

This work is a first step in attempting to revive Freudian metapsychology by moving above clinical content to the operative processes of our methodology. As such it was written timidly by a novice and remains tentative and provisional. But its goals were clear from the start: to free us from the jargon of physicalist metaphor and analogy and move psychoanalysis into the common scientific vocabulary of general knowledge, where our field and its findings rightly belong.

I am deeply grateful to Arnold D. Richards, editor-in-chief of International Psychoanalytic Books (IPBooks), for undertaking the republication of my two revisionary volumes and heartened by his belief in these works.

—Anna Aragno
August 3, 2015

Preface

We are all children of our age, in one way or another, destined by the social climate and milieu we happened to stumble upon, to be molded by the stigma of our time, distinguished by its particular emphasis and ethos. Our thoughts and theories, likewise, emerge as the outcome of this confluence of impressions and experience, in both form and stylistic presentation, and in content. Whereas it is not difficult to recognize in oneself the impact of family and culture, nor is it a mystery to us why our lives are so greatly affected by the political and economic environment we come to, yet with regard to our thinking, our opinions and positions, our moral moves and choices, we are often loathe to recognize how these, too, are creations of compromise, indelibly marked by the tenor of the times in which they were developed.

I say this partly in defense of Freud's conceptual kingdom, with its wealth of metaphoric depiction, its vast topography of uncharted terrain, its fluid, poetic, literary vision, eloquent prose and elegant scientism, this monumental foundation. I say it partly to introduce myself in recognition of the fact that what I will expound in the body of this work is of necessity a reflection of who I am, my personality, unique history, and individual heritage, and my aspiration to further the cause and understanding of psychoanalysis.

It is, I believe, a truism that the subjective world of the theorist will inevitably come to bear on his or her conceptualizations and views about human nature and the particular place of humans in nature, bringing to these ideas hues that are the unique expression of the theorist's personal existence. In psychoanalysis, we construct our paradigms and theories according to the scientific molds that make most sense to us as explanatory models with which to organize, name, and explain phenomena which are primarily invisible, frequently untestable, and, for the most part, hitherto unformulated in linguistic terms.

Whether we call this process of "simplification of the phe-nomena" a "fairy tale," as Sir William Napier Shaw did in his 1932 treatise on meteorology, or, together with Frank Kermode (1966), urge ourselves to remember that our theories should be viewed as fictions, as an "organized set of story lines, rather than a picture of reality" (cited in Schafer [1983, p. 283]), or whether we believe our constructs to be valid, worthy formula-tions for the data of our observation, ultimately we must own that these are constructs, and only constructs.

We are living in an era of great transition in which it has become fashionable to demythologize those leaders, thinkers, and ideas that have hitherto been regarded as great. Within this general deconstructivist atmosphere it has been reassuring to observe that psychoanalysis has been able to withstand constant assaults and transmutations of every kind, without losing its es-sential form or power. Freud's brilliant, revolutionary, and accu-rate observations have left us a method of treatment, the foundations of a science of mind, and a cultural legacy of such magnitude and depth as to have colored the entire ethos of twentieth century thought.

During my psychoanalytic education and training, I learned from many journal articles and books that what was needed was a new theory, a new metapsychology. The prerequisite of such a new theory was that it be couched in other than energic, spatial, or otherwise reified terms, concepts borrowed from an epistemology of matter embodied in the principles of Newton-ian physics. Moreover, what was essential for psychoanalysis, if it was to finally overthrow the great biological opposition waged against its legitimacy, was that the principles of its clinical meth-odology be adequately represented and substantiated by its the-oretical foundations. Ultimately and ideally, I learned, these should not only coincide conceptually and epistemologically, but should provide viable hypotheses for testability. Only in such a way could psychoanalysis not only survive but also win its place as a true science within the framework of universal knowledge.

Virulent attacks on Freud's "hydraulic," "archaeological," "energic," and "topographical" models have been published in the literature and even in the media ad nauseum, yet few authors have offered anything better, and fewer still have worked to build upon and reexplain the Freudian edifice. Psychoanalysis has been bent like plasticine, into many shapes by its divergent schools and narrowed to fit the differing prisms through which it is perceived—divergence being a specialty of the post-Freudian era. Everyone has their own version of psychoanalysis. Yet, like the piece of plasticine whose shape is molded by the hand that holds it, its essential constitution survives intact. Pliable and resilient, its principles remain overarching and constant.

This is because psychoanalysis is both a science and an art, a method and a theory, a biological and hermeneutic model of mind. It is a relational as well as an individual psychology, subsuming principles of ethics and aesthetics, phylogenesis and ontogenesis, semiotics and symbolization forged in the fusion of form and content inhering in all expressions of the human mind as these manifest in its traditional methodology, wherein observation and practice are one. Moreover, ideological and philosophical concerns also make their appearance for the purpose of personal reevaluation in the ongoing quest for integrity and autonomy, obtained through an adherence to the spirit of inquiry as Mitchell (1981) commented, which separates psychoanalysis from whatever social context it finds itself in, enabling it to preserve its apolitical and asocial nature.

Indeed, in the principle of inquiry, with its implicit reflective requirement, as in the "free" associations of the patient and corrolary neutrality of the analyst's stance, lie the restructuring potentials of the psychoanalytic method. These become instrumental in linking the intrapsychic with the interpersonal, the presymbolic with the fully symbolized, the reenacted with the remembered, and the hidden with the "telling," as they provide a bridge between the past and the present, the analysis and the individual's adaptation to society. All are rooted in the reality of the analyst's presence and the regularity of time and fee, yet are delivered from the impact of judgments or the influence of conventions, suspended privately within a privileged psychoanalytic discourse and space. And here the "reflective" prerequisite, the central operative tenet of its clinical method, joins diverse cultural domains as exploration is always with respect to the subjective, always unbiased vis-à-vis the individual, his unique history, unique experience, environment and culture.

Inasmuch as I intend to "build upon" rather than demolish, to transpose rather than decompose the bedrock of our theory, and attempt to unify its clinical and metapsychological components, I will be reviewing in contemporary terms much that Freud perceived and conceived of, if only in rudimentary or tentative form. What we now need are new definitions, new frames of reference, and new formulations. Fundamentally, we need a new paradigm within which to rework and elaborate upon the foundations Freud left us, in order to refine and update these, bolstering them with contemporary research and scholarship from the diverse disciplines of infant and child development, the neurosciences, sociobiology, semiotics and linguistics, cognitive psychology, as well as social psychology, the arts, anthropology, literary and narrative theories. In other words, I believe that what is called for is a synthesis.

Most pressingly, we need to move from a paradigm of substance to one of pattern, where the interrelationships of form and content and the configurations of these in transformations of subjective experience are unified in psychological terms and systematized into developmental models which encompass body and mind, and move conceptually from the biological to the psychological.

There has long been a call for a unified theory, a contemporary model, which, in recasting metapsychology from new fundamentals, can incorporate and accommodate what all the disparate, partial theories now account for—but so far, no theory has emerged that is sufficiently encompassing. This work is an attempt to fill that void. And if this seems too ambitious a quest, certainly it strives to move in the right direction and point the way.

The linearity and potential simplicity of such a theory was intriguing to me, more so since the notion of mind as part of nature inevitably poses the challenge of discovering what can be discerned about its insubstantial processes and how these can be identified, organized, and utilized in the way physics adopts supraordinate principles for discussing the functioning of matter. So far, a felicitous marriage between the neurosciences and psychoanalysis, between the functioning of brain and its expression in mind, has offered but dim prospects. In practice, the requirements for interdisciplinarity and the correlation of complex data from diverse but interrelated fields, presents a quite formidable challenge and obstacle to the scholar and would-be theorist.

In order to manipulate information and achieve theoretical simplicity, physics pushes its principles to paradigmatic ideals where, at these high realms of abstraction, the few sparse concepts derived can be made to articulate an otherwise astonishing array of mutually limiting elements. For the purpose of theorizing, I believe there is a valuable lesson to be learned from this approach. In a field in which the proliferation of divergent models has virtually obliterated the notion of a singularly psychoanalytic theory of mind, the tendency has been to move further away from theoretical abstraction and become ever more mired in the details of content. Yet theories are built not on content but out of the distillation of principles derived from the interrelationship of form and content.

Broadly speaking, changes and transformations occurring in the natural world are understood by physics in terms of the dynamic quantities, energy, and momentum, and the combinations and arrangements, the mechanical and thermal properties of matter, of which the basic unit is the atom. In trying to understand the universe, physicists study the intricate interplay of interdependent elementary particles in correspondence with the principles of mass, space, and time (Ridley, 1976).

But the universe of mind is insubstantial. In fact, mind is so hard to grasp or define because it is not a thing at all, but a fluid process. And in this unique inner world of meanings, the only manifestation of change or transformation to which we can refer is revealed in the shifting modes and means through which a person finds expression. These, as psychoanalysis has shown, in both content and form, reflect inner organizations of experience which will be expressive of the particular nature of a singular internal world.

If the atom is the smallest particle of an element, the smallest particle of mind is a crystallized unit of subjective experience:

mind transforms experience, it patterns and shapes feelings out of which are formed concepts, ideas, and the representational vehicles to carry them. We cannot see or measure sentience, nor can we quantify meaning, yet these are the constituent elements of the psyche.

The problem posed by the challenge of a new metapsychology rested on how to find a purely psychological principle of psychic transformation, analogous to the energic and topographic transformational metaphors utilized by Freud. On the assumption that there is some ancient kinship between human form and the elements of the universe, the question to be asked appeared to be: What is the nature of psychic transformation? Or, as Freud put it: What is the nature of the psychical?

Today, one hundred years since Freud brought us the idea of a psyche and laid down the theoretical foundations of psychoanalysis, a science of mind and method of interpretation, we have not, thus far, progressed toward finding an adequate answer. Broad frameworks and paradigmatic models, as Kuhn (1962) demonstrated, influence the entire realm of scientific enterprise, and positivism permeated the very fabric of scientific thought; hence, Freud's early substantive models. Yet, while we may be tolerant of Freud's metaphoric reifications formulated a century ago, which were able to give shape to his observations and enabled him to grasp the transformational nature of mental phenomena, though he clearly cautioned that this was merely "temporary scaffolding," we need not be so lenient with ourselves today in noting that we have moved no further. While adhering too closely to the founder, or exerting independence via dissent, we have not heeded his request, that we find more suitable formulas for the phenomena at hand, that we reformulate and revise and move ahead. The field has fallen into a state of theoretical crisis, and nothing short of a paradigm revolution can revive it.

We are whirling toward the end of a century of rapid change and unprecedented, peripatetic evolution, one in which new ideas, new disciplines, technologies, and paradigms have been born in rapid succession. This accelerated progress has pushed forward the frontiers of science and attuned our sensibilities to new and once unthinkable outer limits. I believe that for psychoanalysis this paradigmatic shift opens the way for and provides the means by which a reevaluation and recontextualization of our theory can take place.

Departing radically from the physicalist epistemology and reified analogical terminology in which Freudian metapsychology is cast, and moving beyond this formulation of "the nature of the psychical" in favor of a view of mind as transformative planes of protosymbolic and symbolic organization, I propose an alternative comprehensive psychoanalytic model of mind providing a new and different theoretical framework for normality, pathology, and our notion of therapeutic efficacy or cure. Central to this new developmental–structuralist model is the process of symbolization as the key to the conscious and unconscious dimensions of all experience and its corresponding relation to the primary and secondary processes.

Correlated with other developmental lines and with substantial interdisciplinary data support, an unfolding developmental continuum crystallizing into hierarchic organization is proposed as an alternative paradigm for a general theory of mind, encompassing extensive and radical revisions for most major facets of metapsychology.

Reconceptualizing mind as meaning, this model operationalizes the modes and ways of expressing meanings in terms of representational stages or steps in the microgenesis of referencing, highlighting the formidable impact of this process on the nature of subjective experience. Such a model provides psychoanalysis with a viable theoretical place for the biological nature of affects and their psychological elaboration as emotions, accounting for the central role and function of language in the therapeutic situation, and unifying its thus far disparate conceptualizations of clinical and theoretical models.

The thoughts that are elaborated in what follows are the outcome of questions I began asking roughly ten years ago, when, due to unforeseen circumstances that were to alter my life's course, I changed course and embarked on what has become a rich internal adventure.

Retrospectively, I can now see I was profoundly privileged to have encountered such questions at a relatively late date, in part due to knowledge accrued in living and added discipline and maturity, but primarily because I already had a vision and a goal toward which I strove with dedication and passion. I had been able to devise a course of study tailored to Freud's recommendations for "a scheme of training for analysts" in his "Post-Script to the Question of Lay-Analysis" (1927) in addition to following traditional training routes, and had been fortunate enough to encounter universities which supported my aim. Consider that an appropriate and complete university program for future analysts is not yet in existence in any institution. The culmination of this course of study was my doctoral dissertation in 1992, from which this book is derived.

This work builds on that of many great thinkers whose scholarship and vision I am indebted to. I am appreciative of the encouragement I received early on from teachers, supervisors, and mentors, in particular from Drs. Robert Sapolsky, Arnold Wilson, Jerome Bruner, Alexander Marshack, Don Shapiro, George Frank, and many other colleagues and friends, all of whom helped me along the way with support, challenges, and demands. In particular, my thanks go to two wonderful, patient, and remarkably swift typists, Sam Chapin and Peg McDonagh, who put all of this on paper, and to my patients from whom I have learned so much. I am grateful to my daughters and those close to me whose unswerving support enabled me to pursue this work, and deeply appreciative of my companion's input, patience, and encouragement, all of which have been invaluable to me. And finally, my gratitude goes to Dr. Margaret Emery, eminent editor-in-chief of International Universities Press, who showed faith in my ideas.

It is undoubtedly true that separation has been the dominant theme in my life, and in what follows I hope to illustrate the central role that separation plays in the development and transformation of psychical experience. Differentiation, separation, and loss are the outward manifestations of an inner transformation. They sow the seeds which germinate representation and, given adequate soil and temperate climate, will blossom and slowly flower into the symbol, fully formed, born, as it were, at the hub of these three. In this sense, all acts of referencing inherently dislodge old unities by the very process which brings

them about; to take a symbolic vehicle as representing or referring to something else, is to hold it within and imbue it with
meaning. Mind comes into being out of the void left by absence,
wherein the experiential world and object were one, fused
within the orbit of an undifferentiated, intersubjective field.
And so, as the old, tangible, sensory ties must be severed, to take
their place there crystallizes an inner representational form, the
symbol. What is lost to the senses, becomes mind. The microgenetic steps in the development of symbolization are therefore the
evolutionary history of mind—phylogenetically and ontogenetically, recapitulated in every individual. I am, therefore, indebted
to my losses as much as to my gains.

1.

Psychoanalysis Observed

> The stage of classical physics where an isolated piece of matter, the mass point, is the representative of a natural phenomenon has been passed. With it the conventional type of energy transmission, or causality, as the basic relation linking points in space, time or events, has been greatly changed.
>
> Meaning rules human action, whereas cause determines physical processes. The rules of meaning rather than the laws of nature explain human behavior.
> [Ernest Hutten, 1981, cited in Pines, 1981, pp. 276–277]

STATE OF THE ART

My goals in this work are threefold: to reconceptualize the notion of the convertibility of instinctual energy, taken to be the bedrock of metapsychology; to contextualize meaning as an operative activity; and, in reconstructing a metatheory from new fundamentals, to bring about a conceptual transformation of how we view the nature of mind.

On the first rests responsibility for the entire "mind as machine" analogue; within the second lies a pathway toward synthesizing the interpretive claim of psychoanalysis with an organismic noninstinctual theory of meaning. My goal, in short, is to provide psychoanalysis with a revised general model of mind which has maximum internal coherence and the closest

1

possible fit to nature. To this end I have formulated a conceptual framework for the singularly mental process of symbolization, or the abstractive process, in terms of stages in its development. Such a model serves the purpose of organizing various strata of experience and characteristic modes of expression as these manifest themselves preverbally, linguistically, as well as nonlinguistically, and come under scrutiny in the psychoanalytic situation. In short, such a model begins to trace the ontogenesis of referencing and the mediating function of signs and language on psychic reality.

Successful integration of these principles might satisfy some of the critics of psychoanalysis and begin to unify its clinical and metapsychological aspects. In addition to necessitating a reevaluation of prior Freudian fact, this requires radical rebuilding from the foundations of the Freudian edifice—a dramatic shift in scientific vision, a paradigm revolution. This far-reaching ambition is fueled by a recognition that the field has been in a long-standing state of crisis which, despite the few publications each year that propose partial revisions, appears ever farther from satisfactory resolution.

In this, I am heartened by Freud's own spunky admonishment in the case of his overly virtuous Swiss colleague, Protestant minister Oskar Pfister (cited in Reiff [1966, p. 107]): "Your analysis suffers from the hereditary weakness of virtue," he writes, "It is the work of an over-decent man who feels himself obliged to be discreet. Discretion is thus incompatible with a good presentation of psychoanalysis. One has to become a bad fellow, transcend the rules, sacrifice oneself, betray. . . . Without some such criminality, there is no real achievement." Words echoed and urged upon us by the erudite and irate Reiff (1966) as he inveighs against today's psychoanalysts: "The meetings of psychoanalytic societies produce boredom; it is mainly psychoanalytic institutes that train these bores . . . (p. 103). A few pages earlier Reiff noted that "Freud's successors know less and less because their knowledge, uninspired by that passion to find faith with which it must merge in order to fulfill its potential of power is not taking them anywhere except where Freud has already been" (p. 98). These "bores," according to Reiff, as he laments the decaying rut of contemporary psychoanalytic thinking, lack the "creative egoism" or "criminality" imperative for our "great and necessary profession." "Orthodoxy, in the pejorative sense, kills a living theory. Old verities become new variables, jargon makes a mystery of the obvious" (Reiff, 1966, pp. 100–101).

Above all, Reiff is adamant on the issue of the unsuitability of the medical degree, with "its long doses of rote learning," which according to him is, "precisely the wrong preparation for psychoanalysis. Psychoanalysts are not medical doctors . . . the absorption of psychoanalysis under the medical rubric has opened the door that Freud once closed so decisively: to a resurgence of physiological and materialistic models—dead theory." Further, he warns, "materialistic medicine has returned to charm the Freudians in a new disguise, parading now as the ambition to quantify and measure" (p. 101). Neither would he have psychoanalysis fall into the hands of educational psychology, second only, according to Reiff, to social work, "intellectually the shoddiest field in the academic world" (p. 97).

To the bold, the mischievous, the creative egoist, the scoundrel psychoanalyst then, is left the challenge of "criminality"—the chance to transcend rules, sacrifice oneself, betray and uphold Freud's doctrines of uncertainty and revision, to embrace his own philosophy of bleak realism, since "It is not required of a realist to be hopeful or hopeless, but only truthful" (Reiff, 1966, p. 34). Freud's therapy may inspire us to tolerate our doubts but his legacy challenges us to revision, holding firmly to our knowledge, now fueled by "a passion" that finds faith in the lesson of Freud's own conviction, as he affirmed, "We possess the truth, I am sure of it" (quoted in Reiff [1966, p. 83]).

Reiff avows the profession's failure to maintain an intellectual level commensurate to its canon despite the optimal circumstances afforded it, and he is not alone; "Psychoanalysis has . . . an authoritative body of writing administered by sanctioned cadres of teachers which provide continuity and justification for lesser research which, were it not part of a greater picture, might remain insignificant" (p.102). But Reiff complains that even in their research:

[A]nalysts have developed a false empiricism, in which the highest intellectual achievement is often nothing more than yet another report to their colleagues of a case history complete with pious cross-references in the footnotes to show they remember the great, who are dead, and the mediocre, who are alive. . . . The movement is softened, its mind lulled by the featherbeds of dead data collected in the ritual act of having been published. While worrying too much about whether they are scientists in any sense of the word acceptable to the most bigoted opponents, the psychoanalysts have become at worst technicians of therapy and at best erudites writing up data without any sense of responsibility for the more general import [1966, p. 103].

Indeed, the predominant focus on content or politicized reality issues, such as gender issues, feminist issues, incest issues, ethnic issues—current trends at conferences and meetings—detracts from the greater challenge of cross-disciplinary integration and the updating of a psychoanalytic metatheory with greater refinement and precision in its application to practice. Paradoxically, the more psychoanalysis has infiltrated the sociocultural infrastructure of the twentieth century, the more it is threatening to become a historical phenomenon, a product of post-Victorian middle Europe. And the more it is preserved as a relic, the less is it equipped to move into the twenty-first century.

Reiff's words are worth noting; we should heed the great sociologist, a man of culture who can place his irate critique within the broader framework of historical knowledge, as culture, thus described, is conceptualized as "another name for a design of motives directing the self outward, toward the communal purpose in which alone the self can be realized and satisfied" (Reiff, 1966, p. 4). He will have understood what others have not, that Freud's psychoanalysis sought to encompass a theory of culture, within which irreducible and inseparable, the complex implications of the evolution of the individual and evolution of the race are recursively shaped and reshaped.

Freud's view of human nature, in line with that of Hobbes and Darwin, has been interpreted to depict the individual as being endowed with a primary hostility toward his fellow man, massing socially in the name of survival, and willing only under coercive circumstance to group together for the sake of self-protection. On closer reading (as with the object-relational debate), one finds his writings replete with acknowledgments and implicit inclusion of the fundamental dialectic inherent in the person, familially and socially embedded. Freud's impeccable consistency on the issue of instinctual renunciation and the individual's encumbent compromise solutions, originating from and rooted in the group setting, reflect a theoretical vision far broader than the individual mind, emphasized in socially aware statements such as this: "One must bind one's own life to that of others so closely and be able to identify oneself with others so intimately that the brevity of one's own life can be overcome; and one must not fulfil the demands of one's own needs illegitimately, but must leave them unfulfilled, because only the continuance of so many unfulfilled demands can develop the power to change the order of society" (Freud, 1905a, p. 110). Such statements are therefore incongruent, perplexing even, when referred to in the words of an otherwise erudite and lucid critic, J. A. C. Brown (1961): "Freud believed in the person as a social atom requiring community only as a means to the satisfaction of his needs . . ." (p. 14). This is not quite accurate, in my opinion: rather, Freud sought a universal evolutionary explanation for the ubiquity of conflict and culture, in an attempt to identify how the human mind could make ideas out of passions. With the notion of culture as constraint, he sought a genetic model for how the mind shapes passions into actions and molds personality through compromise.

The counterpart to cultural narcissism, humanism, as it evolved out of the eighteenth and nineteenth centuries, from Spinoza, Rousseau, and Kant, to Goethe and Marx, may be seen more recently expressed in broad movements striving for global unity and numerous secular bonding coalitions. Out of humanism had come the idea of unification, that mankind is one, each individual carrying within himself "all of humanity" (Fromm, 1964, p. 83). With this new ideology, came a method of responsibility requiring objectivity and realism, one humbled before the facts and their implications: "it is not accidental that most of the outstanding natural scientists of our day are humanists," writes Fromm (1964, p. 84). With regard to the contemporary status of the profession, however, he was none too pleased: "Most professionals have remained technicians and have not acquired a scientific attitude" (p. 84). Not without reason is the wrathful Reiff found likening such analysts to bureaucrats, who "sit behind impersonality and are experts at redistributing jargon and managing case history files" (1966, pp. ix–x). Inheriting an empiricist protocol brought more problems than advantages as it threw the objective observer, striving for empathy, into a professional dilemma.

"The curse of erudition in the 18th and 19th centuries was that it collected trivia and cluttered the humanist culture of the time," writes Reiff (p. 102) as he bemoans the scientism of the new narcissistic psychoanalytic culture, satisfied with self-congratulatory, self-serving, and self-publishing fractionist institutions which neither communicate nor collaborate with each other. Regrettably, this isolation cannot provide an atmosphere of cross-fertilization, and hampers integration which might otherwise promote advancement of theory. More seriously, the psychoanalytic movement is said to train "tame Freudians," and consequently, "few sons remain who are worthy of the father" (Reiff, 1966, p. 99). Freud's vigorous efforts to liberate humankind from the tyranny of the superego and its pathological manifestations in piety and religion clearly were not enough. In absconding from the obligation to develop radical revisions, Freud's more devout descendants have renounced an evolutionary call. Only a rare few have ventured forward; in this, as a radical revisionist, Schafer (1970) has courageously paved the way, believing that: "The high probability of being presumptuous and unfair in the attempt—or of being thought to be so—is exceeded by the even higher probability that in the absence of such attempts psychoanalytic thinking will stagnate in the lowlands of orthodoxy" (p. 425). I know of no other science which, in the last century, has progressed at such a slow rate. Perhaps this state of affairs had, in part, been anticipated by Freud who, in no uncertain terms, had delineated the direction for the ideal preparation and suitable course of training for this discipline. For reasons he spelled out in 1927, this course would require a broad interdisciplinary foundation in the humanities and social sciences, leaning heavily toward psychology rather than medicine.

If Freud so prophetically wanted to prevent psychoanalysis from falling exclusively into the hands of the medical profession, he certainly could not have anticipated what has befallen it today, particularly in America. In New York City, for example, psychoanalytic institutes are distinguished by disproportionately uneven intellectual standards and levels. The elite orthodoxy has well nigh strangled itself by its own closed mindedness, adhering so rigidly to Freud as to rob him of his inventiveness and diminish his own progressive doctrine and scope; while other categories, under the apparent exigencies of licensure requirements, invite through their doors individuals of such breathtaking ignorance and ineptitude as to perplex even the most open minded. There are many honorable licensed professions, plumbing being one of them, which, however, are not presumed adequately to prepare for the specialized training of psychoanalysis by virtue of this license. Surely, licensure implies qualifications to practice within a specified field? Without adequate discrimination or selection according to the principles laid down by Freud, unprepared and unsuited individuals from adjacent "mental health fields" fill the institutes with uninspired readings of psychoanalysis and provide the bulk of candidates in training.

Furthermore, much university and medical school sponsored research is burdened by a preoccupation with positivist empirical methods imposed upon subject matter which it is ill-suited to represent. This research has produced masses of "data" and material, much of it negligible in furthering our understanding of psychoanalysis, or which illuminate it in only very tangential ways. The general concerns with externals endemic to our culture, the behaviors, overt communications, "words," and emphasis on manifest events divert genuine psychoanalytic research from understanding unconscious processes and broad patterns of change pertaining to its principles, and thereby distract it from its primary intent. Psychoanalysis and psychoanalytic theories have to do with internal phenomena and unconscious manifestations, observable only through their most diverse expressions and inferred only through invisible transformations. The psychoanalytic method is based on contextual inquiry; a preoccupation with quantification, measurement, or behavioral change only distorts the basic principles of its approach and intent, one which is centrally focused on its clinical claim to effect deep and lasting change. Moreover, its metapsychology is defined at high levels of abstraction, and the higher the level of abstraction the lower the possibility of obtaining "verification" or disproof through empirical evidence (Ricoeur, 1977; Grünbaum, 1977, 1981, 1984). An immense amount of time is wasted in attempting to handle as general and theoretical what is in fact particular and historical, and, conversely, what might be generalized theoretically has been largely ignored as untestable and therefore unscientific. Small wonder that masses of clinical research, all scrupulously reduced to slices of empirically testable units and statistically quantified, have produced little that is new with regard to what is quintessentially the domain of psychoanalysis, namely, mental functioning with regard to transformations of inner experience or psychic reality. The debate still focuses on how to test the untestable (Edelson, 1984), and where to go in order to get psychoanalysis to fit empirical demands. It is a perilous quandary indeed, since the very methods utilized to support what are considered empirical data only confirm the unsuitability of an epistemology which, in its materialistic orientation, is inappropriate and unusable for understanding the issues at hand. Mind is not quantifiable, nor are subjective "meanings" general. As the singular datum of our enquiry, psychic reality remains an elusive and insubstantial subject, and one which requires another epistemology and another paradigm for its scientific verification (Heron, 1981).

It has been said over and over again that the empirical bed in which metapsychology lies is misleading and its epistemology unsuited for the task of conceptualizing the kind of phenomena it is called upon to describe. Freud's therapeutic method provides no testable terrain or data to satisfy empiricists, and his theoretical ascent to metaphors takes him out of their realm altogether. It is worth noting, however, and particularly in academic psychology, that the criticisms levied against psychoanalysis rest less on disagreements with Freud's observations than on the manner in which these are presented and expressed. Due to its analogical, physicalist constructs and metaphoric reifications, metapsychology seduces but then cannot satisfy hard core scientists, while in addition, it does not adequately account for much that is apparent yet still unexplained in clinical theory. I am thinking in particular of the relationship between language and change, action and reflection, and the linguistic exchange in the psychoanalytic hypothesis of cure. With regard to these and other aspects of the method, Freud's metapsychological conceptualizations have clouded rather than clarified issues of clinical interaction and intent (Fromm, 1980; Barratt, 1983, 1988; Bachrach, 1989).

How is it, we may well ask, that the man who, in linking unconscious signification to symptoms, first and foremost enabled us to view mental disturbances more humanely, is now frequently perceived and discredited as a reductionist or dehumanizer? According to Lomas (1968), that this could happen at all is "due to the failure outside the psychoanalytic movement, to recognize that Freud's findings transcend his language and by psychoanalysts, to reformulate his findings in more worthy terms." In fact, Lomas emphasizes, "most psychoanalysts do not even recognize the pressing need for such radical reformulation" (p. 118).

Many, however, do recognize such a need: "Psychoanalysis is now in serious trouble—at least many of us believe it is," writes Peterfreund (1980), "and many of us believe that to a great extent our current difficulties stem from the anachronistic metapsychology that plagues us" (p. 328). "Freud conferred on us a terminology inadequate to impart clearly his monumental insight," writes Opatow (1988, p. 617), in a paper at the interface with philosophy, designed to "undercut the source points from which the splintering of psychoanalytic theory into diverse and divisive schools proceeds," these being the metapsychological treatment of need, wish, self and object, and what Freud (1940) defined as "the inexplicable phenomenon of consciousness" (pp. 157, 620, 636). And this is only one aspect; many authors of differing convictions (Rapaport, 1944, 1959; Holt, 1965, 1967; Gill, 1967a,b; Basch, 1973; G. Klein, 1975; Schimek, 1975; Schafer, 1976; Steele, 1979; Peterfreund, 1980; Modell,

1981, 1984; Edelson, 1984; Eagle, 1984; Storr, 1989; Bachrach, 1989, to name a few) have highlighted the inherent problems and incongruities within metapsychology as these are closely tied to the "untenable doctrines of psychic energy and drive discharge" (Breger, 1967, p. 1). Listing numerous core objections to several basic Freudian hypotheses, Schimek (1975) calls for the abandonment of the concept of unconscious mental representation as instinctual motivator, reasoning:

> [I]t is directly linked to the idea of psychic energy, the economic drive discharge model . . . with the unconscious as a container of encapsulated mental contents . . . it tends toward a reductionistic emphasis . . . with the implicit assumption that by interpretation we can rediscover past experience in its original form, and it does not provide an adequate approach to the problem of different levels of consciousness, their influence on behavior or their relation to symbolic processes and language [p. 182].

Schimek's succinct repudiation of the notion of "mental representation" and its ramifications, underscores the necessity for a revision of the psychoanalytic view of memory and unconscious fantasy (Arlow, 1969a,b). In their relation to the idea of unconscious determinants, both are firmly linked with the clinical method and theory of cure; namely, to a linguistic reconstruction and/or transformation of unconscious material. In addition, as fulcrum, the mind–body dilemma expressed in the definition of instinct, instigates countless derivative splits. A unitary model of symbolic processes such as the one I present in chapter 4, in my opinion, serves as an effective theoretical framework for a theory of mind and, particularly with respect to the mind–body relation, is more useful to clinical application.

Psychoanalysis is now almost one hundred years old, and many of us are children of a post-Freudian era. As psychoanalysis approaches its second century, however, precariously positioned between medicine and hermeneutics, it does so without an acknowledged metatheory, genuine scientific status, or legislative independence as a separate discipline and profession. The outgrowth of a hundred years of divergent splits has moved the field through multiplication by accretion, splintering its intellectual resources and confusing theoretical focus and clarity, particularly with respect to the requirement for interdisciplinary cross-fertilization and scientific updating of its central tenets.

While there has long been a call for radical revisions of Freud's metapsychology, none has emerged that is sufficiently encompassing, and many theoretically inclined authors seem to have thrown up their hands when faced with formulating a unified theory, which brings together a conceptual model based on the method on which it operates. Understandably, in recent years there have appeared numerous publications with revisionary designs, all of them reflecting their authors' preferred school or theory, and particular way of working. In this vein, revisionary works move further and further away from meta-theoretical, epistemologically sophisticated paradigm change and lean more and more toward reappraisals of clinical approach and theory (Greenberg, 1991).

It will not do, in my opinion, to continue to attempt to revise one aspect of our theory and ignore the other. From the time of its inception psychoanalytic theories were based by their founder on the observations of its practice—the two are inseparable. Method in psychoanalysis derives from and is the operational correlate of the particular view of mental functioning or theory of mind which underlies the treatment situation. Today, as with the early dissenters, the primacy of theoretical controversy remains central to internal disputes. No longer grounded in a common doctrine of the psyche's modus operandi the current morass of internally divisive viewpoints does not bode well for a vision of psychoanalysis as a unitary model, and analytic therapists today who prefer not to fall into eclecticism find they are obliged to endorse one particular model or school and adopt its approach, and reject the others (Richards, 1990).

Distinctions are further complicated, since the same concepts are operationalized and defined in different ways depending on preferred theoretical positions, while many more differences arise out of semantic confusion. Moreover, each school has created its own new language and theoretical world to describe the phenomena it selects and considers to be most relevant, further contributing to the general atmosphere of confusion and controversy prevalent in the field today. "Ego psychology, object relations theory, Kleinian psychoanalysis, Lacanian psychoanalysis, interpersonal psychoanalysis, relational psychoanalysis and self-psychology, are all rival claimants for the analyst's theoretical allegiance as we enter the 1990s" (Richards, 1990, p. 350).

Unlike other sciences, which in the past hundred years have awakened to once unthinkable avenues of new knowledge, psychoanalysis faces its second century mired by antiquated and superseded psychophysiological notions embedded in an epistemology of matter which has long been recognized as ill-suited to capture the insubstantial nature of mental transformations and, more fundamentally, which is unable to provide an explanatory framework encompassing or elucidating of the events of the clinical situation. Still grounded in metaphors pertaining to a physicalist epistemology which divide its clinical and theoretical models, without a viable or integrated theory of affects, of language and its relationship to action, of internalization, development, or the central, transformative, ameliorative function of talking in the talking cure, psychoanalysis enters its centennial as an agglomeration (Richards, 1990) of schismatic schools, with its clinical efficacy as a singular, albeit inexplicable, unifying phenomenon. The mushrooming of a plethora of divergent approaches which fragments the symmetry of its central theory and are divisive in nature, only adds to the growing theoretical fuzziness. These offshoot models offer only partial solutions for major underlying problems and, through ad hoc modifications, cloud more fundamental issues while adding much new jargon to say things which have already been said. In analogous fashion Kuhn (1962) describes that, by utilizing Ptolemy's system prior to the Copernican revolution, the complexity of astronomy was "increasing far more rapidly than its accuracy . . . creating . . . a system so cumbersome it couldn't possibly be true of nature . . ." (p. 68). The same might well be said of psychoanalysis today. "Through this proliferation of divergent articulations . . . the rules . . . become increasingly blurred. Though there still is a paradigm few practitioners prove to be entirely agreed about what it is" (Kuhn, 1962, p. 83). In fact, while falling into two broad opposing camps in theory, surprisingly, most analysts appear content to practice more or less the same method, while continuing to argue about their differences in intent and effect.

Few analysts today are in agreement about anything. Divided by an almost clannish adherence to schools which argue about whether the organism is pushed from within or pulled from without, more recently revisionist (Greenberg, 1991) struggles have turned to how to duplicate Freud's simple conflict model while doing away with his posited mental agencies. Disagreements centering on which are the most irreducible of forces propelling human motivation cloud a more cogent point which sees very few questioning the validity of an interpretive or theoretical framework couched in causal or motivational terms. All analysts, however, have become deftly adept at slanting clinical evidence toward the model of their predilection, with each theory tending toward self-validation. Clinical material is notoriously so pliant and multidimensional as to be compatible with formulations derived from practically any interpretive vantage point. Such rampant pluralism is a far cry from Freud's vision of psychoanalysis as a unitary general psychology linking with "mythology, philology, with folklore, with social psychology and the theory of religion" (Freud, 1917a, p. 167)—in short, a general theory of mind. But supraordinate models require articulation at high levels of abstraction. Theories are built not on content, but on concepts *about* content. In this sense Freud's distillation of the observations upon which he built his psychoanalysis should remain our guiding principle.

Despite the disjunctive fractionist effect of these theoretical splits, phenomena Kuhn identified as symptomatic of paradigm crisis, a state of crisis can also be the harbinger of change, a "necessary and appropriate prelude" to a scientific revolution which simultaneously offers a new theory as it supplants the old: crisis both "loosens the stereotypes and provides the incremental data necessary for a fundamental paradigm shift" (Kuhn, 1962, p. 85). Yet novelty emerges only with difficulty against an often rigid backdrop of entrenched and cherished communal beliefs in which only a pronounced awareness of anomaly, issuing from within the disciplinary matrix, a recognition of mounting problems for which the paradigm cannot provide adequate solutions, must play a pivotal catalytic role. What is at stake here is the very fabric of derivations of meanings, events, and causality, the entire frame of reference underlying a particular way of thinking or world view.

In psychoanalytic theories today internal incoherencies and anomalies abound, and any number of entry points could serve equally well to highlight the puzzling discrepancy between application and theory and the urgent need to reconceptualize the field from new fundamentals. We have no unified model to mend the artificial psyche/soma split or integrate affects and language within a developmental framework of normality and pathology; our schools remain divided around the controversial conflict/deficit dispute and provide no sound theoretical grounding to clarify differences in the effective treatment of the preverbal, preoedipal, nonconflictual and the oedipal pathologies; we are still tied to Freud's energic and economic descriptive metaphors to explain what is transformed when unconscious becomes conscious, and even more pointedly, we are unable to provide a psychoanalytically informed definition of the nature of mind. In the face of this, and in bypassing the challenge of an integrative interdisciplinary interface, the field has failed to weave fresh and evolving conceptual equipment into the fabric of its basic tenets. Even more seriously, very few seem to be aware of the fact that revisions will have to take into account the entire scientific framework in which psychoanalytic tenets were devised in order to recast them in models that more closely fit the facts.

In the experimental sciences, if you keep coming up with inconclusive answers you have to wonder about the questions you are asking; it still remains to be seen if we can formulate questions which will yield comprehensive and encompassing answers. This is no small matter when dealing with mind, and we must be prepared to shoulder the weighty legacy of philosophers and theologians, psychologists and neurologists before us in their struggle to place mind within body, mind in brain, and find human consciousness.

But psychoanalysis was born when Freud unveiled the workings of an unconscious, and psychoanalytic investigation began as Freud found meaning in the disavowed or the meaningless; in what lay outside awareness. In identifying the symptom as a symbolic production, likening it to the healthy symbolic expression of dreams, as something which represents a meaning, and in discovering the importance of putting this significance into words, Freud inadvertently established psychoanalysis as a science of symbolic functioning, concerned with the organization and expressive mode of symbolic systems, their acquisition and ontogenetic development, their function in relationship to feeling and thinking, their communicative and expressive uses (Edelson, 1972).

Without a theory of semiotics, a model of signification, or an epistemological language that could detect or describe organization and pattern rather than energy and matter, Freud left us a metapsychology of motivation which explains human behavior in terms of unconscious determinants, one that dichotomizes inner and outer, reality and fantasy, rational and irrational, need and adaptation; with a principle of inertia, derived from nineteenth century neurology operationalized as pleasure or tension reduction, as its fundament. But motives are not the same as meanings, although they typify our propensity toward giving explanations; and whereas motives lead to causal explanations, meanings take us into the subjective world of an individual and the expressions of this experience. Stripped of the accoutrements of descriptive psychiatry, the single datum of the psychoanalytic endeavor remains the interpretation of subjective meanings, or psychic reality.

A careful reading of Freud reveals his awareness of the limitations and shortcomings of physicalist analogies for psychological phenomena as, even at the end of his life, he was grappling with "the profound obscurity of the background of our ignorance . . . [in approaching] the still shrouded secret of the nature of the psychical" (1940, p. 163). Yet subjective experience and "psychic reality" would seem to come together in the notion of meaning, and a model that operationalizes meaning must intrinsically capture the essence of "the nature of the psychical," a nature which reveals itself in the relationship of reference between manifest and latent, signifier and signified, in something being taken to represent or express multiple referents; that is, in the essential, primary, symbolizing function of the human mind. "Significance, by definition, is not possible unless something can be seen as representing something else" (Rosen, 1969, p. 198)—indeed the fabric of meaning, of thought, of consciousness, comes into being through the relationship between symbol and symbolized. Equally, consciousness is not a "thing" which is arrived at through shifting quotas of "cathexis"; consciousness emerges at a point along the symbolizational continuum in which meaning is carried by a symbolic referent, and used to denote.

Of the many divergent trendsetters, only Lacan (1973), I believe, attempted to straddle the philosophical, metaphysical, and linguistic worlds which Freud had, with such ease, encompassed. It was Freud's genius to return problems of signification and meaning, relegated to philosophy by the experimental mainstream of psychology, to the domain of a psychology which now addressed the personal with respect to both conscious and unconscious aspects (Freud, 1895; Lipps, 1897). In restressing Freud's topographical model, Lacan reconsidered some of the implications of what it means to interpret surface derivatives of meanings which in their deepest layers correspond to the "subject" conceived in a "kingdom divided." Unfortunately, Lacan adopted de Saussure's (1955) turn-of-the-century linguistic model (corresponding more or less to Freud's early topographical concepts) which has now been superseded and proven untenable, first by Chomsky's (1957, 1965) phase-structure grammars (in the 1950s) and more recently by newer models such as generative semantics, discourse analysis, and cognitive linguistics (between the 1960s and 1980s).

Moreover, Lacan presents numerous other major problems, among which are a facile equation of person with language, a propensity for dichotomized thought, and the view of existential alienation as an inevitable human condition. His sophisticated regard of the "eye" and its gaze in relation to the object of Desire, embodies an occidental occulocentrism, and psychology's long-standing preoccupation with perception. But his theoretical orientation is limited by a simplistic Saussurian (1955) topographical perspective and provides no link with the more clinically grounded relevancies of character analysis and the narcissistic pathologies prevalent in contemporary psychoanalytic practice. While his linguistic–philosophical bent has attracted the attention of an elite academic world, particularly in America, the total absence of reference to development in general and particularly to the integration of verbal with other facets of organismic development, strays too far from the biological realities of which human stuff and psychoanalysis are made. His approach moves us backward rather than forward in our general concerns with theory building and with broadening the scope of psychoanalytic therapy, and provides no epistemologically sound, or new, recasting of a theory of mind.

The mind is not a group of functions contained in a dichotomized topography of systems, nor is it fueled by opposing forces, filled with units, complicated pictures, or malleable structures altered by the fluctuations of a libidinous energy. Nor does it house selves or egos—in fact, mind is not a "thing" at all. Freud knew this well even as he "provisionally" adopted a physicalist epistemology for his "intellectual scaffolding," with metaphoric reifications given to *explanation* (Erklärende) rather than *understanding* (Verstehende).

The history of the philosophy of science (Kuhn, 1962; Holton, 1973) is replete with examples of how more than one theoretical construction can be applied to a given set of data, and it does not fault Freud's impeccable observations for us now to redefine the problems, determine new significant fact, match theory with fact, and articulate a theory that can with greater simplicity and precision account for a wider range of phenomena in the psychoanalytic situation (Grünbaum, 1980, 1981, 1984). The existing paradigm can no longer serve in furthering our understanding of numerous aspects of the very models to which it gave rise: "On the most general level" writes Schafer (1983), "the natural science language of forces, energies, mechanisms and the like is now to be set aside in favor of a language devoted to meanings, for a situation is not an object or an environment or an ego function, but necessarily the individual version of reality that is currently understood and experienced by a person, especially unconsciously" (p. 98).

In order to generate a general theory of mind, psychoanalysis must stand firm on its own empirical ground and discover the universal principles derived from, and implicit in, its application in the clinical method; only in this way can our model fit the method on which it is premised. In my view, we must forego the general tendency toward reshuffling surface phenomena, a preoccupation with externals endemic to our culture, which only detracts from the more penetrating pursuit of major theoretical concerns which need to be articulated at higher levels of abstraction for theory building. Nor will it do to additively encumber the central tenets of psychoanalysis with divisive ramifications, or to replace theory with hermeneutics, since the human mind is intrinsically part of nature, irrevocably a biological process also governed by physiochemical laws which can and must be accounted for in line with psychoanalytic principles, in psychoanalytic terms. The psyche–soma rift needs to be bridged not broadened; we cannot afford to abandon the founder's strivings to integrate body and mind. Freud's "drives" at bottom are conceptual vectors *akin* to phenomena in biology, life and death, superordinate metaphors for the polarization of forces in existence; they are metaphors for the life of the body, not actual, and belong to a different level of abstraction. A unified psychoanalytic model needs to account for the biological, but not be defined by, nor borrow, its terms. A psychoanalytic theory must be constructed in terms of conscious and, particularly, unconscious mental phenomena; a theory of mind not an offshoot of behavioral biology.

The current division of psychoanalysis into multiple, divergent theoretical perspectives creates a major cleavage between two more or less broad categories which essentially embody a much more fundamental epistemological rift. At one end of the spectrum there are the hermeneuticists (Home, 1966; Ricoeur, 1970, 1984; Schafer, 1976, 1983; Steele, 1979; Spence, 1982, 1987), who contextualize data yielded from the psychoanalytic situation, considering psychoanalysis to be founded on the observation and interpretation of a reality engendered "in the analytic encounter"; a truth formed within a narrative created by "the co-understanding of analyst and analysand" (Steele,

1979, p. 408). For them, the goal of psychoanalysis, unlike that of natural science, is taken to be understanding and not domination, prediction, or control. Freud, this line of thinking reminds us, removed the psychoanalytic study of psychopathology from the world of science and established it in the world of the humanities, because the contextual coconstruction of meaning is not a search for causes but an empathic attempt to understand the subjective experience of another: "meaning," writes Home (1966), "is not the product of causes but the creation of a subject" (p. 43). From this perspective the search for psychoanalytic metatheoretical models is inconsequential. Method, for the hermeneuticist *is* theory; and the interpretive search for meaning within a newly coconstructed, psychoanalytically informed narrative, is enough.

Empirical science, on the other hand, attempts to dominate its subject matter by isolating and determining the events to be studied and method to be used, for the purpose of either refuting or verifying a testable hypothesis. This highlights the demand expressed by the canons of positivism that a clear distinction be maintained between observation and inference, the first perceived as fact, the second as fancy, whereas in humanistic study the only distinction required is with respect to who is saying what. The one seeks explanation and knowledge, the other contextual understanding. As Home (1966) emphasized, "categories of living and dead are decisive for the methodology of thought" (p 44; see Von Foerster, 1974). Scientific explanations have to be couched in causal terms, since they attempt to explain how things happen, where, by contrast, the humanistic mode "deals with the live object, asks the question why things happen and answers in terms of the subject's motives" (Home, 1966, p. 45). Inappropriate application of the scientific model produces meaningless theories and vice versa, while "abuse of either mode has its own peculiar symptomatology" (Home, 1966, p. 45). Both Home (1966) and Steele (1979) consider identification and empathy to be integral parts of the coparticipation which creates the analytic dialogue, very much along the lines of Sullivan's "participant observer" concept. "The subject of meaning is known to us through an act of identification," writes Home, "and not through an act of sense perception or scientific observation'' (p. 47), and adds, ''objectivity, in treating what is observed as an object, is the cornerstone of natural science, but it is the gravestone of hermeneutics and psychoanalysis'' (Steele, 1979, p. 408).

Unfortunately, using just such an argument, the requirement for the analyst's equidistant, neutral state of ''evenly hovering attention'' has recently been severely criticized. The requisite neutrality advocated by Freud as a technical necessity for an optimal clinical stance is downplayed by interpersonal schools which consider the analyst's real presence and influence to be inevitable. Implied, is a mistaken equation of neutrality with distance. In my opinion, objections brought against this requirement misrepresent what Freud intended by neutrality and indicate a further misunderstanding with respect to what one is required to remain neutral toward (Hoffer, 1985). On closer reading, and on many occasions, Freud depicted the analyst's task as one of extending unconscious sensibilities outward and reaching toward the patient's unconscious communications. Hardly a recipe for neutral objectivity, this is a rather vivid description of an empathic identification, reminiscent of the early attunement of a mother toward her child.

With regard to the central clinical tool of psychoanalysis, the contextual interpretation of meanings, insofar as this leans excessively toward an ''interpretative hermeneutic claim,'' Rycroft, Gorer, Wren-Lewis, Storr, and Lomas (1966) among others, warn against turning away from Freud's unitary grounding in the biological: ''The statement that psychoanalysis is a theory of meaning is incomplete and misleading unless one qualifies it by saying that it is a *biological* theory of meaning . . . psychoanalysis interprets human behavior in terms of the self that experiences it and not in terms of entities external to it . . . it regards the self as a psychobiological entity which is always striving for self-realization and self-fulfillment'' (p. 20). According to the hermeneuticists, data issuing from a coconstruction of narrative comprehensibility and coherence is so resistant to a natural science frame of reference as to make theory building a ''virtually futile exercise in circular reasoning'' (Richards, 1990, p. 352). Narrative truth, in this sense, has more to do with

"sense significance (Loch, 1977) than with a veridical correspondence with facts" (Protter, 1988, p. 498). The quarrel with
correct or incorrect theory is therefore of little consequence to
those who, intent upon and content with interpretative understanding, consider preoccupation with theory a moot point.

At the other end of the spectrum are the empiricists who
require that a science provide evidence of its validity according
to the strict canons of their protocol. They represent a rude
answer to Freud's deeper ambition for psychoanalysis to be considered a general theory of mind, primarily because no metatheory of psychoanalytic principles has been put forward which
can be fit or tested within this framework. A major proponent
of this militant trend, Holt (1985), would declare Freud's metapsychology an unsalvageable ruin, asserting that "metapsychology has been effectively destroyed by a series of critiques . . . and
is virtually dead" (pp. 289–292). The most extreme view from
this perspective claims that the psychoanalytic situation cannot
generate scientifically significant data subject to validation or
disproof according to the canons of science and is therefore
not a science at all (Grünbaum, 1980, 1984). Ferguson (1988),
however, tackles Grünbaum (1977, 1981, 1984) with a counter-
attack criticizing him on his own terms, arguing that the studies
on which he relied were "conceptually inadequate to judge
psychoanalytic therapy" and that he had based his argument
on "an interpretation of Freud that is contrary to Freud's own
understanding of his own work" (p. 536). I cannot attempt here
to catalogue the amply documented pro and con ideological
arguments between those psychoanalytic and philosophical fac-
tions which consider the argument of whether psychoanalysis is
a science or not to be a fertile endeavor; suffice it to say there
have been forceful and eloquent responses issuing from both
sides.

Holt (1967, 1985), who would definitively banish Freud's
metapsychology, admonishing him for his heritage and indebtedness to Helmholtz, Haeckel, and Lamarck is, however, more
benevolent toward the "heart of psychoanalysis," its clinical theory which, he believes "need not be trivialized by being reduced
to a hermeneutic" (1985, p. 289). He advocates an attempt to
"collect and separately consolidate its metapsychological and

clinical-theoretical branches, purging them of all fallaciousness and errors . . . and . . . *restate the theory* in such a way as to make it as testable as possible" (p. 308). Holt's definition of science, however, as Richards (1990) puts it, "is extremely narrow" (p. 352). A more moderate proponent of this view, Edelson (1984), would grant scientific status to psychoanalysis, having confined it in a defining template as the investigation of the relation between imagination and sexual desire. Edelson remains optimistic that the future will see hypothesis testing of psychoanalytic propositions according to the scientific code, the results of which, he predicts, will confirm the heuristic (and clinical) value of fundamental aspects of clinical theory (Richards, 1990).

A most cogent answer to these arguments has come from Basch (1973), who is less interested in resurrecting the ill-fated debate as to whether psychoanalysis is a science or not, than in clarifying some of the questions inherent in the debate. He does this by applying the tenets of scientific philosophy to Freud's own theory formation and essentially expounds the thesis that "the division of psychoanalysis into clinical and metapsychology theories, the former being considered empirical and inductive and the latter speculative and deductive, is neither philosophically correct nor functional" (p. 39). Additionally, he would consider revising the assumption that metapsychology is abstracted from clinical theory.

Out of a well-argued, complex, eight-point list of fundamental principles of natural science, for our purpose, several important concepts may be distilled. These are that there are inductive (correspondence) and deductive (coherence) theories but these are not to be equated with inductive and deductive *inference*, nor are the conclusions derived thereof exclusively the products of either single method. So-called empirical science is also composed of inductive theories, and these can further be divided into complementary *classificatory* and *explanatory* theories; the former being formed through *abstraction from observation*, while explanatory theory relies on *hypotheses about observation*. And finally, the division of psychoanalytic theory into clinical and metapsychological theory is untenable, this being neither functional nor epistemologically correct, since psychoanalysis is taken, by Basch, to be an empirical, though neither a biological nor a physical science, and is composed of inductive theories.

To summarize Basch's argument: in thus dividing natural science empiricism into classificatory theory and explanatory theory, the former utilizing a method of abstraction from observations, the latter forming hypotheses about observations, psychoanalysis may comfortably be placed within the realm of empirical science. Emphasizing that both these aspects are functionally necessary and play a part in inductive theory, Basch highlights the futility of attempting to distinguish or devalue theories on the basis of their origin in either inductive or deductive inference, since no theory can be constructed without both these forms. "Causal explanations seek to answer 'why'? descriptive explanations, 'how'?" (1973, p. 42) and, Basch affirms both aspects, although unequatable, are of equal import to scientific explanations.

His proposed conceptualization of theory formation looks like this:

I. Deductive Theory—(Coherence)
II. Inductive Theory—(Correspondence)
    A. Classificatory Theory
    B. Explanatory Theory
       1. Causal Explanatory Theory
       2. Descriptive Explanatory Theory

He qualifies this by noting that, "the laws of science are descriptive explanatory theories; they account for what happens and what will happen in the future on the basis of generalizations based not on *why*, but on *how* a given set of circumstances is related" (Toulmin [1953] cited in Basch [1973, p. 43]). In conclusion, Basch states that *descriptive explanatory theory* illustrates its postulates symbolically through various mathematical and other modes, or "linguistically through metaphors and analogy" (p. 43)—these being Freud's very own methods par excellence. He would dispel the cleavage between clinical and metapsychological theories on the scientific claim that such a distinction is based on a discredited antithesis between observation and speculation, which his classificatory and explanatory categorizations would adduce as being not only epistemologically sound and correct, but part and parcel of the empirical model.

Another eminently cogent perspective on the problems posed by psychoanalytic theory construction from G. Klein (1973), depicts the key dilemma in efforts to develop a unified theory as "whether to develop a theory of the mental apparatus through quasi-thermodynamic principles (including contemporary, more plausible physical analogies) or to continue theoretical efforts to the enterprise of deciphering meanings" (p. 60). Statements of signification, or the meaning of behavior, he claims, are of a different level of coherence from those applying physiological laws which require causal explanations. Polanyi (1966) drew attention to the fact that "an operational principle defining the structure of the machine is of a different level from the laws of physics and chemistry" and that "while the machine may function thanks to the laws of physics and chemistry, the reverse does not apply" (cited in G. Klein, 1973, p. 60). Klein draws a sharp distinction between the analyst's pursuit of meaning and significance and a specification of the lawfulness of these, and the need for physiologically based data with its own lawfulness, viewing these as two distinct yet complementary levels of observation. This appears to me to be a most cogent appraisal of the implicit, and still current, requirements for psychoanalytic theorizing; a requirement which points the way toward the distillation of principles at superordinate levels, derived from both these vantage points.

Whereas it would be unrealistic and well beyond the scope of this work to discuss the complex ramifications issuing from the philosophy of science, or to examine in depth the profound impact empiricism has had on the fabric of our thinking, one cannot help but note in all of this a highly idealistic, unanalytic preoccupation with and investment in a single, prepossessing "truth," marked by a lack of tolerance for ambiguity, the possibility of fluid truths, multiple truths, or no truths at all (Levinson, 1983). And this, despite the fact that we have moved into an age at the cutting edge of discoveries which have turned our notions of time, space, and causality upside down. These new

organizing dimensions of chaos and disorder indicate a tolerance for suspense and lack of closure implicit in a universe,
which can be understood according to multiple frames of reference. As Basch (1973) remarks, "The search for absolute and
absolutely certain knowledge that preoccupied so many meta-
physicians and epistemologists in past centuries has been shown
to be an unfruitful and perhaps an impossible quest" (p. 39).

Yet, psychoanalysis has been so steeped in concepts related
to truth, integration, and self-awareness, as in the "exalted role
of interpretation and making the unconscious conscious,"
writes Protter (1988), that one can "hardly separate this core
epistemic function from psychoanalysis' very self-definition" (p.
418). Protter traces the philosophical lineage of psychoanalysis
to deep Socratic (know thyself) and Judeo-Christian (the truth
shall set you free) roots (Hartmann, 1960; Fromm, 1964). But
Freud's (1937) keen concerns with truths and truthfulness may
better be understood if we consider that he developed his theory
against a backdrop of post-Victorian currents and a moralistic
cloak of habitual self-deception. Freud teaches it to be intrinsic
to the psychoanalytic ethic that a truth coherence not be confused with veridical absolutism (Spence, 1982): this would mean
having misunderstood the concept of psychic reality and ignored the constant, fluid undercurrents of multiple function
and multidetermination which structure subjectivity, and are
present in all human enterprise. Nowhere is the blunt modera-
tion exercised by the founder of psychoanalysis better illustrated
than in his prudent pessimism describing an optimal analytic
outcome as merely the transforming of neurotic suffering into
normal suffering. Freud's realism is mirrored in the ethical fundaments of clinical intent: "The analyst's expertise lies not in
having the answers for the analysand, but in having the questions that will help him wonder more freely" (Hoffer, 1985, p.
79, cited in Franklin, 1990). Exploration and not explanation
is the spirit in which the psychoanalytic endeavor is best undertaken.

Some view the current theoretical pluralism which perme-
ates the psychoanalytic movement as an opportunity for expansion through cross-fertilization and enrichment through

diversity. Pine (1988), for instance, accounts for four conceptually separate, yet overlapping, perspectives on the functioning
of the human mind, each of these psychologies emphasizing
different phenomena. He believes that each adds something
new to theoretical understanding and, particularly from a developmental perspective, advocates their relevance and integration
for clinical practice. Michels (1988), and more recently Kernberg (1993), have also argued if not in favor of, certainly, for
tolerance toward the ambiguity emanating from the tensions of
pluralistic discourse in psychoanalysis today. Wallerstein (1988,
1989) actively supports such dialogue, as he encourages a unity
that would encompass theoretical diversity through the "common ground" clinical facets of the theory shared by all schools
of different persuasions. Thus, he claims, current differences
need not be "organizationally divisive," in that he considers
various manifestations of the central theory (i.e., ego psychology, object-relations theory, and self-psychology) as merely metaphorical additions, created for the purpose of satisfying
"variously conditioned needs for closure and coherence" (cited
in Richards, 1990, p. 353).

Richards (1990) and Gedo (1991), on the other hand, each
prudently aware of the epistemic implications of a clinical
method based on a "minestrone" theoretical mentality, are less
tolerant of the current prolixity. At the interface with neurophysiology and developmental theories, Gedo invokes Occam's
cautionary razor, calling for the simplest possible model. Distinguishing it from the biological, for the purpose of conceptualizing the etiological differences between deficit versus other
forms of psychopathology, Gedo greatly narrows the definition
of what is "psychological" and to which principles within psychoanalysis this definition would be applicable. Taking method
as the starting point for his discussion and subscribing to a
correspondence theory of truth, Richards advocates interdisciplinarity and the development of a biologically inclusive theory
of mind. He believes the psychoanalytic theory which prevails
will be more rather than less relevant for the method of clinical
practice on which it is based.

The problem with such rampant pluralism, as I see it, is that it creates an atmosphere which continues to undermine what, I believe, should be the primary focus of our inquiry, namely, the distillation of time-honored psychoanalytic principles as these manifest in the method, and, through interdisciplinary cross-fertilization, a recasting of these in the light of contemporary science. In my opinion, empirical research, as it is currently conceptualized, will not yield useful results for psychoanalysis; a multivalenced methodology must require theoretical articulation at higher levels of abstraction in order to meet with the broad, superordinate principles to which its practice applies.

The dialectic presented by a narrative–interpretive approach and physiobiological developmental and causal premises contains the fundamental dichotomy Freud's great discovery would have coexist. Divergence and devaluation are symptomatic of a post-Freudian paradigm crisis which divisively pushes psychoanalysis further and further away from the integration necessitated by a general psychology, pulverizing its progressive potential through internal disputes. It will not help psychoanalysis in the future if isolation prevails over collaborative discourse. Equally, it is not helpful to try to invalidate Freud's impeccable approach to fact finding by demonstrating that he was a man of stubborn conviction (Holt, 1985), nor can it diminish his theory to say that he was a man of his time (Fromm, 1980; Storr, 1989). Rather, as J. A. C. Brown (1961) puts it, "The real criticism of psychoanalytic orthodoxy is not that there was anything wrong with Freud's methods or observations, but that there was something very wrong indeed with the attitude of the group which kept his explanations fixated . . ." (p. 190).

Freud's thinking reflects all the dominant philosophical, psychological, artistic, and scientific theories of his era. He was very much a man of his time, through whom there reverberated many cultural and political strains. The echoes of these are reflected in Dostoyevsky's antihero, man portrayed as torn between propriety and savagery; Kafka's diminished man, by dehumanizing obeisance reduced to dehumanized sacrifice;

Conrad's man divided, living the inner shadow of an outer face; Nietzsche's tragic man, like Gustav Mahler's transcendence, born out of the expressive spirit of music; Darwin's adaptive man, the outgrowth of his own evolutionary strength, as thumb meets finger and transforms him from social beast into skilled toolmaker; and the loud residue of ecumenic, Judeo-Christian man, torn between the affirmation of bodily desires and spiritual renunciation.

Inherent in all of these are concepts of lower and higher order, images originating in our earliest mythologies which depict celestial deities and earthly creatures; the duality of astral gods and man beneath, the body's biological pressure, base, inferior; the mind as ether, spiritual, closer to God, superior. The Cartesian psyche-soma and Christian carnal–spiritual polarizations provide a moralistic ethos for a view of human nature which, in Freud's theories, becomes a model of mankind as the conflicted, pleasure-seeking product of dilemmas between an outer "reality" and inner, animal compulsions. The first mental topography that Freud conceptualized quite explicitly divided the mind into lower and higher systems, providing a framework for a theory of cure in which "talking" functioned much like an exorcism. Indeed, the theory of repression and postulations of mental "censorship" and disguisement, the differentiation between latent and manifest content of dreams, the doctrine of compromise formation resulting from mental agencies in dynamic tension, the superseding of primary with secondary process, sublimation, and the supremacy of a rational ego over an unruly id as adaptive organ of domination (consider Freud's analogy of horse and rider), all stem from this mentality. Striving to explain the mind, Freud's psychology inherited and subsumed a dualistic tradition which pitted "human nature against social order" (Reiff, 1966, p. 3). Character, for Freud, was formed out of a compromise between inner truth and the clash with culture.

Freud's own lineage provided authoritarian and patriarchal traditions steeped in ancient Hebraic principles of lawfulness and lawlessness, defiance and punishment, submission and transcendence. Upholding Western philosophy's pervasive logocentricism, Freud's conceptual constructs support the

rational–irrational dichotomy; irrationality, like passion, understood pejoratively as inferior, primitive, uncontrolled, and of a
lower order; rationality, closely tied to objectivity, idealized as
superior, controlled, of a higher order. These dualistic principles, which underlie much of Freud's thinking, produced ideas
which, I believe, fostered his bafflement before the female, perceived by him as an earthy, enigmatic "dark continent," and
also fueled his more rebellious strivings as a genuine secularist,
guiltless in principle, yet a godless Jew, guilt-ridden in practice.
I think it not insignificant that Freud's voluntary death coin-
cided with the eve of Yom Kippur (Gay, 1988).

Consistently divided by an enduring desire for recognition
and an antagonizing tendency to challenge tradition, torn
within by a propensity for intellectual isolation and an irrepress-
ible urge for intellectual domination, theory, like the man it
mirrors, is constructed to explain such splits in the "terminology of the still unknown topography of the mental apparatus"
(Freud, 1905a, p. 162), utilizing principles of physics in a search
to explain repression in causal terms. Freud (1905a) repeatedly
emphasized, however, that his model was "not to be taken ana-
tomically," but was designed as a "descriptive topography to
service explanation" (p. 162). This notwithstanding, an insistence on literal readings of Freud is still pervasive. The vitality
and usefulness of descriptive metaphor in Freud's theoretical
writings, are fluid and intended to capture by analogy the essential processes inferred behind impeccable observations.

Freud's philosophy of science assumed that neither concepts of purposefulness or meaning could yield acceptable scientific explanations. He believed that scientific explanations
were to be purged of teleological implications and that eventually all mental phenomena would be explained through psychological models derived from physiological understanding, of
which earlier formulations were merely descriptive expressions.
Having conceptualized a dichotomous mind in which the system
unconscious[1] exerted a motivational force, in true scientific fashion, Freud now sought to justify its function with causal explanations. Yet, as Schafer reminds us, "the cause and that which it

---

[1]"People consider a single unconscious as something fantastic. What will they say
when we confess that we cannot make shift without two of them?" Freud was referring
here to a point he brought up earlier questioning whether the day residue was to be

is supposed to explain are not logically independent and often they are identical" (1976, p. 76).

Evolutionary determinism, vitalism, and the strife of being born into a restricting, acculturating social milieu form the basis of a theory of mind which, however, when approaching people with symptoms, adopts the hermeneutic task of "understanding," by interpreting the manifestations of disavowed meanings. The biological-physicalist joins the humanist, as Freud, man of letters, who would receive the Goethe prize, battles Freud, man of medicine, neurologist, schooled in the functioning and anatomy of the brain. Schimek (1975) writes:

> One can see two conflicting trends which pervaded Freud's thinking: a dominant intent to explain mental phenomena in terms of forces and quantity derived from a causal mechanistic model of a "mental apparatus"—in contrast to the search for connections of meaning at different levels of symbolic expression through a new method of interpretation. While the former trend is more explicit in his metapsychology and the latter pervades the spirit of his clinical discoveries, the struggle between these two approaches is evident at all levels of Freud's formulations whose enduring richness can never be reduced to a tightly knit consistent system [p. 180].

At bottom this is an epistemological problem which originates in viewing the body as matter and the mind as air, understandable only in terms of matter. The legacy of this approach and its limitations in providing *knowledge* but not *understanding*, embody the distinction made by the German philosophers between *Erklärende psychology* (given to explanation) and *Verstehende psychology* (striving for understanding). While Freud did much

---

considered "really unconscious in the same sense as the unconscious wish" (1917b, p. 227), to which he himself responded, "This is the salient point of the whole business. They are *not* unconscious in the same sense. The dream-wish belongs to a different unconscious—to the one . . . recognized as being of infantile origin and *equipped with peculiar mechanisms*" (p. 227). And he adds, "It would be highly opportune to distinguish these two kinds of unconscious by different names. But we would prefer to wait until we have become familiar with the field of phenomena of the neuroses" (1917a, p. 227).

to shake the establishment and modify the origins of this thinking with biologistic instincts, infantile sexuality, and an interpretive method based on linguistic exchange, he lacked the epistemic framework for a model of structural *organization* or a conceptualization of symbolic activity in *functional* terms. Understandably, with the great strides made in the fields of neuroscience, cognitive psychology, and infant and child development, today there is further to go and much that requires a radically different epistemological perspective. Moreover, major underlying problems have only been compounded by the multiplication of partial theories wherein partial solutions still need to be redirected and subsumed under radical theoretical reorientation.

I think it not insignificant that Freud wandered from the physicalist ambition of the Project (1895) to take explanatory refuge in the evocative organizations of myth and metaphor, abstractions of the highest order. In the absence of organizing principles which can be accommodated by existing explanatory frameworks, the creative mind resorts to abstractions by analogy. The cosmic appeal of life and death instincts, dual drives—love and aggression pitched against each other—and the infantile "wish" as spark of our ignition are enduring, a legacy unwillingly renounced. Indeed, the ethics and aesthetics of the Freudian canon, with its symmetry and complexity, congruity and dissonance, stands as an exemplary edifice. I am a product of a system I hold dear even as I attempt to recast its central tenets. This is the theory that shaped my understanding and the method which taught me to question further without fear of superego or dogma. If psychoanalytic therapy can confidently boast of anything, it is that it broadens horizons, that it expands and deepens experience, and teaches one to question, to think about how one is thinking.

Understood as a developmental thrust with intent to unify, a task divined by Freud as quintessential eros, this work is undertaken in the belief that it is eminently necessary for our theory to prevail and to withstand growing attacks from within and from without. It is undertaken in the belief that phenomena can always be conceptualized in different ways, that there are multiple world views or conceptual frames within which to shape information, which can accommodate and subsume prevailing research and contemporary knowledge and which do not have to resort to mechanistic codes of reference or make use of militaristic metaphors (Schafer, 1976).

A major stumbling block to radical revisionist aims, in my opinion, is that positivism has left intransigent residues in the way academicians, scientists, and indeed the entire establishment think (Morgan, 1983). One only has to observe the way in which language is used in our field to realize that anything "mental" is still defined in reified terms, making processes, experiences, feelings, and activities into "things" attributed to internal agencies of one kind or another. Descriptive diagnosis carries the same legacy. Moreover university research is still governed by the protocols of positivism and research design often reinforces this mentality. While we may "easily come to think of Mind as 'thing' . . . the analogy does not hold," writes Home (1966, p. 44). Venturing a tentative definition, he states, "we might say mind is the meaning of behavior; or anything that has meaning is mental," and concludes, "If mind is not a thing, then each time we speak about it, as if it were a thing, we are speaking metaphorically" (p. 46). While metaphors may not suffice in the refining or fleshing out process of scientific theory building, they are nonetheless valuable initially in providing an inclusive shape or form out of which later elaborations may evolve. Empirical research and its fragmenting mentality moves further and further away from the abstractive process which distills superordinate metatheoretical considerations. Yet it is only from this high realm of conceptualization that overall patterns and the principles underlying them can emerge. Popper described theory as "a net set to catch what we call the world" (1968, p. 59)—it is a world view, and our field requires a new lens to enable a more encompassing vision.

CHANGING PARADIGMS: PARADIGMS FOR CHANGE

Gregory Bateson (1972, 1979) considered himself to be an epistemologist, and perhaps more than anyone else became primarily responsible for introducing new ways of knowing into the fields of family therapy, biology, and the social sciences. He was, in part, indebted to his background in anthropology and sociology in which he found that the intelligibility and organization of events, whether these were social, psychological, behavioral, or neurological, could only emerge in terms of information, and not in terms of a framework of matter or energy. More substantially, he was indebted to a conceptualization of Norbert Wiener (1948), who coined the term *cybernetics*, for the new way of knowing he had devised. This epistemological shift provided the conceptual base for a new way of thinking about living exchanges in the realm of human communication, in the interactions of families as well as larger social systems.

In the thirties and forties, Wiener was part of a group of scholars from varied disciplines who were studying what McCulloch (1965) called the "embodiment of mind." At the same time Piaget was researching children's cognitive development, McCulloch (1965), Spencer-Brown (1969), von Foerster (1974), Varela (1978), and Maturana and Varela (1980) were examining organization and living forms; Bateson (and Mead) in New Guinea were studying rituals and rites of passage; and Wiener, a mathematician, was elaborating cybernetics, a science of information, a way of discerning *pattern* and *form* as organization—one markedly different from the science of physics. The difference between physics and cybernetics is that of two distinct epistemologies; between an epistemology of force and mass and one of patterns and forms that shape events. Living systems could now be studied in terms of relationships, communications, interactions seen in nonlinear, noncausal terms, in which events take on specific meanings according to the contextual forms of knowledge and frames of reference which engender them. With good reason Bateson remarked that cybernetics was "the biggest bite out of the fruit of the tree of knowledge that mankind has taken in the last 2000 years" (1972, p. 476).

The mechanistic world view which dominated most societies of western culture from the time of the Renaissance until approximately the Second World War (the 1940s), was based on analytical thinking. This way of thinking produces deterministic explanations based on causes. In fact, causality implies determinism; it is an epistemology which defines the application of energy to matter. But causality precludes the human elements of purpose, choice, and free will, all based on subjective experience. Synthetic thinking, which developed as a consequence of this realization, uses analysis to determine how a system works and synthesis to understand its overall functioning. This way of thinking adheres to the idea that a system cannot be divided into parts without losing its essential properties. Therefore, the functioning of a system is best understood through a study of the organization of the interactions of these parts within the system, and in relation to other systems in which it is embedded (Ackoff, 1975).

In the fifties, sixties, and seventies, incited by the Zeitgeist provided by this new general scientific paradigm, those already aware of the "breakdown of a paradigm" (Hartmann, 1939, p. 536) and dissatisfied with the status of metapsychology, began adopting what has been called by numerous closely related names: feedback theory, information or information-processing theory, cybernetics, general systems theory.

Viewing the organism as intrinsically active in maintaining a "disequilibrium called the 'steady state' " (von Bertalanffy, 1968, p. 209), leads to conceptualizations of innate development unrelated to causal explanations. A systems wholeness or autonomy is best understood if one closes the boundaries and looks at it from the inside (Keeney and Sprenkle, 1982). Thus, the intrinsic coherence occurring between interactional systems "needs no explanation other than that coherence is a natural spontaneous phenomenon that arises when living organisms spend time together" (Dell, 1982, p. 36). Such a perspective does not automatically imply favoring the interpersonal in psychoanalysis over the intrapsychic—an epistemological error which only perpetuates our theoretical quandaries. It merely emphasizes the need to reexamine our frames of reference when considering the individual, intrapsychic experience and the phenomenology of the transference in the psychoanalytic dyad. Since to some degree the dialectic of self with other, and outer and inner, will always make of human experience an ongoing exchange of influence and influencing, what has impact and what is impacted upon will always need to be understood in terms of recursivity. What is inside will reflect what was once outside and its assimilation by the subject—this is the stuff of psychic reality in a participatory world, a universe of recursivity.

Systems theory gained increasing influence in psychology and psychoanalysis: the infiltration and impact of these new concepts can be felt in the works of Rapaport (1959), Allport (1961), G. Klein (1970, 1975), Horowitz (1972), and particularly in Bowlby's (1969, 1973, 1980) and Peterfreund's (1980) meta-theoretical reformulations, both of which drew heavily from information and systems thinking. In the opening chapter of a work inspired by "new look" perceptual research, G. Klein (1970) stated the intent of this exciting new trend: "One explicit goal of our work was the reassessment of the concept of personality itself. Instead of a language that would convey no immediate implications of cognitive processes, we tried to develop concepts that could imply both the constant or stable aspects of personality and its specific manner of appearance in the workings of thought and action" (p. 9). And in 1975, von Bertalanffy expressed the hope that the pervasive interest in general systems theory might lead to a conceptually more fruitful framework for the understanding of normal and pathological psychology.

Drive theory takes discharge of psychic energy as its fundamental conceptual building block; its aim is to form a bridge between body and mind. Innate needs give rise to tensions, the force of which "represents the somatic demand upon the mind" (Freud, 1940, p. 148). Freud's use of drive propulsion for principles of homeostasis corresponds to his adopting a scientific value system which sought to explain phenomena by determining the mechanisms that move them—the mind as machine. Thus threading through his entire theoretical system, libido provides internal coherence for a causal model which detects the mechanisms of a "mental apparatus." The mind is conceived as a discharger of internal stimuli, and the mind's work is to find ways to reduce tension.

Offshoots from this central mold have adopted strategies of accommodation; these attempt to reconcile the clinical primacy of object relations with the theoretical primacy of the drive model (Hartmann, 1939, 1964; M. Klein, 1955; Jacobson, 1964;

Mahler, 1979; Kernberg, 1984); strategies of radical alternative, which place relationship with others at the center of theory claiming that all motives derive from the vicissitudes of relational issues (Fairbairn, 1954; Guntrip, 1971; Winnicott, 1965; the British object relationists; Sullivan, 1953); and mixed model theories, in which drive model principles are preserved and mixed with relational model observations (Sandler and Rosenblatt, 1962; Kohut, 1971, 1977, 1984; Loewald, 1971, 1978).

All these formulations strive to account for the two-person, relationally based clinical setting and reconcile this with a theory of human motivation—to unify theory and method. For drive theorists, making the unconscious conscious and structural change, as internal rearrangements, represent the cure; the analyst's function, to furnish knowledge, is external, catalytic. For the object relationists, for whom the relationship itself is primary, the analyst enters the process. In the absence of the category of a dialectic, or the notion of reciprocal recursivity, or a theory of internalization, all these models resort to physicalist premises geared toward explaining how the outside can affect the inside and the origins of human motivation; they generate propositions about what motivates behavior, not about the nature of mind. These differences are indicative of a much broader, more fundamental epistemological problem, one that divides the world of physics from the world of living organisms.

In the world of physics, according to the second law of thermodynamics, it takes energy to maintain structure, without it there is disintegration; the concerns are with mass, force, and entropy; this is the world of Freudian metapsychology. In the world of cybernetics, a science of information, according to the natural history of organisms and aggregates of organisms, the concerns are with "identifying patterns of organization that characterize mental and living processes" (Keeney, 1982, p. 155). The first is a way of studying the laws of matter and the forces that move it; the second a way of discerning patterns of organization in the recursive embeddedness of living systems.

The dramatic shift is from an epistemology of substance to one of form: from a material world and the analysis of its mechanics to an interactive world discerned through the transformation of the forms it shapes and is shaped by. Many theorists today, however, confuse the two by formulating interactional models of internal mechanisms propelled by forces which explain motives. They fail to integrate a more basic paradigm shift—one which moves conceptually from mental structures to structural organization and pattern. The shift in view was made possible by a new scientific paradigm which introduced the concept of interlocking systems and attempted to account for the inseparable process of change in relation to patterns of stability in the organization of living systems.

Cybernetics and systems theory, thinking in terms of reciprocal recursivity, examine parts and wholes in terms of their patterns of organization. In contrast to the scientific method which isolates and objectifies, they place the agent within what is being examined; the investigator is part of the investigative system.[2] Further, the traditional passive–efferent paradigm of information is found to be inaccurate when describing the autonomy of living systems; rather, informing is to be viewed as *con*structive rather than *in*structive, conceived as a "recursive transforming of difference" (Bateson [1979], cited in Keeney [1982, p. 161]). Within the diverse currents of this trend, a common principle can be found: "to take man not as a reactive automaton . . . , but as an active personality system" (von Bertalanffy, 1975).

These models imply a dialectic. Discussions as to whether psychoanalysis is a one-person or a two-person psychology are moot if Freud's structural model is understood within an epistemology of recursive embeddedness. We cannot speak of an "I" without "another" since "I-ness" is a dialectic to otherness—"I" both contains and distinguishes itself from what is not itself. Freud's theory of stages of psychosexual development implied the significance of others in its libidinal, evolutionary design; while rooted in the biological, Freud's theories were operationalized in terms of relationship, and are as much relational as they are shaped by a drive-motivational mold. Equally, the one- or two-theory problem dissolves in an epistemology in which both are conceptualized as inseparable.

---

[2]Heisenberg's uncertainty principle from quantum theory accounts for this, stating that the observation of a phenomenon changes it.

The issues which gave rise to the need for a relationally based model become obsolete in an epistemology of recursivity in which a dialectic is implied. Freud's dichotomizing of inner and outer, fantasy and reality, subjective and objective ways of thinking, and his compartmentalizing psychic agencies with respect to mental contents can now be seen to be misleading foundations. It was this aspect of the theory, one that deals consistently with psychic reality but still attempts to polarize subjective and objective perception, founded on the notion of pleasure versus reality principles, that most misrepresents our uniquely human way of processing experience, one that is always subjective and always constructed and coconstructed.

Systems theory accounts for the interlocking processes of change in relation to patterns of stability and provides complementary perspectives for the psychoanalytic dyad and the study of group phenomena. Principles derived from cybernetics and systems models, accommodate intrapsychic and interpersonal, subjective and objective, acting and interacting, while facilitating the operationalizing of meaning within the contextual frame of the mind of an individual—in terms of purposes—with reference to behaviors in relation to others and their responsiveness. Imagine a series of concentric waves echoing outward and recursively inward. Without the sharp boundaries erected by a physicalist mentality, but rather thinking in functional terms of patterns of organization, the human mind is better understood as a seamless interactive process through which experiences are transformed into concepts.

The organism is now conceived as intrinsically active rather than reactive; stimuli do not cause processes in an inert system but only modify processes in an otherwise autonomously active system (Varela, 1979). Entropy is replaced with negentropic conceptualizations of innate development and naturally occurring "coherence"; the organism even "advances toward higher order organization" (von Bertalanffy, 1975, p. 209). Neither can a "reality principle" be found, corresponding to a fixed external reality as distinct from an individual's personal configurations of psychological experience; in fact, an intrinsic self-righting principle may be manifest in endogenous tendencies toward differentiation and reintegration in the reorganization and expression of symbolic representations throughout life

(Lichtenberg, 1989). Rather than being the result of compromise in a circuitous root toward inertia, activity is often sought for the yields of its own pleasure in self-expression, and is perceived as self-activated and goal oriented. This developmental orientation conceives of the person as intrinsically moving in the pursuit of evolutionary trends toward the fullest realization of innate potentials, in which regression is manifest as diminishing or stifling individuation and pushing back toward dedifferentiation and its correlate desymbolization.

In formulating a motivational theory of causal explanations, Freud inadvertently precipitated psychoanalysis into an unresolvable quandary because *meaning is not the result of a cause* but the private construction of a person (Home, 1966). It has been a misleading axiom, in my opinion, and one resulting from a natural science epistemology, to insist that a psychoanalytic model of mind explain motivation, for *motives are derived from meanings* and symptoms,[3] as we were taught by Freud's great original insight, are the expressions of these meanings. This is a symbolic relationship which reaches to the heart, not of the *cause* of the symptom but of the *means* for expressing its significance.

Psychoanalysis has delineated its field of operation by focusing on psychic reality and its transformation within a contextual realm dedicated to the exploration, understanding, and coconstruction of meanings, through their variegated expressions. And here we reach the central problem of psychoanalysis, an interpretive science locked into a natural science model. While the repercussions of this internal incoherence have led to years of disputes, we need not take this to mean that psychoanalysis is not a science or that an appropriate scientific framework cannot be found in which to organize its fundamental principles, although some theorists would eschew the whole issue. For this grounding we are again invited to examine the tenets and process of our method.

The analyst's interpretative punctuation of the analysand's free associations creates a particular, unique, specialized dialogue in which the dialectic of two subjects reconstructs and

---

[3]Today we would also say character or personality structure, defenses, general behavioral patterns, and style.

recontextualizes the events of the clinical situation in terms of a spontaneous subject and an object in the light of the complex interaction of language, history, current behavior, and reflection. Consequently, any genuine psychoanalytic model must define the pivotal role of language in development and its therapeutic action; reconsider the clinical phenomena of resistance, repetition, reconstructing, remembering, and working through; and encompass the unconscious and conscious dimensions of all experience, adopting both a fitting epistemology for issues of mind and a broad enough theoretical base to accommodate all these general principles.

In order to unfurl from the quagmire of motives, we must be suspicious of questions posed in terms of "why" because they trap us into causal answers and focus rather on generating questions that ask "what," in terms of "what does this mean." The same principle applies to theory building: the psychoanalytic situation generates data that are always variable with regard to content and always consistent with regard to form—it is the "talking cure"—what does this mean for our theory? To my mind it means that we would do well to explore the relationships between form and content—between our medium and the correlate developmental stages and uses to which it is put within the therapeutic situation. Scientific enterprise usually takes a demonstrable phenomenon as its point of departure and must ultimately return to it (Home, 1966). All we really have in psychoanalysis is a method of transformation through the medium of linguistic exchange; this then must be our central, theoretical point of departure. Psychoanalysis, as Freud pointed out, has the added difficulty of being a science which must take as its object of inquiry the very same mind it is trying to conceptualize. Yet mind can be known only through its manifestations. In fact mind is the vehicle by which concepts are formed out of prior knowledge or experience otherwise expressed through direct actions or behaviors.

I believe we will come closer to understanding the nature of mind if we attend to the relationship between the way experiences are being expressed and how these gradually become transformed into concepts, through various modes and channels denoting or expressing these concepts. The mind works neither energically to discharge tension nor motivationally to achieve inactive pleasure states: mind comes into being through symbolizing experience. Further, it seems to me that Freud's descriptive analogue referring to bound and unbound "energy," was an important inroad, albeit a metaphorical one, toward understanding the processes of psyche and the nature of the changes occurring in the clinical method. The therapeutic endeavor strives not for motivational change but for symbolizational transformation, and these transformations, which should be the targets of our metatheoretical focus, come closest to grasping what constitutes the essential therapeutic change in the nature of psychic reality. We are confronted by the simple truth that understanding rests neither in content alone nor form, but in the in-between land of their correspondences. In the social sciences we should be looking not at entities but at functions, not for energy but for structural organization; not for causes which can be found in mental contents (always variable), but in the *overall functioning* of mind itself. Such a model would conceive of experience as the signified and mind as the signifier—a symbolizing process.

Neither a dichotomized mind, biological drives and their energic shifts, nor reified juxtaposed structures or mental pictures appear today as viable postulates for the foundations of a metatheory. Our theory and practice are better served by a hierarchic model of mind understood as stages of symbolic organization, with corresponding modes and means for expressing experience and how these are reflected in behavior. Such a framework facilitates unification of the disparate facets of our model through prior assessment of what constitutes a genuine theory of mind and the articulation of a paradigm which focuses on the stepwise development of the instrument of our singularly human evolution; the symbolic function. Each level of symbolization radically alters experience and the meaning of what is represented for the subject; and the meanings incumbent upon this structurally altered organization bring about a change in the very nature of motives and their modes of expression, in behaviors and interpersonally.

Buttressed by a new epistemological starting point which provides a different way of knowing and understanding the shifting relations between experience and world, this work attempts to reconceptualize the psychoanalytic model of mind in the belief that psychoanalysis is a general psychology, that it urgently needs revitalizing, and that rigorous revisions encompassing interdisciplinary data must reconsider what has thus far been described within the context of an epistemology that has now been superseded.

As was suggested earlier, in the ongoing effort to reformulate psychoanalytic theory one major problem has been the general tendency for criteria traditionally adopted by the canons of positivist research to be applied in the judgment of all knowledge, to allow this frame of reference to govern our definitions of the nature of knowledge itself. The "reluctant mind" or, more benevolently, neo-orthodoxy would rather find compromise through adjustments or modifications that might accommodate Kuhn's "paradigm crisis" without radical change. What is threatened is the entire fabric of a particular way of understanding phenomena. There is massive resistance to strategies that seek to promote different ways of "knowing," that push toward accepting the relevance of different paradigms for conducting research or understanding phenomena, and ask that we shift our perspective to embrace different conceptions of scientific inquiry, questioning the very nature of science itself (Morgan, 1983).

One such approach, in seeking to remedy the assumption that it could be significant, or even possible, to study the social world by "neutral objective observation" devised a method for interpretive research strategies. From this perspective, the scientific protocol is understood to be just one particular kind of interpretive activity that serves to create the myth that one is being objective.

Evolving out of an attempt to counter the limitations of positivism (Dilthey, 1924; Max Weber, 1921, cited in Wellek and Warren, 1977) theorists who founded modern interpretive research, led an approach that focused on the intricate, socially constructed tissue of the social world. They reoriented ideas about research and laid the foundation for an objectivity that could account for the relevance of subjective meanings, the importance of individual actions within human exchanges, and in the processes through which individuals construct their realities. Such an approach favors in-depth analysis, the case study, and sensitive descriptions of contextual, subjective relevancies. Essentially, it rules out large-scale surveys, scrutiny of isolated fractions of phenomena, and measurements, since meaning can never be assumed and is always context bound. While the interpretive researcher is concerned with finding generalizations, the emphasis is on *generalizable processes* that are not content-specific. The empiricist preoccupation with isolation, observation, measurement, hypothesis testing, and prediction outcomes is, quite simply, not applicable to interpretive research.

A more recent and important alternate approach to interpretive research is that of the emergent paradigm or naturalistic inquiry—the two are so close they overlap (Schwartz and Ogilvy, 1979; Lincoln and Guba, 1985). Axioms of the positivist paradigm as derived from Newtonian mechanics stand in stark contrast to the principles advocated by the emergent paradigm (or naturalism), despite the fact that this new trend is being defined in relation to its predecessor under the umbrella of postpositivism.

The basic assumptions of empiricist philosophy, from which the emergent paradigm principles radically depart, are essentially those of naive realism, a universal scientific language, and the correspondence theory of truth (Guba, 1985, p. 81). These assumptions presume there is an external world which may be defined and thoroughly described in a scientific language by the scientific observer who stands outside it. This scientist observer, user of the scientific language, may comprehend external facts and organize these into propositions of the observable world which are proven true if they correspond to facts, and falsified if they do not (Hesse, 1980). In rejecting these assumptions the basic principles of the emergent paradigm, as delineated by Schwartz and Ogilvy (1979), characterize the shift along seven dimensions: complexity, heterarchy, morphogenesis, indeterminacy, mutual causality, perspective, and holography (Lincoln, 1985, p. 138).

Further, the philosophical underpinning of this model, in recalling the "private as political" credo of contemporary social movements, underscores that "on many levels the paradigm shift is with us and people are living it in their daily lives" (Lincoln, 1985, p. 140), as a multileveled new world view. In my opinion, this paradigm revolution presents psychoanalysis with an opportunity to ground its metatheoretical formulations in new epistemological soil which concomitantly enables it to substantiate its clinical method as both a treatment and a research mode. I therefore think it worthwhile to catalogue the conceptual changes underlying this new scientific approach.

The seven dimensions of shift are defined and conceptualized in the following summary of the basic principles of the emergent paradigm (or naturalism) as derived from Lincoln and Guba (1985, p. 88), after Schwartz and Ogilvy (1979).

Out of these 7 axiomatic transformations emerge 14 other logically derived points which bring congruence and coherence to the research enterprise. These are:

1. The naturalistic setting. Naturalists (like anthropologists and ethologists) are interested in contextual investigation, believing that one cannot understand a phenomenon, a situation, or an event removed from its context.

2. The emergent design. Believing in the unpredictable nature of interactional phenomena and the multiple constructs of realities, naturalists rarely predesign specific schemas of investigation. Anticipating an emergent design, the researcher relies on this to emerge or evolve in recursive interactions which will themselves bring forth what is of interest and of importance to the investigation.

3. The human as instrument. In believing that personal knowledge requires more than dispassionate rational analysis, and that the human-as-instrument approach provides for remarkable adaptability and potential for exchange of learning between researcher and respondent, naturalists acknowledge that all instrumentation implies some set of values, but believe that the human instrument is equipped to identify, account for, cope with, and learn from another's overt and covert values and communications.

4. Qualitative method. Methods most congruent to the human instrument are qualitative in nature. These include participant observation, interviewing, scrutiny of nonverbal

TABLE 1.1
Basic Beliefs and Associated Principles of the Schwartz and Ogilvy
Paradigm

New Paradigm Basic Belief	Associated Principle
Complexity	Real-world entities are a diverse lot of complex systems and organisms.
Heterarchy	Systems and organisms experience many simultaneous and potentially equally dominant orderings—none of which is "naturally" ordained.
Holography	Images of systems and organisms are created by a dynamic process of interaction that is (metaphorically) similar to the hologram, whose three-dimensional images are stored and recreated by the interference patterns of a split laser beam.
Indeterminacy	Future states of systems and organisms are in principle unpredictable.
Mutual Causality	Systems and organisms evolve and change together in such a way (with feedback and feedforward) as to make the distinction between cause and effect meaningless.
Morphogenesis	New forms of systems and organisms unpredicted (and unpredictable) from any of their parts can arise spontaneously under conditions of diversity, openness, complexity, mutual causality, and indeterminacy.
Perspective	Mental processes, instruments, and even disciplines are not neutral.

communication, and artifactual analysis, by which is meant the analysis of content, documentary analysis, record usage, and other forms of analytic observation which, naturalists believe, allow for examination of the emergent shape (or resistance to shaping the phenomena of interest take) within interactions with the inquirer. Qualitative methods engender holistic, broad-based understanding and strive to prevent the uprooting of phenomena from their contextual frames, wherein are lodged competing value systems and multiple constructions of different realities.

5. *Utilization of tacit knowledge* acknowledges and legitimizes the inherent utility of knowledge which is "known" or "felt" but cannot be put into articulate language. The distinction between propositional knowledge and tacit knowledge was made by Polanyi (1966). Naturalists support the utilization of these levels of intuitive or tacit knowledge, believing that much nonverbal and interactional activity between inquirer and respondent transpires at these levels, providing valuable clues and cues for framing understanding and further shaping of important questions.

6. *Grounded theory.* Theory construction may proceed out of validation or falsification of a hypothesis; or it may be derived and follow from data. Preferring the second grounded theory approach, naturalists typically construct theory from data rather than beginning with an a priori, constraining bias that might skew the understanding process. While bias, in the form of beliefs or attitudes, is inevitable, grounded theory construction is less amenable to imposing shape on the inquiry and more genuinely anchored in respondent analysis and reflection.

7. *Inductive analysis.* Inductive analysis structure is preferred to deductive techniques by the naturalist researcher, not only because it is more capable of subsuming multiple, contextually constructed realities, but also because it may take into account values that are intrinsic to the inquirer/respondent interactions, as well as those inherent in the explicit data encountered. Further, inductive methods are more likely to yield "thick description" (Geertz, 1973) and therefore strategic information which may be applied to similar contexts.

8. *Purposive sampling.* The naturalists' goal, to achieve maximum scope and range of data collection, is accomplished by casting a net designed to identify markedly opposite, deviant, or atypical constructions of reality in the situations of inquiry. Random sampling increases the likelihood of collecting data which are representative of the entire population of interest; purposive sampling is the appropriate strategy when one wants to learn about, and come to understand, something about particular cases, without the necessity for generalizing to all such cases. The search is for sameness, rather than variation. Purposive sampling maximizes the ability to explore a large range of

perspectives within a given context, and the in situ value patterns and multiple realities which are unique from individual to individual.

9. Problem determined boundaries. The simple solution in focusing and bounding an inquiry is to permit time, energy, and logistical factors to determine the boundaries; the more complex solution is to let the inquiry determine its own boundaries and to let the problems emerge contextually, rather than be bound by preestablished theoretical constructs. Because problems cannot be separated from the environments in which they are found, the establishment of boundaries cannot occur without data that have been contextually arrived at. This implies that both participants gain contextual information regarding conditions, values, and relevant shaping structures which will in turn inform them how long an inquiry should be and when it should stop. Having been thus defined and identified circumstantially, at this point, the inquiry is bounded, as data become redundant and duplicative.

10. Idiographic interpretation. Naturalists believe that it is the particulars of a given context that will shape interpretations and conclusions derived from collected data. Idiographic interpretation is to nomothetic interpretation as the particular is to the general. Different interpretations of conclusions will be significant inasmuch as they express the experience of those in a given context. Moreover, naturalists strive toward meta-analysis of mutual influences in shaping, that may lead to understandings which are cocreated and informative to both inquirer and respondent.

11. Tentative application. Bound by a value structure that does not believe in making broad generalizations, naturalists are cautious and reluctant to enforce sweeping application of designed interventions that tend to ignore particulars and contextual variants. This hesitation is in keeping with the belief that values and realities may be constructed by totally different sets of cognitions regarding meaning, from one context to another.

12. Case study reporting mode. Grounded as it is in the particular of a given context, the case history, as bridge between the humanities and sociology, is favored by naturalists and is always a part, or an end product, of an inquiry. Narrative form demands that the inquirer render experience, focus on description and process, consider patterns of mutual influence, and engage the reader. "To understand why someone behaves as they do, you must understand how it looked to him, what he thought he had to contend with, what alternatives he saw open to him; you can only understand the effect of opportunity structures, delinquent subcultures, social norms or other commonly invoked explanations of behavior by seeing them from the actor's point of view" (J. H. Mead, cited in Reinharz, 1979, pp. 40–43).

13. Special criteria for trustworthiness. Traditional criteria include internal validity, dependability, and confirmability (Lincoln and Guba, 1985). Naturalists reject conventional criteria for their studies on these grounds: (a) internal validity implies an isomorphism between outcome and a single reality onto which inquiry can converge; (b) external validity is inconsistent with the basic principles concerning generalizability; (c) reliability, because it requires absolute stability and replicability, is found to be inappropriate, irrelevant, and, in any case, unobtainable by a paradigm which upholds an emergent design; and (d) the criteria of objectivity are found to be useless by a model that chooses to admit, and attempts to take account of, two well-recognized problems in social science research studies, the role of values and the inquirer–respondent interaction (Guba, 1981).

14. Negotiated results. The arguments advanced in favor of negotiated results are complementary and consonant with principles of the naturalistic approach along moral, practical, and methodological dimensions. Member check (the process of checking findings with relevant coparticipants), as part of the cooperative process of inquiry, serves to determine credibility and to negotiate understandings regarding what is meant by information provided by respondents. Heron (1981) identifies relevant points of this cooperative paradigm, among which are the negotiation of the language of communication, intentionality, axiology (the study of values), and the argument for an extended epistemology, the belief that "knowledge" is best acquired by bringing propositional, practical, and experiential aspects of inquiry to bear on the interpretation of results (Lincoln, 1985).

The above points exist synergistically with one another and in relation to the axioms of this model as outlined above. Schwartz and Ogilvy's (1978) holographic conceptualization argues that rather than appearing concentrated at particular points, information is distributed throughout a system; it is therefore essential to try to understand the totality of a system and the manner in which it works.

My purpose in detailing the axiomatic base of the emergent paradigm and its related naturalistic research philosophy is to suggest that this new model provides a perfect foundation, indeed an ideally suited epistemological bed, in which to place a contemporary metatheory for psychoanalysis. Such a model permits reconceptualization of social science inquiry in general and is encompassing enough to accommodate the psychoanalytic multidimensional approach and stance to the exploration of mind. Moreover, in preferring inductive data analysis, this paradigm upholds (and itself adopts) the original methodology of psychoanalysis which combines research and treatment within a single context, deriving theory from the yields of contextual investigation. Further, this approach legitimizes and unifies the two facets of psychoanalysis, the theoretical and the clinical, without imposing or upholding unnecessary rifts.

Implementing the new paradigm requires rigorous traditional training and immersion in this; a thorough comprehension of the old, as well as exposure to alternate ideas, and a willingness to learn while questioning what is handed down. Perseverance in searching for the new, the capacity to evolve a new consciousness as it were, often lonely and demanding endeavors, are additional personal requirements: "The challenge is not simply to refine a method but to revise the entire paradigm" (Reinharz, 1981, p. 421). And Reinharz (1981) continues, "Socialization towards a new paradigm involves an encounter with and an internalization of a critical perspective vis-à-vis the dominant paradigm. . . . By grounding oneself in specific criticism of the dominant paradigm, the process of demystification with 'scientism' of the dominant paradigm can continue" (p. 421). The call involves continual effort to question assumptions and move through conflict innovatively, rather than regressing to orthodoxy, by analysis and the creation of alternatives, on the assumption that operational constructs come about as the last step in a process that began at an abstract level of conception (Colapinto, 1979).

A further requirement, in my opinion, is continued exposure to and inclusion of interdisciplinary ideas and an inherent responsibility toward cross-fertilization and integration. "The psychoanalytic theory which prevails," writes Richards (1990), "will be one which best explains or converges with data from other fields," and, he notes neuroscience and observational research of infancy and childhood in particular (p. 350); "For recognition of convergencies" is requisite in an epistemologically sophisticated understanding of the mind–body problem. It also requires an understanding of the relations between a theory of mind and theories of a biological or neurophysiological nature" (Richards, 1990, p. 385). This vision of the psychoanalytic theory of tomorrow, Richards believes, will be realized if "we promote vigorous dialogue among the proponents of divergent theoretical viewpoints of today" (p. 362). And if this promises to be a practical impossibility, then the revisionists' responsibility will have to be a vigorous examination of divergent theoretical viewpoints, in order to better arrive at a theory that corresponds to the multiple relevancies of the method.

This work is an attempt to reconceptualize the psychoanalytic model of mind, particularly those aspects currently attributed to energic movements, and to unify incongruous or disparate facets of theory in the implicit belief that psychoanalysis is a general psychology, that it urgently needs revitalizing, and that revisions must reexplain what has, thus far, been described within the context of an epistemology which has now been superseded.

My focus will be on those specific areas underlying our metatheory that rely on energic and economic analogical metaphors to explain mind and will move to a view of mind as a symbolizing process, a relatively simple unitary concept of psychic change at the heart of which is meaning as an operative activity. Our switch in epistemological gestalt opens the way for an experiential developmental model of subjective experience in which human symbolic systems, their stages of development and organization along the unconscious–conscious dimension, and their variegated modes and means of expression can begin to be understood.

The crux of change is from an epistemology of substance to one of living pattern: from a paradigm of "thing" to one of patterns of organization. In our study of mind we need to move from *Pleroma*, the world of thermodynamics, energy, inertia, and reification, to *Creatura*, the world of living pattern, process, relationship, participation (Bateson, 1972). These embody the imperative shift from mind as machine, the "mental apparatus," to mind in nature, a transformational process.

The first is the epistemology of Freud's metapsychology, the second an epistemology for a new metatheory, which encounters planes of organization at different levels of development and of different developmental lines, within a model of mind as organic assigner of meanings, idiosyncratically and contextually elaborated and expressed.

And for psychoanalysis as a whole, a method of treatment, of research, a theory of mind, a community: "The hardest lesson to learn is not how to choose, but rather how to acquire the passionate knowledge which will permit us again to be chosen" (Reiff, 1966, p. 98).

2.

Psychoanalysis Re-Viewed

> There is no need to be discouraged by these emendations. They are to be welcomed if they add something to our knowledge, and they are no disgrace to us so long as they enrich rather than invalidate our earlier views—by limiting some statement, perhaps, that was too general or by enlarging some idea that was too narrowly formulated.
>
> [S. Freud, 1926, p. 160]

In order to better identify and comprehend the loci of confusion in our metatheory, stemming from its epistemological base, I have selected for examination and exploration six major premises which subsume a number of fundamental concepts that underlie Freudian metapsychology. I do so in the belief that greater gain may be obtained by placing these key premises within a historical contextual framework and by following their development and amalgamation into the theoretical body of the Freudian edifice.

My approach will be twofold: first, to identify the origins of these premises tracing their evolution in Freud's thinking as he selectively elaborated upon, abandoned, or revised his conceptualizations, and follow these to contemporary theoretical status; and second, to derive from this a critical discussion of these propositions in the light of contemporary knowledge from the psychologies and related interdisciplinary fields of relevance to psychoanalysis. I have come to consider it the revisionists' responsibility to address the relevant issues from the standpoint of three broad interrelated perspectives, each reflecting corresponding central questions. The perspectives are the contextual, which asks what the relevant issues were at the time the theory was constructed; the epistemological, which asks what kind of world view the theorist was embedded in, and what kind of questions the theory answers and how; and the scientific, asking what we know now that the theorist did not know then. As I see it, the revisionist has an obligation to tackle current theoretical problems only after a thorough examination of these in the light of their origins and their historical development.

I undertake this task in view of the fact that a hundred years have passed since the inception of psychoanalysis, a dramatic period of rapid change; and that having played a crucial, pivotal part in the evolution of these changes, psychoanalysis now warrants a careful rereading of its own basic tenets, with a revisionary eye.

THE PRINCIPLE OF INERTIA

From his neurological and physiological training with Brücke, Meynert, and Breuer, Freud distilled an important principle, that of constancy, which appeared to him to underlie mental functioning. On the assumption that the primary function of nervous tissue is to reduce tension states arising within it, he named this tendency the "principle of neuronic inertia" (Freud, 1887–1902, p. 356).[1] The overall equilibrium of the system was thought to be predicated on a dynamic attempt to achieve the reduction of tension. Thus constancy and tension reduction were the organism's aims.

Understanding the importance of formulating his motivational theory in strictly psychological terms, Freud recast the "principle of neuronic inertia," naming it the pleasure–unpleasure principle. The simple early reflex arc model was now superseded by a basic homeostatic design which provided causal explanations for an organism perceived as seeking quiescence, or pleasure. The motivational spark which moved the organism was thought to be the "wish," conceptualized as the cathected

---

[1]Freud's early *Project* was an attempt to explain mental processes in neurophysiological terms, the only truly scientific etiological scheme apparent to him at the time.

mental representation of an instinctual need which, at bottom, was generated from a somatic source, manifest in an urge pressing for discharge. What had been neuronic cathexes became the "cathexes" of mental representations; the function was the same, although it was now transposed to purely "mental" or psychological phenomena.

Freud also utilized energic concepts consonant with a Newtonian, physicalist epistemology of matter and the forces that move it, borrowing these as explanatory analogies for psychological processes. From Hughlings Jackson (1831), he adopted the concept of dynamically related hierarchies in the central nervous system; from Darwin (1859), the tendency to emphasize evolutionary sequence; the American experimentalists (Thorndike, Titchener, Hull), and primarily Fechner 1860 *Elemente der Psychophysik*, the underlying axiomatic concept of tension-reduction. From such diverse sources emerged Freud's pleasure–unpleasure principle, primary and secondary processes, regression, the central role of conflict and a genetic approach to human development. To these, Freud added the psychologically formulated instinctual drive, *Trieb*, as the mental representation of an endogenous, somatic force, urging motoric discharge. The internal aim of drive was discharge of cathexis; the external aim, the means by which discharge was effected. Drives were defined in terms of their impetus, source, aim, and object.

From these origins there evolved the libido theory, developmentally that of infantile sexuality and its zonal proclivities. It was only after lengthy consideration that Freud found it necessary to give equal weight to a second drive, pitched against libido, that of aggression or destruction. This came about by Freud's observation of the unaccountable evidence (according to the pleasure principle) of a persistent compulsion to repeat painful experiences. This had come to the fore via the traumatic war neuroses. Rather than review the basic premises upon which the principle of "inertia" and pleasure rested, he sought to explain the phenomena by taking his constancy principle even a step further, postulating an endogenous drive toward total inertia, characterized by the destructive elimination of all energies, embodied in the archaic Nirvana principle. The dual-instinct theory, initially proposed in terms of libido and aggression and only much later abstracted to eros and thanatos (life as love versus death), are conceived as two opposing forces inherent in the basic struggle of existence which, at biological levels, find correspondence with the physiological phenomena of anabolism and catabolism: the libidinal and aggressive drives are the psychological representatives of this biological conflict (Freud, 1923). Yet in his theory, the basic motivational spring remains the reduction of tension, serving a pleasure principle that tends toward inertia. How can it be that life, eros, is thus caught up in a principle that tends toward death? This theoretical incongruence captures the essence of a theory caught at many levels between moral transcendence and biologistic fatality, an authoritarian ethic and the life of the body; "But this alternative between submission to authority and response to pleasure as guiding principles is fallacious," wrote Fromm (1947, p. 176). Perhaps, in this pessimistic "nodal core" Freud reveals his general view of mankind as being irrevocably caught in a compromise between desire, the body, and the constraints of culture, the mind.

Integration of dual drive theory was to await the advent of the structural theory (1923) and its later elaborations (Hartmann, 1950, 1964; Kris, 1951) permitting a more succinct conceptualization of the drives themselves as well as the ego's development of mechanisms of defense against these (A. Freud, 1937). The important formulation of a new theory of anxiety, attributing its signal function to the ego, was undertaken in Freud's seventieth year (1926). Structural theory provided a dynamic framework within which metapsychological tenets could be organized, as well as a conceptual model of greater clinical value and theoretical clarity.

At this early stage, Freud conceived of the "immature mind" as containing certain "primary mental processes" enabling it to effect discharge via mobile energies; these archaic modes were superseded by the adaptively molded "secondary processes," which had been modified by an inhibitory structure, the ego (Freud, 1887–1902) conceived as "a group of neurons with a constant cathexis." This relatively stable mental structure "performed" many functions. In addition to its secondary process quality, to the ego were attributed the functions of attention, perception, consciousness, memory, judgment, reality testing, thinking, and the psychological defenses. As a term, however, the ego was also used interchangeably to designate the phenomenological experience of "I-ness," of the self. Only much later did Freud recommend that the ego be understood primarily through the operation of its functions.

While the ego thus conceived stood in opposition to the more archaic areas of the mind, it was believed these modes might come to the fore under certain pathological conditions which induced a regression, wherein overwhelming affects or severe anxiety temporarily impaired higher, more complex psychological functioning. Paralleling Jacksonian neurology, in which such situations automatically call into play more primitive processes, Freud introduced the important concept of regression to his psychoanalytic theory. Obeying the "pleasure principle," and seeking the shortest pathway of discharge, the "wish" is thought to exploit the mind's capacity for "mental representation" and utilize this constructive ability creatively in dreams and fantasy to obtain immediate gratification.

For Freud psychoanalysis was a special psychology, one "which leads behind consciousness" (Freud, 1887–1902, p. 226), and is served metapsychologically, only when a psychical process has successfully been described in its dynamic, topographical and economic aspects (1915b). In this way Freud's theoretical extrapolations from the observations of his therapeutic method, were to yield him psychological explanatory models for human psychic functioning which embodied familiar physicalist principles.

I have had to take a slight detour and digress momentarily because Freud's theories often evolve in complicated, labyrinthine turns according to their own logic and symmetry. Moreover, one aspect of his theoretical thinking usually flows out of the unserviceable aspects of another, in an attempt to break through a theoretical impasse. To return to our theme, which rests on Freud's assumption that overall, organismic psychological equilibrium is premised on the same principles as is physiological homeostasis: Homeostasis refers to an automatic self-regulatory mechanism, like a thermostat, designed to return things to a status quo. In physiological functioning it applies to that internal organization of regulatory feedback loops which gauge the delicate balance of various biochemical, neurohormonal, and other systems, and works to maintain these within a precise vital range. It is a conceptual model which describes the functioning of a system. The term can be understood as being *one aspect* of the internal organization of the system or as being the *very nature* of the system's organization. It may be construed to be a *means to an end* (in causal terms) or to be *an end* (as maintaining the status quo through a resistance to change). For instance, Claude Bernard's milieu internal (1957) referred to the entire organism's internal coherence (I use the term suggested by P. F. Dell [1982]), whereas Cannon's (1932) use of the term *homeostasis* applied to a mechanism by which various variables in the body are maintained within a critical range. Each of these represents a different level of analysis, namely, the behavior of particular components of a system or the coherent functioning of the system as a whole. Freud used the concept to describe an overarching equilibrating mechanism which motivated the organism's overall goal of tension reduction, conceived psychologically as dynamic equilibrium, and theoretically as the "pleasure principle."

Insofar as equilibrium is construed in terms of tension reduction in a dynamic organism, this same organism cannot be conceived as stimulus-seeking or as striving to bring about its own evolution through the active pursuit of mastery. Neither of these pursuits can be accounted for by a primary motivational goal which seeks quiescence or inertia in tems of inactivity. Such intentional interactions, guided by an active, purposeful organism, therefore, had to be ascribed to a compromise structure, the ego. In addition, because instinctual pressures were endogenous and labored only for a "pleasure principle" serving internal gain, Freud had to juxtapose and weigh the ego and its secondary process functioning toward external "reality." This dichotomizing of inner and outer goals has left countless, theoretical problems in its wake. Actually, there is no need for such juxtaposition in a unitary developmental framework. Moreover, the concept of homeostasis itself has been highly criticized and appears flawed when applied to living systems. Derived from a physicalist epistemology, it serves physiological principles but is ill-suited to the "structure-determined" (Maturana and Varela, 1980) ordering phenomena which arise spontaneously in the coherence of living interactional systems (Dell, 1982). Homeostasis as a means is vitalistic and, according to Dell (1982), leads to a causal dualism; thus to reason that the system maintains stability because it is homeostatic is circular reasoning, and, to answer that the system is stable because of an inherent "homeostatic principle" is akin to explaining the phenomena of life by a concept such as élan vital (Dell, 1982). The mentality which seeks reasons and causes for homeostatic mechanisms also tends to isolate variables and to present a view of individual functioning that is detached from its surround, one which does not serve when applied to living exchanges. The same idea is better conceived as one of intersystemic coherence—this conceptualization has the added benefit of implying the person exists in an environment wherein internal and external goals are in constant flux, each impacting on the other as they interrelate. In an organismic–holistic framework, "every act gains significance and status in terms of its role in the overall functioning of the organism" (Werner and Kaplan, 1963, p. 5).

Attempting to encompass both tendencies toward preservation of the status quo and progressive developmental tendencies, Werner and Kaplan (1963) write, "There is, on the one hand, the tendency of organisms to *conserve* their integrity, whether biological or psychological, in the face of variable and often adverse external or internal conditions. . . . There is, on the other hand, the tendency of organisms to *develop* toward a relatively mature state: under the widest range of conditions, organisms undergo transformations from the status of relatively little differentiated entities to relatively differentiated or integrated adult forms" (p. 5). They assume an inherent progressive developmental trend toward differentiation and integration. It is difficult to reconcile the forward thrust of progression with a basic, governing principle of inertia, and even more difficult to justify movement by a force which tends toward stasis or rest. Perhaps it is in the confluence of both tendencies that genuine equilibrium and maturation occur.

   The idea of homeostasis also appears to be closely related to the clinical concept of "resistance." One of Freud's basic clinical principles, often described by him in adversarial or militaristic metaphors (as in fighting the resistance every step of the way), rests in part on a moralistic concept of cathectic forces at work in repression and, in part, on the homeostatic premise that the system will resist change. While this is how things may appear, it has become clear that "energic forces" are not a satisfactory explanation for the characteristically entrenched phenomena manifesting clinically as resistance. The system, to continue this unsavory yet serviceable euphemism for a person, is not so much resisting as operating in the only way it knows how, according to its own coherence. Part of the therapeutic effect in this light might be viewed as having a benevolent destabilizing intent;[2] interpreting the resistance as being a way of changing the coherence or reconstructing a new narrative. The person, or system, will evince a tendency toward morphostasis in integrative attempts to interpret information according to its coherence, and a tendency toward morphogenesis in ongoing adjustments to new input. In attempting to accommodate the notions of intrasystemic and intersystemic change, a principle of coherence ("a congruent interdependence in functioning whereby all aspects of the system fit together" [Dell, 1982, p. 31]), serves us better than homeostasis, and corresponds more closely to the notion of narrative truth.

   In psychoanalysis this agent of coherence has been called the ego which, however, due to its terminological dual service as agent and functional system, still presents too many theoretical problems. Conceptually, however, I believe it is unfortunate that Freud chose to abandon his early postulations regarding the ego's "instincts," those of self-preservation and mastery, since I believe these ideas, perhaps in modified form, together with the topographical model, were of great value for a more unified theoretical approach. If we can conceive of the ego as less of a structure than as the goal-directed, relating, mastering, and signifying expression of an individual's "coherence," then we

___

[2]Heisenberg's uncertainty principle may be invoked to support this.

need postulate no further drive-fueled motivations operating in the service of a principle of pleasure.

We have traveled far from "neuronal inertia," and in so doing have found the organism to be quite the contrary, goal-directed, active, pushing for mastery and development. Such a view questions the basis upon which Freud's fundamental principle is founded. Yet how is the pursuit of quiescence to be reconciled with the great thrust of mankind to understand, to represent, to conceptualize, to create, and build and bring about innovation? Homeostasis and quiescence cannot account for change in a moving model. The adaptive, mastering ego cannot be reconciled with a superordinate "principle" of tension reduction. Generally, the homeostatic scheme is not applicable to dynamic regulations (those that are not based on fixed mechanisms) or nonutilitarian, spontaneous activities. Clearly it cannot account for processes designed to increase tension rather than diminish it, or to processes aiming toward growth, development, creation, or art. We need to be able to account for evolution and activity based on an assumption that people respond to internal strivings which correspond to what can be realized, or can be accomplished in stimulus-filled contexts. People characteristically find fulfillment through shifting the predominant aims of their intrinsic developmental aspirations throughout the life span, goals which are not always or necessarily measured along the pleasure–unpleasure dimension. We need to move from a basic concept of stasis, to one of motus; from a paradigm of inertia to one of goal-oriented movement.

PERCEPTION

A fundamental shift in the way we understand perceptual activity has occurred since 1604, the time when Johannes Kepler equated seeing in man with the way a lens works in a camera, as carrying an image of the world projected on the back of the brain. This, however, was the theory of vision which was to dominate the fields of neurophysiology, philosophy, and psychology for many years. Freud was well aware of the pivotal significance of perception for a general psychology and, as early as 1896 astutely lamented in a letter to Wilhelm Fleiss, "If I could give a complete account of the psychological characteristics of perception . . . I should have enunciated a new psychology" (December 6, 1896, p. 208).

That said and, in accord with nineteenth century association theory, Freud accepted and adopted the prevailing view of perception as the passive, temporary registration of veridical external objects. Providing the foundations for a dichotomous view, which differentiates between perceptions that originate "internally" from those originating "externally," this belief was to have far-reaching implications for his theories. In line with Kepler's theory, he began by seeking an analogy between the psychical "apparatus" and the microscope or telescope, and, to account for the formation of dreams, indeed for all mental activity, he set a psychological stage with "a scene of action in mental, not physical space" (Steele and Jacobsen, 1977, p. 395). Freud the neurologist preserves his concerns with the "mechanical" and transposes the "machine" model from one functional system to another. In this way he also sought functional and causal explanations using identified and familiar mechanisms and processes.

The "perceptual apparatus" was thought to operate like a receptive surface, as the lens of a camera, and to record new registrations but retain no permanent trace of these: "It is clear, then, that, if the Pcpt. system has no memory whatever, it cannot retain any associative traces" (Freud, 1900, p. 539). Freud believed the only way continuity was experienced, or the past permitted to influence the present, was through the automatic storage of specific objects and their recalling. External reality and perception were often used interchangeably by him, perception itself, believed to correspond with veridical objective registration, left a lasting trace or "memory image," which corresponded to a "cathected" mental representation, conceived as an inner copy of the external object.[3]

---

[3]This belief produced a theoretical quandary for Freud (1917a) referred to in his Introductory Lecture (p. 260), necessitating an attempt to divide the spatially conceived of unconscious. It did not make sense to him that the unconscious which housed the "day residue" could be the same unconscious from whence the "wish" springs. He therefore postulated the existence of a second unconscious and said it would be oppor-

In the "psychic apparatus" the progressive function was from perception to motor activity, passing through the mnemic image (memory). Perception → Mnemic Image → Motor. Later, unconscious (Ucs) and preconscious (Pcs) were interposed between the mnemic image and the motor end: Perception → Mnemic Image → Ucs, Pcs → Motor. Stimuli were thought to originate either through perception exogenously, or from the mnemic image or the unconscious, and in either case innervation moved toward the motor end. The "machine" thus construed, in accordance with the pleasure principle, was pushed to action either by "external" objects or their stored internal "mnemic images," which become distorted and imbued with drive cathexes—the "object" refound.

Inherent is a dichotomized "external reality-world" perceived, and an "internal" partially remembered and "wished-for-world," reinvented. To these were added the psychological defenses, the function of which it was to counter and partially suppress "unrealistic" impulses arising from wishful fantasies, and tame these sufficiently to conform with "realistic" fulfillment. For Freud, "Reality (perception) and fantasy (drive cathected mental representation)," writes Schimek (1975), were like "two different and competing languages or currencies, the constantly shifting dominance between the two depending on economic factors, the relative strength of the drive-cathexis and defense counter-cathexis" (p. 174). He did not, apparently, further question or doubt a theory of cognition which "takes for granted from the start the capacity for objective veridical perceptions and their automatic storage as undistorted memory content" (p. 173). Yet this assumption precipitated important theoretical consequences in the search for unconscious motivators, necessitating the postulation of energic cathectic charges which, by virtue of their drive pressure, distort the representation and imbue it with personal meaning.

To summarize: Freud's theory conceives of (1) veridical, objective perceptions and their memory images; (2) distortion of these through drive pressure (and primary process, mobile

---

tune to distinguish these by different names—but then abandoned this dilemma (see p. 28, chapter 1).

energy); and (3) modification of these distortions through the restraining of drive pressure by defenses which modulate the urgency of discharge (pleasure) by adhering to the requirements of reality (secondary process, bound energy). When motoric action is blocked, as in sleep, excitations would be pushed backward toward the perceptual end, to the internal, fantasied world of pictorialized wish-fulfillment: "In regression the fabric of the dream-thoughts is resolved into its raw material" (Freud, 1900, p. 543). Hence, the postulation of latent and manifest content in dreams and the methodological rationale for "interpreting" such latent content or disavowed, repressed thoughts (making the unconscious conscious), which form the essence of Freud's topographical theory.

Freud's adherence to this erroneous theory of perceptual activity, despite the fact that it flew in the face of his awareness of the irrational in man and of his focus on subjectivity, led to his assumption that distortions of "objective" memory contents must be due to drive pressure. This pressure, he thought, produced "fantasies," or wishful thinking, which represented the motor urge fueled by this motivating force. The confusion between "perception" (reality) and hallucinated mnemic images (subjective creations) is attributed to drive distortion.

In emphasizing the constructivist nature of perceptual phenomena, research of the next 40 years essentially turned all of this upside down. Helmoltz' (1910) functionalism paved the way for the work of Ames (1946–1947), Hilgard (1951, 1962), and the pioneering research of Bruner (Bruner and Goodman, 1947) and Postman and Bruner (1952), all providing evidence that "purposes, aims and intentions suffuse the very act of perceiving" (cited in Klein [1970, p. 129]). In an attempt to update psychoanalytic theory and establish a contemporary conceptualization of personality, George Klein's target was "a theory that can lead to laws of *perceivers* rather than to laws of *perceptions*, a theory concerned less with linking generalized field conditions or states of motivation to perception in general than to the organization of people" (1970, p. 129). The implication of this later body of research is that the organism actively participates in adapting to the environment and continuously "constructs" the world it perceives.

"All input arising over our sensory channels is transformed by the nervous system and is integrated into meaningful percepts," writes Davidson (1980, p. 16) from a biocognitive perspective, echoing Pribram (1969a,b), the renowned neurophysiologist, in his reporting of the implications of the results of visual and information storage experiments:

> All these differing electrical responses arose in the visual cortex—the part of the brain that receives the visual input. We are forced to conclude that signals representing experience converge with and modify the input to the visual-input systems. . . . Somewhere between the retina and the visual cortex the inflowing signals are modified to provide information that is already linked to a response. . . . Evidently what reached the visual cortex is evoked by the external world but is hardly a direct or simple replica of it. Further, the information inherent in the input becomes distributed over wide regions of the visual cortex [p. 6].

With this last statement, Pribram, Nuwer, and Baron (1974) introduce their concept of holographic encoding, a holographic model of the brain, reasoning (as had Lashley [1960], another great neuropsychologist) that neuronal events might interact in ways that would produce extensive and complex patterns within the brain. Today this hypothesis has been substantiated. In connection with the storing of information implicating a large network in the brain, he goes on to discuss distribution in space and time, as in long-term and short-term memory encoding. But for our immediate purpose, it suffices to emphasize the predominantly active, subjective nature of our perceptual processes and the continuous selections we make in the ongoing construction of what and how we perceive, what we make of it, and how we will integrate this information.

Accordingly, this processing function of perception, resembles the functions attributed by Freud to the ego (particularly the unconscious ego),[4] since how we construe what we perceive

---

[4]Later to be defined by Hartmann as one of the "autonomous" functions of the same structural ego.

will have an enormous impact on our judgment and ensuing actions. In this regard, the intrinsic role of the central nervous system was stressed by Mahler, in her assessment of the evolving ego in developmental terms, as she asserted "the somatic corollary of ego development is the central nervous system" (Mahler, Pine, and Bergman, 1975, p. 33). In thus joining somatic processes (biological) to a psychologically conceptualized corollary structure, the ego, we can begin to dissolve the confining dualities we have inherited, particularly along the internal–external, subjective–objective, and psyche–soma dimensions.

Emphasizing the confluence of biological, inherited constitutional characteristics and the impact of environmental factors on how we perceive, Davidson (1980) stresses: "Some of the information in a given stimulus array will be accentuated, other information will be attenuated or even eliminated. The hard-wired architecture of the peripheral sensory apparatus, the inherited functional properties of the central nervous system, as well as the learned interpretational matrix (Kagan, 1967), all combine to govern the manner in which we perceive and respond to our environment" (p. 16).

The confusion between perception (as in Keplerian theory) and subjective reality can be found throughout psychology and is indicative of a more basic problem producing fundamental epistemological errors.[5] An "idea born out of the myopia toward personality theory" (G. Klein, 1970, p. 13), this orientation still creeps into current conceptualizations, despite work which has essentially buried the early view of an autonomous perceptual system functionally isolated which can be studied apart from the person.

Freud's juxtaposition of an external, "objective" reality to an internal "subjective" one produced enormous theoretical problems necessitating recourse to energic cathexes, a reality principle, and the confusion of a content-full unconscious with spatial boundaries between memories and drive induced mental representations. It is now evident that his 1896 model of perception as passive-afferent must be supplanted by perception understood as active-efferent (Freud, 1887–1902). Perception is *not* a

---

[5]It is similar to that produced by the quantified measurement of "observable behavior" (taken as data) on the assumption that "behaviors" have a direct correspondence to fixed, preestablished "meanings."

passive event; conversely the eye stands ready to serve the central process. It will follow that the whole person will be involved in the construction of all perception, in which the current state of the entire organism will always exert a significant impact. Memory, like perception, is continuously and selectively constructed and reconstructed. In Piagetian terms, the sensorimotor schemata form the basis for perception and *action*, rather than sensation or imagery, is at the base of all mental activity; the mind's function one of seeking, receiving, and attributing meaning in its processing and organizing of experience. The mind thus perceived, in serving the organism's goals, seeks pattern matching and similarity: we will tend to shape what we see according to what we already know or expect. The central nervous system's intactness is contingent upon efficient and effective internalization of information and of its integration in increasingly differentiated fashion. Cognitive assimilation and accommodation, the ego's mediating function, the mind as transformer of experience, these concepts come together in the notion of an active, constructing, developing central nervous system, governed by a mind which "orders" and organizes sensory input in accordance with the significance it attributes to events and the meanings with which it imbues them. What I hope to develop further in this work is the idea of mind as central nervous system integrator: of mind as organizer and transformer of experience which, by way of being subjectively "re-presented," acquires meaning according to different levels of symbolizational development.

DEVELOPMENT

"I have found love of the mother and jealousy of the father in my own case too, and now I believe it to be a general phenomenon of early childhood. . . . If this is the case, the gripping power of Oedipus Rex . . . becomes intelligible . . . the Greek myth seizes on a compulsion which everyone recognizes because he has felt traces of it in himself" (Freud, 1887–1902, letters of October 15, 1897).

From this momentous discovery, disclosed initially in a letter to his friend Fliess, Freud was to evolve his theory of psychosexual development, the libido theory. It was not until *Three Essays on the Theory of Sexuality* (1905b), however, in the full force of this ground-breaking text, that the psychosexual theory was to make its impact. Declaring the end of the innocence of childhood, Freud courageously disclosed to the world the universal phenomenon of infantile sexuality with all its empassioned and egotistic desires, its possessiveness and polymorphous perverse impulsions. He paid dearly for his brazenness as culture met the demythologizing of its sanctimonious illusions of infantile purity with pernicious resistance and scathing attacks on Freud himself. He must have felt himself to be in good company, however, because he identifies with and reconnects himself to Schopenhauer and Plato (Preface to the 4th edition, May 1920). In this work in particular, one is also aware of a deliberate allegiance to Darwin's legacy, following a Darwinian model which occupies the boundary where biology and psychology dovetail, touching on the complex interrelation between phylogeny and ontogeny. As Freud noted at a later date: "The phylogenetic disposition can be seen at work behind the ontogenetic process" (1905b, p. 131, Preface to the 3rd edition).

Consistent with an evolutionary point of view, *Three Essays* is about origins, and just as Darwin explored transformational developments of the species, so Freud is preoccupied with tracing the transformations of the sexual instincts and accounting for the variations in structure and form these take. More importantly, the work subsumes earlier ideas on the sexual etiology of hysteria and the neuroses and unabashedly declares its indebtedness to the psychoanalytic method—"that this part of the theory is based on equally careful and impartial observation" (Freud, 1905b, p. 133)—with a radical departure from biologically based study to render to psychology what lies "on the frontier" with biology, in an in-between realm. Here again Freud is weaving a thread that binds the body (instinct) and its pressing energy to the mind via transmutations into psychological experience, now observable through the unique avenue provided by his method; "the present work is characterized not only by being completely based upon psychoanalytic research, but also by being deliberately independent of the findings of biology . . .—a study which is concerned with the sexual functions of human beings and which is made possible through the technique of psychoanalysis" (Freud, 1905b, p. 131).

The elaboration of the concept of "psychical energy," its dynamic mobility and "economy in expenditure on inhibition or suppression" (Freud, 1905a, p. 119), was already extensively included in another major work, *Jokes and Their Relation to the Unconscious,* published in the same year (1905a). Here Freud overtly credits Lipps (1897) for his adoption of his energic-psychological conceptualization which was to play such a fundamental part in the construction of his theory.

> The concepts of "psychical energy" and "discharge," and the treatment of psychical energy as a quantity have become habitual in my thoughts since I began to arrange factors of psychopathology philosophically; and already in my *Interpretation of Dreams* (1900) I tried (in the same sense as Lipps) to establish the fact that what are "really psychically effective" are psychical processes which are unconscious in themselves, not the contents of consciousness. . . . My experiences of the displaceability of psychical energy along certain paths of association, and of the almost indestructible persistence of the traces of psychical processes, have in fact suggested to me an attempt at picturing the unknown in such a way [Freud, 1905a, pp. 147, 148].

The "unknown," then quite a vast territory, quickly became dominated by the energic pathways of instinctual drives, in this case the all-important sexual "instinctual energy," which Freud proceeded to arrange systematically according to a classification of the varieties of its components and later of the forms it takes. The sexual drive was described in terms of goals, objects, and sources and particularly its great plasticity with respect to goals and objects.

While the theory of instinctual drives and their transformations, Freud's framework for his entire model, has now been widely criticized, it guided and served generations of analysts in their work. The biologically oriented motivational theory of

instincts and its accompanying energic framework, was widely
accepted as the only explanatory model for the various psychic
transformations observed in the clinical method and upon
which psychoanalytic theory was constructed. Sterba (1968)
epitomizes this view as he writes, "Mental manifestations are so
manifold . . . that even the limitation to a single principle of
explanation, such as the theory of instincts, results in a complicated presentation. However, in order to gain a deeper insight
into psychic material, Freud's theory of libido has become indispensable, no adequate psychological approach is possible without it" (p. 77).

This might be true if explanations are sought in terms of
how and why, in a breakdown seeking origins. The search for
a single explanatory code for the mechanics of the apparatus
and its motivational fuel, might well be constrained by analogies
to a machine. It is less true or applicable, however, to an approach which finds understanding in the processes of mind
itself; in the active confluence and interrelationship between
sensory, interpersonal, and information-ordering processes and
the particular *meanings* and world view that are constructed out
of this complex transforming of experience. Yet the historical
task of a psychological theory in Freud's day was to join body
and mind and mend the artificial cleavage which at the time
was magnified by post-Victorian propriety and prejudice. Neither beast nor spirit, the human body had to be integrated with
the human mind, and nothing but Freudian brashness, with
its forthright presentation of infantile sexuality, its unbiased
approach to the perversions and aberrations, devoid of any pre-
conceptions, and its attempt to enlarge the concept of sexuality,
would suffice. Again and again Freud sought analogical explanations for psychological processes, for origins, development, behavior, transformation—and he did this without the benefits of
an adequate body of research or an epistemologically appropriate language.

His vastly broadened concept of sexuality (it has come to
mean all that is somatic, sensory, pleasurable, sensual, erotic
and its psychic expression) is, even today, as misunderstood as
his closely related Eros, "of the divine Plato" (Freud, 1905b, p.

xviii). Freud's vision produced theories which interweave explanations from diverse planes of discourse and are articulated at
different levels of abstraction. We are asked to follow him in
analogy or metaphor as he denotes, via spatial topography or
physical structure, as energies become ideas and bodily zones
acquire erotic significance, to the highest vectors of anabolism
and catabolism as living and dying forces in nature. However,
I do not believe that we can take the language Freud used to
describe his discoveries to mean that his observations were incorrect. On the contrary, it seems to me that it is our responsibility rather, to recontextualize these concepts and recast them
in a framework compatible with the knowledge afforded us by
contemporary science.

In accordance with the principles of drive theory, which
traced the origins of sexual and other urges to endogenous
somatic sources, Freud's theory of development is essentially
formulated around a five-phase psychosexual developmental
program which occurs spontaneously in early childhood, progressing through stages designated by the erogenous zones which
achieve successive dominance. The movement of libido is fluid
and mobile in childhood: from its origin in "the primal cavity"
(Spitz, 1965), the mouth, it moves to the anal sphincter, then
to the penis and clitoris, and, in optimal development, reaches
the genital organization, a stage equated with normal heterosex-
ual satisfaction. Thus, the oral, anal, and phallic-oedipal stages,
all characterized by their component-instinctual gratifications,
ideally become integrated and subsumed in mature genitality
which culminates in a desire for copulation with a single, post-
ambivalently loved other for the purpose of procreation. In
health, the component instincts find satisfaction in sexual fore-
play, while the myriad variations of this optimal outcome, the
perversions, aberrations, fetishism, inhibitions, and neuroses,
are understood to be fixations, displacements, and regressive
reenactments of instinctual expressions arrested at earlier developmental stages.

The concept of regression is a central idea in clinical psychoanalysis and one for which Freud found evidence in the
empirical observations which led to his psychosexual developmental model. This concept was rooted in ideas derived from

Darwin, Haeckel ("ontogeny recapitulates phylogeny"), Hall's "recapitulation theory" and the neurologist Hughlings Jackson's (1831), who, within an evolutionary framework, had conceived of neurological disease as "the reemergence of intact, older phylogenetic modes of integration, released by the destruction or malfunction of later evolutionary structures" (Bemporad, 1980, p. 6). Within this conceptual framework, Freud identified "libidinal" regressions in his neurotic patients, because individuals in psychoanalytic treatment manifesting a "regression" tended to disclose memories and fantasies pertaining to the earliest stages of their childhood. This wholesale transposition of a neurological idea was to foster the notion of regression as moving backward, along a temporal dimension. Even today, regression is understood in functional terms, as a result rather than in terms of structural organization, as the expression of certain aspects of ongoing experience. Again, the limitations of the causal and sequential constructs imposed by a physicalist science contrive particular interpretations of data which can and might better be understood through other conceptual dimensions which preserve the phenomenology of simultaneity.

True to his dynamic conceptualization, the psychological experience of childhood is depicted as one of conflict and compromise between instinctual pressure and societal constraint. Thus, "character" (Abraham, 1924; Reich, 1933) evolves out of the confluence of compromise solutions and derivative satisfactions elaborated at each psychosexual phase, culminating in the nuclear "Oedipus complex" which, through its requirement for renunciation and resulting intrapsychic restructuralization, induces an identification with the parent of the same sex, producing a new structure, the superego (Fenichel, 1945). In the absence of data regarding the mental development of children or research-based literature on human cognitive development, Freud devised this ingenious psychological elaboration based on the nature of the material his adult patients revealed to him in psychoanalysis. Thus, the internalization of parental rules is attributed to the enstatement of a psychic "structure."

The sexual instinct is believed to be central in the formation and maintenance of neurotic symptoms, providing the "source of energy" for the neuroses in which, to varying degrees, the "sexual life" of the individual becomes expressed symbolically through symptoms. These are found to have psychological meaning which can be understood in relation to the life history, and are revealed in the manifestations of the contents of the "repressed." "In my experience," writes Freud (1905b), "anyone who is in any way, whether socially or ethically, abnormal mentally is invariably abnormal also in his sexual life" (p. 149); hence the neuroses are said to be the "negative of perversions." All the component instincts in their "paired opposites" and all the perversions appear in the unconscious mental life of neurotics. Furthermore, we are advised "to loosen the bond that exists in our thoughts between object and instinct" (p. 148), as the sexual drive is initially independent of objects, it is "autoerotic," and takes its own body for satisfaction (the infant's thumb-sucking is offered as the prototype). Even later on, Freud continues to assert that it is doubtful that the origin of desire is "due to its object's attractiveness" (1905b, p. 148), but rather that it represents a rekindling of passion in an object "re-found." Nevertheless, in its optimal, postoedipal, genital organization, and only at puberty, the sexual drive will become oriented toward an object of the opposite sex, fostering the final rupture of the child's tie to the parents. At this juncture, drive theory is articulated in such a way as to encompass interpersonal and individuating steps which today can be seen as providing their own motivational impact according to other developmental frameworks.

For Freud (1905b) there is no sharp line neatly dividing normal from abnormal as sexuality, "the weak spot" (p. 149) of the species, becomes the great equalizer: "Experience shows that disturbances of the sexual instinct among the insane do not differ from those that occur among the healthy (p. 148). . . . The very remarkable relation which thus holds between sexual variations and the descending scale from health to insanity gives us plenty of material for thought" (p. 149). Freud is able to achieve formidable theoretical symmetry with the help of a developmental theory of sexuality centering on the biological substrate which corresponds to his overall dynamic design for a theory of personality which emphasizes the continual state of conflict and compromise between instinct and culture.

The turbulent oedipal drama, in Freud's scheme, is followed by latency, a time of relative quiescence during which the child, in an outward turning, becomes involved with school, peers, friendships, and others outside of the immediate family. This phase will be succeeded by a recapitulation of earlier intensities during puberty and a final developmental thrust toward unification of the component instincts in "an impulsion with a single aim" (1905b, p. 232), the definition of adult sexuality. While Freud emphasizes the issue of constitution or hereditary disposition, "upon which it is possible that the principal weight falls" (p. 235), he frequently also supports the opposite view: "it is not possible to adopt the view that the form to be taken by sexual life is unambiguously decided, once and for all, with the inception of the different components of the sexual constitution." He leaves the determining influence of experience open and fluid, as he asserts: "On the contrary, the determining process continues, and further possibilities arise according to the vicissitudes of the tributary streams of sexuality springing from their separate sources. This further modification is clearly what brings the decisive outcome, and constitutions which might be described as the same can lead to three different final results" (p. 237). Thus component instincts of excessive strength may be diverted into various other channels (such as repression) or undergo the transformational process of sublimation as in "the origin of artistic activity" (1905b, p. 238). Freud concludes, "The constitutional factor must await experiences before it can make itself felt; the accidental factor must have a constitutional basis in order to come into operation" (p. 105).

This model of development dominated psychoanalysis until a shift in orientation was brought about by the ego-psychological emphasis on understanding the ego and its adaptive functions. This approach heralded the advent of an important new concept introduced by A. Freud, that of developmental lines, and the postulation of a "conflict-free" area of noninstinctual energy in the ego (Hartmann, 1950). With an intent to establish psychoanalysis as a scientific psychology, Hartmann (1939) set out to redefine and refine the theory, providing such conceptual links as adaptation, equilibrium, and maturation, and incorporating several contemporary trends in psychology, among which were development as a process of differentiation and integration (Leichtman, 1990). In acknowledging the influence of significant European functionalist and developmental psychologists, such as C. and K. Bühler, Claparède, and Werner, and with characteristic scientific rigor, Hartmann sought to expand and orient the attention of psychoanalysis to research grounded in developmental psychology and redirect the study of the development of the ego to consider those functions which do not appear to be rooted in conflict. In seeking to satisfy a positivist protocol and promote further advances in the field's scientific claim, Hartmann presented arguments along methodological and theoretical dimensions, as well as addressing the definition of psychoanalysis as a general psychology. Hartmann decisively pointed the field toward empirically testable research based on direct infant and child observation, thereby departing from earlier theoretical hypotheses extrapolated from adult reconstructions of childhood, rooted in the psychoanalytic method. In this way he paved the way for the inclusion of systematized research of the preverbal stages, which he considered to be "prerequisite for theoretical advances in a variety of aspects" (1939, cited in Leichtman 1990, p. 923).

The impact of developmental psychology gained increasing acceptance in psychoanalysis as pioneer analysts such as Brazelton (1973), Bowlby (1969, 1973, 1980), Spitz (1965), Emde (1983), Jacobson (1964), Fraiberg (1969), and Kestenberg (1975), made significant contributions along empirical lines, while earlier M. Klein had developed her idiosyncratic theory derived from the analysis of children in her London practice. The eminent contributions of Mahler (Mahler, Pine, and Bergman, 1975) tracing and delineating the early stages of separation and individuation as the "psychological birth" of the child, embody the flowering results of Hartmann's vision. Integration of psychoanalysis with developmental psychology, in Mahler's work, reinforces a general framework for a new metapsychology. Mahler's theory, essentially confirming but also greatly refining and expanding psychoanalytic postulates, observes three major developmental phases—the autistic, symbiotic, and the separation–individuation process, starting at birth and ending in the achievement of object constancy at around 4 years of age. Mahler's model is an ego-psychology, drive-based theory, which provides a valuable framework in which to organize the characteristic steps in the psychological struggle toward separation in infancy. She has now been countered and criticized by Stern, a contemporary developmenal theorist, who claims the infant shows separateness at birth and evolves through multiple experiences of self with other, in a coconstruction of identity building.

Freud's drive-based psychosexual stages provided the terrain for the developmental orientation in psychoanalytic theory which was later to be emphasized by ego psychology, but other, completely drive-free models have developed since. Erikson's psychosocial, epigenetic theory of personality includes contributions from cultural anthropology and is essentially a phase-specific developmental model which defines nodal conflictual times of crisis and their progressive resolution along an ascending maturational scale. Each stage is qualified by a particular task, requiring encounter with and adjustment to societal mores for its resolution. Just as Abraham had widened the scope of the psychosexually conceived stages to include concomitant interactions with primary objects, so Erikson further expanded the fundamental model to encompass sociocultural and experiential concerns which appear to become dominant at particular stages along the life cycle. Erikson's model covers the life span and accounts for conscious experience and self-referencing within a sociological framework. As "epigenetic," his developmental framework acknowledges the concept of innate maturational stages with their endogenously unfolding crises and resolution, yet his psychosocial orientation is organized around the phenomenological notion of the experience of self or identity. Moreover, while mediated through social exchange, nodal conflicts and resolutions do not modulate drives as much as they determine the quality of self-experience (Erikson, 1946, 1950, 1980).

At the oral level, during which incorporation is the prevalent mode, Erikson posits a stage of crisis around issues of "basic trust versus mistrust," the outcome of which will determine or color the individual's capacities for relating to others, and style for giving and receiving. The anal stage conflict is characterized by Erikson as that of "autonomy versus doubt and shame," and the phallic-oedipal as that centrally concerned with "initiative versus guilt." During the stage designated by Freud as latency, Erikson identifies "industry versus inferiority," and where Freud's pubertal, psychosexual maturation culminates in adult genitality, Erikson stresses the sociocultural demands of adolescence epitomized in the resolution between "identity versus identity diffusion." With reference to the young adult's sense of inner continuity, Erikson views acceptance of a social role and a personally articulated ideological perspective of goals and morals, as the major achievement of this phase.

Implicit in the successful consolidation of personality is an ongoing integration of the sense of self. Throughout his developmental stages Erikson correlates a core conflict with the phenomenological experience of identity and articulates this conceptually around the fundamental notions of Freud's psychosexual stages. Accordingly, the struggle of orality is defined in terms of "I am what I am given"; that of volitional control over one's body, typical of the anal phase, "I am what I will"; the phallic-oedipal identificatory ideal is defined as, "I am what I will be"; the relative poise of latency, its cognitive interests and outward orientation toward peers and others is seen as crystallizing around, "I am what I learn"; and the final challenge of adolescence, corresponding to Freud's mature genitality, is seen by Erikson as the consolidation of an integrated, solid identity (Erikson, 1951). The principal feature of this epigenetic conceptualization is the idea that each successive stage is directly influenced by the outcome of previous phase crisis conflicts. Resolutions range in a continuum from optimal to unsuccessful negotiation and the myriad nuances and solutions play a determining part in differential outcomes, ranging from adaptive to maladaptive or pathological. Erikson's maturational program progresses with conflict resolution points continuing into old age, portraying development as an ongoing life task. In this he greatly expands the Freudian scheme limited to the gateways of adulthood, and provides a paradigmatic life-span model in which the notion of stage-specific crises and resolutions becomes the organizing principle of personality development.

Freud's psychosexual, Abraham's characterological, Erikson's psychosocial, and Mahler's separation–individuation developmental models may all be understood as relevant and complementary, diverse "developmental lines," to use A. Freud's felicitous concept, each of which enriches the spectrum of developmental viewpoints in psychoanalytic theory. They represent important aspects and facets of human development as derived from a psychoanalytic, genetic perspective and, as such, are mutually complementary. Another major developmental theorist, Piaget, who worked outside of psychoanalysis has, in my opinion, not been sufficiently integrated into our theoretical reorientation. Piaget established a comprehensive theory of cognition which traces the developmental stages of intelligence, or cognitive abilities, which by virtue of their competencies determine how the world is understood and perceived (Piaget, 1962, 1970; Piaget and Inhelder, 1969).

Piaget's (1970) term, *genetic epistemology*, which stresses the developmental origins of the structuring of reality, delineates the evolution of cognition, viewed as *the* process of adaptation to the environment. Originating in action, for Piaget cognition is closely linked to successful adaptation and intelligence itself, which is viewed as the outgrowth of the internalization of action, and governed by two fundamental processes: assimilation and accommodation. The epigenetic stages are conceived as age-appropriate ways of experiencing, reasoning about, and dealing with the world, in which earlier forms of understanding lay the foundations for later, differently structured developmental stages. These ascend from the earlier sensorimotor, concrete and formal operational modes, to the full abstractive capacities characteristic of the competencies of adult thought.

The basic developmental principle of assimilation corresponds to the process by which experience is perceived and internalized according to the child's existing mental capacity. That of accommodation represents the process whereby existing mental structures are altered during modifications inherent in the process of internalizing new *schemas*, the term Piaget used to define and describe an underlying experiential structure. A schema is a configuration within the brain that acts as a pattern against which the impact on nerve cells is compared. It is through the interplay of the two processes of assimilation and integration that the development of cognitive structures progresses, and development itself is understood as the increasing capacity to apperceive reality objectively and thereby assess responses to it with increasing veridical judgment. Reality is thus construed according to the basic organizational capacities existing to grasp it which, according to Piaget, proceed hand in hand with a process of decentration.

The works of Basch (1977) and Greenspan (1979, 1982) stand out for their efforts to incorporate Piaget's contributions to the study of mind into psychoanalysis. Basch is noted particularly for linking Piaget's cognitive formulations to Freud's clinical findings (with particular focus on primary and secondary processes and repression); and Greenspan, with regard to identifying different levels of experience and stages of learning as aspects of ego development. Both authors demonstrate the advantages of such integration and how Freudian and Piagetian psychological models may enhance and complement each other. Nevertheless, and along these lines, it is my opinion that further integration and distillation of principles and terms is needed for radical theoretical reorientation.

In a revisionary paper in which he attempts to redirect Freud's metapsychological explanations away from energy discharge and regulation, and toward empirically founded concepts from perceptual and cognitive psychology, Basch (1977) outlines:

> From our point of view as psychoanalysts, Piaget's most significant contributions are his experiments demonstrating that the capacity to organize stimuli, i.e., to cognize, is acquired in a stepwise fashion. . . . Piaget's experiments led to an outlook that is a distinct departure from the developmental psychology that suggests that the infant is an immature (nonverbal) adult and that development is linear, growing from simple and uncomprehending groping to increasingly complex adaptive behaviors guided by words.

> Piaget's findings indicate a hierarchy of cognition, not primarily dependent on words [p. 230].

This statement invites a radical reappraisal of existing psychoanalytic models because it stands in stark contrast to Freud, for whom language and the ascendance of secondary process thought represent a maturational achievement, in the primacy of reality-oriented perceiving and thinking. It remains to be seen, and I will explore this very point, whether the observations of one theorist cannot be reconciled with the formulations of the other in a psychoanalytic model which integrates the two.

Basch (1977), who takes a rather extremist position on this, emphasizes that "brain function" is what we should mean by "mind" and that the concept of "ordering of stimuli, as a demonstrable experimental and validatable brain function, takes the place of energy-discharge . . . theory that has been part and parcel of our metapsychology since 1900" (p. 249). For Basch, the only way to go in a movement away from analogy, is toward physiological functioning. "Brain function" (the brain's innate pattern matching mechanism) or the ordering of stimuli, in replacing energic transformations and biological drives "relieves us of the burden of hypothesizing a mythical mental apparatus whose nature, essence and function must then be established" (Basch, 1977, p. 249). Both Freud's and Piaget's models contain a major division between prethought and thought-proper phases; however, for Freud the origins of thought are derived from the somatic forces of *instinctual drives*, while Piaget identifies a brain *function*, the sensorimotor mode, as the foundation of thought. Freud's division is described in the terms of primary and secondary processes, whereas Piaget's is defined essentially as that between presymbolic and symbolic thought. For psychoanalysis, the problem with Piaget is that his theory tends to ignore the very soil of its premises, affects, and the power of irrationality. For Piaget, the problem with psychoanalysis is that it oriented a theory around content, and explained mental processes according to their manifestations in the mythology of mental places and agencies.

Greenspan (1979, 1989) further elaborates the integration of Piaget's developmental model of cognition by correlating six levels of organization of experience and three levels of learning. The stages Greenspan (1979) delineates interconnect with each other, representing "milestones in human intelligence from an integrated developmental perspective" (p. 298) so that the experience of self and principles of learning coalesce in the organizational mode of each level and correspond to the characteristic ego organization operative at that time. Greenspan proposes a structural model, with certain organizing principles which help understand how internal and external stimuli are integrated with increasing complexity and differentiation (1979). He writes, "each human being evolves a unique identity based on the development and integration of psychic structures and constellations of self and object representations invested with drive-affect dispositions. The particular character and style of these structures are defined by the unique, innate potentials of that human being combined with his life experience" (p. 298). Unlike Piaget, Greenspan differentiates adaptation to the external world from intelligence with regard to the internal world, reasoning, "The character of the integration of internal stimuli forms perhaps a relatively more distinct pattern based on the individual's unique constitutional givens and life experiences (life experiences constitute . . . not only actions *on* the individual by his environment, but actions *by* the individual on his environment)" (1979, p. 298). Greenspan characterizes the organization of experience in six stages from the somatic, to the transformed representational, with corresponding or parallel levels of learning modes. He emphasizes the importance of a structural diagnosis in that "the developmental structuralist approach takes us beyond traditional concepts of defense and adaptation" (1979, p. 375). The value of integrating principles of cognition into psychoanalysis is that it greatly enhances conceptual understanding of ego development as well as offering an alternative drive-free framework for the organization of mentation.

One of the great contributions of Piaget's theory lies in his asserting that cognition and recognition are based in *action* and not on reflection; that early sensorimotor schemata, as chains or sets of actions, lay down neurological traces providing the foundation for all future thought and self-experience: "a logic of action antedates and prepares the way for expression through language'' (Basch, 1977, p. 232) and not the other way around. The fundamental elements of thought are assimilated through action patterns derived from sensory input rooted in activity: ''The sensori-motor conceptualization of development provides entree to understanding the mechanics of phenomena seen daily by the practicing psychoanalyst,'' writes Basch (1977, p. 234). Subsequent preoperational stages (18–24 months initially to approximately 6–7 years) are characterized by an animistic, egocentric and phenomenalistic imagination; a stratum of ideation correlating with ''fantastical'' or what is known psychoanalytically as unconscious fantasy.

The end of infancy is heralded by the capacity to represent. In acquiring the uniquely human faculty of representation, the child centers its manipulation around subjective and immediate needs (the wish). The advent of symbolic play, imitation, gesture, the use of words, and day and night dreaming, all appear with the figurative function in the *preoperative* stage of the evolution of mental life. The period of *concrete operations* (6–7 years to 11–12 years) is called concrete because at this stage the formulation of concepts is closely tied to things themselves and not abstractions of these. Piaget called this egocentric, phenomenalistic, or ''naive'' realism. The decentering which evolves out of cognitive advances during this stage enables greater objectivity, as consolidation of the permanent object and the awareness of separateness this induces enable the manipulation of internal representations in time and space. This further increases the differentiation between self and not self both with things in the environment and interpersonally, which in turn, leads to further abstraction at the level of propositional or formal operations (11–12 years to 11–15 years). For Piaget, formal thought represents the ability to reverse and conserve hypothetical combinations, or to fully abstract, cognition now being independent of sensory evidence at this final stage of the decentering process. Concrete operations made it possible to reason from the particular to the general; formal operations enable reasoning from the general to the particular.

It is not until adolescence that the capacity for purely verbal, mathematical, or abstractive propositions develop. During this final stage of decentering there evolves the capacity to form multiple representational systems which can be articulated according to combinatorial arrangements of reciprocal, inverse, or correlative relationships. Greenspan makes an important point in stressing: "While the capacity for language and symbol formation increases the mobility of operations, operativity exists as an independent mental capacity" (1979, p. 368). Operativity, that is, the structuralizing competencies in the organization of thought, has a direct impact on the figurative aspects of cognition. "In studying the structural properties of cognition," writes Greenspan (1979), "Piaget and Inhelder were impressed with a motivational force that is directed toward adapting the person to reality" (p. 368). I consider this to be an extremely important point and one to which I shall return in chapter 4 in the context of presenting my model of symbolizational development. In this model the correlate to decentration is a desire to understand or to "know"; to organize and represent information, and express this to another, is viewed as the motivating force inducing the continuing function of symbolizing.

I believe it to be self-evident how intimately intertwined cognitive psychology and psychoanalytically based ideas are, and how germane Piaget's model is to further our understanding of the human mind. While Piaget did not always explicitly incorporate the affective dimension—his research was focused on the problem-solving capacities of children at different stages—he did stress that these two aspects are intertwined and interdependent. It seems to me that any serious reformulation of psychoanalysis will have to incorporate the principles of cognitive competencies derived from Piaget's findings regarding the child's development of cognitive structures—without due consideration and careful integration of this dimension of human mentation, there can be no complete or comprehensive theory of mind (see also Beres [1965]).

Another perspective evolved out of the organismic framework of Werner and Kaplan (1963) in the synthesis of two orientations; the organismic-holistic and the developmental. While the psychoanalytic approach to development was heavily influenced by the historical impact of genetic determinism emphasized by Darwin's evolutionary theory, Werner's efforts focused on the investigation of principles of development that would account for changes in an evolving system following the tradition of Koffka and the Gestalt psychologists. The origin of the organismic approach is derived from theoretical biology and its concerns with the organization of living beings. At the beginning of this century, experimenting with embryological growth and exploring the fate of transplanted embryonic tissue, Spemann (cited in Bemporad [1980, p. 20]) postulated the existence of "a developmental organization" which accounted for an innate course of tissue development. During this course, he observed, tissue became unalterable by environmental influence once it had obtained a certain organization. The impact of Spemann's postulate was considerable in that it disclosed an intrinsic organization of tissue throughout development, and further indicated that this organization was intimately linked with differentiation. This led to the idea that the development of biological structures follows "a lawful scheme of organization which orders the eventual fate of all living matter" (Bemporad, 1980, p. 20).

The principles derived from this approach were then generalized to child development. As embodied in Werner's (1940) stated goals, these were: "1) to grasp the characteristic patterns of each developmental level and its own organization; and 2) to determine the relationship between these levels in terms of increasing complexity, so that any general tendencies in the developmental process may be discerned" (cited in Bemporad [1980, p. 21]). Development is viewed as a fluid, creative process with each progression involving transformation of the entire organism and each phase representing a completely new organizational synthesis, different, not superior to that which precedes it. Maturation is understood as moving toward greater differentiation and complexity but not as being more sophisticated; nor are "higher order" modes viewed as simply added to an unaltered organism. Development is all-encompassing, innovative, proceeding from a state of relative globality to a differentiation of parts which themselves organize into hierarchical arrangements.

One of the general assumptions of the organismic approach is the holistic one, which maintains that "any local organ or activity is dependent on the context, field, or whole of which it is a constitutive part; its properties and functional significance are, in large measure, determined by this larger whole or context" (Werner and Kaplan, 1963, p. 3). The second major assumption is that of *directiveness*, which is premised on the idea that an organismic psychological theory, just like its biological counterpart, requires teleological explanatory concepts, assuming that activity is by its very nature directed, and that various organs or "activities of an organism function in the realization of ends imminent in the activity of the organism as a whole" (Werner and Kaplan, 1963, p. 3). Moreover, the holistic framework stresses the reciprocal relationship between an organism and its environment and holds that the analysis of any behavior cannot take place in isolation but must include the organism embedded in its *Umwelt*, its own vital field. To summarize: the holistic approach to development maintains that "every behavioral act, whether outward bodily movement or internalized cognitive operation, gains its significance and status in terms of its role in the overall functioning of the organism . . . [and is contrary to any view that] would treat an element (for example, a movement, a momentary experience) as if it possessed a fixed structure and meaning, irrespective of the whole or context of which it is a part" (p. 4).

There are, of course, many different perspectives from which to consider development, all of which are relevant by virtue of their contribution to a more comprehensive understanding of the complex and multifaceted nature of human maturation and growth. Some, such as the social-behavioral and learning-theorist approaches of Watson (1925), Pavlov (1927), Tolman (1932), Skinner (1938), Bandura (1977), or Miller and Dollard (1941), I have conspicuously omitted because, in my opinion, their operant conditioning models are limited and do not coincide with the more complex, psychodynamic orientation of human functioning, in line with psychoanalysis. I do believe though that information regarding early experience and research of infant and child development issuing from investigations over the last fifty years has greatly expanded the conceptual underpinnings of our model and is worth encompassing in a contemporary psychoanalytic theory of mind. For a more comprehensive and coherent integration, however, our conceptualization of the principles of early development will have to be brought into closer correspondence with the clinical process of the psychoanalytic treatment method.

While many theorists have contributed to our knowledge of development, and all of the above mentioned approaches are useful, complementary ways of looking at the pieces of what make up a complex mosaic of interconnected facets of maturation, the difficulties in integration are compounded by overspecialization. Distinct viewpoints which have focused on any single aspect and tended to exclude other dimensions and their findings, have produced reservoirs of information which are segregated by specialty. To produce a synthesis becomes an arduous ordeal, in which one person's efforts are hardly sufficient. For instance, both Piaget's and Werner and Kaplan's significant contributions are marred by the absence of the affective dimension. A. Freud, who added important dimensions to psychoanalysis in the concept of developmental lines and the systematic study of the ego's mechanisms of defense, as far as development was concerned, stayed exclusively within the existing psychoanalytic frame of reference. Further complications arise out of semantic incongruence produced by the use of different terms and jargon for similar or interrelated concepts and processes. Arieti (1975) was an important exception in attempting to integrate psychoanalysis with cognitive theory and in proposing an affect-based model of the development of childhood experience, but his work has remained outside the mainstream revisionist literature. Similarly, the important revisionary work of Rapaport (1944, 1951, 1959), Holt (1965, 1976, 1985), Klein (1973), or Gill (1967a), has been largely left behind or obscured by current emphasis on clinical concerns.

In an important comprehensive work, another major contemporary developmental psychologist, Jerome Kagan (1984), challenges some of the most basic assumptions held thus far about human development and the nature of scientific research itself, ideas which, as valuable conceptual underpinnings, may usefully be incorporated into psychoanalytic thought. He identifies five deep premises or "themata," so called by the physicist Holton (1973), which currently govern developmental inquiry.

Each theme he identifies is itself defined by a pair of complementary assumptions. The first of these is the balance between
biology and experience which, Kagan advises, should not be
treated as separate, independent forces. The second theme is
characterized by the contrast between the belief in continuity
versus discontinuity in development; this questions the relative
merit of considering growth from infancy to adulthood as linear
and continuous, or to emphasize its disconnectness, whereby
some prior characteristics would disappear entirely and give way
to emergent new ones. A third theme deals with the way we
describe and understand human characteristics; qualities and
quantities, questions the difference between qualitative discrete
properties and continuous quantities in the conceptualization
of the essence of natural phenomena. A fourth theme is concerned with the selection of the most appropriate level of analysis with regard to a given context, procedure, question, and
setting. And the fifth issue Kagan tackles addresses subjective
and *objective frames* (the term he uses for schema) and the interrelationship and difference between these two frames. While
issuing from the field of psychology, this probing approach to
questions of how to view development reaches to the heart of
contemporary epistemological issues and merits further consideration by psychoanalysts because it pushes toward new and
alternate viewpoints.

Another interesting perspective is offered by Slavin and
Kriegman (1990), who propose a new paradigm based on an
evolutionary biological vantage point which purports to integrate drive and relational psychoanalytic schools in a model
which "echoes aspects of both views," while striving toward
something completely new. Adopting evolutionist concerns regarding the functional development of basic structural capacities, they suggest that "a revised understanding of the concept of
repression provides a basic key to the nature of such a complex
adaptive design" (p. 20) as the human child. Such an evolutionary–adaptive perspective encompasses the biological, interpersonal, and what they call the psyche's "deep structure," as it
subsumes and synthesizes the study of how these facets have
been structured and shaped over evolutionary time. In a nut-
shell, Slavin and Kriegman (1990) claim that, "An evolutionary

based metapsychology thus depicts us as innately individual and innately social, as endowed with inherently selfish, aggressively self-promoting aims as well as an equally primary, innately altruistic disposition toward those whose interests we share . . . we are essentially "semisocial" beings whose nature—or self-structure and motivational system is inherently divided between eternally conflicting aims" (p. 27). Again, while approaching the issues from an interesting vantage point, it seems to me that the search for human motivation has again obfuscated the more imperative search for a developmental model of the human mind. Even from the evolutionary biological perspective, which filters through the prisms of adaptation, I believe a functional model for the structural organization of human faculties serves us better than discussions as to whether we are social or asocially inclined.

Most theorists, however they approach ontogeny, seem to agree on the optimal outcome of the human developmental process; and this is for the adult to realize a relative independence from immediate responses to either internal or external pressure and stimuli, and to increase the possibility of choice in directing behaviors to maximize fruitful outcomes in a given environment after consideration of multiple options. Liberation from impulse and the dimension of thought and selection would appear to be paramount.

It seems to me that the intimate connection of psychoanalysis with developmental psychology needs to be differentiated with regard to methods and goals; psychoanalysis includes principles of development and must incorporate contemporary findings from infant and child research, but it must also retain a responsibility to its own, clinically based theoretical premises, assimilating from developmental fields what is directly relevant to the psychoanalytic process and theory of mind (Blum, 1989). To this end we are obliged to build upon a synthesis. I therefore think it valuable to distill a few central principles of development which have emerged in the aforementioned models and attempt to delineate a few essentials. The first is the principle of critical periods; the second, the closely related concept of epigenesis; the third rests on the need for balance and equal consideration of nature and nurture; the fourth is the principle of ascending complexity and differentiation with regard to self and apperception of the environment; the fifth, the concept of hierarchical mental structuralization; and the sixth, the presence of a general "self-righting" principle (Lichtenberg, 1989) or an inherent tendency toward developmental advance and reorganization through symbolic representation—the latter understood as a primary aspect of the curative function of clinical psychoanalysis. These principles are characterized by a circularity of impact and outcome as self-righting, for instance, which results from the recursive effect of the organism's own contributions vis-à-vis those of an environment which responds to it. The organism is understood to be active, purposive, a coparticipant in adaptational actions and reactions to the environment in which it is embedded.

Concepts of change, always of central concern to psychoanalysts, are perforce intimately tied to theories of development. More might be said about a model of crisis as catalytic for change; about transitions, and particularly about the work of "the mourning process as a change-creative gain sequence in the normal situation" (Pollock, 1977, p. 11), which I too regard as fundamental in psychic maturation. Suffice it to say, we have come a long way from the "nirvana principle," the idea that stimulus reduction and drive gratification are satisfactory explanatory concepts for human motives, activity, or developmental gain. Anyone who has seen their infant clinging, felt the powerful clutch of a tiny hand gripping tightly to hoist him- or herself up to the upright position; or observed the expression of desperate thrill in effort and risk color a vital moment of developmental thrust; any parent who has seen their floundering adolescent pitched furiously against one's penumbral authority or watched the fearful challenge to face the world but do it alone, will attest to the inherent turbulence of change, the intrinsic role of volition, the pain of gain, and the inherent struggle toward resolution, completion, and reintegration occurring at each maturational step. Because the psychosexual stages are so intimately connected to drive-gratification concepts, we can no longer usefully embrace this narrow view of development as a foundation for our theory. "Even rats seem to 'look' for problems (Hebb, 1955)'' writes von Bertalanffy (1968), "and the healthy child and adult are going far beyond the reduction of tension or gratification of needs in innumerable activities that cannot be reduced to primary or secondary drives (Allport, 1961, p. 90). All such behavior is performed for its own sake, deriving gratification ('function pleasure' after K. Bühler) from the performance itself" (von Bertalanffy, 1968, p. 209). We are led to a conceptualization of human functioning and development along similar constructivist lines, in which human mentation must also partake of similar underlying principles.

Today, as "age is losing its customary social meaning, and the trends are toward the fluid life cycle and an age-irrelevant society" (Neugarten, 1979, p. 687), developmental study encompasses the entire life span. Psychoanalysis is challenged to expand its parameters and clinical goals, to reorient its meta-theoretical formulations to include all that developmental research has to offer. Further, we are asked to depart from a line of thinking which perceives of the organism as merely reactive, constrained, and compromised between internal and external impingement, to meet the person as vigorously contributing to his or her own development.

THE DRIVES

In the opening lines of his posthumous "Outline" (1940), with reference to the "psychical apparatus," Freud retrospectively delineates his central theoretical problem. He writes:

> Psycho-analysis makes a basic assumption, the discussion of which is reserved to philosophical thought but the justification for which lies in its results. We know two kinds of things about what we call our psyche (or mental life): firstly, its bodily organ and scene of action, the brain (or nervous system) and, on the other hand, our acts of consciousness, which are immediate data and cannot be further explained by any sort of description. Everything that

lies between is unknown to us, and the data do not include any direct relation between these two terminal points of our knowledge [1940, p. 144].

The basic assumption psychoanalysis made was a belief in the existence of an unconscious; a powerful, motivating source determining human actions and behaviors, which lay outside of awareness.

To the oldest of the psychical provinces in this apparatus, Freud gave the name *id*; it is said to contain everything that is inherited, that is constitutional, above all, therefore, the instincts "which originate from the somatic organization and which find a first psychical expression here (in the id) in forms unknown to us" (1940, p. 145). And again, Freud (1940) recapitulates: "The forces which we assume to exist behind the tensions caused by the needs of the id are called *instincts*. They represent the somatic demands upon the mind" (p. 148). It was to be another twenty years or so before Piaget established a primary sensorimotor stage corresponding to this somatic organization of experience which, however, was to be understood not so much as responding to pressing needs, but rather as the primary, substratal form of intelligence itself; a function rather than a force.

The dilemma brought about by a biologically rooted model of human motivation, which finds causal explanations for behaviors and actions, and an attempt to place rational and irrational, conscious and unconscious thought in a "psychical apparatus," produced splits in a theory which, despite its complexity, was carefully constructed to cohere. The organism in its entirety serves the "pleasure principle" conceived as stimulus reduction, and Trieb (moving force) translated as drive or instinctual drive (Hartmann, Kris, and Loewenstein, 1946a,b) (in contrast to Instinkt) is an endogenous force fueling this principle. The task of the nervous system is to master stimuli, particularly those arising from within, from which it cannot move away. In varying degrees, according to their allotted roles with respect to their relation to "reality," the mental agencies id, ego, and superego, respectively, either serve, modulate, or impede these forces seeking discharge by the most direct route in their aim for stimulus reduction.

Instincts[6] (1915a), detectible only by their source, impetus, aim, and constant pressure on motility, originate in the body—the theory is biological. Yet invisible and untraceable except via their expression, drives are the "cathected mental representation" of things or objects in the mind—the theory is psychological. "An instinct appears to us as a concept on the frontier between the mental and the somatic," reasoned Freud, "as the psychical representative of the stimuli originating from within the organism and reaching the mind as a measure of the demand made upon the mind for work in consequence of its connection with the body" (1915a, pp. 121–122). Again, the premise is that body and mind are separate. The tension produced by this theoretical dualism has trailed endless repercussions in irreconcilable divisive splits between psychoanalytic schools, and resulted in Freud being viewed in such contrasting ways as an intractable vitalist or reductionist, and "the first modern theorist of the nature of the soul" (Konner [1982, p. 130]; see also Holt [1967]).

Trained in neurology in the tradition of medical materialism, and thoroughly conversant in the scientific Weltanschauung of his day, Freud struggled throughout to unite body and mind, by transplanting neurological, energic explanations onto his empirical observations of mental life, and translating these into psychological concepts. Schooled in the Brücke-Meynert scientific value system which held as axiomatic that explanations must be purposive and couched in physiochemical terms, Freud sought to understand the mind by detecting "how it worked," using the "impersonal" (G. Klein, 1973) terms of *energy* and its transformations, *tension* and *discharge*, to describe his findings. He continued to believe that gain in psychological analysis would be obtained through increased knowledge from the neurosciences, and, while a knowledgeable and sophisticated critic of the neurophysiology (in particular of cortical localization theories) of his day, he nevertheless thought and conceptualized in terms of systems, functions, and operations (Pribram, 1965).

---

[6]I use the word as translated by Strachey.

He wrote, "I doubt if we are in a position to undertake anything without having an intention in view" ([1905b, p. 195]; see also Tolman [1932, 1959]). For Freud, the origins of this purpose were biological in nature and, in accordance with the "principle" of the economy of psychical expenditure, he believed that all instinctual activity converged upon two fundamental aims: the avoidance of unpleasure and the reduction of tension. This, of course, epitomizes the circular, closed system approach of Freud's drive theory which gave rise to the divergent, object-relationist perspective. "The nervous system," wrote Freud, "is an apparatus having the function of abolishing stimuli which reach it, or of reducing excitation to the lowest possible level: an apparatus which would even, if it were feasible, maintain itself in an altogether unstimulated condition" (1915a, p. 86), and, he therefore concludes that instincts, not external stimuli, are the motive forces in the evolutionary progress of the human nervous system. He later dealt with major stumbling blocks contesting the plausibility of a pleasure principle by incorporating them into a revised and consolidated dual drive model.

There were three stumbling blocks threatening consistency of the primacy of the pleasure principle. The first was Freud's increasing awareness that aggression had been insufficiently accounted for and needed to be elevated to equal rank with sexuality as an independent drive. The second was the phenomenon of masochism, manifest clinically in "negative therapeutic reactions" whereby individuals seemed to opt for unpleasure. The third stumbling block was manifested in the traumatic war neuroses by a "compulsion to repeat" and reexperience psychologically painful experiences. It was through these manifestations that Freud was forced to recognize that something other than the pleasure principle had to be at work instigating organismic activity. He resolved this theoretical quandary by adopting an abstract concept which he called the destructive or death instinct, attributing to it the same malleability as he had libido, namely, reversibility and displaceability with respect to aim.

It is the "power of the id," writes Freud (1940) in the Outline, which "expresses the true purpose of the individual organism's life" (p. 148), a purpose defined as the satisfaction of innate needs. Although they represent the ultimate cause of all activity, drives are of a conservative nature and are distinguished by the reversibility and great displaceability with respect to their aims. They are infinitely malleable. Because the means for obtaining satisfaction is infrequently immediate or directly available, instinctual energy becomes channeled upon objects and activities other than those which directly serve tension reduction, they are "inhibited with respect to their aim," producing an elaborate array of adaptive and maladaptive compromise solutions, characterological traits, and personality organizations, the expressions of which constitute behavior.

Freud's early postulate included the "life instincts," which were believed to serve the adaptive functions of reproduction and the maintenance of life; these had been subdivided into a group of sexual instincts and another of ego instincts, including basic biological essentials necessary for survival, such as hunger and thirst. Initially the term *libido* was used to label sexual[7] energy in order to differentiate it from the self-preservative "ego instincts." But recognizing that the latter functioned more in congruence than in opposition to each other, Freud chose the superordinate Eros, for what for him had come to represent all the energies of the life instincts: "The contrast between the instincts of self-preservation and the preservation of the species, as well as the contrast between ego-love and object-love fall with Eros" (1940, p. 148). He came to view these forces as antithetical to those tendencies toward disjunction and destruction of the death instinct. Thus, he concludes, "After long hesitancies and vacillations, we have decided to assume the existence of only two basic instincts, Eros and the destructive instinct" (1940, p. 148). "In biological functions," Freud (1940) wrote, "the two basic instincts operate against each other or combine with each other. Thus, the act of eating is a destruction of the object with the final aim of incorporating it, and the sexual act is an act of aggression with the purpose of the most intimate union. This concurrent and mutually opposing action of the two basic

---

[7]In his *Three Essays on the Theory of Sexuality* (1905a), Freud adopted a broadened and expanded concept of the term *sexual* to encompass all that is sensory, sensual, or somatic, as well as erotic. The term is used in this broad sense throughout.

instincts gives rise to the whole variegation of the phenomena of life" (p. 149).

Freud's view of instincts as prime movers and his explanatory use of drive propulsion for principles of homeostatic regulation was very much in keeping with views held at the time. Some, notably McDougall (1923), the champion of instinctual theory, had listed over twenty instincts; indeed Freud's settling for a sparse dual drive model may even appear elegantly simple for the times. Every instinctive process was said to be composed of all aspects of mental activity, the cognitive, the affective, and the conative, correlating with innate psychophysiological dispositions manifest in their afferent, central, and motor or efferent particulars. Instinctual pressure was thought to be attended by some emotional excitement, producing sensations or changes in the sensory content of consciousness, characterized by a persistence toward discharge which prompted specific kinds of behaviors, so that "Every instinct" is viewed as a "form of activity" (Freud, 1915a, p. 122). Obstruction of instinctual strivings was thought to be accompanied by painful feelings whereas full progress toward end pleasure yielded gratification.

While a revolutionary formulation, Freud's psychosexual scheme organizing child development around bodily erogenous zones and infantile sexuality, also fit the times. Closely linked to Darwinian (1859) ideas and evolutionary doctrines rooted in the biological concerns with phylogenesis, morphogenesis, genetic and sexual selection, fitness and reproduction, Freud gravitated toward an approach which blurred motivational boundaries between soma and psyche in nonexplicit ways. His focus on genesis, the apparent connection of present symptoms to past events, his awareness of the impact of early childhood on later development, the sexual etiology of neurosis, biologically grounded explanations, and attempts to sift out inherited from learned behavior are all related to evolutionary ideas. Freud's concerns with the "how" and "why" of human behavior led to a search for origins along the historical and developmental dimension.

Libido theory provided a satisfactory integration of the current data of psychoanalytic experience and brought the momentous conceptualization of infantile sexuality to the forefront of psychoanalytic theory. "The aim of the theory of instincts," writes N. O. Brown (1959), "is to build a bridge between mental conflict (neurosis) and human biology, and . . . it ends by finding the causes of conflict in the biological domain" (p. 81). In fact, Freud's biologism "led him to a conviction that the source of man's trouble lies deep within himself . . ." (J. A. C. Brown, 1961, p. 14).

Freud lived in an era barely emerging from dichotomous frames of reference which had clung to polarizations between the world of animals and that of man, the biological and mental, the life of the body and that of the mind or spirit. Not surprisingly, his theory bears the stamp of such dualistic constructions: a Dionesian, dark unconscious, the id, must be counterbalanced by an Appollonian ego that sees the light of "reality." An unbound primary-process is supplanted by a reasoning-bound secondary process. A "life instinct," Eros, serves to neutralize the "destructive tendencies" of its antithesis, the death instinct. While the metaphor of dual drives provides a supporting frame for the monumental latticework of metapsychology, it has continued to be a source of dissention and dispute from the time of its inception, and today it is utilized only partially by the classical school and very little or not at all by everyone else. For many, comments Gedo (1991), dual drive theory "has become an historical relic . . . through sheer disuse" (p. 73).

Derived from the empirical observations of the phenomenology of pathological conditions elaborated in the reconstruction of childhood memories and fantasies of adult patients, these highly abstracted theoretical metaphors often seem to depart from the clinical relevance of analytic work embedded as it is in the interchanges of the linguistic, therapeutic exchange. Nevertheless, it was in this way that Freud conceptualized the interrelation of the perversions and neuroses, the phenomena of masochism and the repetition compulsion, and then moved his focus to vectors of libidinal currents out of which evolved the concepts of primary and secondary narcissism. He believed that the idea of investment and direction of drive energy could serve as an explanatory device for what he perceived as a fluid psychic force with infinite displaceability. This energy could only be described in terms of its source, impetus, aim, and object of satisfaction, the last being the most variable aspect. It is important to remember, however, that Freud was abstracting theoretical constructs to describe human behavior and actions; his metapsychology, despite its obscurity, is an attempt to organize a theory about people and passions.

"Libido is an expression taken from the theory of emotions," he wrote (1921, p. 90), and is regarded as a "quantitative magnitude (though not at present actually measurable), of those instincts which have to do with all that may be comprised under the word 'love' " (p. 90). Moreover, Freud felt justified in stating that self-love, love for parents, children, sexual love, "friendship and love for humanity in general, and also devotion to concrete objects and to abstract ideas" are all tendencies expressing "the same instinctual impulses" (1921, p. 90)—a general psychoanalytic concept of a "love-force" corresponding to Plato's eros. This superordinate force, however, is then operationalized in terms of biological development. Libido passes through psychosexual stages and achieves adult genitality only when fusion between the pregenital and genital drives has occurred: "applicability of the word *love* begins only with the synthesis of all the component instincts under the primacy of the genitals in the service of reproduction" (Freud, 1915a, p. 138). The genesis of character (Abraham, 1924) is conceived in terms of pregenital drives which, under the influence of social pressures, have altered their aim or object or otherwise been modified by learning in the course of upbringing. In its economical aspect, libido is regarded as a closed energy system regulated by hydraulic-like laws of energy conservation, so that withdrawal from one area will inevitably produce effects elsewhere.

Instincts were viewed both as conservative and regressive, representing a kind of inertial force in organic life which tends to resist change; at the same time they were the organism's prime movers, fueling motivation toward satisfaction. In this way Freud depicted the concepts of "repetition compulsion," the automaticity of instinctual activity and its regressive sway, as expressions of tension reduction. The organism thus exhibited a tendency to reinstate the status quo by repeating an obligatory cycle to reestablish that state as soon as it has been abandoned. Although the drive model is a closed-system approach, Freud's theoretical propositions were operationalized in object-relational terms. It is worth remembering that drives are the *mental* representation of somatic propulsions, and that the psychosexual stages of libidinal development, as well as the catastrophic anxiety situations of childhood (loss of object, loss of the object's love, castration, anxiety, and superego condemnation), are all relationally based constructs.

This notwithstanding, "The central inadequacy of Freud's model" is still "deemed to be its assumption of psychic energy" (G. Klein, 1973, p. 47) and its infrastructure of drive tension reduction as a motivational base. The list of dissenters and the arguments brought against it are too lengthy to enumerate here; suffice it to say that to counteract this unsatisfactory closed-system perspective, British object-relationists and interpersonalists founded psychoanalytic schools based on the principle of *relational* primacy: motivation is shifted from drive satisfaction to interpersonal connectedness—people, they claim, are socially directed and invested (for an interesting discussion see Abend [1988]; Greenberg and Mitchell [1983]).

Arguments against dual drive theory have come from an array of diverse perspectives ranging from the foundations of human motives to the function and premise of psychoanalytic treatment. Objections emphasize that tension reduction does not accurately reflect the phenomena of the clinical setting (Holt, 1965; G. Klein, 1976); that psychoanalysis is a hermeneutic (Home, 1966; Ricoeur, 1970, 1977; Habermas, 1971; Schafer, 1976; Spence, 1982, 1987) concerned with the coconstruction of meanings, not the vicissitudes of biological drives; that the preeminence of the self (Fairbairn, 1954; Winnicott, 1965; Guntrip, 1971; Kohut, 1971, 1977) contingent upon another for its development to be restored to a position of central import; that attachment (Bowlby, 1969) itself is psychobiologically primary; that communications organize the individual's interactions with the environment, and finally, that drives neither explain nor account for the multiplicity of internal and external forces operating in human experience (Spotnitz, 1957, 1974). There have also been those (Jacobson, 1964; Mahler et al., 1975; Kernberg, 1984) who have worked to consolidate compromise theories that accommodate both drive and object-relational propositions, and those who skillfully intertwine the two conceptually (Loewald, 1971; Opatow, 1988; Greenspan, 1989). Objections to drive theory are often part of a rejection of the entire thermodynamic model on the premise that it is "simply irrelevant to the clinical psychoanalytic enterprise . . . and not an inevitable deduction from clinically observed meanings of interpersonal relations" (G. Klein, 1976, p. 47). As Klein concludes, objections "that emphasize the inadequacy of drive-reduction models are noisy distractions from the more fundamental, more constructive consideration of whether there is any validity in the first place in this conception of object relations as drives" (1976, p. 47).

If Freud was familiar with the common biological principle of the "exclusive attachment of an instinct to its first-eliciting object" why did he not construct his theory simply around the vicissitudes of early attachment, since this idea already appeared quite prominently in his formulation as "the pertinacity of early impressions" (1905b) or the general "adhesiveness of libido"? The answer is simple: such a theory, akin to imprinting in animals, would preempt the primacy of the pleasure principle. As Mitchell (1988) emphasizes, "ducklings follow their mother around not because she provides sexual satisfaction, but because *she is there;* they are not so much pleasure seekers as object seekers" (p. 78). I am not convinced that because ducklings follow their mothers (and as Lorenz demonstrated, almost any object will do), this proves that they are object seeking. I doubt that we can really define early attachment behavior as object seeking (the word *object* used in the psychoanalytic sense) as libidinally invested. Rather, it would appear to be object needing, a genuine instinctual need, considering the prolonged dependency of the young of certain species. Freud's concern at the time, however, was the coherence of a model rooted in the vitalistic principles of biology (Holt, 1965); even object need, as primary motivator, must have appeared secondary to tension reduction. The notion of a "sexual instinct," served on two counts. Freud's libido provided stages of development toward mature love; to the drives were allotted motivational and emotional content, thus libido traces the course of the "love life."

Freud had good reason to "loosen the bond" between drive and object, for only thus broadened could the theory encompass the vicissitudes and plasticity of behaviors encumbent upon emotionally driven motives and place the source of sexuality securely within the "spontaneously arising expression of instinctual pressure" (1915a), from within.

The concept of drive satisfaction, however, insofar as "every instinct is a form of activity" (activities being infinitely plastic), is both excessively broad conceptually as well as too constrained by implication, to account for the gamut of what are often goal-directed, purposeful human expressions requiring teleological perspectives and explanations. And, to make matters worse, an activity of any form is not a "thing," with attributes, but always something someone is doing. Moreover, the concept of drive satisfaction neither distinguishes clearly between what is phylogenetically inherited, hardwired, or preprogrammed beyond reflexes and what is acquired or learned, nor can it truly offer explanations for anything other than its own end: "That a drive seeks its own gratification is a banality, it is part of the definition of drive" (G. Klein, 1976, p. 47)—the discussion is circular.

But it is important to remember Freud had other concerns—the assumption of a biological substratum was obvious, while attempts to explain this in psychological terms represented a formidable challenge. To encompass the bestial and the sublime and explain these in language never before conceptualized, was Freud's task. He did this by postulating that a stable, associative link is set up in the mind as a "representation" between the internal perception of the somato-affective experience of satisfaction and the memory of the object which had originally provided the drive satisfaction. While firmly rooted in the body, "There can be no question but that the libido has somatic sources, that it streams to the ego from various organs and parts of the body" (Freud, 1940, p. 151); what were bodily "needs" and "tensions" become "wishes," via their transmutation into cathected *mental* representations. Drives become directional and object-oriented via the subjective valence of the inner image they create—a subjective *construction* rather than an objective memory. The sexual instinct is now defined as the *psychical* representative of an "endosomatic" source of stimulation (1915a) from within, rather than a response to a single stimulus issuing from without.

"Drives," writes Schimek (1975), "distort the content of memories and cathect their contents so that they supersede or at least interfere with the objective information provided by perceptions. . . . The basic and primary effect of a drive [then] is the confusion between perceptions and hallucinated memory images" (p. 173). A bodily urge produces an image in the mind experienced as "a demand for work" which prompts an action designed "in every instance" to obtain satisfaction referring back to the body. Thus, drive, object, and subject have become one through the wish that threads through them all. The process is self-contained. It might seem that Freud had attained his goal.

Yet the internal coherence of this construct has come about through two subtle polarizations: that of inner (fantasy) and outer (reality), and body and mind. It is not the object outside but the mental representation within, which produces continuous drive pressure: it is not the mind but the body which imbues and subjectifies the image it creates with drive energy. The shift from biological to psychological might have occurred when the "wish" replaced the purely physiological "need." But here we stumble on the crux of a dilemma encountered by the adoption of a physicalist philosophy requiring causal explanations for motivation, namely, that purposive principles and physiological principles are two mutually exclusive ways of understanding the workings of the body. They require a different observational stance. The physical "need" and the psychological "wish" are in two separate domains. It would be senseless to discuss the "meaning" of hunger. Tension reduction does not explain subjective motives because it overlooks the uniquely human interpolation of meaning attribution. Nor does it account for the plethora of goal-directed outer oriented human endeavors elicited through external stimuli and triggers. Nor does the juxtaposition of outer and inner and this contrived unification of body with mind hold up if due weight is given to the singular import of subjective experience for the entire individual. Moreover, the "love life" unfolds in the psychoanalytic endeavor more as the expression of deeply affective behavioral constellations related to current meanings and their historical antecedents, than hypothesized component instincts attached to erotogenic zones from stages of infantile development. And fundamentally we find psychoanalysis to be the coobservation and counderstanding of the pathways of an individual's subjective experience in light of the meanings and beliefs of this unique individual as these are expressed in reactions, words, conscious and unconscious behaviors, demands, wishes, and dreams. Much more seriously, for years this skillful amalgamation of the psychological with the prepsychological, distracted the focus of generations of analysts from addressing the implications of this crucial differentiation for our theory.

Freud's search for biologically based motives is very much in keeping with and antedates the premises of behavioral biology and of the ethological position, both of which consider adaptation and evolutionary concerns. In their enumeration and classification of instincts, ethologists start with the concept of a motivating core (the endogenous energy of the instinct proper) out of which a complex and fairly diverse array of appetitive behaviors may develop wherein learned responses can play a role. Ethologists maintain that unlearned species-specific fixed action patterns are based on bodily structures and physiological mechanisms; correlation of morphological characteristics and specific behavior is taken as evidence for their innate basis. For their part, learning theorists (Miller and Dollard, 1941; Dollard and Miller, 1950) who would assign responsibility largely to learning, do not deny the role of innate factors. The heart of the nature–nurture controversy is thrashed out at the nucleus of these two very interrelated aspects of human functioning. Nevertheless, noteworthy contributions from ethology such as the concepts of fixed action patterns (inherited motor sequence behaviors), the innate releasing mechanism attuned to its own specific environment stimulus complex, instinctual inhibition, displacement activity, and the importance of stage-specificity or critical periods for environmental triggers, are all important markers for identifying neurohormonally based, inherited, species-specific behaviors. By their specificity, however, they tighten rather than loosen the connection between instinctual behavior and environmental triggers (drive and its discharge) and, because they pinpoint automatic, neurophysiological underpinnings and preprogrammed sets of motor actions, they take us farther away from the infinite "plasticity" of Freud's instinctual model for humans. The concept of "instinct" thus broadened has lost its "instinctual" meaning.

While the ethological theory of instincts, like Freud's, is a motivational theory in every sense of the term, accounting for the arousal of behaviors, it does so with respect to animals. Ethology, per se, does not address the great human difference in the capacity to represent, to weigh options, to attribute meaning, and to communicate this. Nor does it address the great semiotic particulars of signification, denotation, symbolization, and the great cortical advances that distinguish man from animals. In addition, the ethological definition of instinct would need to be further questioned if applied to man. While language is preprogrammed, as Chomsky claimed, has localizable brain centers (as Broca and Wernicke first discerned), emerges during a critical period according to a maturational timetable, and is contingent upon stage-specific environmental stimuli (Lane, 1976) for its acquisition, it is considered a human faculty, a species-specific inherited ability—not until recently an instinct (Pinker, 1994).

Despite the delicacy of transposing by analogy from animal studies to mankind, the ethologists Tinbergen (1951) and Lorenz (1952, 1977), both Nobel Prize winners, did have something to say about humans (Lorenz, 1970). After selecting patterns of locomotion, sexual behavior, food seeking, sleep, and care of the body surface as instinctual behaviors, Tinbergen (1951) makes very explicit his view that an objective study of the instinctual basis of motivation in man must proceed independently from the psychological study of subjective motivational experiences. By implication he is drawing a very important line that separates the innate from what has acquired signification via symbolizational processes. This is a central point for a psychoanalytic theory which does not adopt energic explanations for mental processes and transformations.

Lorenz, on the other hand, does not hesitate to assume that all the instincts allotted to animals exist in man. While

Tinbergen and Lorenz coincide in their reasoning by analogy and agree on there being an instinctual inhibition of aggression in man, they disagree on the positing of a separate, innate aggressive instinct. Lorenz (1958) frequently alludes to the endogenous nature of aggression in man but does not elaborate the concept beyond its intrinsic ties to hostile connotations. Ardrey, author of the *Social Contract* (1970) on the other hand, viewing man as "the supreme learner," emphasizes another facet: "There is aggressiveness coded into our genetic beginnings—in less or greater measure, just as all characteristics that enhance our original diversity by driving us to develop our peculiar endowments" (p. 87). Earlier he says: "as psychology today denies the principle of innate aggressiveness in man, it denies . . . an innate drive to learn and to master the problems of the environment" (p. 83). There would be no advantage to prolonged youth, he argues, were it not that the inner urge to activity accrues knowledge and skills. Aggressiveness is equated here with a "force," reminiscent of Winnicott's concept of a muscular or motoric urge—a drive to activity, as it were.

One of the most interesting and relevant of biological propositions studied by the ethologists is imprinting, thus named by Lorenz because it is formed in a very brief encounter. This very powerful early attachment, formed during a critical period for this singular experience, appears significantly and permanently to affect later social behaviors, impacting particularly on the character and type of sexual object which will later be chosen (Hesse, 1958, 1962, 1972). The time of appearance and duration of the critical period are governed by the onset of locomotor ability and the appearance of the fear response. The most fascinating thing about imprinting is the potential variability of the attachment object—as was demonstrated in the 1930s by Lorenz (1952, 1970) who imprinted geese on humans, Ramsay (cited in Hesse [1962]), who imprinted fowl on green boxes, and Harlow (1959) whose famous wire mothers of the rhesus monkeys in attachment studies made research history. All of these studies emphasized the power and supremacy of attachment needs. The strength of this phenomenon and the way in which phylogenesis has provided for its indelible hold, such that punishment during imprinting only enhances attachment, and the indiscriminateness of the bond (almost any object will do) I believe, are indicators that early attachment in the young of dependent species is primary and indisputably instinctual.

It was through the great contribution of Bowlby and his three-volume opus, *Attachment* (1969), *Separation* (1973), and *Loss* (1980), that a body of biologically based research became formally included into the psychoanalytic literature. Borrowing heavily from ethological concepts Bowlby's studies of infantile attachment and reactions to separation, mourning, and loss, form the basis for a reconsideration of the drive fundamentals of classical theory. In explicitly departing from the language and premises of drive theory, like Fairbairn and Guntrip, Bowlby devised a "relational/structure" model (Greenberg and Mitchell, 1983, p. 184) based on the actual experiences of the child with early attachment figures, adhering to the genetic principle in psychoanalysis which proposes that these will have lasting effects on behavior. Bowlby's argument is that this is because these are fundamental instinctive systems and not derailments of internal drive satisfaction. The child's attachment to mother is primary—gratification derived from her, secondary.

This "new type of instinct theory" (Bowlby, 1969), emphasizing the phylogenetic, instinctive underpinnings of human emotional life, identifies five instinctual responses, components of the early attachment constellation; these are sucking, smiling, crying, and following, which become organized into behavioral systems patterned and coordinated on inner controls and feedback, and coalesce into general "proximity-maintaining" (Bowlby, 1969) or approach behavior. It is worth noting here that the facial musculature is fully formed and functional at birth, implying a readiness toward affective expressivity as a signal and primary communicational vehicle (Darwin, 1872). Bowlby expanded the implications derived from attachment theory to explain all affectively charged behaviors, using this frame to account for virtually all types of anxiety, anger, and the psychological defenses. Because his theoretical focus leans toward phylogenetic and evolutionary functionality he tends to omit an all-important "human" propensity for ascribing signification or meaning to experience. His propositions are more purely biological than psychoanalytic, since they ignore the ideational and subjective construction in imagination, with reference to real experiences of early attachment and loss. He fails to account for or consider the uniquely human symbolic elaboration of instinctually based phenomena. And while his theory is used by object relationists to support their basic premise, I believe a more careful distinction still needs to be made between physiologically based instincts serving survival and behaviors issuing from these, and the subjective elaboration of these in ideational constructs expressive of meaning, as manifest in verbal and other symbolic forms. At bottom, this is the fundamental distinction to be made between "need" and "wish"; another all-important differentiation is that between affect, a physiobiologic term, and emotion its psychological, ideational derivative.[8] A unified psychoanalytic theory must account for these distinctions and encompass the myriad modes of expression issuing from these diverse layers and facets of human experiences.

Ironically, this is precisely the distinction that critics of drive theory (Klein, 1973; Holt, 1976) would like to abolish by placing "needs" in biology and "wishes" in psychology. "Even if finer levels of physiological occurrences *were* measurable during the analytic hour," writes Klein (1973), "physiological theory would never be primary . . ." (p. 49). These are words echoed by Holt (1976) as he objects to the physicalist language of instinct, drive, libido, energy, and force, and concludes: "drive is dead; long live wish!" (p. 194). Or, as Klein (1973) summates, "The essential clinical propositions concerning motivation have nothing to do with reducing hypothetical tension, they are inferences of *directional* gradients in behavior and of the object relations involved in these directions" (p. 48).

These are crucial concerns for a metatheory which attempts to encompass clinical data within its formulations, insofar as many patterns of affective responses, the complex defenses against these, and their emotional elaborations may be understood as expressions issuing from these two fundamentally different motivational sources—the fusion or blurring of the distinction between "need" and "wish." This bears directly on

---

[8]For this distinction I am indebted to Mark Shobin, in a personal communication. These terms will thenceforth be used throughout, in keeping with this definitional differentiation.

implications for technique and parameters in therapeutic approach. It is well-nigh useless to "interpret" deficits of psychobiologically based developmental needs for which only a prosthetic therapeutic "function" may initially suffice, while it is quite helpful to understand the elaborate psychological defenses and ideation contrived to compensate for an unsatisfied wish, and this, notwithstanding their interconnectedness. This same distinction serves advantageously in the diagnostic division between neurosis and psychosis—neurotic-level disturbances having to do with purposive ideoemotive problems, the psychotic implicating more basic physioaffective processes. A clearer theoretical understanding in which to ground these issues might further widen the scope of psychoanalytic treatment and orient toward appropriate techniques. In this, a better understanding of the expressive uses of language, still the only medium of our method, I believe, might provide a rewarding research avenue (Shapiro, 1970).

To speak of a single motivational program for humans is to ignore that there are multivaried motivational vectors involved at each developmental level, that these continue to change, and that as the person evolves and acquires cognitive and symbolizational capacities, these in turn give shape and meaning to new goals. Recognition of the ongoing meaning-elaborating and choice-making aspects of development are important considerations which have, together with responsibility and volition, long been neglected and overshadowed by unconscious determinism and the closed system perspective of psychoanalytic drive theory. "Drive" in this sense is better adopted as a general term to denote pressure or persistence; as a driven quality or the property of drivenness, as a characterization of intensity. Human motivation requires teleological conceptualizations which are never reducible to any single or highly abstracted biological or psychological principle. Moreover, I believe far too little emphasis has been placed on affects, emotions, and their expressive repertoire and development in the framework of the multivaried forms of human expressivity. I therefore turn my attention to these, our earliest and most pressing "somatic demands upon the mind" (Freud, 1940, p. 148) with the intention of redirecting our thinking from concepts of "drives" as motivating source, to affects as organizing, motivating, and expressive indicators (see also Shapiro and Emde [1992]).

The search for the emotions in a bodily locale is as ancient as human existence. The idea is often expressed poignantly by children who will describe their affective experience in terms of personifications, metaphors, and internal entities. Perhaps this is because emotions "overcome," "well up," and "spill out" or need to be "vented"; they prompt to actions of unbound heights or plummet the spirit to abysmal depths. The madman was said to be "possessed"; emotional outbursts "erupt" and "explode" from within. Emotions antedate and supplant reason, they drown out the rational; they are powerful and whimsical, are said to have a life of their own, and are often inexplicable. Emotions frequently determine our choices and course, they color the fabric of our earliest experiences, and define what we know and think of ourselves. They are a powerful, effective, and unambiguous means of communication. And apparently have a way of pressing to expression—not only is it salutary and beneficial to own and express them, it may even be life saving. Lastly, much of the misery which brings people to seek psychotherapy is centered around them—too intense, not intense enough, painful, frightening, inhibited, inhibiting. To "dominate the humors" is often a lifelong task.

It was Darwin who, in a preliminary contribution to ethology, addressed the study of emotions in his lesser known *The Expression of the Emotions in Man and Animals* (1872). In this work he emphasized the functional relevance of expressive movements and facial expressions; "He wound up . . . and set in motion the study of social behavior as adaptation," writes Konner (1982, p. 148), an approach which led sociobiology to the vital new subfield of behavioral biology (Weinrich, 1980; Plutchik, 1980). Agreeing with Darwin and McDougall, the ethologist Lorenz, who subscribed to a drive model for emotions, acknowledged the utility of an approach which sought qualitative distinctions between emotions as clues toward determining the number and nature of instincts, for the purpose of deriving a taxonomy of these. Earlier, Darwin had even proposed a tentative physiology for emotional expressions and actions, which were thought to be elicited by an "overflow of nerve force" from the central nervous system, transmitted through the spinal cord to peripheral organs. This resembles a premise of the theory Freud was to propose in his Project less than twenty years later. Although Freud never investigated the emotions per se, both Darwin and Freud held a view of emotions as discharge phenomena.

Abandoning the physicalist strivings of the Project, in recognition of the scant information available to him from the neurosciences, Freud, however, formulated explanations which have deepened the gap between neurobiology and psychoanalysis (see also Hebb [1949]). His "drives" at bottom, are conceptual tools to bridge biology and psychology, body and mind. They serve a conceptual descriptive framework rather than a practical purpose. A clinical interpretation in terms of drives is ludicrous. These metaphors were conceived abstractly, metapsychologically, their clinical relevance limited to viewing human behaviors as manifest derivatives of these two broad conceptual vectors. Even so, the concept has not explained the phenomena since human emotions are immensely more complicated than any simple dualism. Moreover, the model has distracted us from focusing attention on the seriously neglected need for a theory of affects and emotions along developmental lines; and so psychoanalysis today still lacks a viable, integrated theory of affects.

It is useful in this regard to keep in mind that Freud's drives were essentially derived from a theory of emotions viewed as discharge phenomena: "The forces which we assume to exist behind the tensions caused by the needs of the id are called *instincts*" (Freud, 1940, p. 148). This "somatic demand" became implicated in human motivation through the circuitous biological route of tension reduction, but libido was for Freud an emotional, affectively driven current. It might be helpful for us now to return to affects again but with a new view of these as core organizers, and begin to identify how a differentiation between innate behaviors, affects, and emotions and their relationship to the uniquely human capacity to represent and denote, can all come together in a recasting of our theory of mind.

For the benefit of background, in a brief discussion of the emotions, we may start with the William James/Carl Lange theory. Devised in the late 1800s, this grounded the emotions in physiological functions, accounting for the involvement of peripheral organs in their connection with the viscera; "The feeling, in the coarser emotion results from the body experience" (James [1884], cited in Konner [1982, p. 137]). *Results* is the key word here, as the theory claimed that emotions come from bodily experience; the mind is circumvented. This claim was criticized and carefully countered by the eminent American physiologist W. B. Cannon (1927), with conclusive evidence proving the opposite to be true—emotions are controlled by the central nervous system—they come from the mind. While the James–Lange theory had located emotion in the periphery, Cannon returned the emotions to the brain. In a 1928 paper he located emotions in the thalamus, where they were said to evolve through a relay of circuitry which passed through this organ: "the peculiar quality of the emotion is added to simple sensation when the thalamic processes are roused" (in Konner, 1982, p. 141).

The next leap in development toward a theory of emotions came through the contribution of J. W. Papez (1937), a physician–neuroanatomist. Papez isolated a circuit for emotions and their expression in a grouping of interconnected structures at the core of the brain, in what is now known as the limbic system (MacLean, 1949). This circuit system involved parts of the thalamus, the cortex, and the all-important hypothalamus, through which occurs regulation of the hormones of the pituitary. Working in the forties and fifties, and a major heir to Papez's neuroanatomical model for the emotions, MacLean (1949) proposed a bold hypothesis for overall brain evolution and structure (confirmed in the 1970s by Nauta and Domesick [1980]), which he called the triune brain. Having first identified an intimate connection between the frontal lobes (involving foresight, causality, and meanings) and the archaic limbic system, MacLean's model of the brain presents three coexisting evolutionary levels of development. The earliest of these, involving circuitry functioning to store and control instinctual behavior, he called the "reptilian brain"; the second, corresponding to the limbic system, the "old mammalian brain," which according to MacLean affords particular emotional qualities to what would otherwise be purely instinctual functions; and the third he called the "new mammalian brain," corresponding to man's unique evolutionary acquisition implicating the complex integration of the entire human brain.

While this model is very appealing in proposing anatomical correspondence with psychoanalytic structural concepts, I believe its spatial and functional connotations interfere with an organismic approach in which the neurophysiological substratum might rather be conceived as spread throughout the system. Functional differences in the brain over the course of phylogeny are presumed to be the result of changes in the overall organization of the central nervous system—this way of looking at it tends to unify psychological and physiological principles, with emphasis on the uniquely human processing of experience through a uniquely human nervous system. And, as I have pointed out before, the psychological correlate of the central nervous system in psychoanalysis (Freud's "cortical layer"), is the ego—body and mind, anatomical and psychical, always problematic dichotomies are thus explicitly undermined.

Since Freud's time, emotions have been defined and described as mechanisms for motivating or facilitating behavior (Weinrich [1980, cited in Plutchik [1980]): as knowable only through inference; as the result of conscious and unconscious decision-making processes; as primary communicational channels and signals and as our genetically programmed adaptive inheritance. It is Tomkins (1984), however, who makes the most decisive statement with regard to their motivating function. He views affects as the primary innate biological motivating mechanism, more urgent than drive deprivation or pleasure, more pressing even than physical pain. He claims that while this is not obvious, it is readily demonstrable. Tomkin points in an important direction. The only emotion psychoanalytic theory truly addressed was anxiety, and while Freud explicitly tied the origins of his libido concept to "a theory of the emotions" and described this as related to "quantitative magnitudes," he bypassed the critical issue of affects as motivational springs and centrally organizing forces, through the device of a much higher abstraction.

There are numerous perspectives from which to view the emotions, and Plutchik (1984), an authority, delineates four major traditions which evolved during the last century. The first of these traditions is the evolutionary, identified with Darwin, who believed emotions were appropriate reactions to emergency events in the environment; as signals of future action or intentions they increased the chance for survival. The second tradition is the psychophysiological, derived from the work of William James (1884), which, aside from its chicken-or-egg concerns, spawned the development of important psychophysiological research. The third tradition is the neurological, identified with Cannon, who believed emotions were emergency reactions arousing the organism to fight or flight responses and who placed the "seat" of the emotions in the hypothalamus. The fourth tradition is the dynamic, associated with Freud, for whom emotions could be repressed, distorted, transformed, and otherwise disguised.

"It seems reasonable to conclude," writes Plutchik (1984), "that an emotion is a hypothetical construct or inference based upon various classes of evidence" (p. 199), and that some emotions must be primary and others secondary or derivatives of these. Within an evolutionary framework, he proposes eight basic prototypical patterns of adaptive behaviors or reactions, all having a function for survival. These are: incorporation, rejection, protection, destruction, reproduction, reintegration, orientation, and exploration, and he adds, these behaviors are not merely responses, but, as in Tolman's (1932) terms, "responses as affecting stimuli" (Plutchik, 1984, p. 202). This comprehensive array of human reactions is subsumed by a more basic triad which can also be found in lower animals: "All organisms, in order to survive and maintain their population, must find and ingest food, avoid injury, and reproduce their kind" (Plutchik, 1984, p. 201).

These then are primary instinctual behaviors, as derived from an evolutionary perspective, out of which issue many derivative emotional expressions. Freud's dual drives have little in common with this distillation of inherited, adaptive behavioral patterns relevant to survival. "Perhaps," writes Kernberg (1982) in a paper designed to integrate new neurophysiological and infant-developmental research, "a failure to re-examine instinct theory, . . . particularly an insufficient re-examination of the relation between affects and drives, has contributed to the uncertainty in our field regarding the motivational forces of earliest development, and the origin and development of drives as overall motivational systems . . ." (p. 906). In a searching attempt to redefine the concept "drive" and place affects somewhere in the framework of his object-relational drive model he asks, "Is the biologically determined activation of affects a reflection of the activation of libidinal, aggressive (or still undifferentiated) drives, or are affects themselves—rather than drives—the essential motivational forces?" (1982, p. 907). One might have supposed that "arousal" of behaviors can harbor no such schematic division, rather, that these are gradients of activity along a continuum, pertaining to one of the primary behavioral patterns. This is yet another version of the chicken-or-egg dilemma engendered by reification of "drives" and "affects," and reflects Kernberg's adherence to this tendency. He reaches the conclusion that affects are the primary motivational system because they are "intimately linked with the fixation by memory of an internalized world of object relations" (p. 907). "Affects," he concludes, "are the building blocks or constituents of drives; affects eventually acquire a signal function for the activation of drives" (p. 908). Freud had placed the signal function of anxiety in the ego: Kernberg places all other affects in the same structure, and adds, "drives are manifest not simply by affects, but by the activation of specific object-relations, which include an affect and wherein the drive is represented by a specific drive or wish" (p. 909). Kernberg's is a reexplanation of classical drive theory with the addition of an internalized object-relations component. But the relational component in drive theory is already implicit in the "wish," indeed the wish came about through a relational concept and is itself the psychological representative of the drive's urge. We have gained little by further reification.

Moreover, the discussion further perpetuates the mind-as-container problem with fixed memories and their attendant affect dispositions, while losing Freud's primary idea regarding the mobility and transformability of drives or instinctual "energy," the concept around which pivot principles of transformation in the "talking cure": "to restructure lower order motivational forces (such as instincts) by making possible the transformation of a share of these into forces of greater complexity which can be re-deployed within the nexus of higher levels of motivational organization" (Loewald, 1971, p. 103). The theoretical link can be sought in the events of the clinical situation, in the fluid interplay of current affects rearoused in the light of the past, and their working through in the process of verbalization and awareness. This would seem to have to do with how affects retain their somatic charge until they have been processed cognitively or expressed and represented in a verbal narrative in order to become memory. A sensitive interpreter and synthesizer of psychoanalytic theory, Loewald (1971) insists that the "mind's work consists in 'representing' (in the wide sense of representation)—and not in getting rid of stimuli that reach it. . . . The mind's interrelation with the body is twofold: mental work is *powered* through neurophysiological process; and this work is *stimulated* by organismic needs" (p. 108). Instinct, for Loewald, is a *mental* stimulus, the most primitive element of motivation, "a psychic representative of biological stimuli" (p. 108). It would seem that a developmental model accounting for the gradual differentiation of emotion (psychological) from affect (somatic) would be more clarifying, theoretically. The central role of talking would again appear to play an important part in this.

In moving toward a psychoanalytic theory of affect closely aligned with infant research, Emde and Buchsbaum (1980) emphasize the biosocial as well as biobehavioral aspects of shifts in organization of early life: "these organizational shifts are central in affective development and provide the framework for the ontogeny of affect structure during the first year" (p. 208). Due to their early, organized appearance and importance in crystallizing the prerepresentational core self (Emde, 1983), Emde and Buchsbaum view infant affects as central in biobehavioral development from the start: "Affects do indeed serve to organize mental functioning and behavior" (p. 215). Moreover,

Emde (1983) elsewhere emphasizes the cross-cultural universality of both the expression and recognition of certain basic patterns of emotions and their facial and vocalic manifestations. Discrete affects and readiness for expression in the infant include: happiness, fear, sadness, surprise, anger, disgust, and pain (Emde et al., 1978) Their presence and availability as communicational tools are taken as proof that discrete affective expression is part of our biological heritage, with which all members of our species are born.

Emde and Buchsbaum further claim that affects initially operate as biosocial motivational signals prior to becoming psychological; this is not unlike Freud's latter model, postulating the signal function of emotions in the ego. In their reading of Freud, however, these authors note that "affects do not need to be 'tamed,' they don't *become* signals as a consequence of socialization. Rather, they are signals to begin with" (p. 216). With this, they turn away from the drive reduction model, claiming that socialization needs to be thought of from other perspectives. They emphasize that affects are active participants in negotiating social interactions, rather than "chaotic structures needing to be shaped" (p. 216). Their proposed organizational model for biobehavioral shifts, the core affective self (Emde, 1983) and social referencing, are important pointers toward future reformulations, the former developing according to three biological principles, self-regulation, social fittedness, and affective monitoring.

There have been numerous other prominent motivational hypotheses put forward which explicitly avoid reference to drives. These hypotheses include hierarchical schemas, epigenetic life developmental models, relationally based object-relations models, "constellation of forces" concepts, self systems. More recently, Lichtenberg's (1989) carefully integrated theory of structured motivation, proposes "a series of systems designed to promote the fulfillment and regulation of basic needs" (p. 1). Lichtenberg's sophisticated, comprehensive model, in addition to encompassing five systems of basic human motivation (including attachment and affiliation), is developmental and integrates intentionality, wishes, and the sense of self in relation to activities involving all of these. It still remains to be seen if motivation per se is a central concern for a theory of mind which must primarily address and account for subjective meanings. It seems to me that motives must be contingent on the underlying structural organization that elaborates them, and that they will therefore always be subject to the attribution of meaning of which a particular representational level is capable. Affect tolerance and complex emotions would appear to have a place in this model of levels of organization in which these will be expressed according to the degree to which an experience is still somatically felt or to some degree represented symbolically. In chapter 4, I will propose a model of mind in which developmental stages of symbolization account for the gradual modulation of affects into emotions through changing levels of symbolic representation which structure the very nature of subjective experience and the meanings encumbent upon this.

To the degree that Freud shaped psychoanalytic theory through a biological mold, he obfuscated the events of clinical psychoanalysis; and because his explanations were embedded in physicalist concepts, they were not sufficiently inclusive of the signifying, linguistic, and symbolizational dimensions of mind. While the theoretical monument he constructed was a brilliant, comprehensive, and cohesive explanatory vehicle, its cohesion rests upon certain principles which lead us in the wrong direction, to remain sheltered in a collapsing edifice. Energic transformations of "drives" in their circuitous paths toward stimulus reduction are two such principles. They cannot explain or account for the uniquely human way of processing experience as expressed through many different symbolic vehicles and modes at different levels of structuralization, and they do not adequately mirror the transforming events of the "talking cure." "We need, in fine, a metaphysics which recognizes both the continuity between man and animals and also the discontinuity. We need, instead of an instinctual dualism, an instinctual dialectic" (N. O. Brown, 1959, p. 83).

MENTAL REPRESENTATION AND INTERNALIZATION MECHANISMS

From the time of its inception psychoanalytic terminology has been an ongoing source of debate; indeed, much confusion and disagreement often arises precisely over conceptual arguments embedded in semantic disputes. Mental representation, originating in Freud's *Vorstellung*, "idea, representation, imagination" or his basic "memory image," is a case in point. Considerable ambiguity as to the meaning of unconscious representation is compounded by its overlap with fantasy, image, and memory. At different times, it has been used to refer to: the ideational component of drive pressure; the contents of ideas that lie outside awareness; an organization of mind; eidetic images, mental pictures, or units of interpersonal interaction; schemas in the classical sense as in "unconscious fantasies," or even as underlying constituents of all memories and thoughts. Connotations range from the metaphoric to the veridical, from a hallucinated figment of a "wish," to memory itself.

As the term indicates, for Freud *representation* was something created internally by the mind. This stood in stark contrast with what was believed to be an objective, external "reality," or a veridical internal memory of something that had actually existed in reality. The problem with this conceptualization is that all mental processes are fluid and are constantly being constructed and reconstructed according to a subjective present. Mental representation was used by Freud to denote primarily unconscious mental "contents," a problematic notion which conjures image of the psyche as "receptacle," with spatial departments containing cathected or decathected fixed, mental representations. Assisted by the constructivist underpinnings of a cognitive perspective, I will attempt to redefine this concept, placing the mental representational mechanism within the context of ongoing, continuously reconstructed and changing mental activity, whereby fragments of experiences and memories become organized and reorganized dynamically according to current cognitive competencies at different levels of organization of meaning.

The concept understood today in contemporary psychoanalysis as mental representation can be traced to Freud's original "hallucinatory wish fulfillment," embodied in the idea of the hungry infant's creation of an inner image of the desired mother's breast—hallucinated, inasmuch as it is called up in its absence, but also "remembered" as having been a real source of gratification. Today we know it to be unlikely that a tiny infant is capable of evoking an internal image, this competency evolving quite a bit later. But the central problem with Freud's conceptualization is that he explained a mental "function" with a cause; as he thought, the fulfillment of a "wish." The mental image, however, is not created out of drive pressure; it represents the essential functioning of the mind. Without a functional approach, mental processes and phenomena are understood in terms of their results. In this way Freud differentiated mental representations (which could be unconscious) from veridical memories, creating a division between "reality" images, and "fantasy" images. Actually there is no such functional division in a mind which essentially comes about through its function; to "represent" is the process of signifying meaning. To speak of "mental" is to speak of representation—and to speak of representation is to speak of meaning. Mind and meaning are one. From this point of view the theoretical requirement is simple; to formulate a developmental model of levels of mental organization. But psychoanalytic theories have evolved without the benefit of a radical reevaluation of this core concept, and by their adherence to a focus which emphasizes the "contents" of representations rather than the function, they forego the necessary theoretical shift. The door to this, however, has been definitively opened by the work of Piaget, through which the Freudian use of mental representation, with its energic connotations, may undergo a radical revision.

The term *mental representation* has continued to be used in psychoanalysis while undergoing numerous conceptual transformations, and has currently been harnessed by object-relationists primarily to refer to internalized units of interpersonal interactions, or as a gauge of self esteem, as an image of the self, the "self-representation." Numerous authors refer to mental representation broadly as "forming the unconscious base of all conscious psychic-activity" (Novey, 1958; Beres and Joseph, 1970); these authors apply the term rather loosely to a "postulated unconscious psychic organization capable of evocation in consciousness as symbol, image, fantasy, thought, affect or action" (Beres and Joseph, 1970, p. 2). Others, notably Pine (1985), Fraiberg (1969), and McDevitt (1975), pair its achievement with separation–individuation issues, emphasizing the attainment of libidinal object constancy in the separation–individuation process as the culmination of the child's attempt to internally evoke an absent and needed object. Here, the concept appears to be akin to evocative memory. More recently and from a decidedly interpersonal perspective, Stern (1985) asserts that the infant's capacity to recognize another as differentiated from the self, is present at birth; he focuses on the representation of generalized interactions with others, drawing a distinction between this and a specific memory: "it contains multiple specific memories but as a structure is closer to an abstract presentation, as that term is used clinically" (p. 97). Sandler and Rosenblatt (1962) pointed out that mental representations are not merely images, but "schemata constructed out of a multitude of impressions" (p. 133). As it is referred to here, adopting Piaget's term *schema*, the concept is identical to the general idea of internalized experiences. This points in the direction I suggested earlier, to the mechanism itself. Further, it points to its origins in the sensorimotor schema rooted, as was Freud's ego, in the body.

Adhering closely to Freudian notions (energic and drive concepts) Beres and Joseph (1970) speak of "freely mobile" and "bound" psychic energies, "the cathexes of objects, of organs, of functions" with "libidinal or aggressive energy of the mental representations of the items listed" (p. 4). These authors also address the correspondence between mental representation and the primary and secondary processes and their relation to various regulatory functions, but do so using explanatory notions of different modes of discharge of "psychic energies" rather than in process or developmental terms. In so doing, they obfuscate the particular significance of the mental "image" in psychoanalysis and how this partakes in the ongoing construction of meanings. They make a particular "thing" of a process that constitutes it depicting various activated pictures charged with varying degrees of drive energy, controlled by a central, governing switchboard—the mind as "apparatus." The language of reification in which these papers were conceptualized, I believe, fosters ideation that moves away from understanding the mind in functional terms, as an organic process whereby experiences are transformed into concepts, and therefore promotes little further clinical or theoretical understanding of these phenomena.

The traditional psychoanalytic point of view adheres to three major assumptions, initially promulgated by Freud, later elaborated upon by Jacobson (1964), Fraiberg (1969), Mahler et al. (1975), and more obliquely by M. Klein (1945), Balint (1960, 1968), the British object relationists, and recently Sandler and Rosenblatt (1962) and Kernberg (1984). These are that (1) at birth the infant cannot phenomenologically distinguish another from itself until the achievement of the separation–individuation process; (2) that mental representation is a relatively advanced accomplishment, appearing only toward the end of the second year when abstraction through language and the capacity to symbolize consolidate; and (3) that representations are in part products of psychological defensive activity and are affected by these. So closely has the notion of mental representation come to refer to a general internalization process—whereby representations form the constituent units of all mental contents—that the term is now virtually interchangeable with schemata. This takes us to the doorstep of a view of mind in developmental–structuralist terms, as stages of competencies which determine levels of representational organization. Mental representation, as such, has become obsolete. In fact, as Piaget pointed out, the advent of the semiotic function in the course of development corresponds to object constancy, with its correlative nascent capacity to "represent"—to evoke the mental image. As such, the mental image is always subjective, always constructed, and always current: it enters into the very fabric of memory, of subjective experience, and the personal narratives that are elaborated out of these (see also Arlow [1969a]).

Incorporation, introjection, and identification all closely related psychoanalytic metaphors, have been defined primarily as internalizing mechanisms. Each of these experiences is characteristic for a particular stage of development and is believed to exert a marked impact on the inner life of the subject, particularly with reference to the construction of the self representation. These concepts are essentially descriptive terms for fantasies or ideation pertaining to the phenomenology of ways in which the mind takes in what is outside. As the most advanced and final result of a process which begins with perception and moves through various stages, according to Hartmann, Kris, and Lowenstein (1946a), internalization is when regulations that occurred in interactions and interpersonal exchanges with others are replaced by inner regulations. They are alluding more to a superego structure than to the broader meaning now attributed to this internalizing process. Beres and Joseph (1970) assert that only identification is observable as clinical manifestation. I have found, however, that hearing a parental voice of reprimand or prohibition (an internal audition) is a fairly common clinical phenomenon and does not necessarily represent an identification, but is more akin to a superego introjection.

The earliest forms of "taking in" occur at the beginning of life, considered by psychoanalysis as an undifferentiated phase, and by Piaget as the sensorimotor stage. The predominant incorporative orifice at this level of experience is the mouth. When the "taking in" of stimuli is by the sense organs, as in the sensorimotor child, we call this organismic analogue "incorporation." The result of this process will be expressed in a fantasy of incorporation or introjection which highlights the somatic orientation of experience of which this stage is capable. Sensorimotor experience is one of organismic involvement; undifferentiatedness one of merger. Clinically, this often appears as the expression of the self as harboring the presence of another—of an unmetabolized "other," dominating the self from within, or of the projection of this experience into someone else. Concepts of introjection and projection, I believe, are meaningless unless we understand the phenomenon of merger or the undifferentiated sensorimotor experience, a realm without consciousness in which the absence of clear boundaries between self and other are such that we tend to contain and express part of someone else's feelings and attitudes, or alternately, in which we attribute to someone else what we are unable or unwilling to integrate within ourselves. To call these "defensive" mechanisms at these early stages is, I believe, imprecise since at this level they are the normal consequence of undifferentiation. When these experiences linger into adulthood as the manifestation of a breakdown in differentiation or of enduring desymbolization, however, they are indicative of pathology, possibly of psychotic processes.

The concerns here are with inner and outer, perception and fantasy, consciousness and unconscious processes, and, as Freud saw it, with the difficulty we seem to have in giving anything up—the ego is the precipitate of lost objects—that which was outside is held within and becomes part of the construction of a self: "a portion of the external world has, at least partially, been abandoned as an object and has instead, . . . been taken into the ego and thus become an integral part of the internal world" (Freud, 1940, p. 205). This is a description of internalization and representation—the way the mind transforms experiences into concepts. To hold mother, the child learns to represent her, to evoke her in her absence, to behave like her, to become like her. Here is a clear developmental progression which can be directly correlated to the advent of the symbolic function in the capacity to evoke a representation, and the subsequent imitative and unconscious identificatory processes of internalization through which all children pass. For Freud, however, internalizational processes spring from the constitution of the "wish," to create images, a precipitate of loss. He writes, in "Creative Writers and Day Dreaming" (1908):

> But whoever understands the human mind knows that hardly anything is harder for a man than to give up a pleasure which he has once experienced. Actually, we can never give anything up; we only exchange one thing for another. What appears to be a renunciation is really the formation of a substitute or surrogate. In the same way, the growing child, when he stops playing, gives up nothing but the link with real objects; instead of *playing*, he now *phantasies*. He builds castles in the air and creates what are called *daydreams* [p. 145].

The fantasy is equated dynamically with the substitution of a real object, while the ego, in its connection to reality, is formed out of identifications and internalizations.

"Identification," writes Beres (1965), "is a basic characteristic of the human psyche, a form of object relationship expressing a fundamental need of the child to be like the parent . . ." (p. 179). Psychoanalytic authors have tended to stress the object relational aspect of these internalizing processes while neglecting to trace their stepwise developmental evolution in functional terms. I would argue rather that internalization mechanisms and representation are the quintessential faculties of psyche and the basic nature of what constitutes mind. Thus defined, the mind is understood as a transformer of all experiences into ideas. The carriers of these ideas are symbolic representations. Kohut based his whole theory of therapeutic gain on the concept of "transmuting internalizations" as these occur during the process of therapy. Thus, interpersonally, we are primed to "take in" what we currently need according to our developmental status and condition. Analogous to Piaget's assimilation and accommodation paradigm, the processes of internalization are twofold; taking in and sorting out. The mind does indeed transform experiences according to its own representational activity and in this sense, the ego is formed out of the experiences which have become internalized representationally. At these levels of high abstraction Freud's concepts can be found to conform with contemporary understanding. Today we are in a position to translate his concepts and apply them to the vicissitudes of separation and individuation which are intimately intertwined with processes underlying the construction of representations.

In a probing paper, Friedman (1980) criticizes attempts to categorize representations, as well as what he considers to be the loose or imprecise use of the concept itself, questioning its clinical usefulness, unless "it is held fast to the high-level abstractions it labels" (p. 217). With a strong penchant toward clinical integration, Friedman continues, "Just as the people we study have more or less abstract ideas in their minds, so also representations exist on many levels of abstraction. We are asked to regard these as the subject's subjectively experienced and lived-with abstractions, rather than categories imposed by the theorist" (p. 217). He states, "The trouble with representation is that it means so many different things (c.f. Fraiberg, 1969) and almost all of its meanings are vague. Since mental life is practically equivalent to signifying activity, the term 'representation' is almost synonymous with 'mental.' In the broadest sense, the language of representation is merely an atomized way of speaking of meanings (c.f. Modell, 1968)" (p. 216).

Precisely. Mind as a *signifying activity* is central to all our theory building, and whatever else we may focus on, memory, cognition, or affects, meaning and mind remain virtually synonymous and necessarily at the center of our discussion. If this is the case, then we need a more comprehensive term and framework for the general abstractive tendency of mind.

Friedman (1980) is perfectly right when he contests, "What about a primary process presence? . . . What about a voice of conscience? What about a spontaneous image of a commending or a condemning parent? . . . a hallucinated voice? Are these also to be considered representations which have, somehow come to subsume understanding into a single phenomenon?" (p. 221). How useful is such a broad and imprecise term, psychoanalytically—why do we need a concept such as mental representation? (see also Linnell [1990]).

The notion that the young human, as distinct from all other species, can and does gradually begin to use representational vehicles depicting units of experience is, I believe, beyond dispute. No comprehensive theoretical paradigm has been proposed in psychoanalysis, though, that could account for the changing manifestations of this underlying mechanism, or that might organize a phenomenological developmental model of how these different configurations of experience become represented. Psychoanalysis has lacked a crucial definition for this process and has lagged behind information issuing from other disciplines. Yet, I believe that in a new and comprehensive developmental model of symbolization there lies a framework for a new metapsychology, one which does not take recourse to constructs of mind as containing forces, counterforces, cathexes, or any other type of energy flow (Holt, 1967). Such an approach focuses on the unconscious–conscious dimension in terms of the way originally unconscious, sensorimotor patterns and protosymbolic, preverbal organization may become conscious as these acquire degrees of symbolic signification. Schimek (1975) suggests that, "it may be more legitimate to infer unconscious sensori-motor organizers of action at a pre-ideational, as well as pre-verbal level, without postulating that behind the various observable manifestations of an inferred unconscious motive lies an unconscious image or fantasy" (p. 172). This is a very important issue, and one which bears directly on a new model which obviates the need for the concept "mental representation" altogether.

Let me briefly then trace the course of the development of symbolization, a course which will be taken up in greater detail in chapter 4. Piaget's work addressed cognitive functioning and, whereas he alluded to psychoanalytic tenets and encompassed processes that occur outside of awareness, his interest was specifically in delineating operational structures or stages of thinking, and not their emotional implications; the function itself, not its implications for the entire person. Tracing his stages of cognitive development and interweaving these with other psychoanalytic developmental lines yields a comprehensive picture of the subtleties involved in the stepwise microgenetic evolution of signification. In this, the symbolic function plays a central role in mental functioning. At the stage in which the psychoanalytic child is accomplishing a separation–individuation process, intensely involved with a primary "other," caught up in all the attendant emotive dramas of attachment, the sensorimotor child, in cognitive terms, is elaborating a set of meanings associated with particular signs and signals which induce it to respond with actions. The sensorimotor child (roughly from birth to 18 to 24 months) does not hold in representational form, but acts, moves, vocalizes, and expresses knowledge and reactions organismically.

Experiences gradually become subjectified directly through signifiers of significates and, only later, via more advanced symbolization, through signifiers which are distinct from significates or the signified. The scheme of the permanent object appears as part of the developmental achievement of a particular operational mode of thought, just as libidinal object constancy, understood as the enduring internal representation of an attachment figure, appears as part of emotive developmental achievements, and both are predicated on the capacity to call up a stable representation of something or someone not present. The image thus conjured will reflect not only the subjectively felt experience of the person or object that is being recalled, but also the structuralizing competencies of a particular developmental stage. Prior to this developmental juncture, the sensorimotor child reacts to the sight of the father's slippers as though they were father himself, the sound of mother's voice on the telephone as though she were present (i.e., the "sign" or "signifier," in this example, slippers and voice, cannot as yet evoke presence, but only announce it). Only after many comings and goings, absences and returns, will the schema of the leaving-and-returning parent become encoded and integrated into the total organic experience of the "parents." And only later, will the "sign" enable the child to foresee consequences. The crucial distinction between signification prior to the symbolizing capacity and genuine symbolic representation rests entirely on the fact that the former yields only sign and signaling correspondences, while the latter involves a differentiation between signifier and what is signified. This seemingly minor difference, however, impacts quite dramatically on the nature of experience. What I emphasize here is the function itself, and the fact that representations need to be cast in developmental terms, as these will undergo ongoing microgenetic modifications according to the stage of symbolization of which they partake. To discuss representation theoretically is to discuss meanings; and meanings are better organized and understood when they are cast in developmental terms, in a paradigm of symbolizational development.

While psychoanalytic and cognitive perspectives may differ in their approach and focus of inquiry, nevertheless it is self-evident how interlocked their developmental pathways are and how much they impact on each other. It is as misleading to think of these aspects of mind in isolation as it is to perpetuate the artificial psyche/soma split. Likewise, figurative and operative functioning are always interrelated, the symbol and what it represents express meanings, which have been seen and felt. All perception, habit, abstract thought, even motor activity, consists in "linking meanings, and all meaning implies a relation between a significant and signified reality" (Piaget, 1950, p. 124).

The concept of mental representation is intrinsic to a drive psychology in that it embodies the image of "instinctual" satisfaction. But without drives or energic cathexes the term is indistinguishable from evocative memory or the symbolic function. Today's "mental representation" subsumes Freud's unconscious fantasy and the object relationists' notions of internalization; however, since neither of these are elaborated developmentally, they both uphold the idea of a fixed or static "inner image" in a mental container, ideas which are not consonant with contemporary understanding of a fluid, active, constantly reconstructing mind. As representations have been discussed here, however, on a continuum with all symbolizing activity, the term is subsumed within a developmental paradigm of symbolization, providing a unitary base for a revision which lessens our theoretical burdens considerably, and greatly simplifies our model of mind.

THE EGO/SELF

Of all the terms originating in Freud's psychoanalytic concepts, none has become more misunderstood, distorted, used, and abused, both in the professional vernacular and popular parlance, than the term *ego*. Infelicitously translated by Strachey in a latinized (one is tempted to say medicalized) version, *das Ich* (the I) had appeared as early as 1895 in the Project, in which Freud had begun with a neuronic conceptualization of "a group of neurones which is constantly cathected . . ." (p. 323) an organization of the psyche with certain specific functions, primarily an agency of "inhibition" binding the discharge of psychic energies. Right away we are at the heart of a physicalist conceptualization of mind, in which effects are necessarily explained by causes and changes are understood as shifts or modifications of energies.

The "immature mind," Freud wrote, was composed of certain "primary mental processes" providing maximum mobility of cathectic discharge. Subsequently, and due to the impact of external reality, these primitive or archaic modes were thought to become modulated by the more adaptive "secondary processes," which gradually supplanted them (1887–1902). The inhibitory, mediating agency of this process was the ego; first and foremost a "body" ego.

The early view conceived of an undifferentiated drive matrix at birth directed toward the interior of the body: with maturation, the id's mobile energic discharge gradually differentiated, and in varying proportions and fusions, moved toward particular organs at the body surface. As these mobile energies of the id (conceived as a "seething cauldron") became "bound" by the frustrating demands of the environment, there gradually emerged an ego, which, by way of encroaching influences from outer reality, evolved into an organization of specific functions (i.e., control and regulation of the drives, perception, motility). Serving the primacy of a "pleasure–unpleasure principle" (originally the principle of neuronic inertia, 1887–1902) in this early topographical model, systems exist (the id) or are formed (the ego) in order to perform certain functions or to divert and transform the nature of energy coming from other systems. Since the ego was thought to develop in relation to external reality, pathology is defined in terms of loss of contact with or distortions of the sense of reality; it is either ignored or denied in neurosis, while totally abandoned in psychosis (Freud, 1924). In later elaborations, the principal measure of mental health is considered in terms of ego strength.

Freud's (1911) idea was that "the unconscious mental processes" were organized as a "pleasure ego," while their antagonist, the "reality ego," strove for "what was useful" and guarded "itself against damage," for which task it was equipped with the functions of consciousness, motility, judgment, and reality testing. The ego is associated with the secondary process, reality based thinking, in contrast to the archaic "primary process" of the unconscious. To this early ego, Freud had allotted two possible "instincts" of its own, positing that self-preservation and mastery might be such intrinsic forces. From the outset the ego was conceived as pitched against, or as a controlling agency, harnessing the "unconscious mental processes"; it was the "outer rind," a mediating agency which formed out of contact with external reality and emerged out of the id.

Although Freud warned against taking his earlier topographical theory literally, complications stemming from this early model were evident in the ambiguous, double sense allotted to the system unconscious; a descriptive sense, indicating the particular quality of a mental state, and a dynamic sense, which attributed a particular function to this mental agency. Confusion is further compounded by Freud's realization and much of the ego must itself be unconscious, only a small part of it covered by the term *preconscious* (Freud, 1921).

Freud's dynamic topography of the mind evolved into a dynamic structural model in which three agencies, the id, ego, and superego, represented specific kinds of mental functioning corresponding to drive impulses, reality adaptation, and the internalized dictates of parental or societal codes and standards of conduct. The earlier core metapsychological concept of levels of psychological processes was replaced by that of structures; psychic organizations defined by their functions (Freud, 1923). Once the mind's "mental structures" were defined in terms of functions, the study of their interrelationships and dynamic tension was to take center stage. The ego now became the locus of the defenses and character and, after 1923, the legacy of structural theory directed psychoanalytic focus to the study of the ego (see also Rapaport [1957a,b, 1959]).

Ego psychology reached its zenith in the study of this agency's functions and operations, but the theoretical problem caused by its double duty remained to haunt the psychoanalytic theorist. The phenomenology of the "self" known to each of us as "I," "me," "myself," in this conceptualization, has been subtly usurped by the duplicity of a self divested of selfhood, a system of functions which therefore must be reporting to a still more central core agency, the true self. The knotty consequences of such a dissection are being spun out by generations of analysts who, in considering an ego which performs many "functions," are left looking for the person it performs these functions for. Moreover, this conceptualization led to the outgrowth of an entire school of psychoanalysis intent on resurrecting the neglected self as an aspect of human experience and core organizer, with crucial repercussions for psychological stability and well-being. Both the complementarity of the self–other dimension and the impact of early relationships on self-esteem, as well as implicit psychological struggles with separation–individuation issues and the internalization and identificatory processes issuing from these, now come to pose serious problems for psychoanalytic theorizing (Opatow, 1988; Krishner, 1991).

The ego had always been depicted as overrun by unconscious forces, struggling with the demands of superego dictates or of external reality. The tripartite model of mind conceives of three agencies more or less juxtaposed to each other with a central governing ego, "a poor creature owing service to three masters . . ." (Freud, 1923, p. 56). Scant attention was given to "narcissistic" issues, which, in Freud's formulations, had been absorbed by the idea of vectors of libidinal energy distribution. The direction of the flow of libido and a distinction between primary and secondary narcissism addressed, albeit inefficiently, the all-important issue of self-esteem. There is little room in the mind thus conceived for a self, an identity, a center of agency and volition; and if we should find it, we wonder if, thus reified and embattled, we could even recognize it or be able to differentiate it from the other three mental agencies. Taken to a degree of absurdity, this line of thinking only highlights the fundamental problem of adopting such impersonal terminology when approaching the understanding of an individual's subjective experience and sense of cohesion, agency, or self-esteem. Clinically it creates immense problems as we listen to our patient's "superego" and "ego ideal," admonishing and reprimanding or holding up unattainable goals; to their battered "egos," in varying degrees of disrepair, and their "ids,' alternately wailing, raging, and demanding or generally disrupting their everyday lives and the analytic process. These compartmental structural metaphors of personal experience and activity often blur rather than clarify clinical relevance and render the problem of formulating a succinct, experience-near interpretation, practically an impossibility. It is difficult enough to separate a lofty "superego" from an "ego ideal" or a sadistic one from an "id"—even more so to address them independently.

Moreover, this conceptualization accentuates a fractionist, medical approach to the mind as a set of mechanical parts in more or less disarray or malfunction, to be checked, fixed, reen-forced, or reapportioned vis-à-vis each other for the machine to run smoothly. It is at odds with later more unified concepts of "personality" (Rapaport, 1957b; Klein, 1970) and the view of mental disorder as attributable to the entire person rather than to particular isolatable parts: "The 'molar' concept of the psychophysical organism as system contrasts with its conception as a mere aggregate of 'molecular' units. . . . Psychopathology clearly shows mental dysfunction as a system disturbance rather than a loss of single functions" (von Bertalanffy, 1975, p. 208).

The ego, misleading, confusing, and apparently mistrans-lated as this Latin version might be, is nevertheless the term psychoanalysis has used for *das Ich*, connecting the experiential self and the structural "ego," although, as Schafer (1976) com-ments, Freud's concept is not merely ego and self, "it is also 'I,' the agent, the subject who must always be assumed in any psychological proposition" (p. 111). While Freud had adopted a term which was already in familiar use (and is found throughout philosophical writings), the precise meaning which he attached to it, early on, is not unambiguous. Throughout his writings the ego is used to represent both a particular part of the mind with special attributes and functions and, particularly in connection with narcissism, for the entire self: "Freud never separated what we think of as the metapsychological ego from the experiencing self" (Kernberg, 1982, p. 894).

Protter (1988) identifies the core problem of Freud's con-ceptual metatheorizing to be his lack of the dialectical catego-ries that would have enabled him to dispense with "the insufficiency of the static dualism of either/or to apprehend and keep hold of a vital process" (p. 619). While leaning heavily on philosophical concepts and dovetailing Freud with Hegel (1807), in a paper rich with solutions for metatheoretical enig-mas, Protter ably dissolves drives, self, wish, and object into each other, "terms that are naively taken as self subsisting" (p. 620), obscuring problematic dichotomies and illuminating their in-terdependence; "consciousness is both connected to and dis-tinct from its object" (Hegel [1807] cited in Protter [1988], p. 622). It comes into being in an "outward turning," as mind begins in the void which mother left behind—her absence. Thus

Protter reiterates, "the Freudian subject is connected with itself only through the mediation of an object," and "the concept 'self' and 'wish' are bound to each other by mutual implication" (p. 620). The self is desire and, like drive, at the interface of soma with psyche, is both physical and representational. Id, in binding itself, becomes ego.

Freud's subtle ambiguity (the ego as an agency and the experiencing self), however, has created enormous theoretical and terminological confusion, and, I believe, is the origin of much ideological splintering in the field. Object relational theories and self psychology sprang out of theoretical premises rooted in self and other which could not be reconciled within the conceptual framework of structures or drive alone. While arising out of theoretical efforts to redefine primary and secondary narcissism, and refine conceptualizations of the narcissistic[9] pathologies, the term *self* is now reintegrated as referring to libidinal cathexes of the mental representation of the self. This is highlighted by Hartmann's 1950 statement, "the opposite of object cathexis is not ego cathexis, but cathexis of one's own person, that is, self-cathexis; . . . we do not imply whether this cathexis is situated in the id, ego or superego. This formulation takes into account that we actually do find 'narcissism' in all three psychic systems . . . ," and concludes, "It therefore will be clarifying if we define narcissism as the libidinal cathexis not of the ego, but of the self" (Hartmann [1950], p. 127, cited in Kernberg [1982, p. 897]). The self is now found to be a "self representation," located in the system ego, and with this distinction made, Jacobson (1964) is able to offer her crucial contribution to ego psychology, namely the differentiation between the self as person, and the psychic self representation of the "bodily and mental self in the system ego" (Kernberg, 1982, p. 897). This self, however, has come into being in order to give credence to the theoretical bind that the concept of secondary narcissism imposed, namely, to explain how the self can cathect

---

[9]Still one of the most ambiguous of terms, *narcissistic* is currently called upon to mean a "self-cathected" personality, inclined to grandiosity, self-preoccupation, exploitation of others, entitlement, and inaccessibility; and also its opposite, as in the "narcissistic pathologies," namely, developmental arrest, fragile, vulnerable, lacking in self-esteem.

itself. Now it is the ego cathecting the self which is "representational"—an image which, however, is theoretically conceived as a structure.

While Kernberg (1982) goes on to admonish Hartmann for his fateful separation of ego from self and self from self representation and for having created the artificial disjunction of "structural, experiential and descriptive aspects of ego functions" (p. 898), he concedes he has found Jacobson's elaboration of the concept of self representation indispensable for his investigation of neurotic, borderline, and narcissistic pathologies as well as for normal development. "Insofar as the self as person is a psychosocial, behavioral and interactional entity" he suggests replacing the term *self* with the term *character*, and then proposes to reserve the term *self* for "the sum total of self-representations in intimate connection with the sum total of object-representations" (p. 900). And, he emphasizes, he is defining the self as an intrapsychic structure originating from the ego in which it is "clearly" embedded.

I must confess that I see very little advantage (and nothing that is clear) in this rather convoluted conceptualization of mind as collector and processor of snapshots, or of mind as structures containing other structures; nor am I able to follow this game of musical chairs with the self, as it is now apparently envisioned as being contained or "embedded" in an "ego," which experiences and defines "it." In fact, it seems to me, that we could dispense altogether with these terms and metaphors if we adhere to a model of mind as meaning. If we insist on defining mind in concrete terms as an entity, however, surely we must attempt to speak of personal *experiences* when describing the activities of the person whose mind this is.

It seems to me that with regard to the utility of such conceptualizations, we have reached the point of diminishing returns; what were conceived as descriptive explanatory constructs are no longer serviceable, as ego, self, id, superego, drives, and cathected mental pictures collapse into the person and what this person feels, does, says, thinks, or denies. For the sum total of this person's history and the experience of this history as he or she recounts it and lives it in the present, is the expression of this person's identity or self, and not his or her ego, superego, or cathected image. If, as Schafer (1976) claims, "Anthropomorphism in metapsychology is the archaic representation of the theme of human action" (p. 114), then we can only hope that somehow we may find a way out, through this terminological maze of structural confusion, and back to the individual, the subjectively experiencing person who will express the unique meanings of his or her experiences in a unique and idiosyncratic way. For Schafer (1980) "all experience is a construction of the person. . . . The self, then, is not what one has, but what one does: and it is what one tells about what one does" (p. 91).

Inasmuch as we speak of a self, we speak of a construct describing subjective experience—one must stand outside the self to give an account of it. And this reflection can only be described or expressed in terms of actions or personal experience. Again, we are speaking of meanings. We cannot then so simply abrogate this personal narrational device and core identity concept to concretized or localizable metatheoretical structure, and then speak of the "state" of a patient's self or ego, as though these were malfunctioning entities. Nothing could be further from the truth, writes Emde (1983), who emphasizes the self as a process concept, which "refers to a vital set of synthetic functions which increase in complexity and depth as development proceeds throughout the life span" (p. 168). Emde recommends avoiding the notion of a sharply focused age period in which the self develops, as this encourages reification of a process better thought of as a "descriptor of an expanding, individualized and creative aspect of the personality" (p. 169). I see this somewhat differently and will return to a discussion of the intermingling concepts of self and consciousness in chapter 4.

While the structural model as an explanatory construct provided a precise dynamic frame of reference for conflict pathology, and greater descriptive clarity and scope in the examination of the ego's mechanisms, it did so by further entrenching the language of psychoanalysis in a natural science framework, splitting the person further in a continued search for psyche's functional organization and for the loci of experience. One effect of the growth of ego psychology was reexamination of certain key concepts in Freud's theory. Among these were the understanding of anxiety, the study and localization of defenses, facets of object relations, and the idea of a self, while the ego's "integrative" (Nunberg, 1931) and "observing" (Sterba, 1934) capacities could now be identified and clarified. Always an "inhibiting" agency, the ego now became the locus of anxiety, of muted affects, and of the defenses, as well as "the great reservoir of libido" (1920);[10] it binds energies of the id and neutralizes them for "deinstinctualized" expression in sublimation and "signal" versions of powerful emotions. Most importantly the "character" of the ego is "a precipitate of abandoned object cathexes and contains the history of those object choices" (Freud, 1923, p. 29); it is the result of introjection and identification, as well as being coterminous with intentionality and signification, two fundamental concepts eclipsed by a psychology of parts and functions.

It was A. Freud (1937) who systemized the study of ego defenses and Hartmann (1939, 1950, 1951) who, in accord with a biological–adaptational perspective, placed the ego in a central regulatory position as "governing" agency, giving it a set of "autonomous" functions and refining the concept of neutralization. He presented the ego as defined by its functions but at the same time noted that perception, thought and motility often serve the id and superego as well, and highlighted the inevitability of intrasystemic conflicts arising between the ego's defenses and other primary ego functions such as reality-testing and its synthetic function. "How . . ." in the face of this, asks Schafer (1970), "are we to understand . . . 'coherence' as a defining characteristic of ego constituents?" (p. 435). While this metapsychology strives to detail an explanation of the "unitary person" (Schafer, 1980) via the examination of the many high-level organizing functions of the ego, it cannot nor does it, attempt to account for subjective experience, signification, or the attribution of meanings in their particulars, and therefore is incomplete in its explanatory propositions. Moreover its explorations

---

[10]Freud, however, contradicts himself frequently on this point: alternately he allots to the id and the ego the "reservoir" of libido concept. This confusion seems reconcilable on the assumption that for Freud the "reservoir" concept initiates in the original id-ego, undifferentiated matrix and only later is syphoned off, as the ego differentiates and "sends out" libidinal cathexes to objects.

are premised on a method which can only lead to a dead end, searching for further superordinate functions in yet another superordinate agency. When formulating concepts of mind it would be better to move toward generalizable, contentless principles which, while implicitly referring to a unitary individual, stay away from adopting language that makes a "thing" out of processes and explains overall functioning by the categorization of discrete functions.

In conjunction with this trend, the ego's mechanisms were studied in great detail, in the sort of exercise exemplified by Bellak's (1974) twelve-point list of ego functions, now part of any training institute's curriculum. Erikson's (1946, 1951, 1980) concept of ego identity is also noteworthy as, with it, he strove to bridge the gap between a reified ego and the existential self-experience of agency, via an epigenetic model tracing the development of identity. Along developmental lines, Mahler et al.'s (1975) separation–individuation theory also contributed further to the understanding of ego functions in terms of early object relations and structuralization and, most importantly, in the integration of drives into a comprehensive picture of the psychoanalytic theory of libido within developmenal psychology. In addressing the undifferentiated–differentiated dimension, her theory bears directly not only on the formation of the sense of self but also on the nature of the development of the symbolic function itself.

While ego psychology busied itself with the examination of the ego, the restorers of psychic wholeness or the self, Fairbairn (1954), Winnicott (1958, 1965), and Guntrip (1971) in Britain, and Sullivan and Kohut in America, countered with less impersonal, relationally based psychologies emphasizing the coconstruction of self with other. This self, unlike the ego psychologist's self "embedded in the ego," is conceptually closer to the "entire person," Freud's original concept of *das Ich.* No sooner elaborated, however, than we find this self also, rapidly becoming reified and described as an entity. There are the "pathological–grandiose," divided, primitive–archaic, enfeebled, omnipotent, bipolar, infantile, real, false, hidden, core, personal, and nuclear selves, self systems, and multiple other subselves to be found and accounted for. The self is described as striving to "affirm itself," "actualize itself," to develop, safeguard itself, to "cohere." Now, in looking for a unitary concept accommodating issues of self-esteem, authenticity, purposeful action, volition, and relatedness, we are led instead to an implied "superself or superordinate self" (Schafer, 1980, p. 91) perhaps to the philosopher's "humuncular self" hidden behind consciousness (Krishner, 1991), some superentity capable of governing this construction of multiple subselves. The basic premise of the psychologies of the self adheres to Hegel's (1807) dialectic, namely, that the sense of self is dependent on affirmation from another and requires this responsiveness in order to blossom. Without confirmation, or worse, in the face of an unempathic, nonaffirming other, self-depletion and shattering result, or there occurs a defensive flight into illusory self-sufficiency.

Yet both the complementarity of the self–other dimension as well as implicit psychological struggles with separation and individuation issues, continue to pose problems in psychoanalyic theorizing. These are compounded by internalizing and identificatory processes which leave their representational and characterological stamp on the entire personality, again splitting the subject into agent and container of his or her experience. These concerns lead to a more focal problem, one defined by Freud as "unfathomable," that of consciousness, a discussion of which necessarily leads to further problems if conceptualizations continue to be couched in terms of mental places, agencies, and their functions. I will return to this discussion and an alternate approach in chapter 4.

While theoretical focus on the experiential self might have paved the way for a language for psychoanalysis which could return agency to the unitary person (Schafer, 1976), the psychologies of self have essentially transposed old problems with egos to new problems with selves; "now instead of forces or psychic structures autonomously having it out with one another, subselves do the same" (Schafer, 1980, p. 90). In our theories the same problems keep occurring. As I have mentioned throughout, this is because the real problems are epistemological, having to do with "how to formulate theoretical psychoanalytic propositions nonmechanistically far more than . . . with the content of specific propositions" (Schafer, 1980, p. 84). Fragmentation into parts leads to examination of the properties and operations of these parts and of their relationship to other parts, but away from the understanding of, or speaking about a unitary person exhibiting certain patterns of behavior in relationship to certain feelings and experiences, which are the result of unique and uniquely elaborated personal narratives. Perhaps this explains why intentionality and volition, dimensions systematically ignored by psychoanalytic authors, are still absent from mainstream theoretical writings. These eminently psychological, indeed psychoanalytic concerns, have in some way been absorbed or replaced by the systems, structures, and functions constructed to subsume their expression.

In this regard and in its radical departure from customary designations of terms or concepts in psychoanalysis, Schafer's (1976) revision and approach are extremely cogent: he prescribes that we "regard each psychological process, event, experience or behavior as some kind of activity . . . henceforth called action" (p. 9), and generally desist from referring to mind in terms of location, direction, quantity or movement, terms suitable for "things" or "entities." He offers an excellent mandate: "we shall not speak of internalization except in the sense of a person imagining his or her incorporating something" (p. 10). In Schafer's language, it will no longer do to speak of someone as "having" a feeling or an impulse or, indeed, to permit any connotation of substantive properties to what are viewed simply as a person's multivaried activities. In Schafer's action language the self is "an item of experience," and "all experience is the construction of a person" (1980, p. 91).

While proposing this radical departure from customary designations, Schafer (1976) excludes from the psychological what is "altogether unutterable" or "on the level of biological reflex" (p. 9). On this point, I am in disagreement on the premise that we cannot afford to divest the psychological of its organic base, to split the psychobiological unity. On the contrary, I believe the psychological must be woven more skillfully with its biological correlate, the person as an organismic unity, finding explanatory propositions which will accommodate this illusory duality, as well as integrating other issues along the psyche–soma dimension. At bottom, this remains a poorly stitched seam in our thinking, since the person cannot be thus split into binary either/or terms, nor can the symbolic–lexical aspects be divested of their urgent affective connections to primary physiological roots.

It is just because Freud's clinical discussion and approach was not constrained either by the reified orientation congealed in his metapsychology, or by a priori general views of science, but rather focused fundamentally on the infinite "plasticity" of mind and the uniqueness and relevance of subjective experience (psychic reality), that theoretical reification appears so problematic. The materialistic rendition of an agency, the ego and its functions (or the self as a thing) is in disaccord with notions of psychic reality or meanings; the symptom as symbolic *expression* of these. Freud taught that the symptom is the expression in compromise of a person for whom both sides of a conflict carry emotional valence due to their meanings. It is to these meanings that we address ourselves clinically and theoretically, and not the state of agencies or reified systems. "Psychic reality" is the equivalent of meaning, and because meaning is what is implied by "subjective experience," Schafer (1970) pointedly asks, "can it be 'energy' that sees importance, and can it be a 'contentless' function that appropriates relevance, or is it rather the person who does both, since only a meaning-creating person can do?" (p. 442).

Consider the clinical implications for the analyst addressing an analysand, reasoning in the reified terms of our current theory—it is inevitable that the conceptual language in which theory is couched impinges upon the analyst's thinking and on the formulation and intent of interventions: "It is a curious kind of isolating or splitting," remarks Schafer (1976), "to regard one's analysand as an existential person with mechanistic–organismic psychopathology" (p. 120). Moreover, this encourages what Schafer calls "disclaimer" locutions on the part of analyands who, swayed by culture and education to distrust their bodies and their affects, frequently speak as though they were possessed, as in "something made me . . .", or "somewhere I must have known," or "in some part of me," and refer to their own dreams in terms of what "the dream" must be telling them.

We are taught to speak of strong and weak egos; egos with lacunae, fragmenting or bristle; of selves that are undeveloped looking for selfobjects or ragefully and fearfully guarding concealed selves, sometimes encapsulated in glass bubbles. But when all is said and done, is it not the person who perceives, smells, talks, acts, and reflects upon; who conceals or reveals, laughs or cries, in terms of the expression of what has evoked laughter or tears, and not a system, a structure or a representation? And to speak theoretically of functions is to remove the self that moves these functions, just as much as to speak descriptively of a certain kind of self is to ignore the experiences which that self is expressing in the simplest of actions and the most complex narratives. Systems, structures, and functions have replaced subjective experience, meaning, and its expression. For the self is a linguistic construction and comes into being as "I," in the very act of speaking about itself—in the unfolding of its own narrational definition as each "and then" always qualified by "and then I," locates personal experience in time and space, substantiating itself in *shared* participation. The self *is* a dialectic, it is reflective, reflexive and referential, an abstraction of personal experience created by the narrational properties of causality and the subjective interpretation of temporal sequence, and exists experientially in emotional and linguistic expression vis-à-vis another. *How* the analysand speaks of him- or herself is also *who* he or she feels him- or herself to be. Identity or psychological life is always present, in the present, in the narrational thread the person weaves before us. Hence the centrality of talking in the talking cure.

This essay was written in part to examine the history of the concepts ego and self, and the problems that have evolved around them in psychoanalytic theory, and in part to illustrate the ineffectiveness of the natural science language when discussing mind. Meanings are not causes, nor can the ego or self that elaborates them be located in any mental compartment. As will become evident in the course of the elaboration of the developmental paradigm in chapter 4, another possible way of theorizing about mind which captures the phenomenology of the self without reifying it, is to conceptualize developmental planes of organization in which different levels of symbolization determine the very nature of experience and the modes in which this is expressed.

CONCLUSION

Freud found the wish as explanatory vehicle to bridge the biological and psychological for a theory of motivation which, he believed, was to be rooted in biological drives, "for in the psychical field the biological factor is really the rock bottom" (Freud, 1937). It was consonant with the philosophy of science of his era to seek explanations in terms of causes and the operations of mechanisms in terms of the dissection of parts. Freud's formulations were designed to accommodate both his more synthetic hermeneutic, clinical observations and the prevailing analytical requirements of the science of his time. Causality implies determinism and analytic thinking is the logical complement to the doctrine of reductionism (Ackoff, 1975): in subscribing to both, Freud produced a cohesive model which conformed to, and satisfied the criteria of science in his day.

Due to the prevailing understanding of perception, Freud polarized an inner-oriented, pleasure-seeking, and unconscious "irrational" mind to a reality-oriented, adaptive "rational" mind, attributing to these two separate principles of functioning. These were connected via the transformation of drive energy investment—a dichotomized mind containing lower and higher order processes. Motivation was thought to originate in unconscious irrational urges, only secondarily modified by the ego, an agency of compromise which, in turn, is governed by a "superego," an agency of internalized controls. Hence, a dynamic, structural "mental apparatus." Freud gave libidinal urges a developmental scale in which component drives became the origins of the love life of the individual.

Yet neither a dichotomized mind, biological drives, and their energic shifts, nor reified, juxtaposed structures appear

today as viable postulates for the foundation of a general theory
of mind. While a theory of human motivation might answer in
terms of causes, a theory of mind has no such causal requirement. Meanings not causes govern the reasons for human actions, and to speak of mind is to speak of meaning.

While inclusive of the complexities of the entire organism's
functioning, a theory of mind should preferably be concerned
with what is mental, and its unique function in this whole. This
approach will be process oriented, not "thing" oriented. Mind
cannot be understood through concepts related to the application of energy to matter, but rather needs to be conceptualized
in terms of overall processes and patterns of organization; specifically the organization of symbolic activity. In this, the confluence of affective predisposition, developmental level,
cognitive competency, physiological condition, environment,
and experience will all impact, so that "each element of the set
has an effect on the properties or behavior of the set taken as
a whole" (Ackoff, 1975, p. 13).

While it is clear that we are all "driven" in some way, it is
equally clear that "drives" per se do not exist. Would it not be
better to use "drives" generically and descriptively (as in common parlance) to denote quality or degree of manifest persistence of *any* given behavior, inclusive of affects as
communicational vehicles, the intensity of these being determined by predispositional tendencies and environmental responses to these? This perspective is completely consonant with
Freud's view of the ego, "each individual ego is endowed from
the beginning with its own peculiar dispositions and tendencies" (1937, p. 240). Drivenness, thus defined, as a quality describing motivational strength, might be applicable to what thus
far have been understood as "ego functions," for example, mastery, planning, and hence would correspond to Freud's concept
of hereditary endowment of the id–ego continuum. Classification of instinctual behavior might need to be relegated to hard-
wired, inherited, and stage-specific behavioral patterns: early
attachment, emotional expressiveness, sexuality, relational and
group phenomena might enter into this rubric. To the biological we can with confidence attribute one fundamental instinctually based pattern of behaviors, those of primary attachment.

The vicissitudes of attachment, separation, and loss in the young produce the most basic psychobiological and biocognitive repercussions. Human attachment is instinctual and adaptively essential for any species with slow development and lengthy dependency, and may be viewed as gradually reversing during adolescence when peer groupings, sexual behavior, and pairing, together with culturally determined individuating and autonomous strivings, supplant it. The recapitulation of early familial issues might be understood as prototypical for developmental crisis points which thrust toward differentiation and integration at newer and higher levels of individuation in an ascending spiral throughout the life cycle.

The young of our species go through a prerequisite developmental apprenticeship for relational evolution that only begins with instinctual attachment and may or may not flower into loving. Psychological differentiation, with a loosening of early internalizations and separation from affective patterns molded in shared early experiences, form an essential part of transferential working through in analytic treatment. The articulation and verbalization of personally devised aspirations and goals may be conceived as *the* maturational achievement of analytic work joining both old and new theories of what is curative in the psychoanalytic process. Freud's "where id was, there ego shall be" (Freud, 1933) and Gedo's "the gradual elimination of the symbiotic bond through systematic verbalization" (1979) come to mean very much the same thing since verbalization and emotional working through of early affective patterns gradually transform experience through their abstraction at higher levels of symbolic organization.

The stages of life today are no longer as clearly demarcated according to age-specific prescriptions; development is now understood to be an ongoing process with phasic characteristics throughout the life span. Rather than being the result of compromise (although conflict and compromise are present) in a circuitous route toward inertia, activity is often sought for the yields of its own pleasure, in self-expression, and is understood as self-activated and goal-oriented, the agent or person impacting on the environment equally as much as the other way around. This developmental orientation conceives of the person as intrinsically moving in the pursuit of evolutionary trends toward the fullest realization of innate potentials, in which regression will become manifest as diminishing or stifling individuation and pushing back toward dedifferentiation. I believe the instrument of this singularly human developmental potential lies in the mind's capacity for symbolization—the study of which the rest of this work is devoted to.

3.

Symbolization: The Mind's Medium

> [M]ost of us remain excessively timid, reluctant to tackle the grand problems of comparison, generalization and synthesis, even though the certainty of being found in frequent error if we did so ought to be heavily outweighed by the opportunity to deepen, sharpen, and ultimately justify our inquiries.
>
> [Robert McC. Adams, 1968, p. 1192, cited in Marshack, 1972, p. 373]

Except for the immediate satisfaction of biological needs, man lives in a world not of things but of symbols. . . . We may also say that the various symbolic universes, material and non-material, which distinguish human cultures from animal societies are part, and easily the most important part, of man's behavior system. It can justly be questioned whether man is a rational animal, but he certainly is a symbol-creating and symbol-dominated being throughout [von Bertalanffy, 1968, pp. 215–216].

The symbolizational capacity has rightly been defined as the fundamental process of mind, "one of man's primary activities, like eating, looking or moving around" (Langer, 1942, p. 32). Langer depicts symbol making as a human necessity, "a primary need in man; its impairment central to all adult psychopathology." Kubie (1953) calls it the hallmark of man "the *sine qua non* of man's highest psychological and spiritual capacities" (p. 98). "Insofar as symbols enter into the formation of experience and knowledge rather than merely evoking or expressing pre-existing conceptions," writes Barten (1980), "the study of symbol formation in all its forms *is* the investigation of human knowledge" (p. 91).

Language, signification, and the symbolizational capacity, without which neither of the former may fully develop, are core issues at the very heart of any endeavor that attempts to explore the human problems of knowing and meaning. Equally, any in-depth probing into the question of how we know what we know will need to address the nature of consciousness. For the purpose of tracing the phylogenetic and ontogenetic development of human mentation, symbol making or symbolization, as the instrumentation of experiential form and content, represents the stock and substance of our inquiry. As von Bertalanffy (1968) wrote: "probably all emotions used to characterize human behavior are consequences or different aspects of symbolic activity" (p. 216). And the highly subjective, idiosyncratic nature of the relationships and correspondences that enter between experience, emotion, meaning, and its expression is what constitutes behavior. As such, a symbol can be an idea, a myth, a root metaphor, a symptom, a poem, or an act, as Freud illustrated and Langer (1942) pointed out, "every move is at the same time a gesture" (p. 51). We are confronted by the simple truth that understanding rests neither in content alone nor form, but in the in-between land of their correspondences, and that in psychoanalysis we should be looking not at entities but at overall function, not for energy but for structural organization.

This has always been the natural realm of clinical psychoanalysis. The formidable leaps in understanding of the last sixty years, the birth of a new epistemological vision, and dawning of a new Weltanschauung have laid the ground for new approaches to scientific enquiry, as from numerous major disciplines and simultaneously, there awakened a recognition of and interest in the basic mental function distinguishing humankind from other animals—the use of symbols; "the edifice of human knowledge stands before us . . . as a structure of *facts that are symbols and laws that are their meanings*" (Langer, 1942, p. 21).

Everything we perceive and our sense organs process is constantly being transformed into symbols—these constructed vehicles of meaning are our elementary ideas. And this transformational process which constitutes mind, is symbolization.

This generative idea held such promise that from the fields of anthropology, philosophy, art history, developmental and cognitive psychology there grew new focus, an interest so encompassing it might even be called a movement, yielding progressive works designed to study and further our understanding of human symbolic forms. For several reasons, among them a profession divided into multiple fractionist camps and a paucity of interdisciplinary cross-fertilization, psychoanalysis remained isolated and lagged behind this important trend. Yet, in my opinion, it is the generalized use of symbol discerned that is significant for theoretical restructuring of psychoanalytic theory, as it represents the form, content, and medium of mind, and its study promises important inroads.

Every scholar rests, as it were, on the shoulders of the scholars who came before, and is indebted to their teachings. Accordingly, in my integrative efforts, this work builds on the ideas of a group of outstanding thinkers and their teachers gathered from a broad multidisciplinary base. The unifying conceptual thread that runs through their works takes the study of the human mind as being synonymous with the study of the symbolic processes and systems it generates, an intellectual lineage that finds its roots in the philosophers Cassirer (1953–1957), Langer (1942), and Goodman (1984); anthropologists Levi-Strauss (1958a,b, 1983), and Marshack (1972, 1989); the art historian Gombrich (1961); and developmental and cognitive psychologists Werner and Kaplan (1963), Piaget (1962), and Gardner (1982). This work is also influenced by literature from the philosophy of science (Ritchie, 1936; Toulmin, 1953; Kuhn, 1962; Hesse, 1980) and the neurosciences (MacLean, 1949, 1973; Pribram, 1969a,b, 1977; J. W. Brown, 1976; Reiser, 1984; Winson, 1986), and finds correspondence with select ideas of a number of psychoanalytic authors who have given relevance to the symbolic function, most especially Kubie (1953), Searles (1962), Rosen (1969), Edelson (1972), Deri (1984), and Freedman (1985).

Accordingly, this chapter is devoted to tracing the conceptual history of symbolization as it has reached ascendence in diverse disciplines and evolved in psychoanalytic thinking. My exploration of symbolization will be from an interdisciplinary perspective in the belief that a broader base enables us to synthesize data issuing from disparate viewpoints and to cull from these relevant, superordinate themes and principles.

Everyday usage of the term *symbol* refers, more or less comfortably, to the dictionary definition: "That which suggests something else by reason of relationship, association, convention, etc., esp.; a visible sign of something invisible, as an idea, a quality: an emblem, as the lion is the symbol of courage." The word *symbol* in common parlance suggests to us some "thing" which stands for something else, the way a flag represents a country, or a dove peace. Yet closer scrutiny opens up a Pandora's box of questions with awkward answers encumbent upon the "symbol" thus loosely defined. If a red light "stands for" *stop*, is red a symbol or a sign? If the switch from red to green "suggests" *go*, is this a signal or a symbol? Is it the change from red to green that signals, or have the colors "by convention" universally come to symbolize *stop* and *go*? If so, how do we understand green as in envy, or red as in passion? Is a sign the same as a signal or a symbol? If not, how do they differ? What is the relation between symbolism and symbolization? How do we distinguish the pointed figure of indication from that of rebuke? When and in what ways are words signs, signals, symbols? What are songs, sobs, slogans? Dream images, poems, gestures?

These are only some of the questions that spring to mind when approaching the topic of how the mind represents, how it learns to intuit and to construct meanings. The symbolic function, its origin, its forms, its results, its transformational potential, how it has been defined, and how it has been understood to impact on human experience, will be the focus of this chapter. Before proposing a psychoanalytic developmental paradigm of the stages of symbolization I think it worthwhile to peruse what has been written directly and indirectly on the subject thus far.

It is well known that Freud was intrigued by archaeological research and frequently used archaeological analogies when referring to mind. Indeed, he kept a fine collection of ancient statuettes and artifacts in his personal study. Paralleling the study of early man, a psychoanalytic preoccupation with prehistory and origins frequently led to the adoption of the metaphor of mental layers and of digging, when speaking of the unconscious. True to his aspiration, Freud attempted to find "clear and sharply defined basal concepts" upon which to build his theories, believing that, "The true beginning of scientific activity consists . . . in describing phenomena and then proceeding to classify and correlate them" (1915a, p. 117).

I will follow him in his archaeological pursuit but not with similar aim or intent; for if the grouping of phenomena, their classification and correlation, may accrue data and descriptive information, it yields insufficient understanding of the internal processes and meanings of their daily lives and codes of behavior, of their traditions and myths, the essential contextual relevancies involving the life of this data, or the purpose and meaning of the customs and lores in which it was embedded. Rather, I propose to "tackle the grand problems of comparison, generalization and synthesis" as challenged by Adams ([1968], cited in Marshack [1972, p. 373]), from which I believe can be distilled the quintessential property of the human mind; this can be discerned less through classification and correlation, than by the interpretation of its historical and contextual manifestations.

I am referring to the new process-oriented modern archaeology and to Marshack's important contribution, *The Roots of Civilization* (1972). In tracing these roots, Marshack presents hypotheses and evidence for his reinterpretation of Upper Paleolithic, Mesolithic, and Neolithic bone markings and cave art which revolutionize the simplistic traditional categorization of these images into more or less stereotypical "hunting magic" or "sexual symbolism" terms. Marshack's study joins contemporary archaeology's broad ecological concept of time and space, as these correspond to his approach to the deciphering of a complex and sophisticated lunar notational system, previously understood as insignificant groupings and sets of decorative markings. Through careful and unbiased analysis, and with microscope in hand, he reinterprets early cave, stone and bone engravings by noting the different types of points used and painstakingly tracing the temporal sequence of their execution. In identifying their possible and varied uses, the relationship and correspondence between different animals and signs for them, Marshack identifies these to be symbolic depictions relating to seasonal and ritualized elements. He found the hitherto misapprehended "reportorial" images to be related to time-factored, storied, and symbolized representations of repetitive, periodic, and continuing narratives and myths; that is, images which, aside from their exquisite rendition, had relevance and meaning beyond their most apparent, reproductive value, or the mere moment of their engraving. These appear to be representations of sequential events of class phenomena and their mythologized juxtapositions, as derived from observations of animals and natural life, made into narratives and pictorialized by time-factored thought.

Marshack (1972) asked new and different questions and observed these early images with fresh insights, in terms of "the evolving cognitive, time-factored and time-factoring capacities and potentialities of the human brain" (p. 111). He sought and found an expressive purpose in these early depictions which opened a way in which to understand the kind of mind that would create them so that "we may begin to see that a reconstruction of early man's life, which includes the dynamics of his real world, the real and symbolic relations he had to that world, as well as the cognitive processes by which that culture was created and maintained. . . . At the end of almost a century of European archaeology, the mysterious maker of the chipped stone axes is beginning to seem not only human but a person we are able to study scientifically and in depth" (p. 372). The functional similarity between the mind of early man and our own has begun to emerge.

This focus is representative of a shift in concerns from the collection and categorization of data to an ecological approach which articulates the interplay between adaptive responses and activities of humankind at a given time, within the larger natural and social contacts and settings of that period, addressing the widest possible range of interlocking effects. Therefore, Marshack remarks, the "remnant products" of culture or what has been considered archaeological "hard evidence" cannot provide us with process, wherein the organizational complexity of the makers and users of such cultural remnants, by implication, can be understood. This requires more than mere accumulation of factual evidence "the central creative activity in archaeology, like in all scholarship," writes Adam (1968), "lies in induction, in outstripping the narrow base of available facts to suggest new and essentially speculative unities" (p. 1190, cited in Marshack, 1972, p. 373).

The speculative unity Marshack proposes is that despite the inherent limitations of comparison and exposure available to the inhabitants of the Upper Paleolithic hunter and Mesolithic and Neolithic hunter–gatherer cultures, "the processes of cognition were evolved and modern" (p. 373). In addition, the persisting movement of adaptation and evolution in the development of civilization finds its origin in the abstractive and symbolizational processes of which only the human mind is capable. These were already evident and manifest in the rudimentary expressions of the cultural traditions of early man, as distinct from all other species. Moreover, so far as the human brain is concerned, Marshack (1972) writes: "It is the time factored, time factoring and visual–kinesthetic cognitive ability that is the human basis of science. . . . The nature of the problems and the questions varies, as cultures develop and as the levels of reality in which man is interested become more specialized, and as the quality and the amount of the evidence change, but for the brain these are merely differences within a basic class of input" (p. 67).

The unique potential for symbol making, the symbolic function, as the distinguishable genetic advance over a more generalized mammalian capacity for form recognition, furnished Homo sapiens with a mechanism which provides the foundation for evocative representation, the creation of secondary images, the organization of events in time and space, the capacity to hypothesize, plan, and imagine, and the ability to elaborate meaning. And it is again via an innate propensity toward "knowing," by distilling meaning and manipulating ideas, and projecting future results via concepts derived from this knowledge, that mankind has devised and refined skills in utilizing the environment. Adaptation, intelligence, and symbolization are synonymous. So far as thought is concerned, and at all levels of human cognition, wrote Ritchie (1936), "mental life is a 'symbolic process' "; "The essential act of thought is symbolization" ([p. 278], cited in Langer [1942, p. 27]).

Homo erectus was omnivorous and had evolved along these lines for hundreds of thousands of years. This required a knowledge of the periodicities of nature, the range, potential, and nature of resources offered by each season, and the ability to exploit and maximize provisions from these resources by storage. The interrelation of these time-factored and time-factoring processes with the socially self-created and increasingly complex, artificial aspects of culture such as myth, ritual, and tradition, lead directly into the calendric notations and art of early Homo sapiens. As Marshack observes, Neanderthal man, with a larger brain, also a skilled tool maker and user of varied symbols, was, however, not a creator of secondary images or art. To use an object or product for immediate purpose and to derive from this object a sign or symbol of process and story, to give it a contextual meaning, would appear to require two different levels of symbolizational development. In other words, other forms of knowledge are implied beyond the mere manipulation of tool use and tool making. And while paleontologists have written extensively about the development of language in early man in terms of the increasing capacities of jaw and tongue musculature, "communication," writes Marshack, "goes profoundly beyond the physiological ability to manipulate the tongue and articulate words. . . . In my assumed instances, I implied a vast amount of communication—expressed, recognized and understood—which is not entirely vocal or semantic, but which would, nevertheless, have required a near human brain for the expression, recognition and understanding" (1972, p. 117). There is every indication here that language also evolved out of its precursor sign and signaling function, from the same symbolizing tendencies as did engravings and notation. As such, it manifests

in a most efficient instrumentation, the human use of representational vehicles for communicating information and expression in interpersonal relationships (see also Teeter [1973];
Lenneberg [1973]).

One might speculate that this hominid propensity for communication, which would have corroborated a recognition of
feelings and states via affective expressions and possibly alerting
or signaling calls, must have evolved out of communal and
group activity; communication which nevertheless finds its earliest roots in the intuitive interactions between mother and child.
We need only look at ontogenetic development more closely to
find the phylogenetic origins of our prehistory. "Because of this
complexity," Marshack emphasizes, "speech would have been
only one aspect, perhaps simultaneous, of that broad, evolving,
non-verbal process involved in communication and symbol-mak-
ing" (1972, p. 117). Herein is the basis not only for class concepts, sequential time-factored reasoning, notation, and vocalic
communication, but for the sources of human expressivity, behavior, depiction, art, the very inception of conceptualization,
the origins of the entire range of innate mental potential of
early man as this becomes manifest in culture.

Piaget (1952, 1962) noted that ideas are not so much taught
as they evolve through stages of maturation—the potential is
innate. The sensorimotor child is spontaneously acquiring concepts of the permanent object, reversibility, and geometric and
narrative concepts in space and time *before* he has achieved the
capacity to verbalize these concepts. Similarly, "Before a name
had been given to each phase of the moon, the phases would
have seemed 'understandable' to a brain capable of shaping a
form, of chipping a pebble" (Marshack, 1972, p. 135). And,
"against the phases of the moon"—the diurnal cycle—the sea-
sons, his only constants, early man told many stories, held his
rites and rituals, structured his beliefs, his social and biological
life. "The name, then, when it came, could have represented
recognition, a comparison, a process, a story meaningful in that
culture" (Marshack, 1972, p. 135). Perhaps it would have accompanied movement or rhythm and evolved out of dance or
ritual. Words would not have been precise symbolic denoters
with abstracted meanings, as they are in language today, but

would have partaken in a general communication of meaning, comprehensible only within a particular contextual relation or process. Language, thus perceived, is the flowering of only one facet of intelligence and expressivity, an adaptive communicational vehicle of a symbolizing and symbol-producing mind. The entire sway of evolutionary movement might, in this sense, be understood as producing a gradual increase in specialized abstractive processes with respect to the self, reflected in cultural and societal elaborations within and between groups of people.

Among other things, Marshack attempts to shift the emphasis from tool-making and language skills, as primary expressions of hominid culture, to a more generalized and inclusive human capacity. This tendency encompasses the implicit unity and continuity of human evolution, with all its diverse activities and discoveries, creations and remnants, as the products of manifestations of a single, adapting, and basic human brain (see also McCullough, 1965; Bateson, 1979).

Marshack's research into Upper Paleolithic notations and engravings and his hypotheses regarding early cognitive capacities, indicate human mentation needs to be approached "not as an absolute, but as a process that is time factored, evolved, developmental, specialized, diversely structured, limited and potential," and he emphasizes that while Freud pioneered an approach which searches for the genesis and dynamics of emotional and symbolic equations, he did not ask questions relating to the evolution of these processes. "The possible stages in the evolution of this human cognition have hardly begun to be discussed" (1972, p. 130) Marshack concludes.

These questions were approached from the field of philosophy by Langer who, having inherited the new philosophical queries unveiled by the schism between empiricism and transcendentalism and schooled in the enigmas of semantics, logic, and the nature of knowledge, found herself "scouting the possibility that rationality arises as an elaboration of feeling" (1957, p. 124). The entire thrust of her opus rests on this novel idea, as she elaborates and develops her core thesis. "The concept of meaning, in all its varieties, is the dominant philosophical concept of our time. Sign, symbol, denotation, signification, communication—these notions are our stock and trade" (1962,

p. 55). Quick to embrace the advance in imagination that marked a shift from "substance-attribute thinking to functional thinking" (1962, p. 56), with extraordinary scholarship, rigor, and innovative vigor, she took it upon herself to move philosophy into a "new key" (1942), placing her stamp on the formidable issues of symbol and meaning, and the great problems of reference launched to relevance by the brilliant generation of thinkers before her, epitomized in the works of Cassirer, Whitehead, Freud, Wittgenstein, Russell, to name just a few.

She continued to elaborate and develop her ideas in works devoted to the discussion of *Problems of Art* (1957) and feeling and form. These culminated in her three-volume work, *Mind: An Essay on Human Feeling* (1972), an exhaustive foray into the origins of our humanity, our biological evolution into mental expression, and, most specifically, into the singular propensity of the human mind to symbolize. She noted that several major lines of thought had recognized the basic mental function distinguishing man from all other creatures to be the multivaried use of symbols to convey concepts (1962). "What we understand," she writes (1957) "we conceive, and conception always involves formulation, presentation and therefore abstraction. . . . All understanding requires abstraction . . . there is no understanding without symbolization, and no symbolization without abstraction" (p. 92). This is in striking accord with Marshack's conclusions. Referring to Marshack's reasoning that early man's engravings and notations implied the existence of a general mental capacity to process experience in a symbolized way, we may further extrapolate, as did Langer, and pinpoint this process to be an organic *abstractive mechanism*, originating in the essential nature of how we transform experience into knowledge. In other words, in the very nature of mind itself.

Langer's sweeping explorations are prefaced by a careful presentation of her status and purpose as a philosopher. She first demarcates her terrain, in close proximity with and often overlapping other fields, plants the seeds, and fertilizes her ground, and then, with rapture, embarks on the unfolding of an august harvest of infinite complexity and intellectual dexterity.

The philosopher's aim is generality, but his true method is not therefore to deal in generalities. There are two familiar ways of establishing general propositions. One is the traditional method of selecting a key idea . . . and reinterpreting all known facts in terms of this universal exemplified principle. . . . The other method is that of progressive generalization from concepts which prove fertile in a limited way, that is, concepts which tend to expand and gradually become applicable to more and more phenomena, sometimes at different levels of abstraction, but in just as much detail . . . as in its original context [1967, Vol. 1, p. xxi].

She finds that many issues which had appeared to concern the *source* of knowledge, rather appear to refer partly or completely to the *forms* of knowledge, or perhaps even depend on forms of symbolization (1942). And in 1972, her formulations fully ripened, she develops the focal goal of her profound reformulations: "To trace the development of mind from the earliest forms of life that we can determine, through primitive acts which may have vague psychical moments, to more certain mental acts" (1967, p. 310). I have taken up this avenue of thinking, initiated by Langer, one which extends to the concept of mind as symbolizational activity, or transformational process. This represents the central proposition of my thesis, which will be developed in psychoanalytic terms, and is the pivotal concept to be derived from the material covered in this chapter.

Langer (1942) was instrumental in bringing focus to the new preoccupation with symbolization, in announcing its coming of age as it were, as she declared it to be "a commanding philosophical problem" with the "promise of power and versatility" (p. 24), its study bifurcating into two distinct, apparently incompatible yet rich and fruitful courses. One conception led to logic, challenging new problems in the theory of knowledge; the other "to psychiatry, the study of emotions, religion and fantasy" (p. 24), a course which, defined by a discerning eye, can clearly be recognized as the original soil of psychoanalysis. In both courses Langer observed a cohesive theme, that of human responsiveness as a constructive rather than passive process. She believed that in the fundamental idea of symbolization, mystical, practical, or mathematical, lay the keynote of all humanistic problems. In it she saw the possibility of a new approach to what we conceive as "mental," a course which could illumine questions of life and consciousness, instead of obscuring them as had traditional "scientific methods" thus far (1942).

Langer's work, as it developed out of the early questions regarding art and form, logic and semantics, feeling and rationality, is a monumental contribution toward a reorientation of our thinking about mind and meaning. Her emphasis highlights the entire sway of the development of the Hominidae to be "epitomized in the evolution of symbolic activity" (1972, p. 345). In tracing the development of mind and toward proposing a unifying concept of feeling and thinking in line with an understanding of human responsiveness as a constructive rather than a reactive process, she examined the origins and uses of sensory experience, reasoning: "The nervous system is the organ of the mind; its center is the brain, its extremities the sense-organs, and any characteristic function it may possess must govern the work of all its parts . . . the activity of our senses is 'mental' not only when it reaches the brain but in its very inception. . . . All sensitivity bears the stamp of mentality. Seeing is itself a process of formulation; our understanding of the visible world begins in the eye" (1942, p. 90).

Langer believed that our intuitive, habitual hypostatizing of impressions, of "seeing things," depends on the fact that we automatically and unconsciously abstract forms from sensory experience and then utilize these forms to conceive the experiences whole, as entities or "things." To paraphrase Wittgenstein: we create pictures out of facts—and by unraveling this same process we try to interpret dreams. For Langer, symbolization is the starting point of all intellection in the human sense. This is one reason why words and language evolve naturally out of the symbolizing process. To name a "thing" is to give it objective status and equally, why words in their denotive closure, often obfuscate and militate against the profounder "knowing" of Wittgenstein's "unspeakable," encased in nondiscursive forms of expression. Likening the brain to a great transformer, Langer adds, "sense data would be useless to a mind whose activity is through and through a symbolic process, were they not par excellence receptacles of meaning" (1942, p. 90). And, in all the variegated forms of meaning, "Sign, symbol, denotation, signification, communication" (1962, p. 55), Langer identifies the dominant theme of our time. "The human mind requires a more fertile concept than 'individual,' or 'self,' or even 'organism,' not a categorial concept, but a functional one, whereby entities of various categories may be defined and related" (1967, p. 310). Words echoed in the ideas of the anthropologist Marshack (1972). With reference to his findings regarding the earliest expressions of the symbolic function, he remarks, "we are dealing with a tradition of schematic and symbolic representation rather than with a limited language of set forms" (p. 326).

The unconscious apperception of forms, for Langer, represents the primitive root of all abstraction which in turn "is the keynote of rationality"; so, she concludes, "it appears that the conditions for rationality lie deep in our pure animal experience—in our power of perceiving, in the elementary functions of our eyes and ears and fingers" (1942, p. 89). Langer identified that mental life begins in our physiological constitution. Piaget had already shown that "intelligence" or "thinking" does indeed begin in the body, in the sensing, moving body with a sensorimotor stage of development. "A tendency to organize the sensory field into groups of patterns of sense-data," writes Langer (1942) with respect to the quintessence of this process:

> [T]o perceive forms rather than a flux of light-impressions, seems to be inherent in our receptor apparatus, just as much as in the higher nervous centers with which we do arithmetic and logic. But this unconscious apperception of forms is the primitive root of all abstraction which in turn is the keynote of rationality; so it appears that the conditions for rationality lie deep in our pure animal experience—in our power of perceiving, in the elementary functions of our eyes and ears and fingers [p. 89].

Langer identified that mental life begins in our physiological constitution. Several decades later, the notion does not strike us as so strange. In fact, Langer believed abstraction, like recognition of relations and the attribution of meaning, to be intuitive, calling it "one of the basic acts of logical intuition," its prototypical occurrence, the process of symbolization. More than anything else this innate form-building propensity is part of our biological heritage.

Langer's method was predicated on exhaustive and in-depth research into her topic, and her great talent is manifest in a reformulation of the basic questions of philosophy. These were now posed in such a way as to produce a radical shift in focus and emphasis. It had been while reflecting on the nature of art that she had come upon an entirely new conception of the symbol, one that stemmed from the Kantian analysis of experience and had been elaborated extensively by Cassirer in *The Philosophy of Symbolic Forms* (1874–1945). Cassirer had recognized the pivotal importance of symbolic expression in the development and evolution of the "animal symbolicum," and the central role symbolization plays in organizing how events in the natural world are perceived. The abstractive nature of symbols often leads to semantic discussions based on discursive thought and Aristotelian propositions; yet, as Langer points out, as did Cassirer, there may be many ways of abstracting and therefore as many kinds of symbols. This touches on the issue of strata or types of knowledge existing in preverbal or other than verbal forms. A stepwise developmental model would seem to serve here, to fill this void. Langer did not thread her ideas into an ontogenetic developmental framework, however; this work has been left for others to elaborate and expand upon.

As with all developmental processes, the road to the construction of a true symbol is gradual and proceeds hand in hand with (or is perhaps one with) the differentiation–individuation process of early childhood, in a stepwise fashion that moves through undifferentiated protosymbolic forms to more differentiated symbolic forms, which influence the entire nature of subjective experience. A careful distinction between signs, signals, and symbols and the organic effects of such differentiation is therefore central to the understanding of the complex interplay between affective, conative, and cognitive factors which enter into the construction of symbolization and how this process becomes prone to deconstruction or regressive deforming. "[A]bstraction is a process that allows of steps, incomplete phrases to which all sorts of protosymbolic phenomena . . . might be related," writes Langer (1962, p. 64). Works of art, dream elements: neither can be classed as symbols according to the orthodox dictionary definition since neither point beyond themselves in reference to something else, nor do they denote meaning which has been established by convention—yet in their powerful articulation they conjure an expressive form and therefore are symbolic perhaps in another way. In this, a thorough understanding of protosymbolic phenomena would seem to be essential since these must play a crucial role in transforming affectively charged experience into more placated, integrated, verbal articulation—we are looking at an integration which occurs by degrees along a symbolizational continuum.

The symbol proper is a vehicle of thought; symbols are not the same as what they stand for but *represent* a concept of what that means. In fact, symbols are instruments of conceptualization and contemplation; tools for thinking. Signs signify an act or an event—they announce their object. Signals indicate, they command action. Both signs and signals are immediate, still tied to the senses. In functioning at the level of conditioning (between somatic and consequence learning) signs and signals may be learned by animals; they imply a one-to-one correspondence between the sign and what it indicates—no abstracted concept is implied which may elaborate further meaning. The symbol is an instrument of thought—signs and signals are signifiers. Equally, the connotation of a word is the concept it conveys, its implications, the metaphors it conjures, the particular meanings it holds for an individual; its denotation is its specific or direct consensually understood meaning—to denote, the act of signifying (For an interesting Vygotskian view of a very similar concept, see Wilson and Weinstein [1992a,b]). As such, and in development, words are signs before they are symbols and acquire this distinct status only as a result of achieving the full symbolic capacity, a crucial step which the schizophrenic has only a tenuous hold over. In this process, interpsychic separation and its experiential corollary, individuation, play a fundamental part; as Freud identified "the ego is a precipitate of lost

objects''; ''the point of departure for the human ego is object-
loss'' (N. O. Brown, 1959, p. 161). The symbol results from
separation—it transcends loss.

Let me try to shed some light on the interrelatedness of
these complex ideas. Classes of concepts are formed from associated similarities, and concepts are denoted through symbolic
vehicles or abstracted "things"; such as people, objects, or ideas.
No true symbol can be formed without a prerequisite distancing
from that to which it refers, and only that which becomes symbolized can be evoked or articulated mentally. Psychological
beginnings, or incipient mind in contrast to somatic[1] experience, occurs as the dual processes of increasing separateness
and increasingly differentiated internalizations yield representations which are initially protosymbolic phenomena before they
become true symbols for what they stand for. "Significance by
definition, is not possible unless something can be seen as representing something else" (Rosen, 1969, p. 168); meaning comes
into being in the qualitative relationship between a symbol and
its referents. Thus to name a "thing" is to evoke the concept
of what it means, to hold it within. But at the beginnings of this
process the name is close to that which it signifies; the whole
class of transitional objects, amulets, tokens, etc., are equivalents, or stand-ins *for*, not symbols *of*, what they stand for.
Whereas a signifier may function in substitution as an "equivalent," the symbol transcends loss—it evokes the object but never
replaces it; it is constructive, not restitutional. What is renounced by the senses becomes mind. This is a gradual stepwise
abstractive process occurring throughout the life span along
multiple vectors; it is mediated through language and constitutes a basic principle of human development.

We make ourselves understood by adopting shared signs
of communicative expression inherent in the *denotive* function
of language, while we hold within the *connotive* interpolation of
symbol to fill the gap left by separateness and delay out of which
flower reflection and imagination. Symbolization enables this
articulation; symbols are the contents of which symbolization is

---

[1]By "somatic," I implicitly also refer to "affect," a physiobiologic term, and contrast this with "emotion," its psychologically more advanced ideational derivative.

the function. The mark of humankind is that we may contemplate upon our experience, that we may give form to what we perceive and feel, and shape the imaginings of what we desire. There is no functional schism between thought and fantasy, only different avenues for their expression.

By discarding inherited dichotomies Langer took great strides toward unifying what had always been kept separate, thought and feeling, and found the human whole, that our "feelings have definite forms, which become progressively articulated" (1942, p. 100): that thinking comes from feeling. "The perception of form arises, I think, from the process of symbolization, and perception of form is abstraction," writes Langer, and so ventures a new definition of symbol: "Any device whereby we make an abstraction is a symbolic element, and all abstraction involves symbolization" (1962, pp. 62–63).

This concept of symbolization is of a quite different origin from that of common definition or even of the more traditional notions of symbolism of the early days of dynamic psychology. The relevance of the multidetermined, condensed, and expressive power of symbols as inchoate yet profound forms of knowledge emanating from psyche, were generally appreciated by the early analysts, particularly by Jung (1958, 1959, 1964) for whom symbol and archetype represent a prototype for a class of qualities or impressions he called the "motif" and, as such, require no further breakdown. Jung, however, whose work and theory are closely associated with symbolism and the archaic layers of unconscious dynamics, did not address or deal with symbolization per se. It was Freud's penetrating insight that the manifest dream was the expression of latent thoughts and feelings which spurred the dream's formation—that the surface form, although apparently disguised, reflected a deeper meaning to which it was related through the dream's particular narrative creation.

One of the reasons few psychoanalysts have grasped the central theoretical relevance of symbolization, despite this being the natural realm of their daily practice, is that for the most part analysts are still attached to early notions of symbolism associated with dreams, framed within a positivist epistemology which makes "things" out of processes and finds "provinces" instead of organization. Symbols are considered "entities," the figurative properties of archaic mental products associated with fantasies in the ideation of primitive levels of mentation, rather than being understood in functional terms, as the instrumentation of mind—the fabric of the *process* of mind. Without functional concepts which address the mind–body unity and organize subjective experience throughout development as organismic activity, psychoanalysis remains stuck in a theoretical blind spot which maintains both its terminological and conceptual underpinnings tied to reification.

This line of thinking, inherited by Freud through the dominant scientific ethos of his day and handed down through Stekel, Silberer, Jones, Groddeck, and other early analysts, essentially views symbolism as a multidetermined pictorial form of mental representation often related to bodily organs and functions or cathected internal objects, in the service of affects, and regressive in nature. It is likened to the thinking of primitive people and children, and associated with the archaic unconscious where it gives shape to the elements of the dream content, its "latent thoughts." Jones (1916), whose seminal paper epitomizes the theoretical views of his time, goes so far as to reduce this function to a deficiency, "an apperceptive insufficiency" (pp. 106–107) he calls it, rooted in primitive identifications and tendencies to seek pleasure and avoid pain in relation to dealing with reality. Fundamentally, Jones' view is in stark contrast to that presented by Langer (1942), and to which I adhere; namely, his view of the symbol as an "inferior" concretization, a pictorial expressive equivalent substituting for forbidden feelings or ideas, rather than the symbol as an articulate abstractive, developing mechanism stemming from an elementary process of mentation itself. It would be another forty years or so before Piaget would comment on the poor progress psychoanalysis had made with regard to understanding symbolism, despite its methodological immersion in the subject, and this because of its emphasis on content rather than function; the function of symbols is not due to their content, Piaget (1962) remarks, "but due to the very structure of thought." The absence of a clear understanding of symbolic relationships and

their expressive forms as being the very nature of mind, engendered a dichotomized view of bodily urges and their "mental
representations." This dualism can now be seen as the focal
stumbling block in a theoretical compromise which sought a
cause for human motives and tried to account for how the mind
produced pictures out of passions.

Even those late authors such as M. Klein (1930), Sechehaye
(1951), Rycroft (1956), Rodriguez (1956), Segal (1957),
Deutsch (1959), and Deri (1981, 1984), who show a growing
awareness of the importance for ego development in the relationship between object and the degree to which it is symbolized, by adhering to energic and economic implications of the
drive propulsion model, failed to recognize the centrality of the
functional activity of symbolization in the essential structuring
and transforming of all psychological experience. In fact no
clear definitional distinction is yet made between symbolism, as
the early analysts thought of it, and symbolization, a functional idea.

Freud came to the importance of dream symbolism largely
due to the influence of Wilhelm Stekel (1911). In fact, it was
not until the fourth edition of *The Interpretation of Dreams* (1900),
a full fourteen years later, that section E in chapter 6, devoted
entirely to the subject, was added, and, while the topic comes
up in other writings, that discussion together with lecture 10,
"Symbolism in Dreams" (1917a), are regarded as the most important of Freud's presentations on the subject. Perhaps this
was in part due to Freud's judicious skepticism regarding the
scientific basis for approaching dreams which had, since ancient
times, been ascribed to the mysterious visions of soothsayers.
Because symbolism in Freud's day was still conceived in terms
of a one-to-one correspondence between a symbol and its meaning, and because Freud's insights prompted prudence, he rec-
ommended a critical caution in approaching symbols. "Regard
for scientific criticism forbids our returning to the arbitrary
judgement of the dream-interpreter . . ." (1900, p. 353).
"Dreams," he writes, "make use of this symbolism for the disguised representation of their latent thoughts" (1900, p. 352)
and these, he believed, originate in the unconscious from a wish
of infantile origin.

Freud viewed most symbols as "sexual"[2] in nature, derived primarily from the generalized expression of particular cathected objects in the unconscious, whether these appear in dreams, myths, religions, or are expressed in artistic form: "The range of things which are given symbolic representation in dreams is not wide: the human body as a whole, parents, children, brothers and sisters, birth, death, nakedness . . ." (1917a, p. 153). In order to interpret the dream, it was necessary to arrive at an understanding of the deeper latent thoughts, through their disguised representational content. "We are obliged in dealing with those elements of the dream-content, which must be recognized as symbolic, to adopt a combined technique, which on the one hand rests on the dreamer's associations and on the other . . . fills the gaps from the interpreter's knowledge of symbols" (1900, p. 353). Freud remained suspicious of any arbitrary approach to the interpretation of dream symbols, cautioned against it, and insisted on the necessity of obtaining the dreamer's own associations in order to arrive at the subjective and unconscious meaning of the dream images. In this he reveals that he understood but did not recognize a symbolic structure in the very functioning of mind.

These notions of the nature of symbols and contents of symbolism of early dynamic psychology, however, have little in common with the process of symbolization. Likewise, C. G. Jung (1958, 1959, 1964), whose work and theory is closely associated with symbolism and the archaic layers of unconscious dynamics, did not address symbolization per se. Both Freud and Jung addressed the content of the symbolized, while not recognizing the activity itself. It was Freud, however, who most clearly indicated an understanding of a "mental function" performing the "dream-work." Jung, on the other hand, apparently unaware of Freud's vision of a multilayered representational system, would have the dream seen as is. Rather than subdivide latent and manifest forms, he would focus instead on the apparent symbolic meanings and their mythical or archetypal significance in the dreamer's ongoing "individuation" process. Jung appears not to have been cognizant of the symbolization function

---

[2]Keep in mind that by "sexual" Freud intended his greatly expanded definition of the term.

per se, or of the relationship of reference to which it gives rise. Freud, on the other hand, while not identifying the symbolizing activity of mind as such, alludes to such a transformational process and is keenly aware of the need for an explanation for this. With great insight and foresight he recognized that somewhere in his postulated mechanism of the dreamwork lay the key to unraveling the earliest processes of mind, perhaps the essential nature of mentation, so that "if we study the dream-work further we must succeed in gaining valuable light on the little-known beginnings of our intellectual development. I hope it will be so; but this work has not so far been started upon" (Freud, 1917a, p. 199).

Jung differed from Freud in his concept of the unconscious. One of his radical departures from Freudian theory lay in his particular emphasis on the "collective-unconscious"; the beliefs, myths, archetypes, and universal symbols common to the race, which he believed lay beneath the personal unconscious, representing only a minor part of this. For Freud this archaic layer represented the individual's prehistory "insofar as each individual somehow recapitulates in an abbreviated form the entire development of the human race, into phylogenetic prehistory too" (Freud, 1917a, p. 199).

Jung's clinical use of individual and collective symbolism also differed fundamentally from Freud's. Emphasizing the dynamic expression of what he understood to be an archaic heritage, Jung based his theory on three basic points: first, that the content of the fantasies of psychotics and schizophrenics are replete with ideas and images around themes of death and rebirth, similar to those found in mythology; second, that in protracted analyses a particular symbol might continue to recur with persistency, but would gradually be divested of all associative connections to the patient's personal experiences, approximating more and more to those primitive and universal symbols found in myths and legends; and lastly, he noted the convergence and extraordinary unanimity of themes in the mythologies of different cultures (J. A. C. Brown, 1961).

It is not difficult to reason that the deeper an analysis probes the closer it will come to a primary psychobiological level, where shared impressions will be common to all humankind due to the nature of our earliest experiences. These, irretrievable to consciousness due to their encoding at the most rudimentary somatopsychic levels, always consist of archetypal constructions, often referred to as unconscious fantasies. Generated by the universal phenomena of human infancy and childhood, these images are woven into the fabric of mythologized narratives in religions, stories, social and cultural beliefs, and the lores and rituals that flower out of these, all over the world. Freud called these "archaic remnants." Jung, however, developed a whole theoretical system out of the nature of the phenomena and imagery emerging from these psychic strata: an analytical psychology which, in attempting to upturn Freud's biologistic formulations, tried to explain the psyche through its own manifestations, so that, "What we properly call instincts are physiological urges," wrote Jung (1964), perceived by the senses. At the same time, "they also manifest themselves as fantasies . . . and reveal their presence only by symbolic images . . ." (p. 67). These manifestations are what Jung called the archetypes. Of unknown origin, they appear to reproduce themselves the world over and in all ages. The archetypes are understood as an "instinctive trend," "a tendency to form such representations of a motif" (Jung, 1964, pp. 67–69). The symbol and the archetype for Jung represented a prototype for a class of concepts, qualities, ideas or impressions or all of these, the "motif," as he called it, and as such require no further breakdown.

In his 1917a discussion of symbolism, perhaps "the most remarkable chapter of the theory of dreams" (p. 151), Freud finds he is unable to "sharply delimit" the concept of a symbol which "shades off into such notions as those of a replacement or representation, and even approaches that of an allusion" (p. 152). Yet he was very clear regarding his detection of a mechanism involved in the transformation of latent thoughts into manifest contents: "A constant relation of this kind between a dream element and its translation is described by us as a 'symbolic' one, and the dream-element itself as a 'symbol' of the unconscious dream thought" (1917a, p. 150).

He was equally perspicacious regarding the possible origins of symbolic relations: "Things that are symbolically connected today were probably united in the prehistoric time by conceptual and linguistic identities" (1900, p. 352), a notion which corresponds accurately with what is now known about the correspondence between language acquisition and thought in early development—language is a system of concepts, its figures of speech, figures of thought (Langer, 1972). The same idea provides a rationale for Freud's technique of dream interpretation, as it is by tracing images through their "narratized" verbal meanings to the level at which these images are formed and where these are word equivalents (the "thing" presentation) that the idiom of the "dream-work" is revealed. Equally there can be no separation between symbol and "knowing" at this level of experiencing, that is where impressions or protoconcepts are not yet tied to any specific denotive modality.

Herein is the basis for a theory of intuition in that "knowledge" may well exist in rudimentary preconceptual or protosymbolic form, at less differentiated levels of experience before it has been shaped to expression via a communicational vehicle which carries denotive reference. And possible vehicles and expressive modes are varied—gesture, image, song, language, dance—all of these expressive systems carry symbolic valence. The importance of updating our understanding of the complex interconnection between language acquisition, individuation, and the dual forms of experiencing words (affective and cognitive) are highlighted as they become magnified in the interactions of the linguistic medium in the psychoanalytic situation. Nowhere is it clearer than at this most psychoanalytically relevant juncture, in which meanings crystallize into expressive forms, precisely what a new model is required to synthesize and reformulate. For the particular, fluid relationship which enters into experience, meaning attribution, and the forms and modes in which these are expressed, must cut across all human activity, and must be isomorphic to the relationship between the figurative narration of dreams and what these mean for the dreamer.

Freud, one senses, intimated the far-reaching implications of this topic as he wrote, "One gets the impression that what we are faced with here is an ancient but extinct mode of expression, of which different pieces have survived in different fields. . . ," and of its apparent universality he adds, "these symbolic relations are not something peculiar to dreams or to the dream-work, through which they come to expression. This same symbolism, as we have seen, is employed by myths and fairy tales, by the people in sayings and songs, by colloquial linguistic usage, and by the poetic imagination" (1917a, p. 166). Clearly, Freud is speaking of the pervasive presence of symbolic relationships in the general manifestations of human expressiveness.

Thus in his investigation of the "relations between the elements of dreams and the genuine things they stood for" (1917a, p. 170) he distinguishes four relations: "the relation of a part to a whole, approximation or allusion, the symbolic representation and the plastic representation of words" (1917a, p. 170). These complex relations, the mechanisms of condensation, displacement, representability, and regressive transformation he called the dream work, and to explain what he believed to be a dynamic process of disguisement, he used energic and economic formulations.

> It thus seems plausible to suppose that in the dream-work a psychical force is operating which on the one hand strips the elements which on the one hand strips the elements which have a high psychical value of their intensity, and on the other hand *by means of overdetermination*, creates from elements of low psychical value new values, which afterwards find their way into the dream-content. If that is so, *a transference and displacement of psychical intensities* occurs in the process of dream-formation, and it is as a result of these that the difference between the text of the dream-content and that of the dream-thoughts comes about [Freud, 1900, pp. 307–308].

Freud is describing a general dualistic principle inherent in all forms of signification and in all symbolic systems; namely, the correspondence between a single significant taken to represent multiple and multidetermined referents or meanings. What Freud ascribes to a "psychical force," the transferability of psychic intensities and the condensation of overdetermination, although not identified as such, is the symbolizational process: the symbol "throws together" and represents—condensation and displacement are intrinsic to its very nature. And the symbolizing function itself (in its new definition as an abstractive device) is recognizable as Freud's dreamwork. As Langer (1967) pointed out, "Feeling, in the broad sense of whatever is felt in any way, a sensory stimulus or inward tension, pain, emotion or intent, is the mark of mentality" (p. 4)—because the mind gives form to feelings, it works to "represent." And while increases and decreases in quantums of cathectic charge in the service of disguisement are purported to explain the course of instinctual force in its direct drive toward satisfaction, we find emotions and not drives motivating actions, giving shape to ideas; *affects,* not instincts, govern the whole process.

While concepts of disguise, censorship, cathexis, and hypothetical psychic forces hold little promise today for an integrated contemporary theory, if anchored in terms of symbolization, the only activity of mind, Freud's notion of "dream-work" and his concept of the "mind's work," as his detection of various mechanisms intrinsic to its multitiered nature, can now be reconsidered in a new vein and recast in the conceptualization of a revised unitary model.

Of the early papers on the subject, E. Jones' classic "The Theory of Symbolism" in *Papers on Psychoanalysis* (1916, chapter 3), stands out as a comprehensive, probing attempt to attain "a fuller understanding of the theoretical nature of symbolism" (p. 87). Amplified from a paper read before the British Psychological Society in 1916, it presents a thorough overview of the then prevalent psychoanalytic views on symbolism and puts forward a few of its own. In it Jones advances some definitional differentiations with theoretical implications and offers ideas on the genesis of symbolism. He also surveys Freud's contribution, mentions Jung's work, carefully critiques Rank and Sachs, and particularly Silberer's (1905) ideas, and concludes:

> The essential function of all forms of symbolism, using the word in the broadest and most popular sense, is to overcome the inhibition that is hindering the free expression of a given feeling-idea, the force derived from this, in its forward urge, being the effective cause of symbolism. It

always constitutes a regression to a simpler mode of apprehension. If the regression proceeds only a certain distance,
remaining conscious or at most preconscious, the result is
metaphorical, or what Silberer calls "functional" symbolism. If, owing to the strength of the unconscious complex,
it proceeds further—to the level of the unconscious—the
result is symbolism in the strict sense [1916, p. 144].

This exemplifies his position. Jones narrowed the concept of
what he called "true" psychoanalytic symbolism excessively by
differentiating this conceptually from metaphor and other
modes of symbolizing, so that for him, "*true symbolism*, in the
strict sense, is to be *distinguished from other forms of indirect representation*" (p. 90) in that it is dynamically repressed and, in varying
degrees, always associated with regressive expression.

Heavily influenced by Freud's dynamic ideas and theories
and exceedingly loyal in his presentation, Jones' paper is marred
by the restricting view of symbols as "inferior," "primitive,"
"concrete," or alternate modes of thought, the devalued sensorial results of a "perceptual" substitute for "conceptual" thinking—this last, a view widely held at the time. Likewise, the
conviction that symbolism emerges out of repression produced
a theoretical blind spot with regard to finding a possible continuity between the topographical and structural models with respect to the symbolizational function itself. In fact, a work which
starts out by emphasizing the importance of a subject which
"seems to comprise almost the whole development of civilization" (p. 87), and certainly the progress of the human mind,
continues by begging the central questions pertaining to how
this might be, and ultimately suffers by its overconcerns with
categorization and content. Distracted from essentials, caught
up in theory, and busied by "scientific methods," the early analysts digressed in fettered papers attempting to define, segregate, classify, categorize, and place types of symbols and their
origins into a psychodynamic mold; an exercise which contributed much semantic complexity to the content of what is symbolized, while ignoring the essential part played by the
process itself.

One point upon which most psychoanalytic authors do agree is that in its representation, the symbol subsumes often numerous ideas, feelings, and thoughts and that these are, in the main, outside conscious awareness. The symbol is multidetermined and, like a metaphor, it condenses multiple meanings, for which it stands. This tendency to "fuse together different ideas . . . to note resemblances and not the differences," writes Jones, is typical of "the primitive mind—as observed in children, savages, in wit, dreams, insanity and other products of unconscious functioning," and he concludes, "It impresses one as being one of the most fundamental and primordial attributes of mind" (1916, p. 105). Having made this observation, however, and in agreement with the majority of writers who called attention to the "intellectual incapacity for discrimination," hypothesis of symbolism, he essentially reduced this function to a "deficiency," stating that the most general condition of symbol-formation, with respect to health and disease, in the individual and in the race is "—an *inadequacy* of the apprehensive faculty in regard to its object, or . . . in an *apperceptive insufficiency* (1916, pp. 106–107).

These ideas, together with his strict discrimination between metaphor and symbol, and insistence on the symbol as having a constant meaning, are, in my opinion, the least felicitous of his suppositions. All in all, while the paper often points in the right direction, it remains marred by a tendency toward teleological conclusions which bend the subject to fit a procrustean psychodynamic bed, and ends up mired in its own terminological and classificatory confusion. Moreover, it perpetuates a view of symbolism as a concrete expressive equivalent, as in symptom formation, rather than the symbol as an articulate, abstractive mechanism stemming from an elementary process of mentation itself.

Silberer's 1905 paper on symbol formation, republished heavily edited and footnoted by D. Rapaport in 1951, epitomizes the early views of symbolism as "characterized by a tendency to replace the abstract by the concrete" or "the visually perceptible," as the German das *Anschauliche* more accurately connotes (p. 208)—a contemporary propensity to approach the subject by addressing content and form rather than process and function.

Silberer believed that symbolism belonged to a particular "mental level," corresponding to an underlying organization of impulses and affectivity for which this pictorialized form of ideational representation is the natural and logical expression: "It is human nature, psychic lawfulness, that creates symbols, pictorial signs representing something which at a given time for some reason cannot manifest itself in consciousness in its 'true' form," he writes (p. 211). Silberer's view of symbolism is both broader (inclusive of metaphor) and more encompassing than Jones' narrow "psychoanalytic symbolism," and he considers it to be one of the analyst's principal tasks to decipher phenomena which should not be taken at face value but understood as "symbolic representations of something which hides them . . . the manifest expression of something latent" (p. 208).

The symbol, for Silberer, is the medium for a specific mental developmental organization and expresses itself as a necessity, as a form of knowledge, *Erkennen*. In this, it corresponds to the manifestations of dreams, acts of compulsion neurotics, religious ceremonies, myths, folklore, art, and so on, as the outer substantiation of an inner drive, what Silberer calls "essential symbolism," bearing little resemblance to the generalized "diluted" arbitrary sign. "The genuine symbol is the form of appearance of the underlying idea" (p. 211), writes Silberer; however, a person whose apperception is symbolic cannot be aware of this—the implication is that the symbolic equation is created outside of awareness, and according to Silberer, represents the characteristic mode of a particular level or state of consciousness. Its recognition or interpretation thus necessitates the "achievement of a more advanced level of psychological development," wherein the provisional or archaic correspondence between the symbol and what is symbolized may be detected and rendered at a higher level of abstraction, what he calls the level of "truth."

Silberer attempts to answer questions pertaining to the origin of the process, the conditions for the cause and the purpose of symbol formation, and finds partial answers in the economic value of condensation and overdetermination, "the convergence of many association chains onto one point" (p. 215); the appearance of symbols as precursors for ideas which have yet to be comprehended and abstracted "when man's mind reaches out for something which he cannot yet grasp" (p. 217); and finally, in the idea that the "pictorial" represents an "easier mode of thought than the apperceptive one, which can operate at the lower level of energy" (p. 219). Thus, he notes, the direction of symbolic substitutes is regressive in character although, as Stekel had observed, it serves the affects; it is essentially "a play of representations in the service of affects" (1905, p. 224). Adhering to a fundamentally dualistic theory which separates "affective" from "intellectual" thought products, he traces the causes for two types of symbolism in the conditions resulting from an "apperceptive insufficiency," the first on an intellectual the second on an affective basis. In summating he arrives at a causal conclusion; that in "thinking in symbols, the change from apperceptive to associative thought processes corresponds to a regression to primitive forms of thought" (p. 230).

Nevertheless, Silberer concludes, despite insufficient knowledge of the mechanisms of the process, throughout the developmental course of humankind, symbol formation has "gathered the threads of knowledge out of which man weaves his concepts" (p. 233). Without departing radically from prevailing psychoanalytic theory, similar to Freud and Jones but with some differences, Silberer's writings on symbol formation may be viewed retrospectively as historically relevant while conceptually unremarkable. His focus and contribution to the understanding of symbolism, however, should not be underestimated.

In his editorial footnotes Rapaport (1951) cautioned that Silberer's views are better judged if framed against the background of a fin de siècle reaction against materialism. This advice seems eminently appropriate and applicable to the writings of Groddeck, as presented by his student and devotee, Grotjahn who, in a 1945 paper, offers a critique and tribute to his teacher. Grotjahn describes Groddeck as a man "passionately devoted to helping and curing" (p. 11). Influenced by Nietzsche and the acknowledged originator of the concept of the "Es" (the It), about which he wrote a book (1923), Groddeck was an innovative and intense physician with a fervent interest in the unconscious, who became an important and forceful influence in the beginnings of psychosomatic medicine. For Groddeck, the "It" was "the source of life expressed in one form; . . . the symbol out of which psychic and physical life originates as the expression of one and the same" (p. 11).

Grotjahn summarizes Groddeck's entire opus and presents his singular contribution to the literature on symbolization, in an article entitled, "The Urge to Symbolize," in a 1922 edition of *Imago*. Here, Grotjahn informs us that Groddeck highlights man's innate drive, "the natural form and expression of the 'It' in the symbol" (p. 11). To identify the "dependence and the predetermination of consciousness from the unconscious," writes Grotjahn, "is the aim of Groddeck's paper" (p. 14), to emphasize that men are essentially limited by the 'It,' and that the symbol functions to convey the representation of its unconscious charge. Groddeck's views are characteristic of the ideological revolt against scientism, the Zeitgeist of his time, and illustrative of the enraptured idealization of the unconscious embodied by the artists and writers of the French Symbolist and later Surrealist movements.

Melanie Klein's 1930 paper, "The Importance of Symbol Formation in the Development of the Ego," which holds promise in its title, develops the clinical and theoretical aspects of the case of a 6-year-old boy with dementia praecox. The opening paragraphs characteristically inundate one with Kleinian adultomorphic, theoretical constructions of infantile development and psychopathology,[3] imagery replete with sadism, destruction, devouring of maternal breasts, excreta transformed into weaponry, desires for domination, possession, exceedingly premature oedipal wishes, fantasies of parental coitus, incorporation, and the like (pp. 25–26). The paper then unfolds its cogent central thesis, that "not only does symbolism come to be the foundation of all fantasy and sublimation, but, more than that, upon it is built up the subject's relation to the outside world and to reality in general" (1930, p. 26). This statement has

---

[3]A most eloquent critique of this is offered by Kubie (1953), "Klein invests the infant's unmyelinated cerebrum and his partially myelinated afferent and efferent pathways with adult conscious and unconscious symbolic perceptions, conceptions and fantasy formations—in short, with the full complement of adult psychic equipment" (p. 93).

merit in that it clearly ties the development of the symbolizing *function* to the entire spectrum of ego functions which mediate the difference between inner and outer reality, and further, it suggests that this progression is contingent upon a meaningful close relationship. Indeed, the rest of her paper describes a 6-month course in the treatment of this "unloved" child who had all but retreated from relational contacts; who didn't speak, didn't play, displayed no affects, no overt anxiety, and whose adaptation to the environment appeared to be almost entirely lacking.

When he entered treatment, little Dick's withdrawn, indifferent, disconnected behavior apparently had no meaning or purpose; he ran aimlessly to and fro, his movements uncoordinated, his eyes fixed and distant. Klein reasons that Dick's early feeding, somatic, and relational difficulties stemmed from "a complete and apparently constitutional incapacity of the ego to tolerate anxiety" (p. 29) causing a developmental arrest due to his failure to overcome "those earliest steps"—referring to the extremely early oral sadistic impulses and fantasies mentioned at the outset of her paper.

"After a feeble beginning," Klein writes, "symbol-formation in this child had come to a standstill" (p. 29), along with relational communications and, as the treatment disclosed, this was in part due to a stringent defense against massive anxiety elicited by his early destructive impulses. In Dick, symbolism had not developed—the absence of affective investment appeared to have frozen his relation to people, objects, things, words, so that it was "impossible to regard them as having the character of symbolic representations" (p. 30) or any symbolic valence, and therefore rendered language, a symbolic vehicle, unusable for communication or expression. Klein describes the difficulty she had in attempting to engage this autistic child in her analytic play technique or to gain any access to his mind, and how she gradually reached him with very direct id interpretations, in accordance with her theoretical ideas. She remarks, "In general I do not interpret material until it has found expression in various representations . . . in this case . . . where the capacity to represent . . . was almost entirely lacking, I found myself obliged to make interpretations of my general knowledge . . ." (p. 34).

From her theoretical standpoint, Klein claims that even in such an extreme case of defective ego development, it was possible to build both ego and libido simply by interpreting unconscious conflicts. Today one might be more inclined to suppose that this was due to her having been able to engage him at an interpersonal level. Klein concludes that while little Dick's symptomatology did correspond to a diagnosis of childhood schizophrenia, the essential feature in his case was an "inhibition in development" and not a regression; the violent defense having caused a fixation point characteristic for dementia praecox. "The ego's exaggerated and primitive defense against sadism checks the establishing of a right relation to reality and the development of fantasy" (1930, p. 39). Essentially, her paper highlights the pivotal significance of symbolization in the development of the ego and its intimate connection to early interpersonal relationships and their effect on anxiety and affect regulation. The symbolic function itself here is emphasized rather than merely its content.

In a paper read before the British Psychological Society in 1955, Hanna Segal recapitulates and expands on the theoretical integration of symbol formation her teacher Melanie Klein had begun to formulate. With further clarity and focus she addresss the "whole process of symbol formation" with particular reference to the distinct ways in which symbols function in neurosis and psychosis; she finds that for the schizophrenic the word is felt to *be* the thing; for the neurotic it *represents* it. Segal emphasizes that whether a symbol is conscious or unconscious is of less relevance than that in its function it represents rather than equates. Thus, Segal discounts Jones' several points defining as symbolized only that which has been repressed and is therefore unconscious, and that which is not sublimated. She adeptly turns the issues toward (1) a wider definition of symbols, corresponding more to common linguistic usage; (2) the observation of an apparent continuity in development from primitive symbols to those used in self-expression, communication, and creativity; and (3) to the fact that analytic views of the child's development contingent on a series of displacements of affect and interests from primary objects to new objects in the external world would not make sense unless such continuity, as mentioned earlier, existed in the symbolizational process, whereby these displacements are made possible. Symbolization now appears to be central to the whole development of the ego and, if this is taken to be true, she notes, "the processes of symbolization require a new and more careful study" (1957, p. 392).

Segal makes major contributions in this paper. (1) She identifies (after Morris, 1955) the presence of a three-term correspondence in symbolization in the relations between the thing symbolized, the thing functioning as symbol, and the person for whom the one represents the other; in psychoanalytic terms, the interdigitation of ego, object, and symbol. (2) She identifies the logical consequence of this, namely that disturbances in the differentiation between ego and object will lead to deviations in the differentiation between symbol and that which is symbolized, as in schizophrenic concrete thinking. (3) She makes a distinction between very early symbols experienced as being identical with the object newly termed by her "symbolic equations." (4) She notes the gradual development in symbolization from symbolic equations, which still carry the original affective charge, to the fully formed symbolic representation (for her, in the depressive position) as correlate of a complete differentiation between subject and object.

Segal grasps the essence of the symbolic creation from its inception as a means of restoring or recreating the original object within. The symbol arises out of loss, not as a substitute for it; it is reflective, not restitutional. And its precondition is an ego which can differentiate self from other and tolerate the anxiety of separation; as Segal puts it, "The symbol is used not to deny but to overcome loss" (1957, p. 395). Thus excessive anxiety in early trauma can be seen to interfere with this process by its fusing or binding the subject to the object, obliterating the space (Winnicott's place of transition) in which the true symbol may be formed. Intense affects merge subject and object just as they blur the boundaries between the thing and what it stands for and the differentiation between what springs from within and what is perceived externally. Equally, when words are felt to *be* what they represent, in concrete fashion, they become

unavailable for purposes of communication. Here she antici-
pates some of Searle's (1962) ideas on the relationship of language and the use of metaphor in schizophrenia.

Segal highlighted the intricate interrelationship between
ego development and evolving symbolizing capacities as these
impact on thought processes, communication, relationships, defenses and the sense of reality. "The word 'symbol,' " she writes,
"comes from the Greek term for throwing together, bringing
together, integrating. The process of symbol-formation is, I
think, a continuous process of bringing together and integrating the internal with the external, the subject with the object,
and the earlier experiences with the later ones" (1957, p. 397).

In his attempt to propose an explanatory bridge in *The
Mysterious Leap from the Mind to the Body* (1959), Felix Deutsch
puts forward ideas on symbolization as a "Formative Stage of the
Conversion Process" (chapter 6). Though thoroughly rooted in
Freudian soil, his ideas show to advantage an advancing functional approach with regard to encompassing the nature of the
process of symbol formation itself. In this sense, his formulations
are not dissimilar from those of Segal.

Deutsch's emphasis, however, is on the organic base; the
pervasive relevance of the senses in relation to perceptual and
ideational configurations. He writes about somatic experience,
body image, physiologic processes and their symbolic displacements, equations, representations, and "symbolized equivalents," with respect to how these phenomena originate the
conversion process. In a paper thick with physicalist analogies,
anthropomorphic reifications, and biologically based hypotheses, Deutsch relates the development of symbolization to object
loss which, he stresses, is anchored in bodily responses. Incorporation and identification, their ideational correlates, and the
somatic expressions in behaviors of "intersensory perceptions"
he states, correspond to ideational and concomitantly verbal-
ized associated memories in psychoanalysis. To describe this
he presents an illustrative case replete with sensorial somatic
manifestations as these appeared in conjunction with associative
material, in what he claims is a miniversion of the ongoing
conversion process.

This process, he asserts, stems from attempts to repair loss, out of which symbolized body organs, as replacements, are "libidinized" or delibidinized according to the respective force of the drives: "The symbolization substitutes the amount of loss which the lost object represented to the individual" (p. 80), he writes, referring to quantums of cathexes, narcissistically invested in body organs. His presentation, however, is marred by an uncomfortable overlap of neurochemical (p. 43), biological, psychological, and psychodynamic terms, mixing too many metaphors and levels of abstraction with discordantly concretic physicalist correlates. While this interdisciplinarity is, in principle, a desirable approach for psychoanalytic study, it requires vigilance against the temptation to bend diverse models to fit procrustean molds.

Admittedly, the early analysts were hampered by the absence of a conceptual language that could serve their ideas. Nevertheless, behind their theoretically determined lens and terms, lie important and valuable priciples. In a successfully integrative paragraph, Deutsch (1959) writes: "my concept of objects stems from the ego's faculty of manipulating sense perceptions in the earliest cognition of objects and of forming a sensory configuration which becomes specific for certain objects" (p. 92). This notion is virtually identical with Piaget's sensorimotor stage schemas and also corresponds to Kestenberg's (1975) approach, both of which address the body–mind unit as the primary experiential field. "In the course of psychic development, these perceptions become symbolized and evoke the whole past history of a specific object relationship. Thus, the symbolization of sensory perception serves as a feedback for physiologic processes" (p. 92). Here, Deutsch is attempting to integrate classical psychoanalytic theory with object relations, and concepts of the earliest development of cognition, ideas which were to become operationalized in Piaget's work and will be further elaborated upon in chapter 4. By addressing object relations and the ego with respect to sensory experience and symbolizational expressions, despite reified language, Deutsch makes a valid contribution toward bridging the "mysterious leap" from mind to body. Historically, his physiological interests complement the early orthodoxy of Jones and Melanie Klein's emphasis on the impact of archaic relations and affect on the symbolizational function. In subsuming these viewpoints, Deutsch's contribution refined and enlarged psychoanalytic theoretical underpinnings.

By the late fifties and sixties and under the theoretical sway of ego psychology, the psychoanalytic approach to symbolic phenomena had become more encompassing and committed to a systematic investigation of the central role of the symbolizing function, the consequences of its impairment, and regressive breakdown. A tendency toward reevaluating the qualities of primary and secondary process thinking and an integration of the symbolic process yield numerous works. These begin to explore the implication of this function in the regressive dedifferentiation of the schizophrenic process and point to its central role in maintaining perceptual equilibrium between the inner world and outer reality (Sechehaye, 1951; Kubie, 1953; Rodriguez, 1956; Rycroft, 1956; Segal, 1957; Searles, 1962). Thus, Kubie and Rycroft draw attention to the merits of a unitary approach which, in appreciating the full implications of ego psychology, tends to consider symbolization and ego functioning in very similar terms.

In a 1956 issue of the *International Journal of Psycho-Analysis*, two important papers furthered the progress of theoretical and clinical integration: Charles Rycroft considered "Symbolism and Its Relationship to the Primary and Secondary Processes," and Emilio Rodriguez, in a somewhat Kleinian vein, presenting "Notes on Symbolism." In both these papers, the crucial part played by symbolic processes in ego development and in ongoing psychological functioning is implicit, and the general thrust is toward gaining further in-depth clarification and theoretical integration.

Stressing an object relations perspective, Rycroft (1956) first discussed the traditional views of primary and secondary process; "theoretical constructs [are] designed to explain a particular range of facts" (p. 139), and emphasized that the assumed antithesis between reality and fantasy, between the person present and the person imagined implied by these constructs is not always a valid one. In diminishing the sharp distinction between these two mental modes, he suggests that the

essential difference between the primary and secondary processes "can be conveniently expressed in two different ways,
one of which stresses the fate of the impulse, the other . . . the
quality of the relationship to the object" (p. 139). From this
object relations perspective, the primary process is considered
to be "objectively autistic," notwithstanding a subjective internal object imago, whereas the secondary process furthers interaction and communication by way of its subjective and objective
contact with a real object in the environment.

Disagreeing with Jones regarding the necessity for considering "true" symbolism, exclusively associated with unconscious
ideation, Rycroft rejects the notion of two qualitatively different
modes of mental activity. He felt it to be illogical to presume
that there was any such discontinuity in the mind which, despite
its propensity toward disjunction, is a unitary structure and
works as a whole. Rycroft pointed out that it is more logical to
view symbolism as a general capacity which "may be used in
two different ways" (p. 140), rather than subdivide the function
according to the different uses to which it is put. Thus, following
Kubie (1953), Rycroft points to the advantage of thinking of
symbolization and ego functioning in very similar ways. This
approach draws attention to the essential continuity in mind,
in that "unconscious symbolic and imaginative processes underlie the development and maintenance of a sense of reality" (p.
141) quite as much as they impact on neurotic, and particularly
psychotic, dysfunctional modes of thought. In this regard, Rycroft proposes the term *phantoms* to be used for defensively
idealized, illusory imagos of psychic construction, in contradis-
tinction to the internal "imagos" based on memories of real
experiences, and further specifies that psychic reality is itself
formed in part by idealization and in part by developmental
experiences occurring in external reality.

In recasting the distinction between fantasy and reality
within the framework of a unifying theory, Rycroft suggests using the word *imagination* for the elaborations and mental organization characteristic of the secondary process, and "phantasy"
for primary process "imagos" or phantoms. This distinction has
several advantages: it highlights the fact that all reality thinking

is supported by unconscious ideation; it emphasizes the importance of imagination as an essential prerequisite for an appreciation of reality; and, finally, it provides three words with distinct meanings—*illusion, phantasy,* and *imagination*—to cover what have previously been subsumed loosely under the general hazy term *phantasy.*

In his last section, Rycroft considers the theory of symbolism by way of symbolization, that is the function, considering this to be a general tendency of the mind, which may appear in primary or secondary process form and be used defensively or realistically, neurotically or artistically, to maintain regression or to promote growth. In his concluding fourteen propositions, Rycroft makes numerous relevant points which may, with considerable loss for the sake of brevity, be subsumed under three superordinate themes. The first is that the process of symbol formation occurs as a displacement of cathexis from a primary, original idea or object of instinctual investment to another idea or object which operates as a symbol, and carries some of the original affective charge. The second, that the process of symbol formation presupposes some ego development, and that once symbolization has occurred it may be used by either the primary or the secondary process; and the third, that although words, when operating as words, form part of the secondary process, they can, under certain conditions, lose their differentiating or "symbolic" characteristics and show their genetic roots in unconscious meanings which carry the complete cathexis of the objects they would normally merely signify. Thus, impairments in the symbolizing function of language and its mediating metaphorical bridges lead to disturbances in interpersonal relationships, as words may become embodiments of affects and therefore no longer form part of a communicational system. Rycroft ends by emphasizing that psychoanalytic technique "presupposes that the analyst, the analytical situation and the words used in analysis are all symbols" (p. 140). Here, and on other occasions, Rycroft draws attention to the central role of language and issues of reference for psychoanalytic theory, and on the importance of focusing research on the linguistic aspects of the clinical situation.

In his comprehensive "Notes on Symbolism" (1956), Rodriguez covers a good part of the extant psychoanalytic literature which, with the help of Langer's (1942) concept of nondiscursive symbolism, brings psychoanalysis up to date, providing a "much needed logical framework for a psycho-analytical theory of symbolism" (p. 150). Invoking a new awareness of the nature of meaning which evolved out of philosophical thought, no longer an arbitrary *quality* but the *function* of a term always related to at least one other term and a subject who uses it, Rodriguez credits Langer's views for enabling the narrowing of a gap between the divergent ways in which psychologists and epistemologists conceive of symbols.

Rodriguez notes the inherent drawbacks in the obsolete logical theory of symbolism underlying the analytical approach: the notion of symbols as "special entities," he believes, distracted from the consideration of complex symbolic structures, so that "instead of regarding the whole form assumed by dreams as symbolic," Freud concluded that "dreams contain symbolic units in their non-symbolic fabric" (p 150). After Segal (1957) and Milner (1952), he aptly points out the important distinction to be made between symbolic equation and symbolic representation: "in the first the symbol *doubles* the object, . . . in the second, it *conjures it up*" (p. 150)—and stresses the crucial functional importance of the passage from the first to the second.

In further addressing the contributions of Klein and her coworkers in the study of the genesis of symbols, Rodriguez refers to the case of Dick, in whom the earliest process of symbolic equating was inhibited and presents a similar case, that of Raul. In his description, Rodriguez traces the vicissitudes of autism and communication, of Raul's first projections and introjections, his attempts to master massive anxiety and to reexperience repressed affects, and how the gradual progression of the treatment was founded upon this nascent capacity to utilize symbols. Ego development, differentiation, and interpersonal communication progressed simultaneously as the boy moved from symbolic equations of direct sensory–affective immersion (as in the basin–breast episode he describes, pp. 155–156) to genuine symbolic representations which "constitute the turning point in symbol-formation'' (p. 157). And, he concludes, "the internal and external objects have to become differentiated in order that one, the internal, may represent the other" (p. 157).

Of all the papers which converge at this time on the topic, the most epistemologically sound, that offering the most comprehensive coverage and theoretically significant contribution, is Kubie's (1953) seminal work, "The Distortion of the Symbolic Process in Neurosis and Psychosis." Grouping ego functions into perceptual, conceptual, executive, defensive, and integrative, and emphasizing their synergistic interdependence, Kubie identifies the singular ego function which can be found to influence the ego's every aspect, to be the uniquely human psychological process of symbolizing. Using the concept of symbol in a broad and inclusive sense, he presents seven summarizing propositions regarding the symbolic function out of which he derives his central thesis, namely, that "in all forms of adult human psychopathology, distortions of the symbolic function occur which cannot occur in the human infant before symbolic functioning begins" (p. 92). It is futile, if not downright fallacious, therefore, to pursue a Kleinian "fantasy," he writes, which "invests the infant's unmyelinated cerebrum and partially myelinated afferent and efferent pathways with fully symbolized elaborate adult conceptions," and he emphasizes, I believe correctly, that this is yet another example of the lack of distinction between "descriptions of causal sequences and the characterization of resultant changes" (p. 93). A stricter, more precise use of terms and concepts, he believes, would have the advantage of first characterizing a sequence of pathogenic experiences and then clarifying the essential qualities of the distortions they induce.

From the outset, with intent to describe the essential nature of "a change" which, he emphasizes, will subsequently need to be further explained and integrated into a complete picture, Kubie asks four pointed questions seeking to identify where the human psychic apparatus is most vulnerable in a uniquely human way, and how this vulnerability is manifest. He further questions what different kinds of distortions may occur and whether these differences clarify the contrast between neurosis, psychosis, and normality. He will not, he underscores, ask how these vulnerabilities arise, since "Before we can explain the genesis of differences, we must know *what* differences we are explaining" (1953, p. 90).

Framing his essay in epistemic remarks through which he delineates a variety of different psychological and psychoanalytic schools and approaches, Kubie identifies how and in what ways psychiatry has begged the central questions pertaining to the etiology of psychopathology. This he asserts has "led to serious theoretical confusion, [since] to describe the consequences of a process does not reveal its essential mechanism" (pp. 88–89). Furthermore, the absence of a clear view of what characterizes the central deformation of the psyche as pathognomic in neurosis and psychosis, and the failure to accurately identify the essential nature of "the critical change whose development our ontogenetic theories have attempted to trace" (p. 90) has left a "hampering gap" in our basic theory, which his paper attempts to remedy.

Addressing the significance of disturbances at the symbolic level, Kubie gives his definition of symbol as subsuming three closely related processes usually considered part of a more general "symbolic function": (1) its abstractive properties; (2) its relation to artistic, linguistic, poetic, jocular and metaphoric use in which symbolic expression remains relatively transparent; and (3) the strictly psychoanalytic use of the term as an obscuring device, wherein the symbol is a manifest representation of a latent unconscious idea. Kubie emphasizes the conceptual overlap of these three different uses of the term *symbolic* and adopts a single generic approach designed to highlight their essential continuity. Appreciation of this continuity underscores the fact that every symbol is a "multi-valent tool," a "chord," as he puts it, "with a potentiality of at least nine simultaneous overtones" (p. 97). On the unconscious, preconscious, and conscious levels, all direct and indirect representations of any conceptual process will simultaneously and always, if in varying degrees, be literal, allegorical and also "symbolic" as in the purely psychoanalytic sense.

Thread through his subsuming propositions, Kubie advances several additional salient points. He identifies that the capacity to synthesize new concepts out of prior percepts and their abstraction utilizes all of the economic devices characteristic of the primary process, and that when these mechanisms occur predominantly at the preconscious and conscious level, they "mediate abstract thought and language." When they occur at the unconscious level, they determine either the "shape of our dreams" or "the shape of our illnesses" (pp. 98–99).

Early in its formation, every concept and its symbolic representation develops an internal and an external pole of reference so that every symbol is derived from ideation of bodily feelings and needs and experiences originating in percepts of the outside world. The symbolic process functions as a bridge: "every symbolic unit hangs like a hammock between two poles, one internal or bodily (the 'I') and one external (the 'not-I') so that whenever we consciously think and speak of the outer world, we are . . . thinking and speaking of the inner world . . ." (p. 102), and vice versa. This "dual anchorage" of every symbol, Kubie continues, is "inherent in the process by which we acquire knowledge and by which we orient ourselves to ourselves and to the outer world" (p. 100). Evolving conceptualizations of inner and outer experience correlate with each other; the conscious and unconscious transmutations of experience known to us as internalization, projection, introjection, somatization, are contingent upon this "dual anchorage" of the symbol.

With regard to conceptual antecedents having their origin in proprioceptive and exteroceptive experiences, these considerations, according to Kubie, are grounded in physiological and anatomical facts. On both a perceptual and a conceptual level, the symbolic process is itself the bridge between self and other, for which a correlate neuroanatomical and neurophysiological basis can be found in the central nervous system.

Due to its bipolar reference points and its correspondence with the central nervous system the "symbolic process is vulnerable to organic and to psychodynamic injury at both poles" (p. 104); and the precise nature of this vulnerability lies in the occurrence of the distortion of the relation of a symbol to its substrate at either the internal or the external pole of reference. "Psychopathological illness begins in the repressive–dissociative activity which distorts the link between symbolic constructs and their referents in the body. . . ," and the essential difference occurring in neurotic and psychotic processes has to do with "the point at which the relation of the symbol to the substrate is disturbed" (p. 106).

In conclusion, Kubie's elegant theoretical presentation emphasizes the unbroken continuity of all psychological manifestations as he traces these on a continuum from normality to neurosis and psychosis. His formulations successfully join body and mind, perceptual and conceptual, and most importantly securely ground a new outlook on the etiology of psychological disorders in aberrations of the symbolic function.

While Kubie's emphasis on etiology did much to integrate the symbolic process in terms of psychopathology, several papers now appeared which focus on its correspondence with language and thought with reference to their interlocking form and the structuring of their substrata.

Dipping into extensive experience and tracing his conceptual indebtedness to Werner (1940), Searles subsumes the theoretical substance of Kubie's paper in his 1962 work, "The Differentiation between Concrete and Metaphorical Thinking in the Recovering Schizophrenic Patient" in which, in his uniquely empathic and clinically engaged way, Searles describes how it is possible for the therapist to "have the rewarding and exciting experience of seeing a schizophrenic patient become free from the claims of 'concrete'—that is, undifferentiated—thinking, able now to converse with his fellow human beings in consensually validated metaphors, and able, as a result of this same double-edged process of increasing differentiation, to share their recognition of the world of concrete things as being truly concrete" (p. 561).

Aside from Searles' poignant and often profound understanding of schizophrenia and schizophrenic communication, his deep respect for and engagement in the treatment process, his paper is a lucid integration of clinical examples and their theoretical underpinnings, so that we follow him, indeed often sit with him as illustrative verbatim vignettes embody what, on other occasions, are often "static descriptions of a 'disease' which set the schizophrenic hopelessly apart from his fellow human beings" (p. 561).

Through two descriptive cases he delineates the progressive process of thought differentiation in the recovering schizophrenic, focusing particularly on the gradual emergence of metaphorical thinking, or the reemergence of the symbolic function. In so doing Searles highlights three interrelated conceptual points: (1) that differentiation is predicated on relatively firm ego boundaries; (2) that these boundaries come into being proportionately as various repressed emotions can be expressed and integrated; and (3) that these same emotions are unconsciously and defensively repressed due to precarious ego boundaries causing the concomitant use of concrete thinking.

The schizophrenic process is understood as a regression to a level of thinking in which there is a *"lack of differentiation* between the concrete and the metaphorical" (p. 561) as well as an inability to use consensually validated metaphors or to think "in terms that are *genuinely* concrete" (p. 561). Thus, neither is the schizophrenic genuinely concrete, since a "thing" or object and the name given it is, for the most part, submerged by anthropomorphic and animistic qualities due to gross perceptual distortions; nor conversely, is it metaphorical or "symbolic" in a consensually comprehensible way as in the many subtleties of linguistic communication. While, in my opinion, this has its origins in the decompensation of the most rudimentary, abstractive, organizational function by which we hold together diverse perceptions, its reverberations are, of course, felt at all levels of the abstractive, symbolizational continuum.

In his patients, Searles (1962) found evidence for only rudimentary ego differentiation, disinguishing them as human individuals from the outer world, and, at the deepest psychological level, little demarcation between classes of inanimate and animate, nonhuman and human objects. There was, on the other hand, massive projection onto all manner of inanimate things and human objects and in one case onto the climatic elements. A precarious or nonexistent sense of identity, reflecting immense alienation and dehumanizing self-depreciation, is epitomized in the blunt, concrete statement, "I'm like tissue paper . . . I guess I'm just nothing" (p. 563) enunciated by a

small, thin, mute catatonic who for months lay flat and mo-
tionless on his bed, as Searles inimitably describes, "like little
more than an unusually large wrinkle in the bedcover" (p. 564).
Searles notes that while numerous authors, including Ferenczi,
Scharpe, Langer, Kubie, and Little have all emphasized the necessity of firm ego boundaries for metaphorical thinking, they
have not addressed the psychodynamic mechanism he identifies
as the literal mode of thought serving defensively against "a
welter of repressed affects as a product of the tenuousness of
ego boundaries" (p. 565). He therefore concludes that "loss of
ego boundaries is one of the most vigorously formidable *defense
mechanisms* which comprise the schizophrenic process" (p. 566).
This defensive function is well illustrated in the autobiographi-
cal recounting of Renée's repeated relapses, often triggered by
what in her case was a mounting of intolerably intense affects
which she could not herself contain (Sechehaye, 1951). Similarly, Searles comments that he was impressed to note how the
"derepression" of a wide range of feelings correlated with a
steadily growing capacity to communicate metaphorically. One
is again struck by the obvious paring of symbolizing processes
and ego development, a point to which Kubie drew attention
earlier.

Emphatically Searles underscores the gross distortions of
the perceptual experience itself, not limited to the realm of
thought, and states his preference for Hartmann's (1939) term
dedifferentiation over the concept of regression per se. To define
the phenomenology of this disintegrative course he proposes
the term *desymbolization,* describing a process "whereby once
attained, metaphorical meanings become desymbolized."

Searles' central idea is that concrete thinking or literal communication, and the concomitant dissolution of ego boundaries
in schizophrenia, serve defensive functions in maintaining various anxiety-laden affects under repression so that "awareness of
the whole spectrum of emotion—is father to the metaphorical
thought . . . perhaps . . . to all forms of symbolic thought" (p.
572). As the schizophrenic begins to tie his "crazy" communications to the intense affects to which they correspond, so is he
able to separate out the figurative realm from the genuinely

concrete. While ego boundaries are prerequisite for differentiation between metaphorical and literal meanings, it is equally
true that metaphor (or symbol) could not develop if there were
not a time when there was "a relatively unimpeded flow between . . . inner and outer world" (p. 584).

Searles' emphasis on the interrelationship and interdependence of sensory, perceptual, affective, and differentiating processes with the symbolizing function itself, also refers to the
essence of my thesis, namely that symbolization is one with, if
not identical to, ego development and is predicated on a relatively consistent, adequately empathic bond with a primary care-
taker in whose orbit the essential early psychological
differentiation may occur. The disrupting effect of excessively
overwhelming affects which give rise to repressive mechanisms,
would appear to disintegrate and distort an integrative thrust
which paradoxically moves simultaneously in two directions—toward greater differentiation and greater communication—due to the gradual giving way of infantile egocentrism
and concomitant cognitive ability to articulate symbolic vehicles
for denotive reference. My suspicion is that we will come to
understand repression also as an aspect of several complex processes in a memory system, rather than as a single, defensive
function.

As will become more explicit within the articulation of the
model proposed in chapter 4, symbolization is the enriching
by-product, the distillate of differentiation, a biologically based
abstractive process which begins in perception, is dependent
upon psychological separation and its generative articulation in
the use of signs and then symbols, which, in turn, furnish
thought. These processes are so interrelated and interdependent as to be virtually inseparable and, as was implicit in Searles'
discussion of the decomposition and reemergence of this integrative function, are the very threads with which our minds are
woven.

For a firsthand account of what it feels like to descend into
this disintegrative state, I know of no more poignant and vivid
account than that of Renée, in Sechehaye's *Autobiography of a
Schizophrenic Girl* (1951), in which the reader is first led through
the grotesque experiential labyrinth of one who has lost her

faculties of mind and who all the while is aware of this, and then through a psychoanalytic theoretical "interpretation" by the therapist of the course of this long, almost lost case. The dual phenomenological and theoretical perspectives, and the identified "curative" mode of treatment, that of "symbolic realization," are what render this account particularly enlightening. In it can be traced many of the most salient points highlighted earlier in those papers which gave emphasis to desymbolizing and concretization of thought in the psychotic process.

What grips us is Renée's literary liberty, however, her willingness to shape a nightmare into a narrative and give form to her perceptual and sensory delirium, to depict in vivid words and verbal images the content of her misshapen, schizophrenic sphere. With intelligence and insight, Renée traces the process of her perceptual breakdown to an early sense of impending doom and world-ending fantasies; a hypersensitivity to sensorial experiences and fragmentation of these. Renée candidly describes her magical personifications and derealization, her alienated and alienating disconnectedness, and her hidden, unbearable tensions and surging affects.

The eldest of numerous siblings for whom she was precociously obliged to care while still attending school herself, Renée maintained the facade of a responsible, hard-working girl, managing a household of six "on a pitiful budget," and later working as a secretary. Beneath this exterior and her deteriorating physical health, "The fear" (a personified projection) never leaves her and she grows more and more bewildered by the "illimitable vastness, brilliant piercing light, the gloss and smoothness of material things" and the puppetlike automatons speaking in metallic, meaningless words "without warmth or color" with which her desolate "other country," rocky and barren, is populated. Dazzled by the intensity of these decomposed perceptual distortions and projections, Renée, physically fragile and overstressed, descends into a deeper and deeper regression, which Searles would call a "desymbolizational" process, wherein Kubie's dual poles of symbolic communication extending from the inner individual to others in the outside world, break down completely.

Indeed, her analyst, Sechehaye (1951), describes her as regressing to the furthest point of complete infantilism, where nothing but the gratification of returning to the womblike "green sea," of which the method of symbolic realization made use, would suffice to engender a renewed attempt at restructuralization within the shared symbolic participation of her mamma/analyst. During the course of this treatment, Sechehaye observes that Renée's weak and precarious ego decomposes under the strain of a "disassociation of affectivity," deeply disturbed by the "loss of contact with life." This notwithstanding and with retrospective evidence, Renée confirms that even in periods of utter lethargy and catatonic stupor, in which she lay for months in a fetal position, an "impersonal lucidity" still persisted.

"My perception of the world . . . sharpened the senses of the strangeness of things. In the silence and immensity, each object was cut off by a knife, detached in the emptiness, in the boundlessness, spaced off from other things. Without any relationship with the environment, just by being itself, it began to come to life. It was there, facing me, terrifying me. And I said, 'The chair is making fun of me, it is playing tricks' " (p. 57). "From time to time, phrases wandered through my dreaming spirit. 'But you will see,' or 'perfectly,' or meaningless scraps of words, 'Ichtaou, gao, gao' " (p. 56) ". . . things didn't exist in and of themselves, but each one created a world after its own fashion . . . as soon as my gaze fell on a spot of any sort . . . I could not drag it away . . . held fast by the boundless world of the infinitely small" (p. 66) ". . . social relationships did not touch my spirit in the slightest degree" (p. 54), except, that is, for the yearned for contacts with mamma/analyst who, in appearing as life restoring in the most physical way, is the single thread to any attachment and therefore, in Renée's undifferentiated state, to life itself. Here is a palpable description of the dissolution of "perceptual" integration, of which Searles wrote, "representing the very first symbolizational function"; in Kubie's terms, the capacity to create abstract cohesion from diverse concrete experiences.

"In the midst of this agonizing lethargy," Renée continues, "storms of dreadful anger, of bitter vexation, surged up within me," while auditory hallucinations taunted her, sending her into self-destructive, frenzied rages requiring repeated hospitalizations and restraining measures. Through this confusion of voices and orders and delirious stupor, she was consistently unable to "regain the relation" with her analyst, until Sechehaye grasped upon the technique of "symbolic realization," by which she vicariously ministered loving care to various substitute dolls with which Renée identified quite completely. Via these displaced symbolized equivalents and vicariously received care-giving instructions, Renée was gradually able to counteract her rage and fragmentation, by internalizing a "good mother" through the neutralizing effect of these soothing interpersonal experiences.

Her complete identification with the dolls could occur only because she was profoundly dedifferentiated, so that the displacement onto the doll-double was experienced by her not as being *like* her, but as actually *being* herself: "I said to myself, 'I am I and he is he, and there is no relation between us,' however, the confusion as to who is who was complete" (p. 65). The apples and their life-sustaining "maternal milk," as handed to her by the analyst, were a symbolic equivalent (in Segal's terms) and not truly a symbol, yet they provided the essential rudimentary bridge between the two poles of the symbolizational continuum with which she could reconnect to someone and thereby restore differentiation and communication between herself and the environment. This is a cogent illustration of Searles' impression that his patient needed to confirm his ability to connect to the therapist at the most primitive levels of relatedness before he could brave increasing separateness and concomitant increasingly metaphoric and abstracted modes of relating. This also corresponds to Kubie's observation regarding the construction of symbols as being derived simultaneously from ideation created out of bodily needs and concepts formed out of percepts of the outer world. The dislocation of the symbolic function in Renée was perhaps compounded by her continued somatic distress, worsened by the severity of her various illnesses.

While Sechehaye reviews in considerable detail what she considers to be the curative factors of the case, and does so interweaving many salient aspects of Piaget's theories of cognitive development, her conclusions ring somewhat outdated, as she apportions quantities of energy to reified structures: "the first portions of the ego to regress are precisely those closely related to society. Their energy, the libido, drains back to the innermost core of the ego, leaving the social sectors devoid of affect" (p. 95), for example. Or, as in this summarizing statement: "The whole problem consisted in realizing this desire, so that it would not be compensated anymore by delirium, and permit a normal development of dynamic growth" (p. 137); by "this desire," Sechehaye is referring to a "legitimate desire" for maternal love. Her reasoning that Renée's early deprivation had caused a fixation point which prevented her ego from growing and which had to be "symbolically" compensated for by various palpable substitutes such as apples or breasts, is conceptually reminiscent of Alexander's corrective emotional experience, whereas her ideas about how the theory of symbolism is related to the efficacious effect of vicarious "symbolic realizations" straddles old psychoanalytic concepts and newer Piagetian ideas. With respect to Renée's symbolizing capacity, Sechehaye confuses the result with the cause. This notwithstanding, her point-by-point account of the progression in the treatment utilizing symbolic realization and the corresponding evolving changes in newly symbolized and differentiated attitudes in her patient's responses, is of great interest.

With regard to what was understood by Sechehaye to be the essential curative factor in the utilization of "symbolic" substitutions for basic caregiving ministrations and nourishment, I notice a remarkable degree of fit between the intent of the intervention and the patient's current level of communicational abstraction, or lack of it (i.e., to the degree of dedifferentiation or "desymbolization"). This points in an important direction. In a sense, such an approach recapitulates the ontogenesis of early development and of the symbolic function itself, a course which will be delineated in chapter 4. At the most primary levels, words must be accompanied by actions. Referencing begins in the orbit of the first dyad. This may explain Renée's expressed relief on being spoken to "in the third person," as mothers instinctively do around the world, with their infants. The third-person communication provides distancing from the self and objectivization of the circumstance, both of which encourage symbolization. The internalization of caregiving relational units thus carries traces of the subject, the object, an activity, and the affective coloring related to these. The retrieval process of memory calls up a symbolized distillation of what past images and current affects construe (neither of these being fixed) and what all of this *means* to the subject—imago-image-symbol—overlaps. In Renée's case, memory and abstracted symbol were dissolved into dreadful imagos carved out of current anxieties and primal experiences of physical pain and psychic frustration. The vicarious experiences through the dolls, the apple-breast, and in particular the benevolent administration of morphine injections by a maternal hand, were sufficiently soothing to enable reconstitution of a new imago-image symbol with which to mediate proprioceptive and exterioceptive impressions. This in turn reinstated the symbolic bridge between inner and outer, a relational connection which in itself produces symbolizing and symbolized channels (Searles' "metaphoric" communication) reconnecting Renée to a wonderful world of "things" and a language imbued with meaning.

The major psychologists Piaget (1962; Piaget and Inhelder, 1969) and Werner (Werner and Kaplan, 1963) have incorporated extensive work on the symbolic function into their theories, bringing to the topic slightly different perspectives which shed light on diverse facets according to their particular emphasis, within not dissimilar frameworks. Because of the relevance of the yields of their work for the model proposed in chapter 4, a synthesis of their conclusions is included insofar as this bears directly on a revised approach to the theory of psychoanalysis, a trend which has already in part encompassed some Piagetian ideas, but has done so much less systematically with Werner and Kaplan's ideas.

Tracing the ontogenesis of mental growth as inseparable from physical growth, and systematizing the continuous stages of psychological development in the child from the early sensorimotor, presymbolic stage to that of logical thought, its operations and structures, Piaget clearly demarcated the semiotic or symbolic function as the major marker in the differentiating shift from intuitive–somatic toward representational–reflective intelligence. Piaget used a basic unit of experience, the "schema" to organize the workings of mind. Vicissitudes of its assimilation and accommodation, with increasing development of logical–cognitive articulation forming the latticework of mental operations, are designed to further adaptation and ensure equilibrium.

Werner and Kaplan's (1963) views rather, embedded in an organismic–holistic orientation, subscribe to a few basic developmental principles inherent in this approach, maintaining that (1) organisms can only be understood contextually; (2) any aspect of organismic functioning is to be considered in the light of its current goals (i.e., the assumption of directiveness); (3) maturation tends to move from states of relative globality to an ever increasing awareness of differentiation (the orthogenetic principle); and (4) this developmental process serves an innate human orientation toward "knowing" the world. For both major theorists, however, the instrumentality of thought (Piaget) and vehicle of knowledge (Werner and Kaplan) is the symbol. Piaget considers the symbolizing function as it alters operations affecting the assimilation and accommodation of schemas, whereas Werner emphasizes the schematizing or form-building process itself.

The central notion of the organismic view of symbolization is that of "dynamic schematization," a post-Kantian view in direct line with Humboldt (1884) and Cassirer (1953–1957), emphasizing the productive–constructive formation of an object and its symbolic referents in the transformation of material into symbolic vehicles. And Werner and Kaplan distinguish vehicular structures (imagery, visual, verbal patterns, gesture, etc.) which directly "present" a meaning from those that "represent" it (p. 16). Thus, a name, when used or conceived of magically as being the "thing" which it normally represents, is no more symbolic than an inadvertent gestural expression of an experienced emotion. From "true symbols," Werner and Kaplan stress, "we distinguish those productions whereby the vehicular structures . . . directly 'present' a meaning rather than 'represent' it" (p. 16). These protosymbols, "lack the intentional act by which a vehicular form is taken to represent a referent" (p. 17); signs and signals, dependent on arbitrary, preestablished combinations of meanings, do not correspond to the connotational characteristics of a referent and are therefore "no more symbolic than 'Stop' and 'Go' traffic lights" (p. 17)—indicating but not representing meaning. In the notion of directedness toward knowing, "explanation is found for the dramatic shift enabled by the advent of the symbolizing capacity wherein the infant transforms his world from one of 'things-of-action' to one of 'objects-of-contemplation' " (p. 18).

The organic holism of this theory is evident in formulations which consider origins; the unfolding of a microgenetic process encompassing directiveness, activity, and contextual structuralization, with expressiveness and knowledge rather than adaptation as central incentives. "The formation of referential objects starts from a primordial matrix composed of affective intereoceptive, postural, imaginal elements, etc., that is directed or channelized into a full perceptual articulation by the schematizing activity . . ." write Werner and Kaplan. An object as a meaningful entity issues from and remains linked to this organizing process: "If this bond breaks, meaning is lost" (1963, pp. 18–19). Werner and Kaplan identify the microgenesis of symbolization in the primary mechanism of conative perceptual integration. Symbols emerge out of the "primordial sharing" of the undifferentiated child with mother from which arises "reference," the initial invitation to shared contemplation, referring to an object by pointing, looking, or touching, which rapidly gives way to shared communication through symbolic referents such as naming and verbalization. Their theory emphasizes the contextual relevance of early experiences wherein affect, object, and referencing are internalized as a unit. "The constitutive mark of a symbol," for Werner and Kaplan, "is its representational function" (p. 43). Thus, whereas indication involves only reference, symbolization entails differentiation and integration; that is, "reference to an object and representation of that object" (p. 43), expressed or realized in another medium (qua symbolic vehicle). The vocal utterance is detached from things of the environment; unlike imagery and gesture, phonic form lends itself to external "interpersonal shaping."

Like Piaget, Werner and Kaplan emphasize continuity in development; the earliest media of representation are to be found in bodily movements and images wherein the vehicle is taken as a "mimatic facsimile" (p. 47) of the referent. At the earliest stages of phonic representation, the phenomenon of "word-realism" (Werner and Kaplan) or magical phenomenalism (Piaget) prevails, but in the course of development, concomitant to increasing interpersonal differentiation, there occurs a gradual "desubstantialization" of the symbolic vehicle so that it becomes a device for referencing and loses its "thinglike" quality.

Interpersonal differentiation occurs concomitantly to increased polarization between symbolizer and the symbolic vehicles he employs. This increasing polarization plays a significant role in the transformations which occur in the development of symbolization since the more primitive the medium, the more closely will it manifest inner form with outer form, and conversely, the more evolved the medium, the more it is objectified, the more it can be utilized to articulate abstract concepts.

For Piaget, these transformations represent the unfolding of predetermined stages of thought development in which mental operations progressively manipulate the assimilation and accommodation of schemas which are first registered in the body (sensorimotor assimilation), but soon move to operational levels (mental assimilation), articulated via "representation" or symbolization. Mental development of the child, or intelligence, occurs as a succession of "three great periods," each resulting from the preceding one and integrating this as a subordinate structure (Piaget and Inhelder, 1969). "Semiotic relations, thought and interpersonal connections," he writes with regard to the earliest sensorimotor stage, "internalize these schemas of action by reconstructing them on a new level of representation, and surpass them until all concrete operations and cooperative structures have been established" (p. 152). Where Werner sees intentionality in the act of denotive reference as characteristic of the intrinsic expressive quality of signification, Piaget's concept of activity, and the "joy of being the cause" in play and adaptation to reality, encompass and cover interpersonal processes of socialization which are at once cognitive, affective and moral.

In his *Play, Dreams and Imitation in Childhood,* Piaget (1962) devotes an entire chapter to the discussion and reexplanation of early psychoanalytic unconscious symbolism, or what he calls "secondary symbolism," arguing that Freud's notion of a moralistic repression barrier as well as concepts of censorship, disguise of unconscious imagery, and a content-full unconscious that is full of content, are unnecessarily complicated explanations for a mind which works along a continuum of similar, not dissimilar processes. Piaget writes: "A simpler explanation must therefore be found for the unconsciousness of such symbols. These symbols are not understood by the subject, because representation is itself an automatic or spontaneous regulation resulting from the interaction of affective schemas whose roots elude consciousness" (p. 204).

Piaget rejects Freud's clear line of demarcation between conscious and unconscious symbolism. Rather, he is concerned with identifying the continuity between unconscious and conscious symbolism, establishing their intrinsic unity in the manifestations of imitation, play, fantasy, children's and adults' dreams, and emphasizing the fallaciousness of the psychoanalytic view of a dichotomized dynamic unconscious within which are stored "repressed" affects. In reformulating what Freud considered to be the results of censorship or disguise, Piaget illustrates that the incomprehensible nature of secondary symbolism can be explained along the lines prescribed by the central propositions with which his conceptual model of mind is built. Thus, affective schemas are assimilated and accommodated outside of awareness equally as much as are cognitive schemas, since both are but aspects of a whole. " 'Repression,' being a result of the inter-regulation of schemas of affective assimilation" (p. 205), raises no special problem for Piaget so far as symbolism is concerned. He explains the unconscious image as "an image whose content is assimilated to the desires or impressions of the subject and whose meaning he fails to understand. The image is explained by earlier accommodations of the subject" (p. 205). The imagery of secondary symbolism, he reasons, is incomprehensible because it is derived from forms of ideation or early schemas belonging to intuitive–prelogical modes, which in children at play and both children and adults in sleep may be conjured up freely due to the severance of wakeful, socially oriented, logical–reflective thought. In contrast to the psychoanalytic tendency to seek the phylogenetic roots of ontogenetic evolution, Piaget recommends that in order to explain symbolism we confine ourselves to the field of child psychology, since we need look no further.

Showing considerable understanding of the psychoanalytic process and notable reverence for the efficacy of its method, Piaget remarks that it has clearly illuminated how the first personal schemas become generalized and "transferred" to other people, and states that as Claparèd and Janet had shown, "affectivity thus regulates the energetics of the action while intelligence provides the technique." "[T]he function of unconscious symbolism is therefore closely linked with that of affective schemas" (p. 206). Returning to the psychoanalytic approach to questions of unconscious symbolism, lest he be thought of as unilaterally a cognitive theorist, Piaget writes, "Affective life, like intellectual life, is a continual adaptation, and the two are not only parallel but interdependent, since feelings express the interest and the value given to actions of which intelligence provides the structure" (p. 206). "After seeing symbolism in its various forms in action the functional coherence of the various manifestations of thought is all the more striking," and we find that symbolization is "implied in the beginnings of all the child's conceptual thought" (p. 212).

While identifying make-believe play as "the most important manifestation of 'symbolic' thought in the child" (p. 169), Piaget acknowledges that it is not identical with it. He distinguishes a variety of conditions in which symbolic forms and functions are involved in play at various levels of awareness, and weaves these implications into his general theoretical aim. For Piaget as for Freud, the rational-logical operations of thought are connected to and dependent upon cognizance and involvement with adaptation to "reality," its assimilation and accommodation as equilibrating functions. This mode can be suspended voluntarily, as in imagination, creativity, or play, or involuntarily, as in sleep. The essential difference in their models, however, resides in Piaget's rejection of Freud's clear line of demarcation between conscious symbolism and unconscious symbolism, since, for Piaget all symbols are unconscious from one angle and conscious from another (p. 171). Piaget asserts that "no such separation" exists, since "symbolic thought forms a single whole" (1962, p. 170).

"Further," he cautions, "lest we lose ourselves in a mythology of the unconscious," what he delineates here is true of all thought, "rational as well as symbolic," and while the result of mental work is conscious, its mechanism remains hidden. "The unconscious is not a separate region of the mind since in every psychic process there is continual and continuous coming and going from the unconscious to consciousness" (p. 172); while accommodation is generally conscious because it calls forth internal or external obstacles, assimilation is usually unconscious. "The unconscious is everywhere and there is an intellectual as well as an affective unconscious . . . the difference between consciousness and unconsciousness is only a matter of gradation or degree of reflection" (p. 172). That said, he clarifies that symbols can never be categorically classified as either primary or secondary, because every symbol can be both; it may have meanings which are readily understood by the subject, or other more remote meanings, in exactly the same way that a concept may subsume a set of implications of which the subject is unaware—again, it is a question of degree not region.

Similarities between Werner's and Piaget's views are, I think, apparent; both consider the totality of mind–body integrity and continuity in development and find the origins of symbolization in the very structure of thought. The differences are subtle but significant; for Piaget the advent of the semiotic function, like that of the schema of the permanent object, marks the capacity for representation and evocative memory, the cognitive advance which makes all subsequent mental operations possible and therefore the hallmark of intelligence. For Werner and Kaplan symbolization is an intentional act, born out of relational–contextual embeddedness in which the emergence of a basic directiveness toward knowing produces the most "significant of man's instrumentalities," the symbol. Following the general orthogenetic principle, its development colors not only cognition, but the entire realm of understanding, communication, and expressivity. Symbolizing is not merely a stage-appropriate acquisition which enables the particular relationship between symbol and its referent to come about, but a continuous process which has entered into the very construction of the cognitive object in an indissoluble fusion of form and meaning out of which language and other expressive mediums flower. Thus while for both Piaget and Werner symbolization remains the constitutive vehicle of thought, each molds explanations of its central function in consonance with the basic principles of his theory.

In a scholarly and genuinely interdisciplinary vein, the 1971 fall issue of *American Imago* reported the proceedings of a colloquium on "The Symbolic Process." On December 11, 1969, under the chairmanship of Victor Rosen and sponsored by the American Psychoanalytic Association, six eminent representatives of various disciplines gathered for an informal discussion with twelve psychoanalysts. Among these were such illustrious names as Peterfreund, Loewald, Lidz, Knapp, Stern, Rosen, and Shapiro. With minimal preparation, other than the predistribution of two psychoanalytic papers concerning symbolization by Drs. Rosen (1969) and Knapp (1969), the group, which included professors of linguistics, developmental and general psychology, philosophy and semantics, English, and art history, yielded a lively interchange of specialized ideas of which Theodore Shapiro's eloquent summary reveals the essential flavor.

With a cautionary, "Scholarship proceeds by its own rules, and scholars are given to appealing to their own authorities" (p. 196), and indicating quite a sweeping interdisciplinary grasp of the whole topic itself, Shapiro's introduction closed with a conciliatory remark regarding the spirit in which the colloquium was convened: "Neither xenophobia nor reductionism seem to dictate the current scientific scene. We hope differences will not be glossed over, but sharpened for the sake of clarity" (p. 200). Wise words, perhaps premonitory of the unanimous realization for a need for greater cross-fertilization among disciplines. This opinion was voiced by Sachs and countered by a less optimistic Katz, who noted that "each member of a discipline works in a highly refined and idealized way," it is "not so certain that the interdisciplinary application is relevant as surmised" (p. 214).

Shapiro presented a thoroughly psychoanalytic overture, which skillfully wove theoretical and clinical tenets into propositions which satisfy all criteria for a summative metapsychological conceptualization of symbol formation. Comprehensively, yet remarkably succinctly, he reviewed the focal points along the course of the development of the theory in which questions regarding the formation or manifestations of symbolic processes arise; that is, linkage of ideas to affects, making the unconscious conscious, repression, manifest and latent dream content, symbols as compromise formation, primary and secondary process, and the role of the synthetic function of the ego. Relating this to principles central to the method, he wrote, "I hold as axiomatic the notion that the psychoanalyst's beliefs concerning symbol formation are closely connected with the psychoanalytic method" (p. 196). Indeed, if it is the analyst's ultimate insistence upon interpretation which most distinguishes psychoanalysis from other therapeutic modes, above all else, psychoanalysis remains a discipline concerned with the integrative analysis of symbolic manifestations and processes.

In their daily work, analysts observe multiple symbolic substitutes for a single referent, which, Shapiro writes, "suggests a polyphony of overtones" (p. 199). It is generally believed, however, that ontogenetically later elaborations are more abstract than their antecedent concrete forms, those referring to bodily experiences preceding experiences in the environment. Psychoanalysis, he continues, is eager to integrate findings from developmental psychology regarding the hierarchical layering of mental structures and dynamic structuralization (Werner and Kaplan, 1963) as these corroborate a psychoanalytic genetic hypothesis concerning the gradual ascendence of secondary process over primary process thinking and a maturational sway leading toward ego-articulated choices over mere reactions to impingements. Moreover, Shapiro notes, while psychoanalysts have been slow to recognize the need to expand the restricted psychoanalytic concept of symbols (Jones, 1916), the linguists' definition of the symbol as something which has been taken to represent something else, should enable us to view language itself as a medium for psychoanalytic scrutiny.

The vivid description of the proceedings of such an interdisciplinary forum brings to mind occurrences at the marketplace; each vendor sells specialized goods, and if you buy from all of them, you can make a fine soup. The unfolding of this multidisciplinary conference, which yielded many interesting but disjointed points, divided itself into several trajectories of discussion; these were the developmental, the linguistic, the philosophical and the literary, with the psychoanalysts interjecting statements primarily intended to reconcile or unify various threads. While each group tended to uphold its own methodological preference, there was some overlap in the discussants' common interest in cross-cultural similarities with regard to the building of hierarchical mental structures, the development of object constancy, and problems of meaning and language. With regard to symbolization, some interesting ideas were put forward addressing its ontogenesis, functions, forms, and medium, but without a clear, unifying definition stated at the outset, the discussion highlighted just how many meanings the "symbol" has, and how differently the word can be used, rather than yielding any new substantive conclusions about it.

Marcus, a professor of English literature, emphasized that more often than not, symbol and symbolization are intended to convey the "pictorial." He stated that "Symbolization is most central to the construction of the concrete, actual and conventional cognition of the physical and social environment" in early childhood, and is "least important, perhaps even disruptive, to formal, logical reasoning from adolescence on" (p. 206), a view which, I believe, betrays a fundamental misconception about the function of the symbolic process itself. This notwithstanding, and in recognition of the aim of artistic creation, Marcus went on to say that "to be understood, a statue must be danced" (p. 208). While each discussant brought erudition and qualified ideas pertaining to their specialty, in my opinion the absence of a consensual definition for the meaning of the title produced an atmosphere of intellectual synesthesia which precluded advancement of any clear new course. Despite this, as Shapiro pointed out, all the discussants realized the "virtue in carrying out a specific area of inquiry so that the limited truths necessary to further investigation could be described or discovered" (p. 214).

With reference to limited truths, it is worth noting that the two predistributed yet unmentioned papers by Rosen (1969) and Knapp (1969) may be regarded as seminal contributions to aspects of the topic, bearing directly on psychoanalysis and containing a wealth of informed new ideas welding "unlimited truths" to existent ideas. In focusing on sign phenomena, Rosen offers one of the most lucid studies of the differentiation between signs, signals, and symbols, their respective places in primary and secondary process functioning, and their relationship to the understanding of the interpretation of unconscious meanings in clinical psychoanalysis. While Knapp, focusing on inner images as phenomenological substrata, presents a most eloquent, epistemologically sound, and comprehensive integration of the concept of "representation" as symbolic constituent of the construction and organization of meaning.

In "Sign Phenomena and Their Relationship to Unconscious Meaning" (1969) within a broader discussion of meaning, Rosen considers what psychoanalysts intend when they speak of latent or unconscious meaning, and does so with the help of information from an overlapping discipline, that of semiotics.

According to semioticians, signals, signs, and symbols form a continuum, since a signal may function as a symbol and vice versa, depending upon the context; but for psychologists determining their differences is of paramount importance. With signification, or the experience of meaning, as his starting point Rosen goes on to unfold a detailed examination of their differences, the rules, and logic of semantics and syntax, and the problem of consciousness, or becoming conscious as in the psychoanalytic situation.

For Rosen, signal phenomena are identified by a "close temporal or spatial contiguity between the signal and the event that is symbolized" (p. 199). Signals give rise to an expectation, they may be idiosyncratic, systematized, or random and belong to any sensory modality; the sign, on the other hand, is identified by its iconic relationship to what it signifies, in a corresponding similarity of some feature of the sign and its signification (p.

199). The important difference between these and the symbol is that the "relationship between the symbol and its referent in the thing symbolized is arbitrary and assigned by convention" (p. 199)—Rosen likens this to the algebraic equation let A refer to B. Thus the referent of a symbol can be quite abstract, as are phonetic and notational symbols, and words need have no evident contiguous or iconic relationship to the objects of their denotation.

Most symbols, in serving the communication of thought, move toward explicitness and away from ambiguity. Notational and verbal symbols are governed by combinatorial rules which organize infinite possible permutations—in language this is syntax. In contrast to signs and signals, symbols result in an "economy of energy expenditure," both in communication and representation. Rosen details the correspondence between signal and sign phenomena in the structure of language and connects linguistic forms to such characteristic attributes of primary process thought as condensation, displacement, and plastic representation. Two important forms of metaphor, metonymy and simile, are to be found in the relationship of contiguity (and the mechanism of *pars pro toto*) between signal and signalized, and that of similarity between sign and what is signified, respectively—their immediacy precludes concept formation. "A metonymy, like a signal, is synchronous with what it stands for. In simile as well the mental representations to be compared are simultaneous" (p. 201) and underscoring his central thesis, Rosen points out, these are characteristics of the primary process in both functional and energic terms, while conversely "specificity, discreteness, abstract representation . . . and delay of stimulus response" (p. 201) (Freud's concept of bound energy) characterize secondary process functioning and its use of symbols. The amulet, for instance, a metonymy, is a "stand-in" for a powerful guardian just as the totem is an iconic representation—thus, Rosen finds the roots of these forms in manifestations of cultural totems and taboos.

Rosen's central thesis is that what is referred to as the primary process is essentially a signalizing and signifying activity, while what characterizes the secondary process is its predominant use of symbols. The analytic process endeavors to decipher

unconscious meaning by "reducing personal events described
in secondary-process symbols, to signal and sign events; and
by interpreting idiosyncratic signal and sign events in terms
of conventional language symbols" (p. 200)—a reciprocal and
integrative translation into referential language of conscious
information, disconnected from its unconscious referents, and
conversely, of unconscious experiences unarticulated in conscious, consensual communication.

The last section of Rosen's paper is devoted to a reexamination of examples of neurotic symptoms in Freud's 1901 "The
Psychopathology of Everyday Life," from a semiotic perspective.
After a brief overview of developmental aspects, Rosen concludes with an interesting discussion of the advent of language
as symbolic communicational system along a continuum of sign
phenomena, and describes how the analytic process consists of
interpersonal decoding and transforming of idiosyncratic childhood theories, fantasies, and experiences, into conventional
word symbols. "It is my opinion that finding the meaning of a
parapraxis is the paradigm of the process by which we arrive at
most interpretations in the analytic process" (p. 204). Thus,
through free association we are able to follow a series of "seemingly nonsensically connected similes and contiguities to the
point where the autonomous process of symbol evocation went
astray" (p. 205). He likens the whole process to tracing an electric circuit to the causative break in the line. In viewing a parapraxis itself as a sign, he reasons the motives illuminating its
meaning may be "read" by solving the "rebus" of metonyms
and similes created by substitutions and displacements brought
about by free association, "we call this solution of the rebus an
'interpretation' " (p. 205).

In placing sign phenomena and symbolic systems at the
heart of the concepts of meaning, its experience and understanding, Rosen's paper offers a notable theoretical contribution to numerous facets of metapsychology while providing
laudable integration of semiotics with psychoanalytic understanding of unconscious phenomena.

Knapp's (1969) paper, "Image, Symbol and Person," on a
par with Rosen's in its innovative, integrative thrust, addresses

the "shadow counterpart" to manifest systems of communication, what he calls the "cardinal vehicle" of our inner language and its silent, simultaneous companion, "the inner image." Quiet, persistent, varying widely in duration and quality, representations or images may substantiate themselves in multiple expressive ways; and Knapp refers to art forms, emotional outbursts, pantomime, "As mental contents [however] they are more often illustrative and unclear. They may evoke a marked response, or they may lurk in the background, dim and almost unnoticed" (p. 392).

Essentially his paper discusses the centrality of the created image as a symbolic representation born out of the confluence of imagined and remembered constructions and their emotive valence, as these acquire meaning and are "assembled in ways which gain still wider meaning"—in short "images become organized symbolically" (p. 393).

Knapp carefully illustrates the difference between discursive (linguistic) and nondiscursive symbolism (Langer, 1942), emphasizing the gradual evolution of symbolic phenomena, whereby "explicit verbal thought" in adults evolves out of its presentational symbolic background; "as a mode of mental activity presentational symbolism precedes discursive thought ontogenetically and phylogenetically" (p. 394). Indeed, "imageless thought" represents the gradual fading of emotive–pictorial vividness associated with the intensity of earlier forms of mentation, or of an unconscious, nondiscursive "stream . . . saturated with qualities of drive and emotion" (p. 395). This "bleached out" thought is typical of cognitive articulation at highly abstract levels in which symbolic referents are so removed as to have dropped out of awareness completely, although nondiscursive symbolic activities always remain in the background of cognitive operations. The nondiscursive symbol, notes Knapp, is the vehicle of global, emotionally tinged, allusive symbolic processes which govern our personal mythologies and thus condition so much of our mental life.

In referring to the paradoxical relationship of image to emotion, Knapp reminds us that originally these are closely fused together. Similarly, when unconscious fantasies are fully retrieved they carry with them recovery of their full affective

charge. He proposes a neurophysiological explanation for the
psychological aspects of this kind of symbolic activity and further
elaborates on the way "aggregate images" formed out of multiple, continued exposures, produce "general classes" of fantasy
and imagery. These become woven into symbolic representations; "Somehow we make elemental abstractions of imagery
and gain general knowledge, which is still not verbal knowledge" (p. 397).

Turning now to the phenomenology of the self, the central
areas of self–other fantasies and identity, Knapp addresses fundamental problems the field has encountered in striving to
adopt a language which is not a mixture of reified structures,
personified agencies, or energic metaphors, within which to
articulate theoretical and clinical concepts and events pertaining to the subject: "Appropriate methods can be found only
after understanding the non-categorical, connotative symbolic
character of inner regulatory fantasy constellations" (p. 398).
Knapp then outlines a series of guiding principles which system-
atize our understanding of the way systems of representation
operate. The central thread in these appears to be an essential
fluidity, in the interplay of images and fantasies, the reciprocal
and continuous linkage between fantasy and memory, inner
image and outer person, and how all of this bears its stamp
on our defenses and attitudes toward the self and "composite
self images."

Stressing the relevance of images and symbols fusing into
constellations, like Rosen, Knapp argues that difficulties in com-
prehending human psychological organization stem in large
part from attempts to express nondiscursive facets of mental
experience in discursive language. With regard to self–other
fantasies, Knapp emphasizes that it is important to consider all
levels and aspects of representations not as separate elements,
but as part of a total organization in which the deepest and the
highest planes are simultaneously present. "Elucidation of these
fluid, connotative presentational symbolic processes," he writes,
"is essential to the understanding of therapeutic change," as
nondiscursive symbolic imagery "leads from fleeting private experience to enduring social structures" (p. 405).

In presenting inner images as phenomenological data, connecting these to nondiscursive symbolic thought processes, Knapp succeeds in bringing about a conceptual synthesis of fantasy and identity within an interpersonal milieu in addition to expanding a theoretical framework inclusive of symbolic processes and phenomena. This notwithstanding, as he himself remarks, "The task of fully elucidating the organization of inner, non-discursive mentation is largely ahead" (p. 395).

From the outset, in reporting the proceedings of a section of the Kris Study Group of the New York Psychoanalytic Institute, Donadeo (1974) identified the central importance of "Symbolism," the topic which for seven monthly meetings drew some of the most eminent members of the Institute to discussions led by Charles Brenner. Emphasizing the scant attention and unsystematic treatment of the topic in the literature, Donadeo began by expressing the need to establish a terminological base, since meanings springing from deep roots in our evolution for the words *symbol* and *symbolism,* have undergone a "wide variety of usages in prophecy, the wielding of power, in language, religion, magic, play and the arts" (p. 77). The definition he cited is that of common usage, offered by Webster (1947), despite the fact that this group's study leans heavily on Jones' 1916 paper, in which symbolism, in the psychoanalytic sense, has a very specific, circumscribed meaning.

The group's efforts represented an attempt to find answers regarding the phenomenon of symbolism in man, through an interdisciplinary synthesis of biological, developmental, and metapsychological approaches. To this end, and in a genuinely psychoanalytic way, the group gave ongoing consideration to all of these trajectories of inquiry. Donadeo is able to render the various diverse lines of discussion and divergent viewpoints which must have emerged in the content of the meetings. In his summary, he interweaves different opinions skillfully into a readable narrative; his paper is chock-full of information which has been cited in the course of this chapter from other papers. This must have been a keen and well informed group.

Nevertheless, one gets the impression that while some innovative minds ventured forward and outside the mold, in the main, Jones' 1916 work, as orthodox and outdated as it may be, still provided an anchoring foundation (one would have wished for a springboard!) for theoretical understanding. Thus, if one is to take Jones' central ideal that "only what is repressed is symbolized; only what is repressed *needs* to be symbolized" (p. 116), one has effectively foreclosed any possibility of moving forward in the understanding of the function of symbols, let alone of elaborating a theoretical integration. One would rather have expected a functional concept to be at the heart of any psychoanalytic conceptualization. There were apparently some who opposed the narrow, confining view of 1916; nevertheless, the gnawing problems of how to explain "motivated forgetting," the dynamic unconscious, unconscious fantasy, and what to make of repression, remained looming questions without visible answers, beyond Freud's own.

While diligent effort was made to satisfy genetic, economic, dynamic, topographic, and structural viewpoints for a thoroughly metapsychological study of symbols, recognition of their unique and complex activity in unconscious mental life still did not yield any radical or coherent new integration within the structure of the theory. On the contrary, Donadeo reports statements which show an alarming lack of understanding of symbolization, its mechanism, its function, or its impact on mentation. One such hypothesis would see symbols as compromise formations, and include them among restitutional phenomena. "The symbolic function," he reports, "so pervasive in severely ill schizophrenics may represent this aspect of symbolism in its most demonstrable form" (1974, p. 98). Yet, as we have seen carefully elaborated in earlier papers, it is precisely the opposite which has occurred in the schizophrenic process. In view of the availability of such sophisticated and in-depth contributions as presented earlier, namely those of Kubie, Searles, Werner and Kaplan, Piaget, or even Melanie Klein and Segal, in which far greater depth and understanding is evident, one wonders how it is that this group harked back fifty years to a point in our history prior to structural theory, for its theoretical source.

Numerous other highly questionable hypotheses regarding symbolism were proposed. One such hypothesis argued that "true symbol formation coincides with the oedipal period and serves as a defense against oedipal distress" (p. 97). Another suggested that symbols are formed in regressed ego states and situations of sensory deprivation, as representations of the denied percept. In striving for a comprehensive probe into the topic, discussions covered the formation of symbols, their relation to ego development and regression, anthropology and symbolism, and the definition and characteristics of symbols. These would appear stimulating and worthy aspects of the topic in themselves, yet the content of the discussion leaves much to be desired.

For example, while the inclusion of the anthropological dimension is highly desirable (this discipline is noteworthy in crediting the capacity for symbolizing to be pivotal in the evolution of Homo sapiens), the selection of only two papers dating back to the 1940s provides little scope for progressive expansion. Moreover, an insistence on considering symbols in their most apparent pictorial expression at the expense of delving into their function, their effects, and critical place along the course of development, renders the discussion little more than an exercise in redundancy. In sifting out the content of this report, I found that reductionism tended to outweigh integration and synthesis. Furthermore, in language, style, and substance, orthodox "theorocentrism" and hypothesis-throwing outbalanced informed, constructive contributions. It is to their credit that psychoanalysts have persistently and repeatedly striven to grasp the conceptual and theoretical relevance of the symbolic function and symbolism. Yet it is equally striking how, without a comprehensive, interdisciplinary synthesis including a functional definition of the term, such discussions were repeatedly stymied.

On October 16th, 1978, Blum presided over a conference on "Symbolic Processes and Symbol Formation," a meeting designed to provide much needed clarification of the term *symbolism*, and to more rigorously differentiate between unconscious, or "psychoanalytic" symbolism, and that associated with language and linguistic terminology. To this end, participants explored the definition of symbolism in psychoanalysis and the construction, forms, and functions of different symbolic processes, such as the advent of two-word phrases in the 2-year-old (an evolutionary landmark for the author) and the development of what they consider to be advanced linguistic symbols and syntax. Implicit at the outset are a number of assumptions with which I personally cannot concur; for example, that language per se represents a more advanced form of symbolism; that rigorous differentiation between unconscious symbolism and other forms of symbolic expression is desirable or even possible; that two-word phrases, as such, represent a notable developmental landmark in symbolization; and finally, that more evolved symbolic processes are necessarily linguistic. (Such a position, one that is characteristic of the psychoanalytic literature, fails to consider the full implications of the essential feature of "symbol" or "symbolism"; notably: its functional capacity to "throw together"; to condense and abstract experience.)

In differentiating psychoanalytic symbolism from other types, Blum makes the point that psychoanalytic symbols are idiosyncratic, arising out of early, body-centered percepts connected to infantile instinctual aims, and cannot be taught or learned. This is in contrast to communicative symbolism or language, which is acquired socially in consensually shared reality, originating in auditory–visual percepts, and related to the secondary process. Psychoanalytic symbolism is a universal phenomenon related to the primary process in the unconscious, and promotes fantasy rather than reality testing. Moreover, according to Blum, psychoanalytic symbols convey disguised thoughts and affects (like symptoms) representing a compromise formation between a wish and its gratification, and are thus always formed and remain outside of awareness.

While Blum concedes that an absolute distinction between different forms of symbolism cannot be made, he presents his hypothesis that out of an original, undifferentiated symbolic–cognitive matrix, the two forms develop along parallel, yet relatively independent lines; unconscious symbolism representing a drive derivative, linguistic symbolism associated with autonomous ego functions. Blum further emphasizes the adaptive function of communicational symbols while highlighting that unconscious symbolism plays a significant role in ego development, particularly in sublimation, and serves the ego's adaptive, regressive potential in the creation of wit and literature.

He then attempts to pinpoint the exact stage in which symbol formation develops.

As I have written throughout, I fail to see how the artificial bifurcation of psychoanalytic from other types of symbolism can be legitimized in a holistic model; furthermore, in my opinion, the theoretical quandary such a split evokes fairly leaps to the eye. It is doubtful that the mind works so discontinuously as to provide separate or special kinds of mechanisms applicable to our conceptual framework, and not to others. It is even more unwholesome, I believe, to think of mental processes as divided into sectors in which the same process (symbolization) would be operating quite differently, according to its functional relevance. Thus, I fail to see how linguistic symbolism can be considered of a different kind from any other symbolism, conscious or unconscious, simply because it also serves a communicative function. This is to dismember a continuous expressive repertoire because only one facet or medium is in evidence, and represents yet another case of attempting to explain a process by its outcome.

Furthermore, Blum fails to adequately address the important distinction between a true symbol, one which has undergone the differentiating steps which qualify it as a genuine referent and not merely an equivalent, and presymbols, such as the first single-word utterances of small children, which are closer to signs or signals than symbols. In so closely adhering to a drive orientation, he fails to recognize that this distinction is a property of the development of symbolization, the function itself, and not a dynamic result. This key distinction would have highlighted the unitary, continuous, and organic developmental process of symbol formation, which not only cuts across cognitive, affective, and linguistic expressions, but encompasses conscious and unconscious, adaptive and imaginative, primary and secondary processes, and implicates all three psychic structures.

Blum then discusses the interdependence of symbolic and separation–individuation processes and associates emergent symbolic development with aspects of ego development such as perception, memory, schematization of body parts, early defenses predicated on anticipation and delay of gratification. For

Blum, as for Jones (1916), the primary characteristic of psycho-analytic symbolism lies in the severance of links between signi-fier and signified. Presumably, the repressed or unconscious nature of this connection is thought to prove that the symbol is invoked to "disguise" an "illicit" connection—a theory to which I do not subscribe. Nevertheless, on the basis of observa-tion and reconstruction, Blum hypothesizes that the earliest ap-pearance of unconscious symbolism precedes the appearances of the semantic "no" (15 months) and follows the establish-ment of the transitional object (approximately 18 months).

As reported by Vogel, the discussants contributed various interesting points: Weil highlighting mother and child interac-tions, preverbal gestures, and naming as antecedents to linguis-tic symbol formation; Scharfman and Edelheit caution lest the distinction between psychoanalytic and linguistic or other sym-bolism be overdrawn, since unconscious signified and signifier are bound to one another in ways usually attributed to second-ary process functioning and vice versa, as when words become reimbued with primary process. Further, they suggest there might be some correlation between early perceptual image memories, appearing in dreams and hallucinations, in relation to psychoanalytic symbols, and later more complex memories organized according to the secondary process. In view of this fluidity, Scharfman contended that sharp distinctions should be tempered, while Edelheit proposed a better term to designate the symbolism of the unconscious to be Lilli Peller's term, *pri-mordial symbolism* (Panel, 1978, p. 471).

In contrast to the two aforementioned collective efforts, Roland's (1972) and Deri's (1978, 1981, 1984) work, emphasiz-ing the role of symbolization in artistic expression and creativity, add a considerable dimension to our literature on the topic. Deri's encompassing grasp of the significance of the role of the symbolic function in clinical psychoanalysis, acting out (1981), and developmentally, in the formation of the transitional object (1978), directs her toward particular focus on the preconscious as a way station between disorganized, unconscious impulsivity and ordered, symbolic creativity. Roland, on the other hand, focuses on the nature of imagery, its relationship to primary process and metaphoric thought, and its place in both the clinical and creative processes. Both authors offer in-depth and well thought out revisionary critiques with regard to energic and topographic concepts (Deri) and the necessity for upgrading our notion of an "inferior" primary process and the supremacy of language (Roland) within the context of symbolization. Moreover, both present works which comprise broad coverage of pertinent literature from diverse disciplines as well as a thorough knowledge of the psychoanalytic, and are therefore able to make judicious critical points as well as relevant, encompassing integrations.

Roland's (1972) "Imagery and Symbolic Expression in Dreams and Art" starts out by questioning the traditional psychoanalytic characterization of the primary process as a regressive or more primitive form of "metaphorical thought" compared to its abstract, conceptual counterpart, the secondary process. Indeed, he challenges the basic assumption that metaphorical thinking, or symbolic expression, is in any way inferior or less evolved than abstract thought, and casts doubt on the validity of the habitual developmental delineation of thought as moving from metaphorical to conceptual. Citing the historical psychoanalytic view of symbolization as participating in the primary process and therefore serving the pleasure principle, he states that from the vantage point of modern linguistics and developmental psychology, no evidence can be found to corroborate this view. On the contrary, he believes that, "the adult ability to think in metaphors is a much richer, fuller development of a basic integrative capacity of the ego that is earlier manifest in an incipient form in childhood" (1972, p. 532)—a view compelling in its integrative linearity and quite consonant with a holistic, developmental perspective. Moreover, in attributing continuity to the ego's development across topographical boundaries, he approaches the view presented in this work.

Following Noy (1969) in preferring to regard the functional significance of primary process modes as "integrating new experiences" and "giving expression to the self" (p. 532), Roland nevertheless differs from Noy in concluding that there exists a hierarchical organization of direct and indirect expression, an apparent order in the mechanisms of the primary process itself: "from the disguised expression of wishes to a multifaceted symbolic expression of diverse aspects in the latent content as incipient paradoxes" (1972, p. 534), he writes with reference to dreams. Further, he believes that while metaphorical thinking offers rich expression for the psyche, paradox and poetic metaphors need to be substantiated and completed in the integrative process of interpretation within the analytic situation. For Roland, mechanisms of the primary process serve a dual function: that of disguisement and distortion when related to wish-fulfillment, and to give expression to internalizations and childhood memories as these issue from and implicate all psychic structures. "Thus, the creative process in art is present in dreams in only an incipient stage and needs the later creative work of analysand and analyst with associations and interpretations to do necessary integrations" (1972, p. 536).

Deri's (1978, 1981, 1984) work, while consistently anchored in the centrality of the function of symbolization, focuses primarily on the "creative principle," an aspect of human potential she considers to have received scant systematic treatment in the psychoanalytic literature. To this end, and with considerable appreciation and theoretical concordance, she discusses and elaborates upon Winnicott's ideas regarding attunement in the primary dyad, the significance of illusion, and the construction of transitional phenomena, ideas with which she is closely aligned. "For Winnicott creativity was not the production of art objects, but a 'coloring of the whole attitude of external reality' " ([1971, p. 65], cited in Deri [1978, p. 47]), and underscores that these views imply important new areas for psychoanalysis, "as well as a conception of mental health truly different from that of Freud" (p. 47).

I have some reservations regarding her adoption of what seem to me to be misapplied, moralistic terms when discussing the symbolizing process (I fail to see how this mental function can be termed either good or bad) but perhaps this is merely a stylistic bent, a use of language which frequently conceals quite profound insights behind simplistic terms. Despite a lingering tendency toward reification, continued adherence to energic and topographic notions, and a somewhat idealized view of the "role of the preconscious" in mediating symbolization and creative activity (i.e., the preconscious as a "mental territory where form-creating processes take place" [1978, p. 59]), Deri addresses in earnest the concept of symbolization in its basic, generic sense after the great philosophers Whitehead (1927), Langer (1942), and Cassirer (1944), who had addressed it before her.

Deri is the only psychoanalytic author who devotes an entire book to the study of symbolization in relation to creativity, and while she fails to integrate symbolization theoretically—her discussions tending toward clinical and humanistic concerns—she is unique in having pointed the way. Moreover, whereas adherence to earlier metapsychological constructs constrains the full development of the implications of many of her salient points, her incorporation of Gestalt concepts and emphasis on the synthetic function of the ego as part of the general "organizing" and "ordering" process resulting from the symbolic function are relevant precursors to such a revisionary aim.

Her 1984 work, *Symbolization and Creativity*, includes and develops many ideas first presented in numerous earlier papers. Most essentially here she elaborates on the multiple ways symbolization can derail, and fits these "desymbolizing" and "missymbolizing" deviations into preexisting psychoanalytic conceptualizations and explanations for symptom formation and various forms of psychopathology. Her assumption is that psychic structuralization takes place through the symbolizational function as "a kind of mapping," or "isomorphic matching," wherein "a more amorphous content finds abbreviated expression in an isomorphically matching but more articulate structure" (1984, p. 141), the latter being a symbol proper, or a "true" symbol for the former. The creation of perceptual order as well as psychic organization is presumed to occur through a series of such matchings, a process she refers to as centrifugal or internal symbolization. In this way, drives and drive-derivative expressions are given coherent shape and, together with the "inside registration" of the outer world, represent "the cycle of the creative process" (1984, p. 130) that is part of human functioning.

In all her work, Deri offers a lively interplay of conceptual, theoretical, and clinical material, often recounting the latter with warmth and a keen understanding of the pivotal part played by symbolization and its multiple impairments in her patients' various displays. Throughout, she endeavors to weave threads that interlace symbolization into existing psychoanalytic views so that she does not neglect to highlight relevant clinical aspects of the function and use of language in the analytic situation, its inverse relationship to acting out, its "binding" or "symbolized" results, and how these affect behavior within the psychoanalytic process of cure. Most centrally for her the symbol is "a guide toward the missing half that will complete a Gestalt" (1984, p. 51). In this sense, the human search for union is manifest not only through physical closeness, but also through the myriad forms of symbolic expressiveness available to man through the arts, religion, and the world of ideas. Her work is rich and replete with aspects of indisputable truths regarding the symbolic function; yet, from a psychoanalytic perspective and particularly in view of this, one would have wished for a stab at theoretical reorientation. As it stands, her work is a valuable way station toward such a goal.

Suffice it to say, we have come a long way conceptually from the early psychoanalytic view of the symbol as a pictorial entity of archaic or primitive origin, functioning in the service of disguise. The term is now used with functional implications and has been integrated with art and creativity as well as language in development and in the psychoanalytic process.

In a seminal paper on "The Concept of Transformation in Psychoanalysis," Freedman (1985) presents empirically derived findings from his research program on the communicative process in psychoanalysis conducted at Downstate Medical Center, Brooklyn, New York. A special aspect of this paper is that it was partly inspired by research observations, and not the other way around: "Empirical research is often used to confirm or qualify a clinical hypothesis. Here, the research served as a guide for conceptualization, as well as an organizer of clinical material" (p. 320). Not only does this felicitous marriage confirm the efficacy of the original dual psychoanalytic charge in the confluence of therapy, theory, and research method, but the derivation of hypotheses *out* of research is completely consonant with

the new scientific principles of the emergent paradigm proposed in chapter 1 as the appropriate epistemological bed for
psychoanalytic investigation.

The superordinate theme of Freedman's paper addresses
what he describes as having become for him "the hard rock . . .
the central issue deemed essential for understanding human
nature" (p. 317), that of transformation: and his particular focus of study, "the organization of kinesic/linguistic event sequences during the associative process [which give rise to]
hypotheses concerning factors that might facilitate or interfere
with the transformational process" (p. 320).

Freedman first focuses on the process by which transitions
from one stage of mental organization move to the next. Viewed
as the essential process of structure building, this shift is brought
about by a dialectic conflict engendered in the clinical dyad
which leads to reorganization at a higher level: "change comes
through the pathway of thesis, antithesis and synthesis. . . . ,"
and, Freedman suggests, "all human development undergoes
this three-part process" (p. 319). These are ideas that originated
in Hegel and Marx, and have more recently been advanced
by Ricoeur (1970) with regard to psychoanalysis. Invoking the
notion of the centrality of the "disjunctive experience" he
claims that shifts "can only take place after a state of disequilibrium has unleashed dynamic forces" (p. 323).

Freedman's more general thesis concerns a frame of reference for the examination of psychic structures in which transformational activity can be identified as occurring in three spheres.
The first involves the shift from discharge to symbolic equation,
illustrated typically by "encapsulated discharge phenomena . . . seen in patients suffering from psychosomatic disorders
where one can speak of visceral discharge" (p. 320); the second,
from symbolic equation to the formation of symbols (p. 320)
the essence of which, for Freedman, lies in "the finding of the
familiar in the unfamiliar" (p. 325); and the third, the shift
from symbol to sublimated symbolization (p. 320) by which he
intends abstract symbolic constructions in which the original
drives are no longer readily discernible.

I find I am in disagreement with Freedman's understanding
of what the essence of symbol formation is, since I view symbolization as an abstractive process, less a subjective "finding" than

a subjective "generating" of a new significant. Also, the term *sublimated symbolization,* referring both to a mental product and a process functioning "in the effort to transcend the original object" (p. 330), is confusing, in my opinion, if one understands symbolization as the essential activity of mind. Traditionally, the term *sublimation* refers to the transformation of drive energy with respect to its aim. We speak of the goals and means for attaining these as being sublimated, but not the process of symbolization itself, which represents a general principle of mind inhering in our earliest physiologically involved manifestations to the highest realms of abstraction and comprehension. While the notion of transcendence, I believe, is very relevant to sublimation per se, I find little correspondence here with the basic linearity of the representational process depicted in Freedman's earlier spheres. With regard to sublimation, it seems to me Freedman is operating in a drive framework. He is therefore alluding to a transformation of *energy,* while mine is a model of transformational *process,* of structural organizations.

In the model proposed in chapter 4, the higher stages of symbolization are viewed as functionally isomorphic in their abstractive tendency, while structurally more evolved. There is less of an emphasis on notions of discharge, drive or otherwise, as causative than on levels of organization and their modes of expression. Nevertheless, despite terminological differences and a slight conceptual discrepancy, particularly with respect to the notion of "sublimated symbolization" which conjures energic connotations, there is striking concordance in our central concerns with "levels of meaning organization that undergo alteration and move increasingly toward higher levels of symbolization" (Freedman, 1985, p. 317).

In the latter part of his paper Freedman also presents the results of a series of studies (with Brucci) which, in observing body movements and language behavior during communicative discourse in psychoanalytic psychotherapy, disclose an aspect of transformation which can be detected in fleeting units. The phenomenon, an "associative organizer," has been termed the "transformational unit," and is triphasic and structured around "nonfluency" or a pause. The three phases are prerepresentational, a symbol-generating and symbol-deployment phase.

"Thus, what we witness in this sequence of events is the rapid progression by which actions are transformed into images, images are transformed into symbolized thought, and symbolized thought gives rise to more elaborate, higher order associations" (p. 333).

Conceptual correspondence between this empirically observed microsequence, my own overall ontogenetic design, and postulations that account for broad phases of advance in psychoanalytic psychotherapy, is striking. Moreover such empirical research provides solid grounding regarding the implications for applying my developmental paradigm as a conceptual base for clinical work.

It is perhaps due to the advantage inherent in generational advance that we, buttressed by new insights, better equipped, may reflect upon the great thinkers who preceded us and attempt a synthesis of their ideas. Fortified by accrued scholarship, a retrospective critique seems both simple and unfair. And while each in his own way, through the prisms of his field, will have seen and drawn conclusions and laid these down according to his disciplinary bent, each will also have contributed to the cumulative array of knowledge so as to pave a path for those that follow. To all, in some way, we are indebted, to some in particular whose vision overstepped the prevailing circumscribed view and, with a leap of imagination, created new vistas of enquiry.

Langer, embedded in the philosopher's world, despite her sweeping novelty, could not have been so intimately familiar with the most detailed propositions of Freud or Piaget. Nor has it been common for important, focused thinkers to produce studies in which a multidisciplinary or multifaceted view has been sought out and adopted. Rather, specialization has imposed a constriction of our vision, departmentalizing more and more what actually needs to be gathered into larger pictures. Nowhere has the inherent weakness in the overzealous use of traditional empiricism been more evident than in psychoanalysis, a treatment mode and discipline of such dimension and scope as to demand a multidisciplinary perspective to encompass its many ramifications. In the words of Adams (1968), even though "most of us remain excessively timid, reluctant to tackle the grand problems of comparison, generalization and synthesis . . ." (p. 373), the advantage of multiple viewpoints is that out of these emerge different and then distilled propositions which merge into new conceptual form. The study of symbolization, its function, and central redefining place in our theory is just such a concept.

Humankind's symbolizing capacity and the symbol itself have been widely discussed from different aspects of inquiry, multiple disciplines as well as in specialized works relevant to theoretical integration of psychoanalytic conceptualizations which are found to converge at superordinate levels. These universals, the substratal myths and images, the magical idols and beliefs, rituals and dreams, the narrated and pictorial substructures that occur across cultures and across time and recur in each individual, were the material of symbolic expression first studied by those interested in symbolism. It was out of the study of early childhood, specifically of the ebullient first two years, that attention turned to the symbolizing capacity in the uniquely human gain resulting from the development of its function. The capacity to "represent"—to construct and hold in the mind something which stands for something else, is the beginning of referencing and hence of articulatable experience, a capacity which will enable the flowering of everything from language to symphonies.

Despite an attempt at thoroughness in my perusal of the pertinent literature there are inevitable omissions, for example, in the important work of Whitehead (1927) and Levi-Strauss (1958a,b, 1983) and particularly in the scant coverage of the great work on the topic by Cassirer, *The Philosophy of Symbolic Forms* (1953–1957).

In the aforementioned works, treatments of the topic have ranged from anthropological interpretation of the earliest manifestations of our time-factored, storied pictographs to the quintessential abstractive mechanism forming the origin of our capacity to articulate ideas. The symbol has been perceived as an entity, with fixed correspondences of significance, the product of regressive and repressive forces serving drives and emotions; we have read of the conditions for its formation, its

functions, distortions, deviations, and dissolution. Symbolization has been viewed from historical, developmental, pathological, curative, artistic, and autistic perspectives, and its
mechanisms have been traced in the finest, most sophisticated
detail; hypotheses advanced as late as the 1970s indicate that it is
still understood only in its most superficial, pictorialized aspects.
Symbolization has been considered from all structural, topographical, and dynamic perspectives in relation to the primary
and secondary processes and other facets of mentation. It has
been perceived as an image, a semiotic form, an ego function,
a process, an interpersonal bridge anchoring the sense of self
and of the other in reality, a vehicle of thought and communication, of meaning and knowledge; and, most essentially, as that
quality of mind which enables man to realize his search for
understanding things of the world, himself, and others.

It turns out there is no separation between symbols and
knowing, inasmuch as the symbolizational function presupposes
an underlying intrinsic organismic mechanism which gives rise
to representational form. Knowledge, always tied to subjective
meaning, prior to being shaped into any expressive modality,
is there in the essential rudiments of our organic symboling
capacity and only gradually molds itself into communicational
symbolic vehicles such as language, which can be shared with
others. If mind is not motivated by instinctual pressure, we are
induced to understand as mental that transformational process
whereby experience, perception, event, become lodged internally and reconstructed within. This is a process whereby what
was once in the senses is lost to them and gained by the mind;
a process predicated on some interpersonal separateness since
it is in the void left by absence that the symbol is erected. It is
in "reflecting upon" that the symbol is summoned. Mind is
now understood as transformer of knowledge, as concept
maker, whose versatility enables expression in a multitude of
expressive mediums. Its vehicles, modalities, and constituents
of articulation all have symbolic qualities, but it is the symbolizational function itself as the abstractive, concept-creating medium of knowledge which gives shape to what we know, how we
view it, and what it means to us. This is what I mean when I
say that the concept is there without being tied to any specific

modality, and why its expression may take discursive or nondiscursive form, and why a single dream image will contain multiple meanings derived from multiple sources and different stages of development.

Symbolic manifestations are not difficult to understand because they are disguised, but because they are condensed, subsuming in a single image (or word) myriad memories, impressions, feelings, and ideas which form the meaning of a concept. The abstractive process in symbolization produces concepts and classes of concepts which may substantiate in any number of expressive forms. This is no more "primitive" than hypothetical–deductive abstractive mentation; in fact, it follows the exact same principles, only in dreams and artistic expression the symbolic vehicles are idiosyncratic and free whereas in logical–abstractive operations, the symbols are bound by convention, logic and social constraints.

It would follow from this that symbolization, intertwined with but not the same as cognition, and mirroring the morphological principles of all organic growth, will have a corresponding developmental line, influencing the formal structuralization of mind at different stages and in different ways. This development is not so much linear as multivectored and multivaried and quite individual since symbolization is an active construction dependent upon the subject's full participation. While there has been some discussion in psychoanalytic circles ascribing the central role of change to forms of linguistic abstraction, the actual mechanism or pivotal function of symbolization itself has not been developed into a comprehensive theoretical framework based on a schematic developmental model integrating multiple facets of contemporary psychoanalytic thinking. This would seem to be at the very heart of any psychoanalytic revisionary endeavor. Despite the many voices calling for such an organizing proposition, none has appeared. In order to posit a possible reason for this, a slight digression will be necessary in order to recapitulate the ways in which Freud apprehended these concerns. This may also explain the long-standing theoretical stagnation of psychoanalysis, since in dismantling the scaffolding of Freud's edifice, we risk collapsing a structure which was not built on foundations designed to stand for so long.

In 1917 Freud remarked, "What characterizes psychoanalysis as a science is not the material which it handles, but the technique with which it works. It can be applied to the history of civilization, to the science of religion, and to mythology, no less than to the theory of the neuroses, without doing violence to its essential nature" (1917a, p. 389). The essential nature of the technique with which it works is linguistic—the verbalization of unconscious and other symbolic expressions within an interpersonal milieu; putting various nondiscursive symbolic presentations into discursive form. While this transformation of symbolic material has little or no correspondence with shifts in cathectic charges of energic forces, this is how it has been explained thus far, first within a topographical framework and then in structural terms, as subsumed in Freud's famous dictum, "Where id was, there ego shall be."

Were it only in the notion that interpretations are catalytic in joining the unconscious to consciousness and are thus integrative, and that the cure in psychoanalysis consists in talking, we would require some fortuitous explanation concerning the intermingling concerns of language and consciousness, their correspondence, and how they reveal themselves in mental stability. There is now even plausible substratal neurophysiological evidence for this. Yet Freud could not incorporate a proposition for a psychoanalytic theory of language because the epistemology of his day did not provide an avenue for its formulation, and all the plethora of divergent theoretical outgrowths today have still not approached solving the most recalcitrant riddle Freud tackled with regard to what is curative, what this transformational process of mind is about.

Freud struggled to explain the transformation that occurs through talking and, once having erected a *provisional* "intellectual scaffolding," settled on a "working hypothesis" utilizing the notion of "a quota of affect or sum of excitation—which possesses all the characteristics of a quantity (though we have no means of measuring it), which is capable of increase, diminution, displacement and discharge, and which is spread over the memory-traces of ideas somewhat as an electric charge is spread over the surface of a body" (1894, p. 60). This he deemed, "provisionally justified by its utility in co-ordinating and explaining a great variety of psychical states" (1894, p. 61). Once having envisioned a topographical model of mind in which were organized primary and secondary processes of thought, he addressed the issue of mental representations as these shifted from one mental state and sphere to the other, through the explanatory hypothesis of quotas of energic "cathexis." This was designed to explain an incomprehensible transformation: the question of how a psychical idea crosses the boundary of the system Ucs and enters the system Cs (Pcs). He concluded that:

> [T]he conscious presentation comprises the presentation of the thing plus the presentation of the word belonging to it, while the unconscious presentation is the presentation of the thing alone. The system *Ucs.* contains the thing-cathexes of the objects, the first and true object-cathexes; the system *Pcs.* comes about by this thing-presentation being hypercathected through being linked with the word-presentations corresponding to it. It is these hypercathexes, we may suppose, that bring about a higher psychical organization and make it possible for the primary process to be succeeded by the secondary process which is dominant in the *Pcs.* [1915b, pp. 201–202].

A presentation which is not put into words, or a psychical act which is not hypercathected, remains thereafter in the Ucs., in a state of repression. (The final sentence contains a pseudo-linguistic solution equating repression to a cathectic deficiency.)

This change in state he explained through energic and economic concepts, which were subsequently subsumed in the structural model wherein this "binding" of psychic energy is attributed to the ego. Access to consciousness is determined by the linkage of word to "thing," or the replacement of thing associations by word associations, representing an economy of psychical expenditure (1905a). Freud based this formulation on the assumption that "transition from the system Ucs" to Pcs and Cs occurs through a "change in its state, an alteration in its cathexis" (1915b, p. 180).

We now find that neither subdivided mental territories nor energic currents are necessary postulates for understanding that the nature of psychical material alters according to its degree and mode of symbolizational organization, and that a stagewise continuum can be more or less mapped out according to an approximate developmental scale. Intimations of such a model can be detected in Freud's topographic theory, but still the problem of transformation remained unsolved. Little or no discussion is offered by Freud regarding some of the most fundamental of the explanatory concepts of which he makes use, "psychic energy," "cathexis," "sums of excitation," "quantity," "intensity," and so forth, because, I believe, he realized that these were merely descriptive terms for a *provisional* "working hypothesis" which attempted to explain invisible psychic transformations much like electrical currents.

However little this change in state or transformational process has to do with psychic energy, its apparent "economy" is inherent in symbol formation itself, as its etymological roots suggest: the symbol "throws together" and "represents." This is an abstractive referencing process, one which distinguishes the articulated, symbolized idea or feeling from unconscious presentation by its being transmuted into verbal form through a deliberate focus of attention or awareness. Whereas feelings and ideas which remain unarticulated retain their urgent affective and sensory immediacy, as is characteristic of nondiscursive symbolic modes of presentation, those expressed consciously in direct discursive form sui generis undergo a symbolic transformation which at once distances and removes them from their unconscious affective intensity. It is *the symbolization process itself* which induces this transmutation to occur since, as we have seen, the symbol proper does not equate as do signs and signals, but fosters contemplative "representing." In so doing symbolization transmutes the nature of experience and knowledge.

The abstractive process occurring in psychoanalysis translates affective nondiscursive sign and signaling pre-symbolic manifestations into discursive-symbolic form in shared participation—shifts in representational levels are always mediated through relationship. How we know what we know is determined by the stage of symbolizational development, or referential level, in which we can articulate, express, or depict this knowledge and, as we know from the psychoanalytic situation, psychic strata coexist: primordial imagos, memory, and symbol overlap and often appear simultaneously. There are no discontinuous dichotomies in mind, only modes and means for expressing different levels in the organization of experience. Discursive symbolic form, that of the psychoanalytic method, subsumes in its narrational fabric both the gathering and abstracting processes inherent in symbolization, and therefore brings about what Freud perceived as a "binding of psychic energy," the secondary process. Even today, this particular transformation is described in terms of Freud's concept of bound energy. It is the mechanism, or process of symbolizing itself, however, not "hypercathexes" which brings unconscious experience into consciousness and performs an integrative function. This is because the very activity of symbolizing, the struggle to give representational form, provides the transformative step (none other than our notion of the "ego"), a step which must therefore be taken by the individual, not for him. As the poet W. A. Auden discerned, "What we have not named or beheld as symbol, escapes our notice."

Thanks to Freud's acuity and to the fact that whenever he approached these issues he overtly stated that his knowledge to date was incomplete, in the hypostatized ideas he did advance may be traced an avenue to more contemporary formulations. It does not condemn psychoanalysis or refute its validity, I believe, to question thus and redirect its metatheory; it merely pushes the requirement that psychoanalysis reevaluate its general propositions so that these may be reviewed and recast in forms consonant with a unified theory. Indeed, since the ambition was greater, it pushes the requirement to move toward the founder's original wish; to weld a theoretical base worthy of a general theory of mind. It is to this end that I tackle a synthesis.

What I am proposing is a model of mind in which development of symbolization replaces energic and economic conceptualizations, a model which, I hope, will help us think of the configurations in the organization of "psyche" in a different way. The proposed model includes and operationalizes meaning and subjective experience, which extends beyond the interactions of the psychoanalytic situation in looking for the form and content of inner experience, "the nature of the psychical" which, as Freud wrote, links "with mythology and philology, with folklore, with social psychology and the theory of religion" (1917a, p. 167). In short, a way of thinking about psyche which corresponds to what we know about its unique and uniquely human medium, symbolization. "If it is indeed a generative idea," wrote Langer in 1942, "it will beget tangible methods of its own to free the deadlocked paradoxes of mind and body, reason and impulse, autonomy and law, and will overcome the checkmated arguments of an earlier age by discarding their very idiom and shaping their equivalents in more significant phrase" (p. 25).

4.

Psychoanalysis Reworked

> The life of mind is a totality of levels, which on one hand exist side by side, but which on the other, appear transitorily one after the other. The moments which the mind seems to have left behind actually exist in it at the present time in full depth.
>
> [Friedrich Hegel, 1807]

Diverse modes of thought and a psyche divided into conscious and unconscious are characteristic features of the psychoanalytic approach from its inception. The conceptualization of mind as a multitiered, transformational process, however, distinguished by stages of symbolic organization and diverse modes of expression, is new. A consideration of the gradual development of symbolization as it unfolds along a continuum from prerepresentational somatic, through sign, signaling, and protosymbolic phenomena, to the full flowering of the symbolic function proper, puts us in a position to reconsider various questionable facets of our theory, facets which Freud had approached primarily in dynamic, economic, or energic terms. In particular, it provides a structural model of psyche, or inner experience, concordant with cognitive and neurological models of mentation and brain functioning, which facilitates reformulation of the unconscious–conscious dimension (and what it means to make the unconscious conscious), reintegration of primary and secondary processes, prerepresentational and representational expressiveness, and the pivotal, structuralizing significance of language in development, in psychoanalytic theory, and its clinical method.

233

Many problems concerning these issues seem to have their origins in the semantics of specialization; for instance, designation of terms defining the parameters of a discipline also tend to delimit the perspective of that discipline's particular approach. While all study the mind or what is mental, they do so from different angles, often using different jargon for the same processes. Moreover, theorists tend to select functions that are most congruent with their perspectives. Frequently the focus of metapsychological interest has been confused in psychoanalysis, either due to the theoretical penchant of a particular school or to the unspecific use of words; such words as cognition, mentation, the unconscious, intellect, experience, or mind, are all used interchangeably.

Despite the close interweaving and interdependence of numerous developmental vectors, particularly at the outset of life, these lines are not identical: cognition or mentation is not exactly the same as experience in its emotive entirety, just as realms of fantasy, art, dream, metaphor are not interchangeable with those of logical operations, mathematics, or grammar. I believe it is important for our discipline, insofar as it holds responsibility for the most comprehensive synthesis, to reiterate its directive and goal; we ask questions not in terms of how or why or what a behavior is, but in terms of what this means to a particular individual—in terms of the quality of internal experience. We should strive toward understanding more than toward knowledge. Therefore our model of mind must provide a tabloid encompassing enough to accommodate the subjective, that is, meanings elaborated at multiple developmental levels of inner experience and the modes in which these are expressed, as well as a formula for how language and its underlying process, so central to our method, moves motives and connects all these levels together.

Yet in the previous chapter, numerous calls for a developmental model for what is clearly discernible as symbolizational activity have been variously called intellectual development, the transferability of psychic intensity, cognition, nondiscursive mentation, or semiotics. It is Langer who defines the forms of expression of symbolization as forms of knowledge in a transformational process, but she does not venture a developmental

model. Already in 1917, Freud was cognizant that further elucidation of the mechanism of the dreamwork could lead to the
understanding of our earliest intellectual development, but remarked, "this work has not so far been started upon" (1917a,
p. 199). Still, in 1965, Knapp, a psychoanalyst, notes, "The task
of fully elucidating the organization of inner, non-discursive
mentation is largely ahead" (p. 395), words echoed in 1972
by the anthropologist Marshack, "The possible stages in the
evolution of this human cognition have hardly begun to be
discovered" (p. 130). It is Schimek (1975), who most clearly
and explicitly declares the need for a new psychoanalytic approach to "the development of cognition . . . an approach that
distinguishes different stages and levels of symbolic [or more
accurately, semiotic] functioning as the key to the meaning of
the unconscious and conscious aspects of every experience. A
consideration of the development of the symbolic function must
obviously include the central role of language and the motivational and interpersonal aspects of such development" (p. 184).

In this regard, and with particular emphasis on the transformative dimension from unconscious to conscious, it is important not to forget our uniquely psychoanalytic focus of
inquiry wherein the nature of the subjective is unknown even
to the subject—the unconscious; ". . . so psycho-analysis warns
us not to equate perceptions by means of consciousness with
the unconscious mental process *which are their object*" (Freud,
1915b, p. 171; emphasis added). Faced with the indisputable
evidence of an unconscious, it was consciousness, "a fact without parallel, which defies all explanation or description" (1940,
p. 157), that was Freud's great stumbling block. Attempts to
explain their interrelationship formed the originating core of
the topographic theory and such causal postulates as repression,
resistance, censorship, the dynamic unconscious, and its infantile motives.

A revisionary model therefore cannot abstain from this primary directive; it must address this particular psychoanalytic
focus and if possible comprehend and reformulate a theoretical
framework to encompass it. This is why neither cognitive, behavioral, neuropsychological, nor hermeneutic explanations in
themselves are sufficient. They provide corroborative models

for data, filling in aspects of psychoanalytic concerns, but do not delineate a sufficiently comprehensive model for what is exclusively psychoanalytic terrain. This, in my view, corresponds to realms of subjective experience expressed in different modes and at different levels of symbolization.

Throughout Freud's writings, ambiguities and uncertainties appear to reflect a fundamental schism in his thinking, which manifests on the one hand in his dominant intent to "enrich science" by explaining the psychical in terms of a "mental apparatus" powered by displaceable energies, and on the other, to seek out relationships of reference appearing in different modes of symbolic and presymbolic expression, by way of a new method of exploration and interpretation. These two conflicting trends were never reconciled. Although he framed his hypotheses in an edifice fortified by formidable "intellectual scaffolding," at the end of his life, he himself looked forward to "this being modified, corrected and more precisely determined as further experience is accumulated and sifted" (1940, p. 159).

In his posthumous *Outline of Psychoanalysis* (1940), Freud summarized the multiple aspects of his theory, recapitulating these in abbreviated form. In a mind structurally divided into id, ego, and superego, three qualities are attributed to psychical processes; these are conscious, preconscious and unconscious, and "The division between the three classes of material which possess these qualities is neither absolute nor permanent" (1940, p. 160). The preconscious becomes conscious without undue difficulty; what is unconscious can, after overcoming strong resistances, become conscious. Freud struggled with the topography of the mind, concluding that consciousness and memory were not operating in the same system, consciousness substituting for the memory trace. Memory was believed to be encapsulated in mnemic traces in the unconscious, a notion which topographically separates conscious and unconscious records of the same content (Freud, 1915b). Part of the clinical problem was to provide conscious reconstructions that might reconnect with the original unconscious memories, "Actually, there is no lifting of the repression until the conscious idea, after the resistances have been overcome, has entered into connection with the unconscious memory-trace. It is only through the making conscious of the latter itself that success is achieved" (Freud, 1915b, pp. 175–176). Via the preconscious, the conscious idea could be reunited with the genuine unconscious memory trace.

The unconscious then, for Freud, contains both the repressed and the original drive-cathected "thing"-presentation, whereas preconscious and ego represent the quality and agency which articulate "word" or "idea-presentation." What is readily discernible, I believe, in Freud's formulation, is actually a description of two levels of symbolic representation, or a relationship of reference.

The phenomenology of the unconscious, insofar as it remains enshrouded, is in the multiple meanings and encumbent motives encased in sign, signaling, and variously presented iconic and pre-symbolic referents which can only be inferred and disclosed in an ambience of contextual relevance. A new model must accommodate the essential continuity between unconsciousness and consciousness and encompass the centrality of language both intrapsychically and interpersonally, within its framework. And while Freud provided vivid and compelling descriptions of the different laws, modes, and qualities which characterize unconscious and conscious processes, devising a system of structures of ingenious clarity to explain conflictual psychopathology, he remained cognizant to the end of the fact that the essential nature of the psychic transformation which occurs in the transition from unconsciousness to consciousness, continued to elude him. Subsequent focus on the ego, its development and functions, has not filled the gap left by a psychology of the unconscious which cannot adequately explain its connection to consciousness. This essay is an attempt to fill that gap; and I believe a developmental model of ascending planes of symbolic organization provides psychoanalysis with an appropriate unifying paradigm.

What has been largely ignored, even by the most sophisticated of the critics of Freudian theory, is the implication of such a revision, which necessitates a radical reevaluation and

remodeling of Freud's entire theory of cognition and dichotomous model of mind. "Any reformulation will have to take into
account the observations which Freud's concept of displaceable
quantities of energy and unconscious mental representations
tried to account for" (Schimek, 1975, p. 182). The observations
which Freud accounted for in terms of energy have to do with
psychic transformations; the kind observable in clinical work
related to changes encumbent upon a particular insight, working through of a constellation of issues, putting something into
words, or an interpretation which frees the expression of hidden
material. Because the method is linguistic, all of these processes
become channeled through language and, in this sense, relate
to a system of referencing: the mind as symbolizing process.

Freud's central concern remained the apparent mystery of
this transformational process brought about by the very method
he had discovered. In his final work he emphasized that having
identified the different psychical qualities of the conscious and
unconscious, these are "to be regarded only as an *indication* of
the difference, and not as its essence." He then asks:

> What if this is so, is the true nature of the state which is
> revealed in the id by the quality of being unconscious and
> in the ego by that of being preconscious and in what does
> the difference between them consist?
>
> But of that we know nothing. . . . Here we have ap-
> proached the still shrouded secret of the nature of the
> psychical. We assume, as other natural sciences have led
> us to expect, that in mental life some kind of energy is at
> work; but we have nothing to go upon which will enable
> us to come nearer to a knowledge of it by analogies with
> other forms of energy. We seem to recognize that nervous
> or psychical energy occurs in two forms, one freely mobile
> and another, by comparison, bound; we speak of cathexes
> and hypercathexes of psychical material, and even venture
> to suppose that a hypercathexis brings about a kind of
> synthesis of different processes—a synthesis in the course
> of which free energy is transformed into bound energy. . . .
> Further than this we have not advanced [1940, pp.
> 163–164].

organizing construct presented in my stages of symbolization is a step toward such an integration.

It has been a misleading axiom in my opinion, and one resulting from a natural science epistemology, to insist that a psychoanalytic model of mind be explained in terms of motivations; for motives are derived from meanings, and all human behaviors, actions, affects, or representations and depictions, as mediums which give shape to experience, are the expressions of these meanings. Where theory has been directing our focus onto energic vectors, internal motivational structures, and their primary biological sources, the process of cure has consistently pointed in another direction. Interpretation never directly seeks to disclose or "explain" motives; it strives instead, through a symbolic system, to promote the understanding of a person, particularly of the feelings and disavowed ideas of this person, and how these feelings have been engendered, and themselves engender, all manner of personal meanings. In other words, it recognizes or affirms the analysand via a denotive medium of communication. Interpretations seek to encourage further expansion and elaboration of these feelings in a shared context and in linguistic form. The therapeutic endeavor strives not for motivational change, but for symbolizational transformation, and these transformations of mind, which organize meanings, are what constitute the "nature of the psychical."

The mind works neither to discharge tension nor to achieve inactive pleasure states; it works by symbolizing experience. Each level of symbolization radically alters the meaning of what is currently represented for the subject, and therefore the nature of psychical experience. The psychic reality, or the meanings incumbent upon this structurally altered organization, bring about changes in the very nature of motives and the modes in which these will become expressed in behaviors, actions, or relationships. Our theory and practice are about degrees in a continuum of symbolizational development, and the diverse modes in which experience finds expression in the content of human symbolic systems.

The persistent emphasis on mental contents and a current descriptive nosological frenzy continue to obscure the clinical

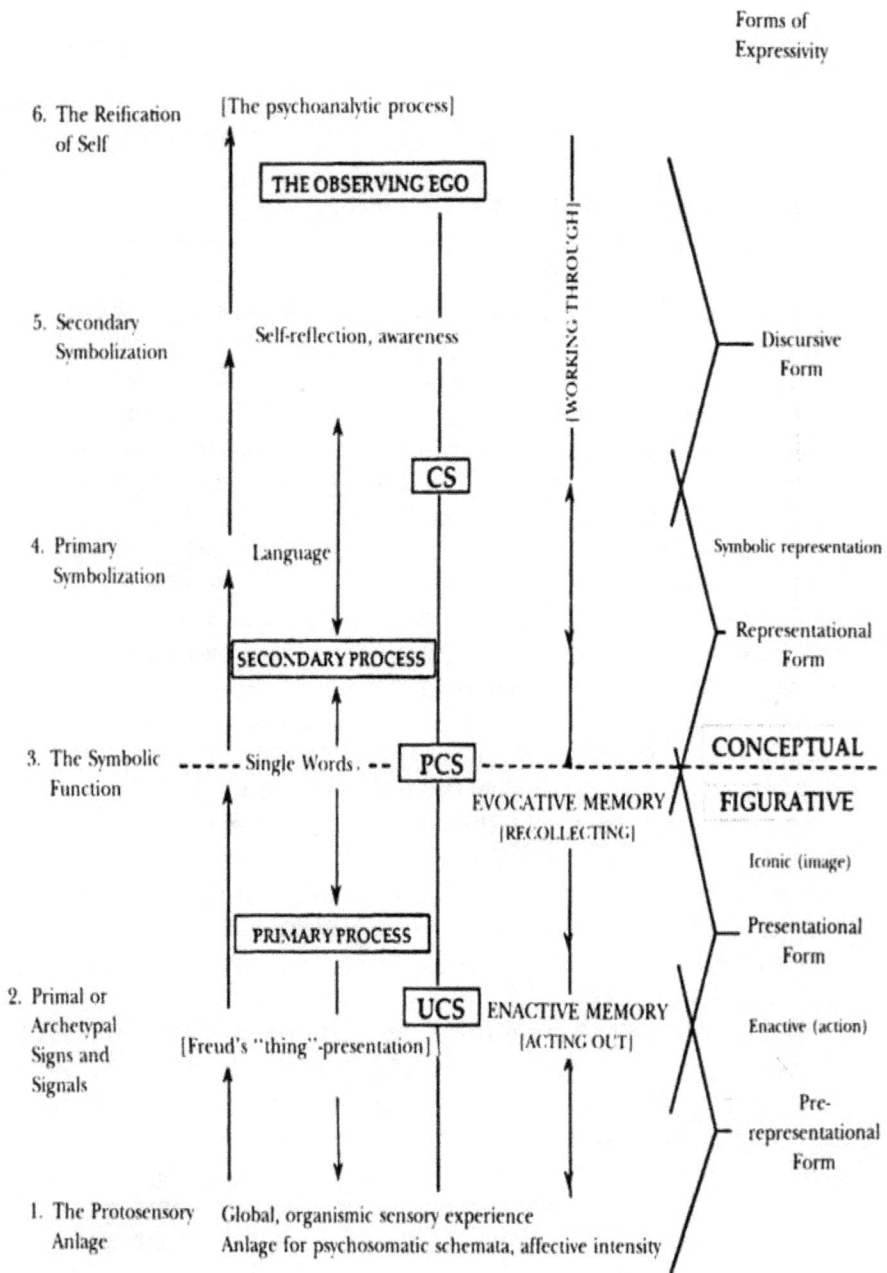

Figure 4.1 Stages of symbolizational development

The advance would have required an appreciation of the symbolic function, and today is predicated on a complete overhaul of such concepts as displaceable quantities of energy, cathexes, and unconscious mental representations so that new emphasis may be laid upon mind in a unitary framework, in which constituent units of internalization—schemata, memory traces, and current motives—crystallize into symbolic-representational vehicles for affects, concepts, experience, and self-expression. Herein is an explanation for the meaning of the simultaneous presence of conscious and unconscious aspects of every experience; and in this, I believe, is the essence of "the nature of the psychical." The key to this reformulation is a paradigm which operationalizes subjective experience and incorporates the abstractive/interpersonal role of language. "The main empirical referent of the unconscious is the concept of interpretation, the process by which psychoanalyst and patient construct new meanings and relationships from the patient's predominantly verbal productions" (Schimek, 1975, p. 182). The clinical process is embedded in symbolic processes and imbued with its function.

Freud's revolutionary departure had been to introduce the notion that what is mental is not necessarily conscious; one of his pitfalls was to dichotomize the "instinctual base" or "somatic discharge" and ideas: body, and mind, attributing the former to the id, the latter to the ego. This bypasses the entire issue of affects—both somatic and later, as emotions, also an ideational expression. He found the "wish" as explanatory vehicle to bridge the biological and psychological for a theory of mind which, he believed, was to be rooted in biological drives, "for the psychical field, the biological field does in fact play the part of the underlying bedrock" (Freud, 1937, p. 252). Due to the prevailing understanding of perception he polarized an irrational, pleasure-seeking infantile and unconscious mind to a reality-oriented adaptive rational mind, attributing to these, two separate principles of functioning—a dichotomized mind containing lower and higher order processes in which correspondences between psychical qualities and provinces or agencies operate in dynamic tension. Instincts, for Freud, the somatic corollary of "what is truly psychical," could never become conscious, only the ideas that represent them. Hence, we have a schismatic psyche and a theory which explains "unconscious" by erecting a (moralistic) barrier between feeling and thinking.

But this dichotomous arrangement is quite inconsistent with the now generally accepted view that psychical, indeed all mental, processes range along a continuum within a unitary model in which thinking, feeling, perceiving, conceiving, and experiencing move together. Moreover, this view of the unconscious as a receptacle of stored memory images contradicts contemporary knowledge of the selective, constructive nature of memory, such that we tend to recreate and lay emphasis on certain past experiences in terms of current cognitive capacities and emotional needs.

Whereas Freud used an economic concept, cathexis, to explain affective import, today we know that subjective meaning and the motivational valence of an object or idea is an inseparable part of our total current perception of experience and not something tacked onto an otherwise objective content (Schimek, 1975). Perception, memory, our entire understanding of experience, is marked by the emotional currents these experiences evoke in the present. The infantile wish, Freud's central concept designed to bridge somatic and psychological, in its inception, attributes to the infant a capacity to distinguish between the object and the experience of satisfaction; to differentiate self from other, register a perception, and retrieve it to recreate an image of hallucinatory wish fulfillment. But we know today that none of these competencies has yet developed in the infant. There is not yet any experience of the world or the environment extrinsic to egocentric need; separation of self from other has not yet occurred. This is a lengthy, laborious, interpersonal, and active construction, the product of developmental, differentiating processes including memory systems, cognitive decentering, and the elaboration of meaning and the symbolic function. Moreover, the reduction of current behavior to a breakdown ending in unconscious infantile wishes is less credible than a conception of coexisting, multiple strata of psychic organization in which current meanings are layered over other early experiences for which similar affective constellations provide the prototypes. It is the pattern or configuration of current experience which recalls the earlier one: and because it has been stored in some form, this does not mean that the original motive is still operative in the present. Psychoanalytic time is always now, meaning is always in the present. "The influence of the past is carried on through the modification of action patterns not through memory images of absent objects" (Schimek, 1975, p. 183).

As the royal road to the unconscious, the dream is regal not because it leads to a childish wish but because it crystallizes the entire spectrum of these psychic layers and creates a narrated distillate of current concerns and their antecedent similarities, and does so in the only form available to a silent, sleeping person, figuratively, that is, in plastic imagery. This does not make the dreamer or the form archaic; in fact, reflecting the entire personality in holographic fashion, the dream will be as primitive or as evolved as its dreamer and will also often express what is "known" but not yet symbolically represented at denotive–abstracted levels of articulation. The images dreams create are complex because they are multilayered, compressing memories, affects, experiences, current concerns, and future hopes, and all of these will reflect the defenses, character style, and unconscious beliefs of their creator. They are difficult to comprehend because the form they take transforms and constructs according to affective valence—the narrative pictures thus fashioned are embodiments of meaning.

As outlined by numerous psychologists (Piaget, 1962; Werner and Kaplan, 1963; Bruner, 1964, 1973; Freedman, 1985), thinking moves developmentally from enactive through iconic to symbolic representational. In the first it is expressed motorically, in action; in the second it represents in plastic imagery; and in the third it articulates at verbal abstract levels. Ontogenetically, each form necessarily develops out of the preceding one but once hierarchic organization coalesces, the stratifications cross-fertilize and all levels are implicated at full maturation. The three modes initially correspond to degrees in the abstractive continuum but later structural organization will be reflected in the relationship between content and form rather than mode of expression. The entire functional structure is always involved, regardless of the mode of expression—a child is after all not a "small" schizophrenic, nor can a mature work of art be dismissed as "primitive" because it is an iconic production. A model of psychic organization developing along a continuum serves us better than one in which diverse modes of functioning are dichotomously opposed.

I am referring to the primary and secondary process. Virtually all aspects of cognitive functioning are implicated in the distinctions between these two modes of thought, and, while the great descriptive value of these different processes remains one of Freud's profoundest insights, their sharp division by a repression barrier, their differentiation in terms of "lower" and "higher," and the notion that in adulthood the primary process is virtually supplanted by the secondary, have all been issues of considerable debate (Gill, 1967a; Holt, 1967; G. Klein, 1970; Basch, 1977; Noy, 1979).

For Freud, the principal defining characteristic of these two diverse modes of thought was the way in which they discharge psychic energy. The first "charged with uninhibited energy" and freely mobile discharge, functions for the pleasure principle; the second, by a quality of being "tonically bound" serves the principle of reality. Descriptively, these ways of thinking are distinguished by different formal and content properties. Associated with the id and the unconscious, the primary process is viewed as archaic, irrational, nonreflective, illogical, tolerating the coexistence of contradictory ideas simultaneously, infiltrated by "drive" qualities, neither ordered nor altered by temporal concerns and "just as little related to reality" (Freud, 1915b). The secondary process, associated with the ego, employs rules of logic, propositions, relationships, anticipation, gives evidence of judgment and temporal order, is reflective, conceives, and reasons in relation to actualities, and serves the "reality principle."

The "distinguishing marks" of the primary process, wrote Freud (1915b), are due to the easy "transvaluation of cathexes," which bring about displacement (when one idea may surrender to another its whole quota of cathexis); condensation (whereby "it may appropriate the whole cathexis of several ideas"); and indirect representation (whereby an image subsumes the formal features of various similar others, disguising dynamically meaningful ideas). The vivid manifestations of these unconscious mechanisms are prototypically evident in the dream which represents a "pure culture" of the essential nature of the primary process.

Freud believed the primary process antedated the secondary both phylogenetically and ontogenetically and was destined to become gradually supplanted by the second, or held at bay by repression. The central thread that runs through these conceptualizations is the notion of psychic energy and its expenditure. Indeed, it is difficult to pry these concepts loose from the fluidity of their "cathexes" and "dischargeability" in order to clearly detect their functional and structural properties. In numerous ways, however, Freud continued to imply a continuum between id and ego suggesting there might be other more differentiated structures in addition to these two general processes. It must further be said that Freud recognized an "intuitive knowledge" at the core of the unconscious (1917a) and emphasized that "these processes which are described as irrational are not in fact falsifications of normal processes—intellectual errors—but are modes of activity of the psychical apparatus that have been freed from an inhibition" (1900, p. 605).

The theoretical debates fueled by the need to recontextualize these processes without the help of psychic energy have, in part, been aroused by the fact that the primary process is intimately linked with such culturally sanctioned, indeed prized, qualities as artistic creativity, scientific inventiveness, inspiration, intuition, and empathy, in addition to regressive phenomena, our dream life, and schizophrenic decompensation. Therefore, it would appear to be imperative to reconceptualize the formal characteristics of these diverse modes within a unitary model which emphasizes their functional–expressive organization and course of regressive dissolution, without implying their current "lower" and "higher" connotations. I believe it will continue to become clearer that such phenomena are better delineated in a hierarchic model of psychic organization, which substratally, however, is understood as being spread throughout the system. In accordance with the principles of developmental structuralization, it would appear that both types of thinking will coexist throughout life, and, accordingly, will continue to partake of the individual's overall development. If we may assume a certain continuity and isomorphism in the processes of mental functioning then it follows that, in keeping with their distinctive features, both forms will unfold in a person's expressive and adaptive course and that it is in the balanced integration of their confluence that vibrant, mature functioning occurs.

The terms *autoplastic* and *alloplastic,* suggested by Noy (1979), better reflect the directional vectors and general orientation of a primary mode wherein motivational thrust is satisfaction of free, uninhibited self-expression in an egocentric reality; and a secondary mode wherein self-expression is adaptively inhibited and modulated toward social interaction and exchange in a decentered reality—the former faces inward, as it were, the latter outward. As Freud put it, "A dream does not want to say anything to anyone . . . it is meant to remain ununderstood" (1917a, p. 231).

I think it justified to reconceptualize these different modes in terms of the first as orienting experience independent of feedback in private idiosyncratic expression; and the second, as orienting experience in physical time and space, vis-à-vis and among others. It is evident that both are necessary and that both nourish different facets of creative adaptation. The former, facing inward, tends to adopt prelogical, uninhibited forms that are expressive rather than communicative. It depicts and responds to idiosyncratic signs and signals and figuratively presents salient events, relationships, impressions, and associated memories charged with affects; it gives form to the senses, shapes impressions that seek organization, and constructs new concepts out of these. The latter, oriented outward, is public, interpersonal, communicative, follows laws of temporality, logic, social order, adopts consensually arbitrary signs and cues, and utilizes abstract symbolic systems to manipulate concepts based on logical propositions. The first becomes expressed in nondiscursive symbolic forms, and is connotive, the second articulates discursive–symbolic systems and is denotive. The first gives figurative expression to personal–affective themes—the second crystallizes concepts for communicational purpose in consensually understood terms. These coexistent aspects of all experience serving different functions, reflect different degrees and types of symbolic organization which crystallize at different levels of the abstractive continuum. What then can be said of the particular mechanisms associated with the primary process, and how can these be understood as constituent steps within a unitary conceptualization of mental processes?

In a detailed study of the primary process Gill (1967a) concludes that most of the specific mechanisms ascribed to the primary process are formal, structural, or phenomenological characterizations of what can be explained and reduced to two primary energic formulations: condensation and displacement; these are "the genotypes, as it were, of which the others are phenotypes" (p. 266). Gill further demonstrates that all the various mechanisms Freud (1900, 1905a) identified as occurring in jokes and the dreamwork actually prove to be form varieties of condensation and displacement.

Another mechanism considered a hallmark of primary process functioning is symbolism. From the earliest formulations the term *mnemic symbol* was applied to signify any aspect of experience which later came to stand for its totality; in this sense symbolism is equated with a displacement. Understandably, Holt (1967) asks: "How does a symbol differ from displacement?" (p. 357). Apparently Freud (1917a) was quite aware of the necessity for a clearer understanding of symbolism and how it differed from other forms of indirect representation; "You see, then, that a symbolic relation is a comparison of a quite special kind, of which we do not as yet clearly grasp the basis . . ." (p. 153). Freud was not able to "sharply delimit" the "concept of a symbol" (1917a, p. 152) because he did not have a functional hypothesis of symbolization as an abstractive process. As Holt points out, Freud could not conceive of symbols as idiosyncratic creations, newly constructed by every individual according to personal experiences, but thought of them (as was characteristic of the time) as "stable translations" (1917a, p. 151), as correspondences, not as a function. Therefore he attributed the manifest content of the dream to the dreamwork, "the *form* into which the latent dream thoughts have been transmuted" (1917a, p. 183) and this, he carefully and scientifically subdivided by qualitative differentiations into categories of mechanisms.

This is part of a larger epistemological error in which concern for categorization and differentiation obfuscates structural patterns and overall form—what is lost is the proverbial forest for the trees. The whole relationship of latent to manifest, which gives rise to reference, is a symbolic one: the manifest subsumes and represents multitiered signifiers or referents. This is the prototypical activity of mind, so that plastic representation is not *a* mechanism of the primary process, but *the* abstractive form at nondiscursive symbolic levels. Presentational ideation, without linguistic expression, *is* iconic; it takes a figurative referent, like a metaphor, to depict multiple meanings. The dream is a plastic representation because it occurs in sleep, when enactive, linguistic, and other motoric expressive channels are blocked, but the basic functioning is the same. The mind is a pattern maker and works to represent. Freud's dreamwork is none other than symbolization—the dream form, similarly, an iconic, protosymbolic form—a depiction of feelings and ideas.

Although they focus on different mechanisms, both Holt (1976) and Gill (1967a) concord in finding that the many distinguishing features of the separate mechanisms of the primary process listed by Freud are more or less subsumed under condensation and displacement. My thesis is rather that both condensation and displacement are inherent in symbolization, in its new paradigmatic definition as an abstractive device. The symbol condenses and displaces by its very nature, inasmuch as something which stands for something else is both a signifier, subsuming multiple things signified and, formally, a different structure from what it represents.

Interestingly, it appears that Freud sensed that the compressed nature of dream imagery had more to do with a mechanism than the "censor's" disguisement: "But although condensation makes dreams obscure, it does not give one the impression of being an effect of the dream-censorship. It seems traceable rather to some mechanical or economic factor . . ." (1917a, p. 173). Earlier, he wrote, "The dream-work put these thoughts into another form, and it is a strange and incomprehensible fact that in making this translation (this rendering, as it were, into another script or language) these methods of merging or combining are brought into use" (1917a, p. 172). Again, Freud is identifying the symbolizing process in its presentational, referencing function. In referring to the previous chapter, I believe this phenomenon may appear less strange and incomprehensible to us if we remember that this gathering and abstractive process is inherent in symbolization itself, as its etymological origins suggest; the symbol "throws together" and "represents." A picture is worth a thousand words because, unlike language, it is not bound by sequential organization; it reproduces by simultaneity in time, so that many ideas become telescoped into one expression. This is partly what makes iconic form so difficult to decipher and why the dreamer's subjective, associative thoughts are essential to its understanding, as they lead to meanings which are unique for each individual.

The defining differentiation then between primary and secondary process modes, would seem to have more to do with their qualities of being unconscious or conscious rather than their traditional differentiation as more archaic and "advanced" levels of thought. Again, the communicative bridge and cognitive valence of language plays a crucial theoretical role here. In their substratal impact, action is not the same as iconic presentation, and iconic representation, both structurally and functionally, is not the same as verbal–symbolic expression. To enact is not at the same level of symbolic organization as to represent or to recount; similarly "repetition" precludes "recollection." Meaning always implies structuring organization. Equally, meaning alters according to the structural–functional expression in which it is cast.

The mind's central organizing principle is that of form shaping; internalizing and organizing experience entail an ongoing dynamic process of category building. This tendency toward formalization is evident in our earliest biological, perceptual functioning—form-perception, as recognition of sameness and similarity, is intuitive. "In this sense," writes Alkon (1989), a neurobiologist, "a human being is a pattern-recognition device created in the course of evolution, and memories are the patterns that are stored" (p. 42). Pieces of patterns are linked if these are associated in time, and the pieces are stored in combination not individually; memory storage is pattern storage, and patterns evoke other patterns. Moreover awareness of a small portion can trigger awareness of a whole; "The formation of associative memories appears to involve a sequence of molecular changes at specific locations in systems of neurons" (Alkon, 1989, p. 42). It has only recently become known that it is a coordinating organ in the limbic system, the hippocampus, which links all the separate sensory signals, and, as it were, instructs each of the original cortex storage sites to retain selected percepts for later retrieval. Imbued with affect (the gauge of valence) by the adjacent amygdala, a single moment or sensation can evoke recall of an entire memorable event (Blakeslee, 1991). The prime literary example is Proust's renowned catalytic madeleine dipped in his cup of coffee evoking at once an entire experience and an entrée into the realm of remembrance of things past.

A proliferation of terms, ranging from unconscious fantasies to pooled representation or schematic prototypes, are currently used by psychologists and psychoanalysts to describe primary mental organization and the way mind crystallizes experience. It would be helpful to have a consensus regarding these definitions and more discrete differentiation between these terms, since there appears to be an inverse relationship between undifferentiated and unconscious protosymbolic forms and the availability of general classes or categories of experience which can become consciously expressed through a symbolic vehicle of denotive reference. In this sense words, initially invoking an entire sentence, only gradually detach from the global experience of the things they stand for. Language only assists thought in becoming conscious; it facilitates the necessary abstractive step. This entire progression is marked by stages of symbolization which characteristically move from somatic–enactive channels, through iconic presentation, to discursive–abstract symbolic forms.

Conceptualization of this process is assisted by the term *schema*, to denote an elemental unit of experience, so that Werner and Kaplan (1963) speak of dynamic schematization and Piaget refers to the assimilation and accomodation of schemas according to stage-acquired development in a program of cognitive operations rooted in activity. This ordering activity begins at birth and schemata involve auditory, olfactory, tactile, and visual sensory modalities: "the schema represents that pattern of physical qualities in the original event" (Kagan, 1984); most children have a schematic category for a general class of events before they learn to name these or apply words to signify their meaning. As Piaget showed, schemas are internalized and organized according to current cognitive capacities; it will require continuous mental activity to elaborate and organize impressions which are assimilated unconsciously but must be processed, categorized, and defined denotively in order to become accommodated consciously. This might be another aspect of "mastery," or our notion of the "ego." Ascendence in the abstractive scale always requires a focus of attention in order for amorphous experience to become symbolized, and as Piaget noted, figurative presentation rarely becomes adequately represented through language which, being conceptual, is emotionally pale by comparison. Perhaps this is where the emotive bursts of expressivity associated with art take flight. This may also explain why experiences related to action schemas or vague, primarily somatic memory engrams are so difficult to articulate and put into words or discursive form, and why frequently sensorial imagery or metaphors are chosen to convey what is not thought but felt.

Once the capacity to represent has been attained, stagewise increases in levels of symbolization enable the articulation of experience and concepts in increasingly differentiated ways. The construction of categories of experience also form the groundwork for systems of belief about how the world works and what to anticipate, providing a basic conceptual framework within which to imagine, reason, and organize behavior. We can envision a primary mode which initiates categorization around immediate, self-centered criteria, articulating impressions unconsciously perhaps through the iconic image of dreams, as these press toward organization and expression; and a secondary mode of categorization accommodating and elaborating experience according to logical operations, concepts which are decentered and increasingly differentiated from subjective

needs and affective coloring. Noy (1979) describes the first as
ordering phenomena according to experience and the second
according to knowledge. Further, he suggests that any single
item of information is categorized twice, "first as a subjective
experience and then as a piece of objective knowledge" (p.
180). Rather than envision a dual encoding, I would suggest, in
a unitary mind both aspects are part of a whole pattern, and
out of this whole, which reflects what is known as well as what
is felt, the construction of protosymbolic and then symbolic
representations are formed. Depending on the nature of the
socialization process, certain kinds of personal responses will be
inhibited in their expression or, conversely, due to their affective intensity, others will require repeated expressive attempts in order to become symbolically denoted. Traumatic
reenactments and repetition, even working through, might be
envisioned in this way.

A certain synesthesia prevails over the way in which experiences are internalized and memories are recalled. The same
event or phenomenon may appear in iconic, phonic, linguistic,
or abstracted form according to the available expressive channels; it will also have its emotional, imaginal, abstractive, and
fantastical facets and will have been assimilated in each of the
modes characteristic for each strata of psychic organization. As
a conceptual unit, the schema subsumes what an experience
means to an individual, and this, in turn, gives rise to and evokes
symbolic referents or representational sequences. These are the
constituents of experience, the building blocks of meaning.
Moreover, in the spectrum of available associative triggers, any
one side of this prism can spark illumination of the whole pattern imbuing it with a slightly different hue. Any aspect of an
experience can become expressed through diverse channels or,
in becoming articulated linguistically, will acquire that particular precision associated with the denotive function of words.
Through exploration and joint investigation of these multiple
facets of memories and current experience, psychoanalytic investigation invites the expression of their affective coloring and
meaning through the linguistic medium, and as such is integrative.

Such a conceptualization obviates the need for notions of stable "mental representations" or fixed "unconscious fantasies" in a mind which is fluid, unitary, constantly internalizing, constructing, and reconstructing symbolic referents newly minted, as it were, according to contemporary events. The epigenetic quality of this dynamic process of categorization may be subsumed in a hierarchic model of stages in a symbolizational continuum. In this, Kagan's (1984, p. 212) inclusive listing of the classes of shared features which, in various combinations, constitute categories, comes to look remarkably like Freud's characteristic qualities of primary process thought.

Due to their relevance in this discussion, their correspondence to Freud's basic primary process operations and the implications of reformulating an explanation of their workings, I believe it is worth dwelling for a moment on Kagan's (1984) inclusive listing of the classes of shared features which, in various combinations, constitute categories. These include: (1) perceptually available qualities like form, color, pattern, movement, pitch, loudness, and taste (particularly in infancy); (2) functional qualities which include possible activities of objects, actions imposed on them by others, and their possible uses by people or animals; (3) mental states evoked by events, which can refer to private, internal feeling or ideas; (4) the names shared by events; and (5) relations between schemata, words, or ideas, namely, complimentarity, opposition, inclusiveness, relative magnitude, and spatial location—these can form the basis for categorical concepts associated with similes and metaphors (derived from Kagan [1984, p. 212]). It seems to me, beyond a doubt, that these same classes of categorical constituents which Vygotsky (1962) also refers to as "relations to generalities" and "systems," correspond to the various combinatorial mechanisms of the primary process as identified by Freud (1900). These may now be understood as initial stages in the fundamental dynamic schematizing process of mind, as the elemental protosymbolic constituents of meaning, through which experience is known and will become crystallized symbolically.

It is generally recognized that a certain synesthesia prevails over the way memories are recalled and that the senses can readily evoke entire scenarios, recollections, and knowledge simultaneously and with great intensity, and all in silent imagery—not all meanings reside, or can even be expressed, in language. In their evocation of concepts, words are used to arouse correspondent understanding, at best to ring a concordant note, as consensually shared, symbolic referents, but can never completely match the richness of variegated aspects of private experience; "words evoke concepts, they do not represent them" (Clark [1983], cited in Kagan [1984, p. 212]). Freud had noted that what lay beneath the repression barrier, although symbolically pictorialized or otherwise reenacted, were contents which only with great difficulty and resistance would participate in the transformation which made their verbalization possible. In other words, although the contents of unconscious organization are depicted in nondiscursive symbolic form, and therefore are to some degree represented, somehow they do not lend themselves to translation into discursive symbolism.

In this regard, Freud had spoken of the existence of two different types of unconscious (1917a, p. 227), and of primary and secondary repression. This division in the unconscious supposedly marked the difference between one "recognized as being of infantile origin" (1917a, p. 227) wherein the "wish" originates, and another containing the day residue, all of which represented the contents of the repressed. "This is the salient point of the whole business. They are *not* unconscious in the same sense. The dream-wish belongs to a different unconscious—to the one we have already recognized as being of infantile origin and equipped with peculiar mechanisms. It would be highly opportune to distinguish these two kinds of unconscious by different names. But we would prefer to wait..." Freud (1917a, p. 227). These observations might better be understood in terms of stages or degrees of symbolic organization. The first unconscious, like primary repression associated with infantile material, corresponds to a primal protosensory level in which experiences are organismic, organized in actions or through affect, and therefore not represented at all; the other unconscious, locus of "the secondarily repressed" might be understood as experiences which were momentarily recorded but which due to personal or extrinsic interdiction quickly underwent an inhibitory process of associative severance within the memory system, rendering them not readily retrievable. This takes the view of memory as a system of a variety of functions involving long- and short-term storage processes; processes that convert experiences to mnemic triggers which are retrievable in a number of different ways.

Unconscious knowledge, organized in nondiscursive symbolic form, would correspond to private, phenomenalistic, and affectively charged strata of experience which is loathe to being shaped by the pristine linearity of discursive form, in the light of propositional logic. Therefore, the psychoanalytic enterprise meets with an apparent resistance. Aside from the fact that a dislodging shift in representational mode and organization entails an upheaval of the very fabric of meaning, it is often painful and always difficult to revisit and disclose this intensely charged, often frightening, shameful, or grandiose private world, and to translate its affective significance into consensually understood linguistic signifiers.

Nondiscursive symbolic form retains its close connection to idiosyncratic, intensely affective evocative imagery; it is personal, fluid, egocentric, free. Language partakes of this cognitive form to which Vygotsky (1962) referred as "word meanings." Discursive symbolism, based on learned systems of impersonal, arbitrary, and abstract denoters, gives shape to public vehicles of communication which link inner with outer knowledge and experience. Unconstrained by time or reason, this inner side makes abstract what is concrete and concrete what is abstract, personifies the inanimate, and mythologizes animate and narrative sequence. It retains simultaneity in its intermingling of signs, signals, archetypal prototypes, and symbols, and coexisting contradictory feelings and ideas. In it, nothing is just what it seems. Conversely, linguistic communication restrains this inner nebulous stream harnessing its ideation in giving discrete form and denotive distance to its vivid, emotive elusiveness. The symbolic function detaches thought from action, equally, if by degrees, from intense emotion.

Language, the paradigm of symbolization, is the great divide beyond which only sentient Homo sapiens wanders. This is not so much because it substantiates consciousness, which it merely assists, but because it materializes meaning. Meaning implies the existence in mind of a reciprocal relationship between symbol and the symbolized, or, in language, the "mutual evocability of name and sense . . ." (Rosen, 1969, p. 198). The natural biological development of language promotes this leap in symbolization, due to its very function and structure. The word, when it becomes a symbol, stands for something which has no correspondence to it other than its denotive reference. (Unlike the sign and signaling function of word meanings in their connotive expression, the denotive word is detached from what it signifies.) As the outgrowth of ongoing dynamic schematization the distancing inherent in this act of symbolizing, and its attendant focus of attention, marks the advent of a structuralization of meaning in discursive form manifest as conscious knowledge. This evolution reflects developmental degrees in the abstractive continuum and is isomorphic to a basic pattern-making or unifying propensity in brain functioning, the formalizing characteristic of mind.

Nondiscursive symbolic form, as part of prelinguistic experience, subsequently remains in the background and ordinarily fades in intensity; however, its dramatic, fantastical, and emotive qualities may be captured for artistic purposes. Discursive symbolic form may be used as a vehicle for nondiscursive expression, as when language is reimbued with affective evocativeness. Art expressly harnesses the dialectic of subjective and objective feelings and forms, and, in life, language constantly fluctuates between these different levels and expressive forms and functions. Psychoanalysis makes the unconscious conscious through the transformative effort of verbalization. Its curative value lies in shaping significance or meaning into denotive linguistic form and sharing this with another. So, to sum up, "*exemption from mutual contradiction, primary process* (mobility of cathexes), *timelessness,* and *replacement of external by psychical reality*" [are the characteristics] we may expect to find in processes belonging to the system unconscious" (Freud, 1915b, p. 187). By contrast, consciousness is accompanied by discursive forms of symbolization, through an act of denotive reference which imbues a signifier with a specific meaning. To be aware, or to become aware, often implies outer communication as "explicit verbal thought evolves from its presentational symbolic background" (Knapp, 1969, p. 394).

Before presenting my model of evolving stages of symbolization (Figure 4.1), I would like to reiterate a few basic principles derived from the holistic–organismic (Werner and Kaplan, 1963), and developmental–structuralist (Greenspan, 1989) approaches, which underlie them. The new paradigm incorporates a number of key developmental assumptions, the first of which subsumes two fundamental notions. The first of these notions is that of the holistic-orientation which assumes that all organismic activity is always contextually embedded and that every aspect will affect the whole. The second notion is that of an inherent developmental directiveness by which organisms progress naturally through a series of transformations which tend to move from undifferentiated states of relative globality toward states of increasing differentiation, discreteness, and hierarchic structuring. Further, it is assumed that each developmental level achieved is defined by certain characteristic capacities for organizing experience according to age-expectable emphasis and criteria.

With reference to the fate of earlier modes and levels of organization, it is maintained that with the gradual achievement of higher stages earlier ones are functionally superseded but not lost; hierarchic structuralization ensures a coexistent stability of multiple layers and modes, any one of which can be harnessed for expressive purposes, or conversely, in which dissolution will be expressed in the regressive dedifferentiation of all modes. Experiences in the environment are viewed as becoming gradually internalized according to developmental transformations involving an intertwining of continuous and discontinuous change—a constant, ongoing manner in which new features emerge together with specific qualitative discontinuities in the forms these changes take.

Development proceeds according to an assumed orientation toward knowing or understanding, a trait uniquely characteristic of humankind, which promotes the exploration of options opened by learning from past experiences and planning for future action; that is, cognition is time and space oriented, and always contextually organized (Marshack, 1989). In order to contemplate and manipulate a world that is known rather than merely reacted to, and consonant with a primary form building, organizing tendency, mankind evolved the capacity to represent—an instrument of thought and an assigner of meaning—the symbolic vehicle.

It is assumed that the symbolic function flowers out of a continuous, underlying, dynamic regulative process of schematization which is constant and upon which depends the ongoing construction of meaning. And lastly, it is assumed that no entity, in itself, is a symbol. A functional concept, the symbol must be recreated anew by each individual through the activity of symbolizing, which originates in a primordial sharing situation out of which arises the first gesture of reference. Therefore, the intentional act of denotive reference, a prerequisite for symbolization proper, is embedded in a relational matrix, upon which its development will depend. Neither signs nor signals, although they indicate and present, are the same as the symbolic vehicle which, uniquely, represents: "theoretically, the locus of symbolization lies in the intentional act of a human being and not in the material which is utilized qua vehicle" (Werner and Kaplan, 1963, p. 333).

Symbolization is a mental activity which distances, organizes experience, and serves expressivity, and in these, increases both mastery and integration.

The stages, their titles, and characterization of unfolding new representational capabilities are designed to organize emergent strata of symbolization, structuring an ascending continuum of gradual transformations which evolve seriatum out of one another.

The emergent stages are continuous and contiguous, and all remain active in their characteristic mode after having reached functional dominance. Transitions from one stage to the next are gradual and uneven, and aspects of earlier functioning are welded and partially subsumed into the most recently acquired level, but not lost. While development proceeds favoring more advanced levels, all modes of symbolizing are retained and coexist simultaneously, and can be tapped (as in artistic creativity, intuition, empathy, inspiration) or may re-emerge in varying forms (as in sleep, altered states, and regressive desymbolization).

I will describe each stage according to the characteristic content-form which appears with each new plane of symbolization but will not emphasize expectable ages at which these appear as my focus is on structural transformation rather than development per se. Content-form will correspond to the particular symbolic configuration of experience and phenomenology of which that stage is capable; this is in order to attempt to render the developmental achievements as they first appear in forms and modes which may be viewed as markers for a given stage. But I urge the reader to keep in mind that there are no sharp demarcation lines between any of these stages, that mind is a seamless organismic unity, with multiple layers continuously and actively intermingling in which only interpretation through modes of expression can serve as a useful tool for understanding.

As emphasized throughout, hierarchic structuralization does not preclude the simultaneous existence of numerous levels of symbolic organization, all operating at the same time. Mental contents, therefore, may, and often are, concomitantly enacted, figuratively presented, represented, and abstracted at different levels and in different modes once development has attained the structuralizing competencies of the highest stages. And while the small child must move developmentally through each successive stage, once achieved, the whole person responds at all levels to all things; these, as William James put it, "being woven through the whole texture of the works" (1842–1910, p. 219).

STAGE 1: THE PROTOSENSORY ANLAGE

—But for those first affections,
Those shadowy recollections,
Which, be they what they may
Are yet the fountain-light of all our day,
Are yet a master-light of all our seeing. . . .
[William Wordsworth, 1807, p. 88]

Forms of
Expressivity

6. The Reification   [The psychoanalytic process]
   of Self

THE OBSERVING EGO

5. Secondary   Self-reflection, awareness   Discursive
   Symbolization   Form

[WORKING THROUGH]

CS

4. Primary   Language   Symbolic representation
   Symbolization

                                                                          Representational
SECONDARY PROCESS   Form

3. The Symbolic   ---- Single Words -- PCS --------------------- CONCEPTUAL
   Function

                                        EVOCATIVE MEMORY / FIGURATIVE
                                        [RECOLLECTING]

                                                                          Iconic (image)

PRIMARY PROCESS   Presentational
                                                                          Form

2. Primal or   UCS   ENACTIVE MEMORY   Enactive (action)
   Archetypal   [ACTING OUT]
   Signs and   [Freud's "thing"-presentation]
   Signals
                                                                          Pre-
                                                                          representational
                                                                          Form

1. The Protosensory   Global, organismic sensory experience
   Anlage   Anlage for psychosomatic schemata, affective intensity

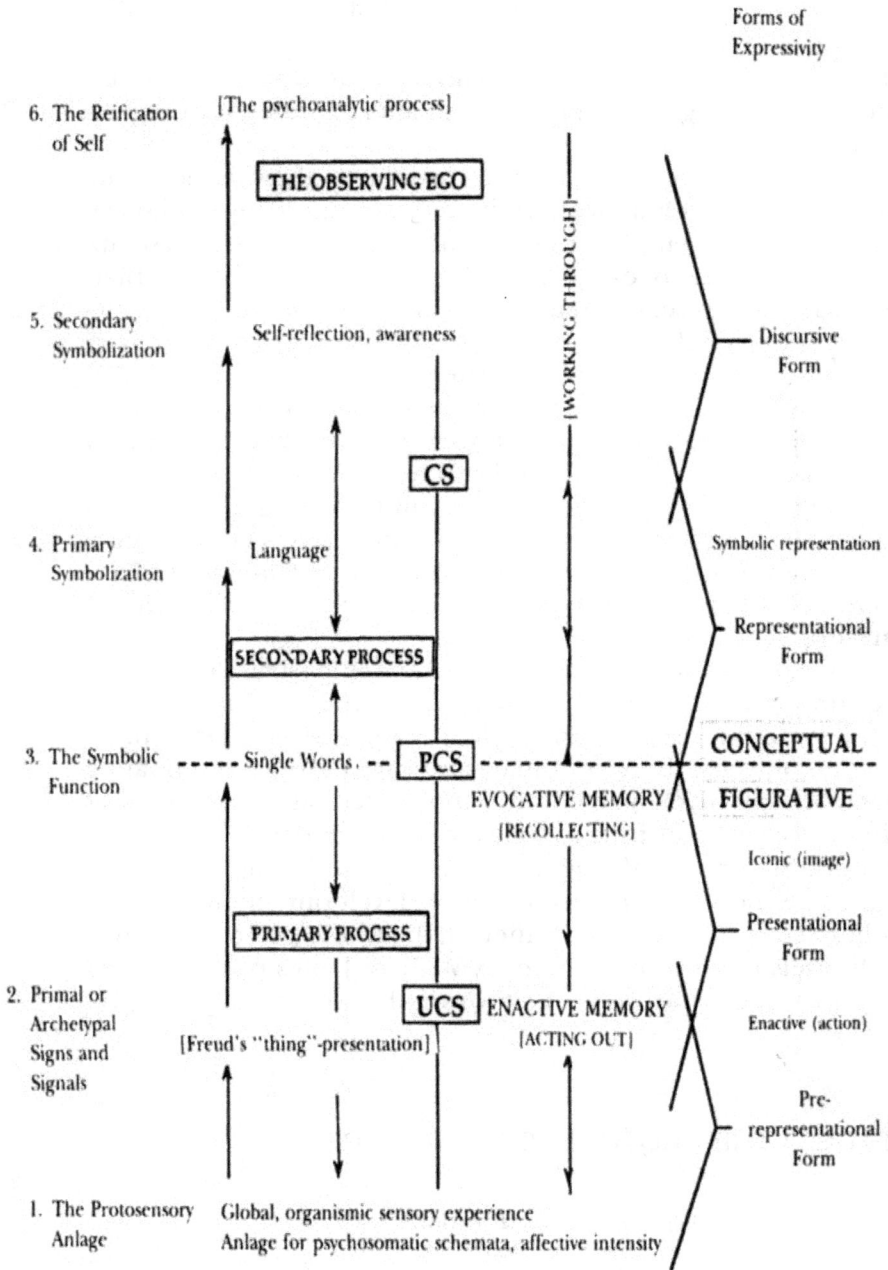

Figure 4.1 Stages of symbolizational development

What we first know of life is taken in, experienced, and organized through the senses; it is undifferentiated, diffuse, coenesthetic. Although our retinas are not fully functional at birth, and maximal intensity in all sensory modalities has yet to be reached, we are equipped to see, hear, smell, move, and, in particular, to suck and grasp; these are our first gropings in the world. We are a somatopsychic unity, already endowed with constitutional proclivities and temperamental dispositions which, in accordance with the tenor of exchanges we encounter in the environment, will lay down the foundations of our most basic physiologic and affective patterns of regulation. Further, we are gifted with an array of affective states along with myriad elusive degrees and nuances of intensity and coloring which are expressed in all manner of postural, kinetic, and organismic attitudes, not the least of which is the powerful vocalic one!

We can only imagine this early experience as a global blur of surging and subsiding intensities in waves of feeling states; of fluctuating patterns and temperatures, lights and shadows, shapes and noises; of degrees of alertness and nebulous quietness, jolts of unexpectedness and sudden bursts of affective effusion; of internal and external percepts without contour or definition, of ill-defined sensations, postures, movements, stimuli. All the vital processes of life, the great cycles of wakefulness–drowsiness and sleep, hunger-satiety and elimination, of lightness and darkness, closeness and aloneness, comings and goings, give rise to forms of feeling which are closely intertwined with motivational states evoked by arousing appetites and tensions. Gradually, we imagine, for all these rhythms and patterns and movements and sensations, broad categories begin to coagulate into "islands of consistency" (Escalona [1953] cited in Stern [1985]), as contours of experience and reciprocal responses coordinate patterns of reflexes.

Stern (1985) distinguishes between these first "feelings of vitality" in infancy, for which there is no existing taxonomy or lexicon, and the more traditional, discrete "categorcial affects." "Affect acts as the supra-modal currency into which stimulation in any modality can be translated" (Stern, 1985, p. 53). From the start, we are endowed with a general, innate propensity toward synesthesia, known as amodal perception; information is intuitively transferred from one sensory modality into another. A central dynamism, evident from birth, toward constructing and testing hypotheses about how things occur in the world, appears as a drive to organize information into units of knowledge. Therefore, cross-modal similarities, constancies, and patterns are beheld; we seek invariance, find consistencies, and are suspicious of incongruence in the new, and through rhythms, cycles, movements, percepts, and feelings, begin to form categories of actions consequent to their effect, in spatio-temporal sequence (Kagan, 1984).

The sensorimotor schema is the abstracted unit of experience organizing knowledge at this somatopsychic level where the sensory event and motor response constitute a whole unit, as it were, for action engrams. Information is "incorporated," as the maturation of motor patterns and corresponding sensations begin to shape a logic of egocentric activity. As such, however, this organization is unconscious, awareness being limited to perceptions of immediate current experiences, and significance attached only to motives directly connected to the cause and effect of action sequences. Experience is immediate, nonideational, affective, and its forms of knowledge and expression equally global, organismic, enactive, sensorimotor configurations. This somatopsychic substructure of ordering and schematizing is prototypical for all later mental organization and provides the affective–expressive foundation upon which all future psychological functioning is built.

Defined by the somatic mode in which assimilation and accommodation occur, this stage describes how infantile experience is expressed and laid down in terms of things-of-action. Accommodation implies some unconscious process by which these action experiences become encoded in the brain, where they become the anlage for further assimilation. As these begin to organize into general categories of space, time, and causal action sequences, these schemata become the prototypes for later internalizations which are corroborated through repetition, imitation, social transactions and later through practice and fantasy play (Piaget, 1937; Bruner, 1973).

The basic neurophysiological channels for regulating stimulation are determined at this stage and nascent, habitual ways for titrating alertness, attention, distress, delay, and effort are established. While experience, like volition, is embedded and programmed in the bodily event at these primal levels, it is not lodged in the muscles alone, but in mnemic sequences of motor configurations in the brain, which form part of our basic, somatic core self. Equally, the conditioned response, habituation, and other early modes of learning which are essentially organismic signal and sign responses, have corollary patterning in the brain. Experiences of learning, mastery, and relatedness begin in the moving body, and somatic engrams contain all aspects of an event; that is, degrees of pleasure-unpleasure, control or lack of it, and affective tone, but the schema itself, an abstracted sequence of experience, is also a mental phenomenon which may find transferability from one set of actions to quite a different set for its execution and expression (Stern, 1985).

The developmental accretion in memory systems of recognition, retrieval, and active memory enable comparison between past and present, similar and dissimilar situations, and afford new integration of separate experiences. The infant's rudimentary construction of notions of causality and contingency awareness (who is causing what) increase new cognitive competencies which produce, among other things, stranger anxiety and attachment patterns, and also lead to an innovative capacity to search for new means to attain familiar ends. This further differentiates environment from infant and shapes the capacity to learn by consequence (Greenspan, 1979).

Emde (1983) refers to three basic principles which underlie the prerepresentational core: self-regulation, social fittedness, and affective monitoring. The first two refer to the innately social orientation of the infant, for whom psychological experience will flower out of a determining interpersonal matrix. The last refers to a fundamental nervous system gauge for regulating adaptive behaviors, measured along the pleasure–unpleasure dimension, and operating outside of awareness, in which affects are the key calibrators. Affects imbue and infuse all subjective experience and are therefore a fundamental aspect of every self-regulatory process, self-regulation being one of the primary achievements of this somatic level of organization. In all of this it is important to remember how much the innate biologically determined predisposition impacts on the nature of subjective experience (Escalona, 1953, 1962, 1968).

The infant has moved from diffuse, coenesthetic chaos toward relative organization in patterns of somatic coordination vis-à-vis internal and external stimuli occurring in an active interpersonal milieu within which many expressive cues and signals have crystallized. Great strides have been made in self-regulation with regard to responsiveness and a basic acquaintance with the logic of movement. Along with an immense amount of learning and coordinating, assisted by social interest and a propensity for eye-to-eye contact, the infant has bestowed on delighted parents the social smile and entered into a remarkably adept communicational system of reciprocal expressiveness and responses with close caregivers. This intensely affective language of signs and signals, rich with intuitive, expressive exchanges, mirroring, and pitched noises, flowers within emotionally charged, daily interpersonal exchanges. We may presume empathy, intuition, attunement, even inspiration to be lodged at these nondiscursive levels, in affective patterns of apprehension. Since affective and cognitive processes are but two sides of one coin, the entire event is swallowed whole, as it were. Experiences fusing form and meaning still reflecting proprioceptive and exterioceptive confusion are incorporated as units, and laid down as such. Stern (1985) writes of this primal phase:

> This global, subjective world of emerging organization is and remains the fundamental domain of human subjectivity. It operates out of awareness as the experiential matrix from which thoughts and perceived forms and identifiable acts and verbalized feelings will later arise. It also acts as the source for ongoing affective appraisals of events. Finally, it is the ultimate reservoir that can be dipped into for all creative experience [p. 67].

Reflex schemas have evolved into habit schemas, and in our search for invariance, as we try to relate current perceptions to earlier schemas, repeated exposure to any constellation will coagulate to form the contours of the schematic prototype, an idiosyncratic creation corresponding to the crystallized average of a particular class of events or category of experience. I think it not difficult to find, in what for Kagan represents an inexplicable "addictive tendency to create categories" (1984, p. 215), the embryonic roots of the prototype for the symbolic function, to "throw together," to condense, and fuse form and meaning.

Experiences thus early laid down in terms of affective, sensorimotor actualities will soon become directed inward where they will be shaped into forms, classes, categories and objects of contemplation. In this inward turning they will become infused with subjectivity. Sensorimotor patterns will acquire forms and contours of significance through a dynamic schematizing process which commingles all sensorial, affective, postural, kinetic, and motor constituents into internalized components of imaginal possibilities. These form the basis for the realm of human subjectivity. At this dim threshold, as in actuality we have acquired certain patternings, gained the capacity to search for new means to achieve similar ends, we begin to create forms from experience. And our propensity toward ordering and form building now crystallizes into vague figments of subjective archetypal presentations, which are the hallmark of the next stage.

Many phenomena which unfold spontaneously and sequentially as behavioral gains within the first two years reflect the maturation of the central nervous system. The emergent organization of perception and ordering of sensory stimuli and motor coordination, recognition, retrieval and active memory, facial and postural expression, stranger and separation anxiety, attachment, play, words—all are correlates of evolving cognitive competencies (Kagan, 1984). Their appearance as external markers, by implication, denotes underlying distinctive changes in the quality of internal experience. Indications of surprise and anticipation, for instance, which appear between 9 and 10 months, suggest there is something to be surprised about, that there is a nascent capacity to organize expectations. In all spheres, behavior is becoming more differentiated, social, and organized (Greenspan, 1979).

While the first year is enveloped in the immediacy of somatic embeddedness, entrance into the second heralds the beginning of a conceptual attitude, with the appearance of "inference, the amplifier of knowledge" (Kagan, 1984, p. 201). Gathered inward, information is now transformed and expanded into concepts and principles of how things of the world work—this increases organization, intentionality, gestural expressiveness, and social communicativeness. Categorizing and classifying will lead to relating events sequentially, adding a temporal dimension—things are organized in relation to a past, a present, and a future, and the great human passion for creating narratives begins in the earliest explanations of causality in which the self is always so central.

Organically, pronounced increases appear in the density of web and fiber connections in cortical regions during the first two years; while subcortical portions of both visual and auditory systems are myelinated shortly after birth, myelination from subcortical to higher bundles of the cortex in the auditory and other systems, is delayed and complete myelination of the highest bundles extends over several years (Konner, 1982). To the complex confluence of environmental impact upon temperamental tendencies, add the gradual struggle toward separateness and individuation, and the complicated interconnectedness of genetics and learning loom large in the effect experience has on the brain—this is to alter structure. The ongoing flux and complementarity between maturation, experience, and development produce behavioral fluctuations reflecting the transformations which are occurring in internal experience (Kagan, 1984). All of these conditions and their impact change the brain, where visual and motor patterns and other sensory stimuli are converted into sensibilities; where the formation and expansion of general classes of states of feeling and concepts become recursively shaped and reshaped into further ideation. Not only nerve cells change, virtually every system in the body responds to experience and use—and all are intertwined.

Dynamic schematization provides us with a mentation which imbues factual traces with elements of imagination, as motives mix with moods, perceptions, hopes, and expectations to produce abstracted experiences charged with significance. "As fast as objective impingements strike our senses they become emotionally tinged and subjectified . . . every internal feeling tends to issue in a symbol, which gives it objective status. . . .

It is this structure that constitutes what we mean by the 'life of the mind' " (Langer, 1972, p. 342). It is this inner life which is the natural domain of psychoanalytic inquiry. We are, of course, in the unconscious, that unconscious of Freud's, "recognized as being of infantile origin and equipped with peculiar mechanisms" (1917a, p. 227), of which the dream is the prototype. Its medium is iconic, yet the image at this stage does not represent knowledge, so much as present it. These motor or kinesthetic images (Bewegungsbild) (1985) which are comparable to those in hysterical "reminiscences" (Loewald, 1971), are not yet either veridical representations or ideas. But Freud had neither sensorimotor conceptualizations nor symbolic systems at his disposal, and therefore found explanation for these phenomena in the energic and economic hypotheses related to the primary process.

STAGE 2: PRIMAL OR ARCHETYPAL SIGNS AND SIGNALS

> The little, or almost insensible impressions on our tender infancies, have important and lasting consequences: and there it is, as in the fountains of some rivers, where a gentle application of the hand turns the flexible waters into channels, that make them take quite contrary courses; and by this little direction, given them at first, in the source, they receive different tendencies, and arrive at last at very remote and distant places. I imagine the minds of children as easily turned, this way or that way as water itself [John Locke (1690, p. 151), cited in Mandlebaum (1971, p. 151)].

Somewhere, along the developmental continuum between somatic undifferentiatedness and whole differentiated representations, as more and more pieces of units of experience, bits of memories, and constructions of impressions are strung together, there emerges the capacity for inner presentation. To be sure, it is nonlinear, amorphous, of a nondiscursive kind.

Characteristically, it is a distillate of the expressive features of
things seen and heard and done and felt, yet it is iconic, and
of the mind. Accordingly it "evokes," in an undifferentiated
manner, not the absent figure formed, but bits and pieces and
particles of features of what are fragmentary experiences. Of it,
Greenspan (1979) writes: "it is unclear from current research
findings exactly when this capacity for internal representation
begins" (p. 301). He notes that "probably [it] begins early in
the first year and continues to develop throughout life" (pp.
302, 306). Clearly, we are speaking of a continuum from imageless to imaginal.

Yet developmental psychologists have tended to establish
as markers those functions which exhibit sufficient organization
to be identified as manifestations of a particular psychological
achievement. Thus, the famed perceptual constancy of the inanimate object and the permanence of the emotional figure of
attachment—the first occurring during the first year, the latter
not before the third, or later—are but two aspects of one
lengthy, multifaceted process of decentering. Equally, the representational capacity, heralding the possibility for an entirely new
order of psychological organization, has sometimes been
treated as analogous to and concomitant with object permanence, or even the acquisition of language, which in neither
instance is the case. Rather, language is to be viewed as the
outgrowth or manifestation of an evolving symbolizing capacity
of which its antecedent (presymbolic) signal and sign variety
are microgenetic steps along the way. Development of the symbol out of these protosymbolic phenomena, is slow and must
be reworked along multiple vectors of experience, cognitive
operations, and expressive modalities. Moreover, as emphasized
throughout, shifts in representational levels are mediated
through relationships.

We assume that mental evolution is continuous and could
not therefore suddenly evoke an image of verisimilitude without
first having undergone a sequential process which only culminates in this event. The concept of "mental representation," if
conceived only in its accomplished, evocative capacity, makes
little sense. Rather, like all development and experience, it is
better viewed as only gradually including objective perceptions,

and only gradually achieving integration, in which earlier, less crystallized, more subjective versions will be less veridical, less cohesive, the mere constituents of later more differentiated forms. The mental image, after all, is woven out of the same threads of which the entire fabric is made.

Perhaps the special role of perception, and its relative weight in contributing to sensorimotor structuralization, has been underplayed in developmental approaches integrating cognitive psychology and psychoanalysis. Sensorimotor development facilitates coordination between visual and tactilokinesthetic sensation, and both enrich each other. The special contribution of perception in action patterns lies in picturing reality in its figurative aspects in contrast to experience in operative-motoric terms, which transforms reality. It is important, therefore, when discussing nondiscursive forms, to balance the relative roles of perception and action, insofar as their functioning, at this stage, is highly interrelated and will impact considerably on the balance between subjective and objective, egocentric and decentered, fantastical and veridical elements in the ongoing development of dynamic schematization (see also Bruner and Goodman [1947]). Accordingly, I have posited this intermediary stage, interpolated between somatic, nonideational schemas and the full conceptual, symbolic representational capacity which, in form and content, corresponds to the organismic sign and signaling interchanges and patterns of knowledge of which this stage of experience is capable.

To capture the phenomenology of this underside, I invite the reader to shed all notions of discursive, linear, linguistic logic and drop upon the threshold of this stage all thought of rational order, of social or temporal constraint. For in the great tide of mind which flows outside of our awareness, where nothing has been lost or can be hidden, laws of different conduct and causality prevail. This realm, shaped purely by its subject, is timeless, immediate, diffuse, fluid, its course abandoned and free; given to reviving all manner of fleeting scenes perceived, impressions felt, hopes anticipated, and these, the earliest and its latest form, welded into one. The dream, of course, is the emblem of the unconscious, as difficult to capture and recount as it is to hold, it must be understood on its own terms; amorphous vaguely conceived, intensely felt, terms in which not *instincts* but *affects* shape its form into patterns expressive of meaning. Its system, a primary, egocentric, phenomenalistic one, follows early dictates, figuratively rendered out of sensual expressivity.

This is a world of possibilities only, where every stifled impulse frees its full form, where disappointment dies in action realized, and desire, cast in strange surreal shapes, weaves fantastical stories of immense import; a world of airy flight and turgid dissent, of sweeping monumental plans as real as the pictures they paint. Significance, imbued with fantasy, collects unto itself a subjective labyrinth clipped out of figments of events, fleeting images, flights of fancy, all coalescing into forms of feeling depicted in our nocturnal figures and their unlikely narratives.

Timeless as affective relevance, the image does not explain; it bespeaks itself and is accustomed to having its way. The rebuking mother of earlier in the day is unrecognized as the evil witch who, cackling with her toothless grin, has found her way into the child's dream. The image is an amalgam of imago, identification, idealization, and the remembered, in which affective tone and motor components all coalesce. Invoked through emotion, it is a composite melody intoned by the senses. Here we may dance our tears, orchestrate our revenge, own a rainbow, erase an unwanted presence, fly above and from our earthly fears. This rapturous realm of metaphor and simile, of teleologic sequence designed to keep the regal "I" in its central, heroic role, is as irresistible as sleep itself; in it, nightly, we regenerate the stifled self, within a narrative order that balances out the constrictions of reality. The basic communicational mode of childhood is encased in affective signals to which gestural imitation adds acquired signs. Later, linguistic form will supersede these earlier expressive modes, but not supplant them. Therefore, will the adult dream, with added, complex, symbolized concepts, return to this animistic, magical–phenomenalistic realm, where shapes of expressivity freely invite the flights of emotive and volitional ascent which typify our inner life.

Organization at this level is structured around affectivity. "If inherited mental formations exist in the human being—something analogous to instinct in animals—these constitute the nucleus" (Freud, 1915b, p. 195). The dream, like symbolic play according to Piaget, serves an emotional function in psychic equilibrium, namely to aid in the assimilation of life's events and travails, with respect to their private significance (see also: Freud, 1900; Roland, 1971; Winson, 1986, 1990). Thus, imitation and practice play (both forms of identification) refer outward to a different pole of accommodation than that of symbolic or fantasy play, which creates symbols and narratives at will, centered around the self. A means of self-expression, it is indispensable for the child's affective and intellectual equilibrium that there be an area of activity, self-constructed, devoid of coercions or sanctions, capable of being bent by personal desire.

Hence, the "subjectivation" of what outwardly proceeds as the gradual process of acculturation finds expression in a parallel, private line. The outer, arbitrary sign forms an inner, correlate symbol, richer, more condensed, and complex, imbued with meaning; the outer form acquires vibrant color as it moves inward and toward the self. And here, at the source of some basic principle of design and primal symbolic formative process, pictorial presentation depicts these expressive depths, grasping their essential features, and projects them into the phatasmagoria of the dream. It is not difficult to see how art itself springs from the same expressive source.

The child's main communicational system now is gestural and tonal, wherein expressive and interactional cues with important people occur in affective signals and signs. "Gesture, the indissoluble unity of form and content, predates the 'pervasive interpretation' (Humboldt, 1884) of sound and significance characteristic of human speech. . . . The non-representational construing of *objects as expressive* is basic, and generally prior to the use of expressive properties in representation" (Werner and Kaplan, 1963, p. 20). Mental functioning early in life is essentially different in kind as well as degree, primarily because at each developmental plane considerable cognitive competency is added, encompassing ever greater integration of reality factors. Therefore, early in this stage we find that organization is still fragmentary, split, love and hate sharply divided; it is animistic, alternately concrete and abstract, diffuse, things and functions interchangeable, obeying sensorimotor notions of causality, given to sudden appearance and disappearance, magical transformation, the world, a subjective universe in which nothing is but the personal frame of reference. Unequivocally, Freud (1917a) had stated as fact that *what is unconscious in mental life is also what is infantile,* explaining that this "mode of expression is incomprehensible to us owing to many of its features. We have said that it harks back to states of our intellectual development which have long since been superseded—to picture-language, to symbolic connections, to *conditions, perhaps, which existed before our thought-language had developed.* We have on that account described the mode of expression of the dream-work as *archaic* or *regressive*" (1917a, p. 199; *emphasis added*). Moreover, "dream life knows how to find access" to the forgotten earliest years of childhood, to shrouded memories which have lain in the unconscious under the veil of infantile amnesia.

It is hypothesized today that consciousness is less an underlying system than a mode of presentation characteristic of a particular phase. Since awareness is tied to the contents of a particular level of organization of experience, it can only know of itself. It will follow that only in dreaming, when this nonlinguistic, iconic mode is tapped, may we revisit experiences which have occurred prelinguistically, and which, accordingly, have left memory traces expressible only in affective-pictorial forms.

Iconic presentation, at this level, is predicated on some concrete similarity between the form and its meaning, it is an affective equivalent, not yet a representation, but a substitute or distillate of the essentially felt features of the original. Accordingly, these images retain the full charge of their affective vitality, indeed they issue from and are expressive of it; Freud identified this as the *idea of the thing* (concrete ideas) (1915b), and described the Ucs as containing the "thing-cathexis" of the first and true object-cathexis, related to the remote memory-trace derived from nebulous images of the first objects. Freud's "thing-cathexis" corresponds to a level of undifferentiated, affective equivalency; a plane of organization in which experience is tied to a sensory sign and signaling variety. If, however, as

Langer declared, the genuine symbol "is above all an instrument of conception" (1972, p. 289), then the pre-symbolic forms of this stage have acquired neither their "conceptual," nor their status of instrumentation—they are depictions, not yet *vehicular structures*, carrying assigned significance for their referents. They partake of significance due to their expressive form but this has not been assigned them specifically; it has erupted spontaneously and creatively, out of the senses. I believe that it is to this level of desymbolized reconcretization that the dedifferentiation of schizophrenic processes returns, similarly producing emotionally charged imagery which, were it not to have broken the boundaries of sleep, might be but a normal dream.

And this is really the crux of the whole thing; primary process mechanisms and presentations are already symbols, but only in statu nascendi. They are symbolic only in appearance, because they have not yet undergone the intentional act of denotive reference, whereby something is taken to represent something else. Therefore they reflect the sign and signaling organization of experience of this stage, although superficially they have the same iconic form of later representations, they have not undergone the process of denotation, whereby a vehicular symbolic form is adopted to signify a referent. They are protosymbolic, evocative rather than denotive, and mark a step in the unfolding of a "microgenetic" process of inner dynamic schematizing activity (Werner and Kaplan, 1963). The essential qualifying difference lies in the intentionality of the act of denotive reference which, through its productive, creative nature, extracts and "brings to the fore latent expressive qualities in both vehicular material and referent" (Werner and Kaplan, 1963, p. 21), which will lead to the establishment of semantic correspondence between two entities, culminating in the flowering of language.

Out of this dual structuring source, one directed toward the referencing of meaningful objects (denotively), the other inclined toward the shaping of patterns of expressivity (connotively), the entire spectrum of human symbolic activity can be organized and understood. Of central import is the process of dynamic schematization which exerts a directive, orienting influence on organismic states and is critical in binding the vehicular symbolic form to its organismic matrix, where it is embedded in personal significance. Referencing, whatever form it takes, can never be a passive, static event; it is interwoven with sensory, affective, postural, imaginal, and interpersonal components, all of which form constituent aspects of the organismic shaping of the symbolic entity as a vehicular form. When the verbal utterance occurs, the word, a sentence, it will be imbued with the significance ordained it by the entire structure, not just the vocable, and will continue to function as a meaningful vehicle as long as it retains its connection to this organismic matrix as a meaningful vehicle of expression.

It is not by chance that Freud wandered into a discussion of schizophrenia in his work "The Unconscious," contemplating the strange decomposition of language characteristic of this decompensated state. He remarked, "In schizophrenia, *words* are subject to the same process as that which makes dream-images out of dream-thoughts, the one we have called the primary mental process . . . the process may extend so far that a single word, which on account of its manifold relations is specially suitable, can come to represent a whole train of thought" (1915a, p. 199). Here, the breakdown of the denotive structure reveals an underlying multiplicity of connotive nuances which have been compressed into a vehicular form. The true "symbol" is a slow acquisition, organismically constructed and maintained, and follows the same gradual process of differentiation and organization of unities characteristic of all development. Freud was correct, of course, in comparing the processes occurring in language and dreams, as they are uniformly the process of a single, symbolizing mind in its evolving construction of symbolic, vehicular forms for expression and communication. The desymbolization of schizophrenia is caused by the disruptive toxicity of unmetabolized interpersonal internalizations and their overwhelming affective connotations, which dedifferentiate an already fragile structure, dislodging the firm connection between the two symbolic poles of reference, that is, between self and other, object and significate (see also Kubie, 1953; Arieti, 1975). The whole process is interwoven with the gradual separation and individuation of child from environment and child from mother, and is contingent upon the vicissitudes of early interpersonal relations which can facilitate or prevent gradual decentering, a prerequisite in the child's ongoing effort to "know about" the world.

At this stage, however, of central import is the essential "transcendence of expressive qualities" (Werner and Kaplan, 1963), discerned as similar features of otherwise dissimilar objects, out of which a pattern is constructed, which is connotively expressive of meaning. In our characteristic search for invariance and propensity toward expressive shaping (or form building), we are now finding similarities in the dynamic properties of people, things, and events and forming expressive patterns gesturally, behaviorally, tonally (and later verbally) that convey internal states intentions and meanings. It is in the transcendent quality of expressiveness, as well as the lack of firm differentiating boundaries, that we find explanation for the animistic, shifting, mobile quality of dream imagery—the interchangeability of one figure or the features of a figure for another, the mixing of animate and inanimate, the subsuming into an archetypal form which seals within it similar characteristics of an entire category. This is the realm of kings and queens, of giants and gnomes, of magic and ritual and repetition, of Jung's archetypal form, which holds entire constellations of primordial significance within its shape. It is the source of narrative genres, here closely aligned to the fairy tale, the nursery rhyme, and later to legends and myths in which we can already discern the underlying linguistic, analogy, onomatopoeia, metaphor, simile.

Later on to this compelling realm of patterns of malleable, plastic unities, language will be added, consolidating both the symbolic function as it flows out of it, and fastening the tight relationship between words and their denoted meaning. Rooted in a deep unconscious structure of semantic, syntactical, and phonological rules, language also generates out of the same basic semiotic constituents that spring from the connotive and denotive aspects of form organization. While the dream creates idiosyncratic patterns that are connotive of personal meanings, words strung into sentences are constructed patterns of consensual signs, denotive of significance; both are spun unconsciously; the one faces inward, the other outward.

Presentation at this level corresponds to signs and signaling phenomena associated in psychoanalysis with the unconscious, primary process. Iconic form is derived from personal experience and based on some concrete or central dynamic similarity with its object. It is an affective equivalent, an instantaneous substitute, for which no delay is required. The relationship between signal and signalized is one of contiguity, and that between sign and signified one of simile; both are important forms of metaphor, metonymy and simile (Rosen, 1969), but neither is a true symbol. The signal announces, it heralds expectation of action or presence; the sign indicates and similarly triggers an activity or presence—both are immediate. In their signification, both imply a one-to-one correspondence between themselves and what they signify, they are synchronous with what they stand for, instruments of conditioning, not conceptualizing. For the small child, the sound of the doorbell announces Father's arrival, his slippers *are* his presence.

Primitive belief systems correspond to this level: magic and ritual, embraced with fervor equal in strength to the fearful superstition and cherished illusion, exist in the same realm of magical realism out of which totems, taboos, amulets, and all other emblems of "equivalency" are created and used. Untested by conceptual doubt or distanced by the speculative intrusion of reality, their meaning is of the senses—affective rather than cognitive. Undifferentiated, they stand proxy for their objects of significance, not in contemplation but in *experience*. All of these phenomena correspond to this stage in the development of symbolization (Lévi-Strauss, 1958a,b; Vignola, 1972).

"Metonymy," writes Rosen (1969), "is that form of metaphor which utilizes the familiar mechanism of pars pro toto or a contiguous object as a means of reference. . . . Simile, on the other hand, is a verbal form of iconic repesentation" (p. 200). In the various other remarkable attributes of metonymy and simile, such as condensation, displacement, plastic representation, generalization, and rapidity of response, we can recognize many of the operations Freud listed as characterizing the mechanisms of the primary process (Rosen, 1969). Metaphor, by its "application of name and descriptive term to an object to which it is not literally applicable" (*The Concise Oxford Dictionary*, 1958) strives for symbolic expression. In its personal, independent, and connotive amplitude, it resembles the expressive potential of the image, and perhaps for this reason is so often the vehicle of poetic evocation. Perhaps it is the linguistic, descriptive materialization of this iconic form. In this it is more depictive or figurative than abstract, more evocative than denotive, and therefore evolves out of our expressive repertoire rather than our logical abstractive conceptual articulation.

Knapp (1969) refers to the inner image as the "cardinal vehicle" of private mental events, when describing the silent, persistent phenomenological substrate of our outer, ordered patterns of communication. He likens this inner universe to a "shadow counterpart" of the manifest exterior. Vivid images imply organization at this iconic level of presentation and implicitly suggest strong emotional currents—equally, powerful emotions are usually coupled with or evoke vibrant images. "A striking image, like a striking percept, entails some degree of affective involvement," writes Knapp, "Yet, the two can become disengaged" (p. 393), or, as he puts it, "bleached," in their movement toward abstraction.

The highly personal, condensed, allusive nature of the image, particularly in its reliance on quasi-imitative approximation in its tendency to portray, renders it exceedingly idiosyncratic and ambiguous and therefore less suited than discursive, linguistic form for purposes of communication (Knapp, 1969). Explicit verbal thought in adulthood, however, typically evolves out of this presentational foundation, and consciousness arises out of processes issuing from this primordial underlay of imagery. Nondiscursive form, in its simultaneity and condensation embodies the interwoven nature of the mind's hierarchical organization, as each level is both an independent construction of experience and part of the unified whole. Psychic constellations superimpose upon one another in an ascending design leading to greater discreteness, specificity, and abstraction. Nevertheless, due to the unending interplay of stimuli and impressions impinging on our senses, to which we cannot readily attend during the course of our days, there is always a proliferation of unmetabolized material with which to spin the images of our dreams. We do not return to childhood, but we return to that vivid form of imaging each night, within which to play out, alter, relive, and expand our current motives, aspirations, fears, and ideation.

At this point, it is important to emphasize that the exact developmental stage at which a dream narrative as we know it begins is not clear. It is doubtful that a discrete, comprehensible, formal dream can occur prior to the acquisition of language competencies. Yet I have included the dream form at this level because its iconic mode of depiction and affective realism typify this stage in symbolizational development, somewhere between imitative accommodation and conceptualization. Moreover, as an expression of the unconscious, it exhibits the properties and formal features of what will become language and its grammatical structure. Every sensorimotor assimilation implies the attribution of significance to the components of schemas-of-action (including the perceptual), and therefore to the establishment of some relationship between an action and what it means. In the earliest part of this stage, the relationship is so undifferentiated that the index of significance partakes of some aspect of the signified and, by way of this connection, constitutes it. With maturation, greater differentiation accompanies separation, and through various imitative and play behaviors, there begin to elaborate the formation of signifiers which are distinct from significates or the signified. It is important, however, to keep in mind that although the stages are sequential, they also overlap and evolve gradually, and that while more advanced development partially subsumes earlier functioning, all stages continue to coexist; the later, dip into earlier modes, as in creativity or dreams.

I am convinced that things must evolve in a stepwise fashion, and accordingly that there will be fragments of images and dreams just as there are gesture and tone before single words, which only gradually gather into clusters and concatenations of new units in images or language. Despite our occidental logocentric emphasis on language, there are forms of knowledge that shape experience into forms which neither spring from nor are determined by the linguistic definitions we later afford them. It is, after all, an ill-determined constructive drive which

urges us to put them into words. Symbolic form finds its prototype in language but it does not consist exclusively of words,
since words, as we have seen in schizophrenia, can lose their
denotive distance and become dangerously empty and concrete;
it is an abstractive relationship, one that binds a concept to a
form with which it is not identical. Dreams may become *repre*-
sentational, as this function matures, but they are also *presenta*-
tional, at the outset.

The developmental steps leading toward the expression in language of the symbolic function evolve out of deferred imitation,
symbolic play, the appearance of the graphic image (rarely before 2 or $2^1/_2$ years of age), internalized imitation, the internal
image, and finally, the nascent form of verbal evocation. Imagining a movement entails an internal reiteration, an inner sketch-
ing of that movement. Neurophysiologically, the imagined
physical act consists in activation of the same electrical pattern
in the brain (Piaget and Inhelder, 1969, p. 68). Thus, each of
these activities incrementally contributes to the mental capacity
for evoking the absent object; that is, the capacity of the mind
to conjure up an image of what is not perceptually present.
Practice has begun in the body, in movement, as deferred imitation cements lasting internalizations and identifications which
then spread and are taken up in all expressive modalities.
    While constancy of the inanimate object consolidates
around 18 to 20 months, permanence of the loved object,
bound by attachment and wrought with intensely aroused conflictual affects, may take quite a bit longer. The vicissitudes
around this process and its outcome impact quite formidably
on symbolization and the many subtle and gross consequences
encumbent upon it. Intense emotions disrupt differentiation
and produce imaginal distortions which increase separation
anxiety and attachment needs, and, as we have seen, because
strong affects substantiate into fantastical imagos, such delays
in differentiation also delay reality testing, which impacts on
more veridical internalized memory traces. Of relevance to py-
choanalysis is precisely this affective component of the schema,
which by its tone and strength largely determines the entire
phenomenology of a given event or experience.

The child has now internalized a variety of imitative, identificatory, and nascent semiotic configurations, which are enacted and articulated within the magical phenomenalistic logic of early somatic intelligence. An increased capacity to distinguish means from ends and to learn from experience, to separate self from other and from things of the world, has produced new levels of reality awareness which, in becoming internalized, lead to what Piaget has called "concrete operations," or the mental manipulation of cognitive constructions. "The decentering of cognitive constructions necessary for the development of the operations is inseparable from the decentering of affective and social constructions" (Piaget and Inhelder, 1969, p. 95), and the first step consists in "mentally representing what has already been absorbed on the level of action" (p. 94).

Separation and internalization, in a dynamic sense, are two facets of a unified duality for us, who, as Freud so aptly remarked, have great difficulty in giving anything up. What is renounced to the senses becomes mind, where it is held and transformed subjectively. Meaning and mind are one. Therefore, the separation–individuation process, and implicitly, decentering, is accompanied by a gradual capacity for *re*presentation. The advent of this new and remarkable level of symbolization, one which only the human child can acquire, heralds the beginning of the instrumentation of conceptual thought, the true symbol. With it, it brings the capacity for the retrieval and contemplation of events and the uniquely human symbolic system of language which leads to consciousness.

As long as experience is retained in the senses, of the senses, it *is* us and is therefore unconscious, not yet of the mind. We have not distanced ourselves from it or taken something to represent it and therefore have no means by which to make it comprehensible to ourselves or others. It is *of* us, not yet *beheld*. Only when we have, as it were, lost it, organically separated ourselves from the experience or object, and perceived it as other, beheld it, and given it a name by which to refer to it, only then can we be conscious of it. This is what marks the human difference; animals remember, humans recollect.

STAGE 3: THE SYMBOLIC FUNCTION

> Nil est in intellectu quod non prius fuerit in sensu.
> [Leibnitz, cited in Piaget (1969, p. 28)]

> If one possesses the picture of a feeling very exactly within
> oneself, then the word must follow.
> [Flaubert]

Evocative or retrieval memory, internal image, and the beginnings of language, evolve more or less simultaneously; armed
with these new competencies, the mind makes a quite formidable leap. From the coconstruction of denotable objects of reference within a gestural language, we now move to adopting a
"means within a medium" (Werner and Kaplan, 1963, p. 19) for
representing these—the symbolic vehicle. Despite a remarkable
versatility in manifestation and diversity of form, the symbolic
function, attained at this stage, presents an underlying uniformity—it enables the representational evocation of things which
are not present. It lifts thought out of action and replaces it
with a representation of the mind. The integrity of body–mind
unity and continuity in development and the genesis of symbolization are the very structure of thought, and therefore of the
psychological.

How is it that we can take a material pattern—phonetic,
pictorial, mimetic—substantially different in quality and design
from which it comes to represent, and learn to exploit it in
symbolic use? How do we move from this transitional place of
illusion where, by reason of its partaking in some way of the
original, something *is* what it stands for, to the transformational
act of adopting something completely different from the original and taking it to represent what it stands for? The seeds of
explanation can be found in the intrinsic progressive tendencies
of our maturational design which, at every step, require active
organismic participation. We have seen thus far, that the child
partakes in the development of a world of shared, common
referents expressive of the affective–sensorimotor orientation

of the earliest stages; in this, the denotive gesture cannot be isolated from the entire context—the *whole* child is involved in the act of referencing. We have also seen how, by gradually internalizing knowledge of things of the world, the child expresses this in organismic acts of mimetic and gestural depiction. The child uses his or her body and all possible modalities for the purpose of presenting and expressing experience. Now, in the constructive, imitative, and communicative thrust of motivational sources converging at this time, this expressive tendency culminates in an entity (here a vocable) being taken to designate another, thereby transforming an expressive form into a symbolic vehicle (Werner and Kaplan, 1963, p. 21).

The act of referencing does not merely consist of passively learning and adopting preestablished expressive similarities between entities; rather, these connections have to be consolidated personally and anew by every individual. The very *intentionality* of the act is what makes the difference, as correspondence between pattern and object is found and both are embedded in similar organismic states to become rooted in an organismic matrix. The productive and dynamic nature of this process of denotation is such that connections between latent expressive qualities in both the symbolic vehicle and its referent are formed, enabling the establishment of semantic correspondence between a word and what it means. This is why at the deepest levels words retain their "thing-cathexis" (Freud) or, in other words, their affective, organismic intensity. A vocable can be reproduced in imitation, yielding a phonetic unit which may be tagged onto something, much like a label in a behavioristic mode, but the sound will hold little expressive meaning. Conversely the word may be embroiled in an affective matrix which renders it equivalent to, rather than representative of, what it stands for. Establishment of semantic correspondence requires the "construing of a pattern *qua vehicle* so that its expressive meanings correspond to the connotational structure of the referent" (Werner and Kaplan, 1963, p. 20; emphasis added). It is not in the sound itself in which meaning is encased, but in expressive threads of signification with which we imbue it, organismically. Only when a vocable has become integrated within the regulative and form building directive of dynamic schematization as a vehicular structure can it enter into a stable semantic correspondence with its referent, and only then is it transformed from status of sign to that of true symbol.

For this to occur, actual differentiation and separation cannot be excessively wrought with anxiety, since affective and cognitive experience are interwoven and move hand in hand, two aspects of one person, two facets of one dynamically determined process. Referencing, in its initial pragmatic form, emerged out of a primordial sharing nexus, usually between mother and child; now, with increased separation and locomotion, sharing can begin to occur through symbolic media—verbal symbols, naming. The symbolizational capacity is progressing concomitant to the separation–individuation process, and "even as we lost the old empathic bonds, the symbolic function has moved into the place of our broken unity" (Langer, 1967, p. 313). We are not poorly rewarded: in its place a form of comparable magnitude appears which, in augmenting our connectedness to others, also gives us more of ourselves, as clearly, more distinctly, it leads from one mind to another. The symbolic vehicle, harbinger of consensual sharing, bridges the self to many others, who, having now been named, appear as "subjects," themselves collaborators in a new level of exchange. Genuine symbolic activity provides a new level for organizing and understanding experience—it represents a *structural* as well as a functional change, reflected organismically, and in the brain; neither "economic" nor "energic," it does, however, partake of the general dynamic form-building tendency of the entire organism to condense knowledge, in which multiple meanings, connotations, and nuances are subsumed into a single expressive entity.

The verbal symbol, words, when they appear, are pursued with avid enthusiasm by the new speaker. In their capacity to fuse form and meaning they not only afford a new flexibility of expression, but free the impulse from obligatory response. From the wellsprings of undifferentiatedness and attunement came an empathic sensitivity to the expressive features of things, an awareness of their essential qualities. Now out of the "great individuation made by subjective activity" (Langer, 1962, p. 319) springs an ideation which seeks to establish an expressive medium for the purpose of "talking about" things in shared contemplation. Language, wrote Humboldt (1884), the symbolic form par excellence, comes into being "in the very act of its production"; in its essence it is "not a product but an activity . . . the ever-repeated workings of the mind towards making the articulated sound capable of giving expression to thought" (cited in Werner and Kaplan [1963, p. 22]). This is the essential function of symbolization, and, like any symbol, the word is actually both—it is distinct from what it is taken to represent, and as an entity, condenses meaning. Its *vehicular* function lies precisely in the symbolic value with which we are able to imbue it. Words lose their significance for schizophrenics or become *things*, because the dual points of reference which would enable the creation of symbols due to their separateness, have collapsed into themselves. The schizophrenic has either only himself to refer to or an affectively dulled and destroyed world devoid of significance with which he has severed most meaningful communicational threads—merger and isolation destroy that space within which the word as symbol is constructed. In essence, the schizophrenic's defensive desymbolization returns words to their empty status as phonemic entities, possibly to prevent the massive affect and anxiety flooding associated with their expressive meanings and use. Defense against affect or affect flooding has erased the spontaneous abstractive process in which rational thought is founded.

But for the toddler, the word, a new power, offers a remarkable avenue for communication and expression. Initial "one-word sentences" (Stern, 1985) often express an entire range of observations, desires, directives, and emotions—the sum total of an experience, in a word. This begins to introduce a conceptual relationship to things of the world which slowly cements not only denotive correspondences, but connotational links between objects and their names, enabling these to be "thought about" in contemplation. The connotational aspect of a word, the concept it conveys, is what is retained in mind when neither utterance nor object are present. It is this genuinely *symbolic* conveyer, the vehicle of thought, which leads to the whole generative potential of language. The word enables experience to detach from itself, as it were, offering an arbitrary symbol for consensual referencing—things are no longer part of a self-in-action, but now become known as objects of shared communication or private reflection. One pole of reference embraces the vehicle as a communicational bridge, the other faces its connotational, idiosyncratic matrix within ourselves. Symbolization entails differentiation and integration, "reference to an object and representation of that object" (Werner and Kaplan, 1963, p. 43). In this, the semantic "I," assisted by negation, the great "not-I," enable the organization of thought and then reflection to occur. A uniquely human experience, the awareness of significance, has begun.

And who of us cannot recall in the dim and distant penumbra of our faintest recollection that vague dawning of consciousness brought about by the learning of words: the thrill of finding in a differentiated phoneme the formal shape for an amorphous experience, a demand newly issued in an utterance, instead of a cry; of enunciating a first noun and transforming our understanding of a "thing" by reason of our having named it. And of how, having now this name to hold it by, we could recollect and ponder about it in private, and reiterate the sound in public, and repeat that name, which had made a thing into a thought. My own life has been such that I have had the opportunity to witness in myself the renewed experience (as much as any recapitulation can ever resemble the original form) of this same awe and wonder, numerous times over, as struggling to acquire new languages, I have relived the effort and thrill of giving new and alien shape to significances known to me and familiar in other sounds. With the privilege of consciousness, I have been keenly aware of how a newly patterned sound, freshly acquired, quickly forgotten, must steadily, insistently be brought to mind in order for it to become embedded semantically. Only with repeated vocalizations can we imbue the alien sound with meanings carried from its contexts to ourselves, and vice versa, from ourselves to others, in shared expression.

For the child in the early stages of this transition, from the experience of things-in-action to that of their apprehension as objects of cognition, the degree of differentiation between name and referent is still slight. Considerable confusion between physical and psychological properties is reflected in an animistic attitude which attributes live qualities to things and people alike. The name is treated as though it were the thing. During the process of naming and concomitant increased interpersonal separateness, a gradual all-around developmental differentiation occurs as the vocal utterance now becomes the primary medium of representation. The symbol and its referent have become more distinct and the word has lost its urgent "realism," becoming more and more "desubstantialized," an *instrument* of reference, description, and expression rather than an *aspect* of it (Werner and Kaplan, 1963). With the advent of invariance and categorization, words attain even greater discreteness; their connotive features retreating inward, their denotive–lexical features more clearly differentiated, now quite independent from external, concrete referents. This is one of the manifestations of increased object and internal constancy.

This is also where we can observe how the interpenetration of "reality," or acculturation, impacts on the advent of secondary-process thought as it is led along by language. The bifurcation of the two aspects of the word as symbol, the connotive and denotive, can be envisioned as two facets of one dynamically determined unit of experience. The former, unusable for realistic purposes, moves outside of awareness and may retain many of its emotive, idiosyncratic, fantastical features; the latter, oriented outward, with consensual use crystallizes into conventional form, acquiring the necessary lexical precision for communicating to others. The connotive aspects remain in the service of the primary process, the denotive encompass secondary process ideation. Piaget cautioned against reifying these or thinking of them in isolation; operative and figurative functioning are interconnected and both will always remain aspects of one verbal symbol.

Unlike gesture or imagery, phonic form is both external to the signifier and functionally superior to both. It is discrete, specific, efficient, and lends itself to interpersonal shaping: "Not only does speech cost little effort, but above all, it requires no instrument save the vocal apparatus and the auditory organs which, normally, we all carry about as part of our very selves, so words are *naturally available* symbols, as well as very economical ones," writes Langer (1942, p. 75). Moreover, language is not only generated, but is itself generative. In language, the child will find a preexisting, socially elaborated system for an array of cognitive propositions, as well as an instrument for self-expression, both of which enrich the child's repertoire of thought and imagination. Freud named this symbolizational stage *the preconscious* and envisioned it to be a system, or way station, with censorship on either side barring access to and from the unconscious and conscious systems. Only by overcoming the "resistance," and with great difficulty, could unconscious contents become conscious. He hypothesized a model in which it was the shifting valence of "cathexes" which, by connecting to the unconscious "thing" presentation, could become attached to "words" representing them in the preconscious. By overriding another censor, they could be fully articulated in language and thereby become conscious. He described this transformation of content in energic and economic terms because he did not have a semiotic system available to him; it is now clear, however, that these are transformations not of energy but of symbolic articulation.

There is a remarkable functional unity underlying development, manifest at each phase and subphase, which binds affective, cognitive, social, and moral concerns and aspects into a unified whole. Development moves consistently in the direction of internalizing what has been external, and through a gradual decentering process, toward greater integration (of multiple aspects and vectors) and differentiation (between these and from the environment). The process is isomorphic in that it reproduces and elaborates in mentation what has earlier taken place at the sensorimotor level, while this sensorimotor nucleus continues to operate as organization becomes structured hierarchically.

This remarkable uniformity has more to do with an innate human propensity for forming systems of representation or the expression of the symbolic function itself than with the vocalic medium of linguistic production. It is now universally acknowledged that the emergence of language during the course of early development, as a basic feature of human biology, is primarily due to a genetically coded maturational plan (Chomsky, 1965; Lenneberg, 1967, 1973; Geschwind, 1972). What is less frequently emphasized, is that this is because its roots, or "deep structure," are in the symbolizational process itself. I quote Konner (1982) who, in referring to Chomsky (1957), writes, "Genetically determined neural structures would account for the 'deep structure' of languages as well as for mental capacities for semanticity, productivity, displacement and the *generation of surface structure from deep structure*" (p. 156; emphasis added). In this generative correspondence one can readily recognize a symbolic relationship and design. Symbolizational development, neurally based in the brain, is part of our evolutionary heritage and can be equated with what psychoanalysis has called "ego development." Konner hastens to add that the learning environment merely "fills the gaps" in this self-propelled program; "its impact on language, superficially impressive, would be of small formative importance" (p. 156). This is because what is of the essence is the maturational propulsion toward representing, referring to, or constructing symbolic systems, not language itself. Actually, there is no substantive difference between different symbolic modes and vehicles. The difference lies only in the degree to which a symbol is truly formed as a distinct vehicle or still embedded in protosymbolic expressions. This can be attested to through cognitive implications and by the fact that prior to the age of 10 or 11, there is no significant impairment in intellectual development in deaf children. The deficiency in linguistic experience at this level of maturation does not preclude its effective substitution by other vehicular symbolic modalities (Furth, 1970). These follow the same developmental sequence of symbolizational stages which normally culminate in linguistic expression.

For Piaget, if we are to continue borrowing and integrating his cognitive model, the balancing interplay of assimilation and accommodation during intermediary steps leading from the initial stages of representational thought to its full manifestation in the capacity to conceptualize, can only find equilibrium in the direction of "decentration" (Piaget, 1962, p. 242). Indeed, the starting point for concrete operations of thought which enable the construction of constancy, displacement, conservation, inverse and reciprocal relationships, and later seriation and classificatory correspondences, is rooted in a gradual organismic decentering. The intermediary stages leading from preconceptual to operational thought (between approxiately 4 to 7 years of age) Piaget described as "intuitive," stating that these higher forms of articulated intuitions remain linked to a configuration or image as part of a schema, due to the as yet insufficiently decentered process of assimilation at this stage.

The symbolic function depends on the capacity to construct differentiated signifiers; this is a gradual process. Signification, an aspect of every schema, in Piaget's terminology, refers to "operative" knowing, that part of a sensorimotor event which has been acted upon to alter reality. Representation refers to figurative knowledge, that perceptual aspect of a schema which corresponds to form. The latter, in its capacity to mentally abstract the structural form of operative activity, eventually leads to reflective or formal abstract thought. The constituent operative and figurative aspects of symbol formation are interrelated, in fact, inseparable. The former is derived from operative experience and will reflect the meaning, the connotive aspects of a symbol; the latter, derived from figurative shaping, will correspond to the medium, the vehicular form or denotive aspects of a symbol. These facets of the word as vehicular symbol are particularly important for a psychoanalytically informed investigation of language and a psychoanalytically based, unified model of mind, because both reflect nuances in the instrumentation of exchanges within the clinical process, and both are always present as two sides of one symbolic expression or communication. As discussed earlier, primary and secondary processes may be reconceptualized in the light of these dual aspects of processing experience. Picasso's famous declamation, "I paint not what I see but what I *know!*" comes to mind in this context, and can be understood as his choosing to depict or represent what was connotive and operatively known to him qua expression, rather than to reproduce the figurative, veridical, perceptual reflection of what can be seen.

Piaget highlighted both the functional continuity between earlier somatic and conceptual intelligence and their structural dissimilarity, and postulated two conditions for effectuating the transition from one to the other: (1) a general system of mental operations internalizing mobile and reversible actions; and (2) the social consideration of these operations which ensure general reciprocity of viewpoints and a correspondence of terms and results with those of others. These two processes are interdependent and, despite functional continuity, the child will now go through a period of slow structural evolution, in which these socially bound and internal operational processes of thought must be integrated into and through the linguistic medium at this new plane of symbolization: "Before equilibrium can be restored . . . a road similar to the one just ended must thus once more be travelled" (Piaget, 1962, p. 240).

STAGE 4: LANGUAGE

> It is a peculiar fact that every advance in thinking, every epoch making new insight springs from a new type of symbolic transformation. A higher level of thought is primarily a new activity; its course is opened up by a new departure in semantic [Langer, 1942, p. 200].

With the advent of the initial stages of genuine symbolic representation, the mind acquires a tool of infinite dexterity, and words, concise, efficient, self-contained, and vocally aesthetic, are ideally suited for the general uses to which they are put. "A new vocable is an outstanding Gestalt. It is a possession too," writes Langer (1942), "because it may be held at will. . . . It is the readiest thing in the world to become a symbol when a symbol is wanted" (p. 125).

From the earliest period (between 8 and 10 months), infants all over the world spontaneously emit the most charming gurgling, babbling, and lulling sounds and gradually engage in all manner of vocalizing which, in all probability, will be reflectively mirrored back with similar sounds and vocalic intonations by all who willingly enter into this universal language of babyhood. From these colorfully inflected tonal conversations and the vocal play of infancy have jelled differentiated patterns learned in imitation, and out of these have emerged one-word and then two-word sentences. Articulate language flowers during the course of the second year, and having made its appearance, usually flourishes. From the outset, the human infant has developed within the familiarity of vocalic expressiveness and due to a pervasive, exquisite sensitivity to expressive features of any kind, the child's impressionability intuits a vague sort of meaning in these auditory forms. Sounds, in all their patterned intensities, have surrounded the infant from birth. It is only to be expected that as the symbolizing capacity, vocalic articulation, and increased social involvement converge, the child will leap into this new medium with which, in a novel way, to grasp the world. Indeed, the child grabs this opportunity and repeats the new vocal treasures incessantly, at every occasion and in all possible tonal variations. Language is not merely a means of communication, it is an entirely new perspective of world and self order.

In this regard, it is worth noting a few poignant lines from P. J. Bonnaterre's (1800) vivid account of *Le Sauvage de l'Aveyron*, the study of a boy of about 13 who was found in the late 1700s living alone in the wild in a French forest. He writes: "consigned by nature to instinct alone, this child performs only purely animal functions: he has no knowledge whatever of those artificial passions or those conventional needs which become as demanding as natural needs . . . his desires do not exceed his physical needs. The only blessings he knows in the universe are nourishment, rest and independence" (cited in Lane [1976, p. 38]). With regard to speech, Bonnaterre remarks that without any means for communicating his feelings, deprived of gestures and sounds appropriate for the expression of ideas, his wild boy did, however, learn to employ some signs immediately relevant to having his needs satisfied, but remained unable to communicate, except in cries and inarticulate sounds: "His expressive sounds, rarely emitted unless he is emotional, are rather noisy, especially those of anger and displeasure; when joyful, he laughs heartily; when content, he makes a murmuring sound, a kind of grunting. He does not utter raucous or frightening cries. Almost all are guttural and depend only slightly on the movement of the tongue" (p. 37).

The optimal, biologically determined time for the shaping of language having lapsed for this child, he was also arrested in the whole symbolic potential which its interchanges afford. Rather wistfully, Bonnaterre comments, "The mind of a man deprived of the commerce of others is so little exercised, so little cultivated, that he thinks only in the measure that he is obliged to by exterior objects. The greatest source of ideas among men is in their human interactions" (p. 38). Without an interpersonal frame for the verbal accomplishment of symbolization and its ontogenic relationship to signification, which can only evolve in interactive, coconstruction, there is also no articulate instrument for conceptual thought, no development of the symbolic function: "Without language, there seems to be nothing like explicit thought whatever" (Langer, 1942, p. 103).

The meaning or meaningful adoption of symbolic form is dependent upon and subordinate to the existent, underlying operative organization and level of symbolization; therefore the significance of a symbolic vehicle varies according to the symbolizational and operative level to which it is attached. At the beginning, in their immediacy, words are scarcely more than conventional signs or signals of the protosymbolic variety, only with time will they become increasingly "interiorized" and abstracted, as instruments of thought. Meaning is an operative activity, and the significance and use of symbols varies according to the operative organization in which experiences are structured.

"A mind to which the stern character of an armchair is more immediately apparent than its use . . . is over-sensitive to expressive form," writes Langer (1942) as she recounts her early recollection of chairs and tables as being remarkable due to the awesome sameness of their appearance: "They *symbolized* such and such a mood . . . a look—dignity, indifference, or ominousness—[as] they continued to convey that silent message no matter what you did to them" (p. 123). From the dawn of memory "where we needs must begin any first-hand record to adolescence, there is a constant decrease in such dreamlike experience, a growing shift from subjective symbolic, to practical associations" (p. 124). At this early stage, dynamic, connotive features of the symbol are almost completely externalized in visible or audible expressiveness, the inner and outer form of the vehicle still undifferentiated. The preconcepts of this level are still only on the way to making full use of symbolization and conceptual articulation and await further interiorization to become abstracted. If a "general class" existed now the *conceptual* identification of the objects, by reason of their belonging to the same class, would serve to differentiate the denotive, collective signifier from its connotive, egocentric, referents derived from individually intuited expressive features and operative aspects of personal understanding. But this conceptual experience is slow to evolve.

On the other hand, were it not for this personal, sensorial, and expressive font, a natural source from which language is always replenished, words might be a dry, brittle, empty, and meager commodity, useless for the embellishment of either an inner or an outer life. To what degree, we might ask, could an impersonal, static, collective code of vocal denoters come to life without its vibrantly individual and subjective underside, infused with meanings and expressivity? The roots of this vocal form are always grounded in expressive acts which retain their organismic connections to the matrix of meanings, at the heart of experience. Therefore, what we know and how we know it will reveal itself in the very linguistic shape in which we choose to articulate our knowledge; both form and content will reflect level of symbolic articulation and only therein reveal meaning. The psychoanalyst's freely floating attention and third ear, indeed the entire empathic instrument of psychoanalytic listening, might thus be viewed as requiring special tuning in order to resonate with the degree to which experience is still organic or is on the way to becoming represented. Von Humboldt (1884) wrote that, "Men do not understand one another by causing one another to produce exactly the same concept, but by touching the same links in each other's sense perceptions and concepts, by striking the same key in each other's individual instrument. Whereupon corresponding, but not identical, concepts arise in each of them" (cited in Werner and Kaplan [1963, pp. 50–51]).

Moreover words themselves induce conceptualization. Nouns, the structural pillars of our vocabularies, by their denotive designation, attribute substantive properties to things which can then be placed and thought about in time and space. Symbolization is implicitly involved in the construction of the cognitive object and quite determining in the way events are organized, integrated, and memorized, and in the meanings which are given them. Similarly, the personal name both frames a form and a relationship mentally, yet removes it from participation. The utterance is also other than itself; Langer (1942) writes: "true language begins only when a sound keeps its reference beyond the situation of its instinctive utterance" (p. 105). Only in detaching the felt presence of "Mommy" from the name, can Mommy also become the concept "mother"; and from that a whole group of other people's mothers, the abstracted attributes of "motherliness," and thence to the relationship of all mothers, as a general class. Due to their vehicular function words naturally increase the distance between the subject from referential objects; the vocable carves itself out in space and time. A word fixes some aspect of experience to the center of signification and crystallizes memory, yet in and of itself it can also be articulated as a phonic entity.

From the earliest manifestations of the symbolic tendency nestled in the sense of significance, to the gradual presymbolic sharing of denotive referencing on to the articulate use of abstractive symbols in linguistic form, our minds work to "represent" knowledge and to express this at various levels of symbolic depiction, until language, in facilitating the transformation of experience into concepts, becomes the dominant form.

Not without reason. Words are speedy, spunky, rhythmic and fun; they are economical, expressive, distinct, equivocal, specific, public, personal, and interesting. They can be strung together in long chains of infinite variability, played with, accompanied, abstracted or made concrete; they can be jostled with, stolen, broken, offered, shared, and their deliverance can be whispered, sung, screamed, declaimed, and used for all manner of contrivance and deceit. Words can caress or kick, praise or insult, imprison or set free; they can parade, hide, beguile, enchant, bewitch, tease, embrace, or torture. By the nature of their instrumentation, they can lead into a whole new world of propositional concatenations which, strung together by a magical syntactic and grammatical glue, make sense of even the most senseless combinations. Words enable us to average and select, to organize and collect whole new groupings of meanings and implications simultaneously, and to lay these out in linear narratives or to muddle them in linguistic labyrinths of vocable webs, spun for others to hear. The power of language lies not only in its embodiment of things and concepts, its metaphors and similes, but in its self-generative, combinatorial strength, which potentiates greater complexity of thought and expressivity and propels us toward abstraction and conceptualization, to the highest realms of hypothetical thought.

But language is also ambiguous, often carrying multiple meanings and diverse levels of symbolic relationships, containing and expressing representational experience from stages prior to its own, compounding impact and confounding intent. In its figurative and operative aspects, it portrays as it declaims and alters its significance according to the contextual conventions and implications in which it is embedded. Language is slippery, it can say one thing but mean and imply something quite different. In its syntactical structure, language contains the seed of deceit as the selective placement of a verb along a chain of informative propositions can alter both the essential nature of the communication as well as its authenticity. Language unfolds a dangerous new dimension, that of truth or falsity. It conceals as it reveals, and in its disclosure can steel sincerity from its content by the fleeting gesture, unintended inflection, expression, or tone of the speaker. It is an inviting avenue for duplicity, for the plethora of psychological defenses to which it lends support and provides cover—language can be pseudorational, the mind's disguise for an action, a weapon, or a shield of defense. It can sustain an apparent aura of display behind which the self can covertly lie hidden.

Language can be on target but it can also misfire: saying what you mean and meaning what you say are frequently not the same thing. On the other hand, leading as it does into the very heart of connotive nondiscursive sources, its contrivance transforms our deep, amorphous experience in the very act of its pronouncement. In its quintessential task, the communication of ideas, it is as much shaped by our inarticulate depths as it shapes what we denote of these, since for the task, we have only preexisting lexical models to choose from.

Langer writes (1942), "In its literal capacity [language] is a stiff and conventional medium unadapted to the expression of genuinely new ideas, which usually have to break in upon the mind through some great and bewildering metaphor" (p. 201). As the expressive embodiment of symbolizing tendencies, language epitomizes the general principles of symbolization itself, and metaphor, by its pictorial, conceptual evocation, is "the law of its life" (Langer, 1942, p. 141). Metaphor throws together and condenses, as it summons image, idea, feeling, and concept into one fused body of figurative ideas; in its creative impulsion it conjures up the new. It is an audacious, aesthetic as well as linguistic device; forceful, enriching, poetic, profoundly communicative. Langer has referred to metaphor as the most striking evidence of our "abstractive seeing" (p. 141), the outcome of imaginal and conceptual representation captured within linguistic form. With its evocative visual and pictorial connotations, it is not difficut to understand why metaphor is favored by the poetic imagination.

Language patterns and transformations grow or shrink with intellectual needs, according to the expressive or expository requirements they have to meet. While single words hold concepts, language must articulate whole groups or units of concepts which, in order to unfold significantly into a chain of comprehensively conveyed ideas, must be held and extended sensibly in temporal sequence. Time and causality are the new dimensions which verbalization and its underlying abstraction, narrational structure, impose on human thought. And with the word, a concept to hold and recall at will, one cannot but suppose that language must play a complex and central role in the formation of mnemic processes.

According to recent studies (Damasio and Damasio, 1991, cited in Blakeslee, 1991), language ability is localized in several discrete brain areas in a pattern that varies from individual to individual. Compact areas correlate with greater language skills; however, while the brain has special areas for processing language, these do not constitute an independent language organ with "storage boxes" for nouns, verbs, and so on, or grammatical structuring. Rather, the Damasios' new theory holds, these essential areas are better conceived as "convergence zones," where the key to the combination of components and features of words and objects is stored. Knowledge of words and concepts is widely distributed throughout the brain, but requires mediation—the convergence zone—to collect this knowledge and activate it in the production of a word. When calling to mind a styrofoam cup, for instance, we do not go into a filing cabinet in the brain and come up with the "ready-made picture of a cup," state Damasio and Damasio (1991), but rather we compose an internal image of a cup, drawn from its features or its attributes.

"In reactivating the concept," state Damasio and Damasio, "you draw on distant clusters of neurons that separately store knowledge of cones, the color of white, crushable objects and manipulated objects. These clusters are activated simultaneously by feedback firing from convergence zones" (1991, cited in Blakeslee, 1991). We can attend to the revival of those components in our mind's eye and thereby construct an internal image of the whole object. The Damasios' claim that the process for activating words is the same; there are no neural filing cabinets for words in the brain; rather, distant neural clusters storing the phonemes C, U, and P are processed in convergence zones for the word *cup*: "You can perceive their momentary revival in your mind's ear or allow them to activate the motor system and vocalize the word cup" (Damasio and Damasio, 1991, cited in Blakeslee, 1991). To read, speak, or make other lexical operations about styrofoam cups, the brain needs a third system, a way station or convergence zone, that mediates between word and concept: "Only then can we operate linguistically and evoke the word from the concept or vice versa" (Damasio and Damasio, 1991, cited in Blakeslee, 1991). Convergence zones are probably established in early childhood during language learning as memories are formed; while new ones can form and existing ones be arranged, throughout life (Blakeslee, 1991).

The notion of convergence zones bringing together many disparately stored facets of a word, concept, or memory, correlates with the idea of a schema as being formed by and including multiple aspects of experience. It is useful in this context to imagine the schema, or unit of experience, as round like a ball, comprising cross-sections of multisensory, affective, cognitive, and conceptual facets, all forming components of a unique schema. The Damasios' interesting notion for language recall as the "reactivation of the image in the mind's ear" corresponds to developmental notions of interiorized operations, as this minireactivation highlights how the structuralization of knowledge is rooted in activity. The meaning of words and language and how these are used cannot be separated from the active agent, the speaker. Meaning does not reside exclusively in words themselves, but is connected to the cognitive and symbolic levels to which their significance is tied and of which they are an expression. In this connection, language is affiliated with the secondary process, partly because its representational capacity reinforces discursive or literal thought but principally because it provides a medium for articulating propositions, abstraction, and socially consensual exchanges which strengthen awareness of others and the environment. Language can also be harnessed for primary process expressivity, however, and often, inadvertently, partakes of both. Secondary process ideation is less, or not at all, due to the bound nature of psychic energy or the presence of a reality principle, or even to language per se, but rather is due to the representational and logical processes which the conceptual and social aspects of language enable.

A number of intermediary phases between primary symbolization (stage 4) and secondary symbolization (stage 5) see development continuing to move in the direction of differentiation and decentration with an increasing capacity to organize experience and information more objectively, in both cognitive and emotive–interpersonal realms. Consolidation of elaborate and reversible internal representations along multiple vectors achieves planes of relative equilibrium at around ages 7 or 8, at the level of concrete operations, and at 11 or 12 in that of formal operations (Piaget, 1962, p. 287).

The balance between assimilation and accommodation with respect to cognitive structures is reflected in the reintegration of play and imitatory processes at 7 or 8, at a more complex level intermingling fantasy, reality, identificatory, and defensive aspects, and at around age 12, when the last forms of symbolic play gradually come to an end. Imitation has become internalized unconsciously as identification, and is now subordinate to goals and ends dictated by the use and articulation of representational–structural intelligence, which must integrate multiple new and extended representational systems (Greenspan, 1982). Toward the end of the egocentric period development enables a capacity to distinguish between different points of view and therefore the recognition of one's own as being distinct from other possible viewpoints. A sense of agency in volition and motivational choices increases as awareness of one's own distinct position diminishes impressionability and heralds the progress of reflection. Reinforced by a sharpening of the processes of selection and rejection, the sense of self further develops along multiple vectors, all of which define and consolidate identity—the hallmark of the developmental struggles during adolescence.

In both adaptive orientation and intellectual growth intelligence continues to broaden and expand, moving toward continued structuring of a permanent coordination between assimilation and accommodation processes. The establishment of these in constant equilibrium is the resulting integration Piaget recognized as formal operational thought (Piaget, 1962).

A final decentering occurring just prior to adolescence, leads the way to the liberation from concrete operations (a type of thinking which is constrained by the articulation of interiorized concrete actions), to an orientation in reflection of hypothesized transformations; that is, a new level of abstraction. During adolescence the mind makes another leap which enables the elaboration of hypothesis construction, organized around logical reasoning, and the formulation of propositions according to reciprocal, inverse and correlative relationships removed from the concrete or present location (Piaget and Inhelder, 1969, p. 131).

In liberating thought from concrete operations the formal level culminates in the establishment of multiple classificatory and combinatorial abstract systems (mathematical, geometrical, algebraic, and forms of probability) which include inversions, reciprocities, syntheses, and completions extended in spatiotemporal dimensions, integrating all of these possible transformations into a new, operationally fused whole (Piaget, 1962). In psychoanalytic terminology, this provides the ego with flexibility and greater options for dealing with internal and external circumstances (Greenspan, 1979).

Decentration widens and deepens the impact of reality; accordingly, this phase is heavily influenced by new social and cultural factors. Formal thought encompasses the possible transformation of a reality which is now assimilated according to incremental increases in complexity and flexibility in personal, affective, cognitive, and hypothesized or projected terms. Morals and ideological conflicts appear, often fueled by the channeling of turbulent adolescent emotions. The emotive transformations of this stage encompass a dramatic change in perspective, as goals, values, choices, opinions, and volition begin to consider a multitude of moral, interpersonal, and societal possibilities and their implications.

The gradual evolution from egocentric, preconceptual, prelogical thought to the decentering which leads to the articulation of hypothetical–deductive structures of logical thought, has been slow, often discontinuous, and never uniform. We have only to consider the degree of upheaval in the neuroendocrine balance during the adolescent passage to recognize what a struggle for reintegration must be occurring organismically at this stage of rapid and quite tumultuous change (Leshner, 1978).

Operativity or cognitive structure, impacts on both figurative and linguistic aspects of mentation, and while symbolization and language have increased the flexibility of cognition, operativity itself continues to exist as an independent mental capacity (Greenspan, 1979). From a psychoanalytic perspective, it is helpful to consider this model as complementary or supplementary in terms of the additional information it affords regarding what constitute actual cognitive competencies. It equips us with a sophisticated and informed framework for orienting our understanding toward the *kind* of reasoning and thinking of which a certain stage of cognitive articulation is capable. This in turn provides a precise diagnostic tool and the possibility of orienting interventions tailored to the appropriate cognitive level. From a psychoanalytic point of view and with reference to stage of symbolization, however, when full hierarchic organization has been achieved, it is more helpful to think of the human mind as characterized by parallel lines on numerous planes rather than being uniformly sequential. Levels of learning and the development of cognition are intertwined with and impact upon the gradual evolution and maturation of an abstractive symbolizing capacity now flowered into full-fledged linguistic expression, but will also continue to find expression and seek integration in nondiscursive modes, at unconscious levels of experience. Secondary symbolization (stage 5) marks a deepening and broadening of the abstractive potential and a subtle, new representational structure, that of the awareness of or attention to the experience of one's self.

STAGE 5: SECONDARY SYMBOLIZATION

> O, what a world of unseen visions and heard silences, this insubstantial country of the mind! What ineffable essences, these touchless rememberings and unshowable reveries! And the privacy of it all! A secret theater of speechless monologue and prevenient counsel, an invisible mansion of moods, musings, and mysteries, an infinite resort of disappointments and discoveries. A whole kingdom where each of us reigns reclusively alone, questioning what we will, commanding what we can. A hidden hermitage where we may study out the troubled book of what we have done and yet may do. An introcosm that is more myself than anything I can find in a mirror. This consciousness that is myself of selves, that is everything, and yet nothing at all—what is it?
>
> And where did it come from?
> And why? [J. Jaynes, 1976, p. 1].

While the achievement of early childhood might be considered mastery and self-regulation of the body, that of childhood and preadolescence a balanced mastery of and adaptation to the environment, that of adolescence lies in the regulation and control of emotion and the integration of a solid identity (Erikson,

1951, 1980; Blos, 1962). The new task requires a new symbolic dimension—awareness of self. "Is the sense of identity conscious?" asks Erikson (1980, p. 127), and answers, "the still experimenting individual may become the victim of a transitory, extreme *identity consciousness* which is the common core of the many forms of 'self-consciousness' typical for youth" (p. 127). The mere fact that the two concepts are mentioned together gives cause for thought. Suddenly, out of a new cognitive dimension, a maturing body and an increased awareness of separateness, comes a loud cry from the "I" to formulate a sense of inner-core experience, a central organization which defines one's difference, and roots the hubbub of existence in "a Self." This new mode of thought "bestowed on us like a gift" (Langer, 1942, p. 201), is in charge of taking inner experience and formulating a conceptual boundary around a self that is different from that of others; the task represents a new level of symbolic expression. This symbolizing act, distilling subjectivity, fuses the form and content of oneself and one's experience, and in its integrative, abstractive potential, contributes to a dramatic structural change—the formulation of a "self." The sense of identity is born out of objectivation of personal experience, a distancing brought about by the recognition of one's difference and separateness from all others, and the requirement to identify in what ways this is so.

Exploring the origins of consciousness, Jaynes (1976) finds the race obscurely darkened in the "holy brightness of the unconscious world" until, in the second millennium B.C., finally the screening off of the tyrannical merger with the gods is "effected by the invention on the basis of language of an analog space with an analog 'I' " (p. 204). Ontogeny recapitulates phylogeny, and a new stage of symbolic representation is called into play. Certainly, increased precision and flexibility in the use of language in adolescence affects the conquest of reality as it facilitates clearer formulations; but the real new challenge is in being able to integrate that one has now become aware of all of this. Consciousness and identity could therefore be said to be interwoven: what good is an identity, if we are not aware of having one? As illustrated earlier, the boy of L'Aveyron was lacking not only in the capacity to train in vocal articulations and interpersonal connectedness but in the whole civilized dimension of awareness of self and other, in the awareness of what feelings or expressions might mean. He was deficient in the whole realm of symbolic valence and therefore the possibility of knowing the conscious experience of "being."

Neither consciousness nor identity exists as "things" until we think about attending to their relevance and, even then, they are phenomenological, experience or content dependent. Both come into being by way of our awareness of them and both, like our bodily organs, serve us best when they do their job quietly without intruding upon our daily lives. We do not need a sense of "identity" at every moment in order to proceed in our existence; yet neither would it do if we did not gradually form such a sense through integrative experimentation and contemplative pondering about ourselves in time and place and who we strive to become as individuals among others. We do not need consciousness to think, reason, feel, act, discover, or create, yet we must exercise our consciousness of these in order to reflect upon what we have felt, reasoned, done, discovered, created, or will do, and to understand what these things mean to us, thereby sealing them in memory and learning from them. Without due attention, neither of these integrative functions could provide anchorage for our subjective experience, nor could our experiences become locked into personal narratives or contexts of any significance out of which to further weave our special and unique continuity, whatever this consists of. Both are therefore crucial aspects of the new dimension cast upon us by a mind which transforms experience into concepts and has now become aware of itself.

Who am I? asks the adolescent, suddenly weighted by an expansive new abstractive cognition, a cumbersome, curvaceous maturing form, a burdensome bursting in of new and unknown emotions and impulses. What do I want to look like, be like, have, do, not do, asks the adolescent, as the fearsome dimension of reflectivity thrusts upon consciousness the awareness of a present, a past, a future dizzy with hopes, desires, doubts, choices, obligations. And the disequilibrium of all this! Having to balance continued schedules of learning replete with responsibilities, achievements, and parental norms, with the magnetic pull toward self-scrutiny in isolation, or self-effacement at the hub of uproarious peer groups. How do I define myself asks the adolescent, and expresses this in, What shall I wear? What clothes express the person I am or want to appear to be? What statement shall I make? What hairdo makes me look the most how I want to feel within myself; which way shall my handwriting go? How shall I talk, smile, walk? What shall I, or can I, do with myself, as the subject of the greatest fascination becomes the construction of one's persona. How do I feel being such-and-such a way? Shall I conform or confound, defer or defy, asks the adolescent, in search of a demarcation line between self and others, while emotions respond with unmistakable authenticity as the self struggles to construct its own ideal. And as the questions manifest in often chaotic or experimental behaviors, there generates a new metaphor to tie the loose ends, that of a nucleus inside, a little "corner" which crystallizes experience into a new unity—the awareness of self, experienced as identity. Now the pronoun "I" acquires a new dimension.

Answers also often come by way of discovering what one is not. "The observation of difference may be the origin of the analog space of consciousness," writes Jaynes (1976). "It is thus a possibility that before an individual man had an interior self, he unconsciously posited it in others, particularly contradictory strangers, as the things that caused their different and bewildering behavior" (p. 217). Awareness of difference, of course, presupposes separateness, and as we have seen throughout, each new referencing differentiation along the course of development produces a new symbol in its wake. It is possible that the awareness of self is a relatively recent acquisition in our phylogenesis, and that identity is predicated on the paradoxical duality of a subjective awareness of the uniqueness of one's experience as singularly different from all others, while being simultaneously aware of being among, and one of, many others. Identity within oneself reflects an appreciation of identity in others. Like the two poles of reference of any symbol, here too, the developmental step is rooted in a dialectic.

The word *identity*, in and of itself, however, does not explain the process by which this experience of consolidated integration, of having a "voice," comes about. Nor does it indicate in what way the possession of an identity can be known to exist. Just like consciousness, I believe, it relies less on awareness per se than on a particular reflexive awareness of being aware. The self has become the symbol for inner experience and volition, and the concept itself provides a space in which to formulate itself—this is the great new symbolizing achievement of this stage. Identity is consolidated when the person can move inward at will, to a mental attitude which can reflect upon personal experiences, desires, plans, and find a familiar continuity in time and space, from which to figure out how one is feeling in order to further articulate experiences, ideals, desires, goals, and future plans.

This mental attitude has necessitated a symbolizational step, that of the transformation of subjective experience with regard to oneself (as one among many different others) into a concept about who one is, how one will proceed, and who one will become. The self has been taken as an object of interest for the developmental purpose of differentiation and reintegration as a denoted other vis-à-vis others. We become aware of who we are as we define our differences and formulate our preferences, and we acquire a sense of separate identity as we abstract a self which has defined these preferences and differences. The heightened importance of an expanding ego ideal is apparent at this juncture as many defenses will now crystallize around issues of self-esteem.

In all of this, the utterance becomes an important means for accessing and communicating what emanates from our central experience. Similarly, recounting references the preliminary stages in a private world reflecting the consciousness of self. Many adolescents today appear to have the telephone grafted to their ear, a costly alternative to the close companion of days of yore, the diary. Both attest to the importance and need for the referencing of personal experience through language, which reinforces an abstractive processing of inner space. According to J. W. Brown (1976), it is through language that purpose becomes volition. He writes, "It is in the idea of will that one sees the microgenetic advance over representational level cognition afforded by language" (p. 86). The adolescent's strident "I will not," is perhaps an articulation of the loud attempts to find this new voice of volition, which represents the demarcation of the beginnings of consciousness of a newly differentiated self.

The very first differentiation played itself out at the level of cells; the development of an embryo, a fetus, then a baby, and the culmination of a first separation in the act of birth. There followed a second differentiation, one brought about by the awareness of absence, a psychological marker in whose wake the inner evocation of an image was left. Gradually, through increased internalizations and differentiations between things in the environment, their relationships to each other and to oneself, there emerged a ripeness for another differentiation, that between the cognizance of otherness in others and the need to construct an inner selfness of self. We gather up the multiple subjective experiences strewn about freely and affectively in unconsciousness and find we must attend to their integration. The symbolized yield of this harvest is the autonomous self.

Erikson describes an increasing sense of identity as a feeling of being at home in one's body, a sense of "knowing where one is going," an "inner assuredness of anticipated recognition from those who count," experienced preconsciously as a sense of "psychosocial well-being" (1980, pp. 127–128). All of these are the correlates of what is presumed to be part of the result of owning a wholesome identity. Yet there are individuals whose identities are formed precisely out of feeling they are not assured about being recognized by those who count, of neither feeling at home in their body, knowing where they are going, or having any sense of psychosocial well-being. Indeed, if these sound like the earmarks of personal misery, they are nevertheless not the measure of having or not having an identity. A sense of identity, moreover, can be as much rooted in the conviction of being unique as it can be tied to an experience of not being unique at all. These affective dimensions, I believe on the contrary, as core organizers, are often tenaciously and insidiously grafted deeply within identities which are therefore painful and often disliked, yielding disintegrative and dissociative experiences. Identity, like consciousness, is a reflective, fluid, ongoing construction, affectively vulnerable, which knows of itself only in the very act of reflexivity and is dependent upon the development of narratives which are constantly reconstructed in time. Preoccupation with an ideal self prominent at this time, is the very product of this ongoing constructive process.

Distinguished by the taking of personal and subjective experience into oneself and abstracting it in terms of a self, this stage is not merely a question of identifying, organizing, and objectifying experience but of coining a private, abstracted center from which it is presumed to originate. This is a symbolizing step, one that is greatly assisted by language and the reification it generates. An often difficult achievement, this new level of consciousness germinates out of a pause arranged by independent experimentation which questions how one feels about a given task, look, event, or person. Hard won, a sense of identity is the reflection of a new dialectic which pins one pole of the new symbolic expression in the irrevocable otherness of others and one at the center of one's singular experience of oneself. Other people's identity often appears more delineated or is more clearly detected than one's own, because other people are observed from afar, whereas the self is caught up in the tensions and tribulations of subjective feelings, known firsthand and from within. Above all, then, a sense of identity is defined by knowing about oneself; the integrated, fused conceptualization which correlates inner experience with volition—possible actions, choices, hopes, and plans and the constellation of affects aroused around these issues. Self-awareness, initiative, and planning are the uniquely human qualities which have been traced to the complex involvement of the prefrontal cortex, or the frontal lobes. Their implication in the continued capacity to reason, plan, decide, coordinate activities and memories fluidly, and learn from experience (Luria, 1966a,b) was discovered obliquely by the dehumanizing consequences of lobotomies routinely carried out in the 1940s.

A typical adolescent proclivity toward acting out has been understood in the light of the basic dilemma between passivity and activity, an antithesis which, via projective mechanisms, forms part of the focal conflicts and negativistic traits characteristic for this developmental stage (A. Freud, 1937; Blos, 1962). It can, alternatively, be understood as the counterpart reaction to or escape from a new inward pull, a contemplative turning in at a new level of organization as the self becomes a reflective abstraction of what had thus far been unconscious experience. This conflicted step is mastered with effort, even painfully, as the pull toward immediate discharge of various somatic and psychic tensions in action is more readily satisfying and accessible than the struggle to organize inner experience contemplatively. In fact, the urge to express in action reaches a peak in adolescence. While this antithesis remains, to some degree, a general human trait (as the principles of clinical psychoanalysis have amply revealed) due to the particular confluence of developmental phenomena which come together now, the struggle between these two modes of self-definition is particularly charged at this time.

The fine-tuning and curbing of impulsivity required for deliberation before taking action, for reflecting upon possible alternatives, and the capacity, once determined, to remain committed to long-term plans, are developmental achievements that stretch cognitive as well as emotional facets of personality to new dimensions of behavior. For this cluster of self-organizing principles appearing at the end of adolescence, psychoanalysis has used the term *ego functions*. These coalesce to form a sense of ego identity (Erikson, 1946, 1950, 1951) indicating a comprehensive gain in increased differentiation and in preparing for the tasks of adulthood. The particular quality of equilibrium or personal stability derived from this integration is attributed to the "synthetic function of the ego" (Nunberg, 1931). Without querying too much about what an ego is or how it mobilizes its functions, one can better try to understand these phenomena as the results of a new level of symbolic organization achieved by our ongoing, persistent mental efforts to represent, to arrange knowledge by transforming experiences into concepts. In order for us to become capable of accountability, deliberation, and consistency in our actions, we have to struggle through a phase in which long-standing impulsions, urges, and affects become reflectively abstracted; the self and its ideal become the symbol for such subjectivity, and are now seen as representing this. The self, having now acquired objective status in the very process of being thought about, becomes the locus for identity.

So strongly does this objective status of core experience invoke the notion of an "inner" presence, that for centuries we have resorted to imagining the idea of a soul, the philosopher's homunculus, Freud's ego, the self, seated at central controls. We have inherited the problems of explaining the experience of experience, possibly without reified concepts which only push us further into infinite regress, "with homunculi embedded in homunculi like an image ricocheting between mirrors" (Johnson, 1991). Identifying the fact that our minds primarily represent experience ought to be a help, that a functional-process concept must replace the fantasy of an inner agency to explain this awareness of experience. A meager substitute for the soul, all we really have is a symbolizing means which transforms experience by representing and referring to it.

The experience of identity subsumes consciousness of self extending along temporal dimensions as well as providing a distinct sense of volition. Just how important an integrated sense of volition is in forming part of a stable identity is evinced by the great battleground of wills which plays itself out domestically, often mercilessly, in the formidable rebellion which young people, "torn between the double prongs of vital inner need and inexorable outer demand" (Erikson, 1980, p. 127), wage during this phase.

Each level of symbolizational organization contains an inherent potential propelling toward the next. While the new mode of thought might well be "bestowed on us like a gift," as Langer remarked (1942, p. 201), it is a gift well earned. Far from coming about spontaneously, the new conceptual plane is reached only with considerable restraint and psychic effort. At each stage much is lost which was familiar; the balanced patterns of impulse and activity, the fixity of acquired knowledge, and the carefree trust in an earlier reality. The new symbolizational step shakes this equilibrium, shakes the very foundations of reality as it forces new differentiation and transforms another loss into another metaphor, a new form of knowing which, ever expanding, will generate new terms for its expression to assist in the ongoing task of mastery and understanding.

The individual has now reached a stage in development wherein equilibrium through self-regulation, the formative process of structuralization, has crystallized into characteristic ways of approaching life which manifest in typical behaviors and patterns of actions and reactions. Equipped with a dexterous mentation which can articulate and transpose almost limitless numbers of relationships in multiple, extended representational systems, the mature person has achieved complete adult status with all of the unfolding expectable, phase-specific relevancies. In this, emotional and cognitive aspects form an inseparable and irreducible unity.

Optimally, development has produced a harmonious, sturdy hierarchic organization, in which all the particular processes of previous levels are effectively integrated, procuring flexibility and resilience within a general capacity to endure and assimilate a broad range of pleasurable and painful experiences. Each level of symbolization has changed the relationship to reality and ways of interacting with the environment, the experience of objects and self, and of what and how meaning and valence are attributed. Each level, moreover, has expanded the possible modes and forms for expressing this knowledge and oneself. Each stage in the organizing and abstracting process has raised mental structuring to a new and transformed level of consciousness which is not reducible to notions of disguise or distortion of contents from levels before it. Each level of symbolization has made possible a new degree of awareness which alters the very nature of purpose and the meanings and motives which prompt and influence behavior. And finally, each stage has altered the dimension of awareness and experience, just as every mirror in a hall of mirrors will add another perspective and image to that initially reflecting a single self. As we have seen, with each gain there is also a partial loss, as in delay or diminution of urgency we lose the intense immediacy of more concrete, global forms of experience.

If, at this point, all has progressed well, the individual is now equipped with a psychical armamentarium rich and ebullient enough to weather all of life's charges and blows. The "executive functions" click in at all opportune moments and in optimal ways, and the individual's autonomous, integrative capacity is commensurate to the demands placed or forced upon it by circumstance. If, on the other hand, feelings falter and the center cannot hold; the old will not be put aside for the new, strains of disequilibrium push backward to earlier levels of expression, and pull beneath levels of adaptation, and failures in integrative functioning erupt into dysfunctional behavior, then a new effort in integration will be called upon, necessitating another push toward a new degree of symbolizational structuring, a new level of awareness.

People do not come for psychological help because they are disturbed, they come because they are unhappy. Innumerable individuals are the cause of great misery to others, yet, because they are quite satisfied with themselves, will never feel the need to seek assistance. The criteria for mental health, therefore, will have to remain fluid enough to encompass gross dysfunction which, however, is not subjectively experienced as such. It is always personal misery, dissatisfaction with oneself, insecurity, overwhelming emotions, inhibitions, failing relationships, dying hopes, fear, despair, which compellingly prompt people to seek a *therapeia*, a process for healing. Nevertheless, the interpretation of subjective experience is the relevant focus of psychoanalytic scrutiny in an endeavor which pits one aspect of self objectively across from subjectivity and, due to the particular nature of the process, calls upon yet a new level of symbolic reflexivity.

While it is rarely events themselves which hold conceptual status but more relevantly the interpretation of what they mean to the experiencing individual, the desire to reorganize, to review, and reconstruct or heal oneself, forces a new advance in reflection and conceptualization. The psychoanalytic dyad opens just such a reflective realm. The symbolic step embodied in the psychoanalytic process uniquely requires that one willingly embark upon an adventure analogous to the disquieting experience of walking in a hall of mirrors, in which the image of oneself is multiplied again and again in infinite, reflective regress. The analogy serves to describe the unique reflective stance required for doing analytic work: one in which significance and its web of interconnections will generate ramifications and integrations extending in time and coalescing into a new level of organization. While it is language which delimits and gives form to consciousness, it does so only to the degree that symbolization can abstract experience, as this strives for interpersonal expression. The psychoanalytic enterprise will engender a new level of abstraction. Awareness will imply differentiation, symbolization, and interpersonal communication—it is born, as it were, at the hub of these three.

The metaphor of a journey has often been harnessed, and fittingly, to depict life's persistent, ongoing time-bound travails; we embark on this or that enterprise and mark its end, by analogy, to have undertaken a trip. Homecoming is implicit in this metaphor, as is a sense of adventure and completion, but more importantly, the picture of oneself as a journeyer. These are the lines with which Kagan (1984) closes his book:

> My own image of a life is that of a traveler whose knapsack is slowly filled with doubts, dogma, and desires during the first dozen years. Each traveler spends the adult years trying to empty the heavy load in the knapsack until he or she can confront the opportunities that are present in each fresh day. Some adults approach this state; most carry their collection of uncertainties, prejudices, and frustrated wishes into middle and old age, trying to prove what must remain uncertain while raging wildly at ghosts [p. 280].

The next stage is embarked upon not just by those whose knapsacks have become too heavy, but by those who are aware that they are carrying too cumbersome a load; those who recognize that yesterday's railing has clouded this morning's dawn, and whose ragings have not yet scared away the ghosts. The inner journey is not sought by everyone, nor is the next symbolic leap a natural step, although awareness may be present and manifest in many different forms and express itself in different modes. The next stage is achieved by those who enter into a particular process, in which frequently they seek to retread where they had slipped before and in which the weighted wares of unwanted current wailings are dispersed in the very act of being disclosed.

STAGE 6: THE REIFICATION OF SELF: THE PSYCHOANALYTIC PROCESS

> [F]or symbols, the spawn of such tropes as arise in the interaction of men and women alive, metaphors, synechdoches, metonymes, new minted in crises, so to speak, really do come to serve as semiotic connectives among the levels and parts of a system of action and between that system and its significant environment. We have been neglecting the role of symbols in establishing connexity between the different levels of a narrative structure [Turner, 1976, p. 141, cited in Mitchell, 1980].

"At the time of her falling ill (in 1880) Fräulein Anna O was twenty-one years old . . ." (Breuer and Freud, 1895, p. 21), begins the case history of this remarkable young woman described by her physician in the most glowing terms. In finding that her "evening narratives" (p. 29) recounted to Breuer brought solace and an apparent cessation of her acute and multivaried symptoms, she named the process "the talking cure," and in so doing inadvertently directed the course for understanding mental functioning toward the mind's symbolizing capacity. Narratizing somehow restored order; somewhere hidden in the process of recall lay the secret to mental stability. Breuer writes (Breuer and Freud, 1895), "—A few moments after she had finished her narrative she would wake up, obviously calmed down, or, as she called it '*gehäglich*' . . . —If for any reason she was unable to tell me the story during her evening hypnosis she failed to calm down afterwards, and on the following day, she had to tell me *two* stories in order for this to happen" (p. 29).

Anna O's variegated symptomatology, including, at one point, the complete breakdown of her ability to use language, would appear today to correspond more closely to a psychotic break than to hysteria; nevertheless, in the late 1800s, seeking to discover the etiology of these disorders, Breuer and Freud believed they had found a cause. The psychical trauma, or more precisely "the memory of the trauma—acts like a foreign body which long after its entry must continue to be regarded as an agent that is still at work" (Breuer and Freud, 1895, p. 6). The illness begins with an inhibition, a severance in associative links and a dissociation between an idea and its emotional valence and expression. It may therefore be said that: "*the ideas which become pathological have persisted with such freshness and affective strength because they have been denied the normal wearing away processes by means of abreaction and reproduction in states of uninhibited association*" (Breuer and Freud, 1895, p. 11). In other words, having been prevented from free expression and subsequent integration, they had also been prevented from becoming conscious. In the complicated case of Anna O, each independent symptom was "taken separately in hand" (p. 35) and traced in reverse order to the occasion in which it had first appeared. As she remembered, she reintegrated; clearly, it was concluded, "hysterics suffer mainly from reminiscences" (p. 7).

The two physicians believed that to achieve a completely "cathartic" effect, an adequate reaction implied one that was necessarily energetic. Instead, they found that language could serve as a "substitute for action; by its help, an affect can be 'abreacted' almost as effectively" (Breuer and Freud, 1895, p. 8). Language, in its representational function, serves to signify, it substitutes for action inasmuch as it represents what was expressed in action. This is a symbolic relationship which reaches to the heart, not of the cause of the symptom, but of the means for expressing its significance. To their initial surprise, they found that "*each individual hysterical symptom immediately and permanently disappeared when we had succeeded in bringing clearly to light the memory of the event by which it was provoked and in arousing its accompanying affect, and when the patient had described the event in the greatest possible detail and had put the affect into words. Recollection without affect almost invariably produces no result*" (Breuer and Freud, 1895, p. 6). It is not merely remembering, therefore, which serves to restore mental coherence, but the integrative process of "putting affects into words." In some cases, they report, the relationship between originating cause and symptom was quite clear, while in others it was obscure and consisted only in "what might be called a 'symbolic' relation between the precipitating cause and the pathological phenomenon—*a reaction such as healthy people form in dreams*" (Breuer and Freud, 1895, p. 5; emphasis added). Symptoms could be the symbolic expression (mnemic symbol) of their unconscious signification; they carried and expressed meaning. When the mode of their expression was transformed through the medium of language, and uttered to someone else, they disappeared. Talking cured—but how?

Remembering or reconstructing and recounting the path of her symptoms, talking about these with revived emotion, was curative for Anna O. What she did not talk about, the intense transference which she had developed toward Breuer, became an exacerbating factor. In this initial, iatrogenic outburst, however, were revealed the remaining crucial pieces of what would become the psychoanalytic process. And out of the entire puzzling experience of this case, Freud derived the fundamental principles of clinical psychoanalysis. The notion of instantaneous abreaction or catharsis was to evolve into a more radical and lengthy process of working through, free association substituted the hypnotic method; and explanation for the miraculous effect of words was found in bound versus free forms of psychic energy. Nevertheless, the context, the medium, the method, and appreciation of the awakening potential of the experience and use of transference provided the foundations for psychoanalysis as a treatment modality.

From the very beginning we are in the symbolic realm of language, of meanings and their communication. In identifying the symptom as a symbolic entity, likening it to the healthy symbolic expression of dreams, as something which represents a meaning, and in emphasizing the importance of putting this significance into words (of *re*-presenting), Freud effectively established psychoanalysis in the terrain of "a science of symbolic functioning, which studies symbolic systems (organizations of symbolic entities), their relationships to each other, and their acquisition and use" (Edelson, 1972, p. 204). Consequently, it will follow that the nature of the therapeutic action of talking in psychoanalysis and the theory of cure, likewise, will be found to correspond to the same developmental processes that evolve during normal mental development and with which integration and coherence are maintained. We have followed this symbolizational process from its inception through its stages of organization, and are familiar with its potential for deintegration. Now, in the psychoanalytic process as it is currently practiced, the reification of self extends the symbolizing process to another dimension, as this particular reflective introspection pushes understanding and the abstraction of one's own experiences, past, present, and current, to a new threshold of consciousness.

When explanations were to be couched in causal terms, the theory of cure referred to a topographical switch, that is, making the unconscious conscious; as systems gave way to structures, it became viewed as structural change. Impersonal forces—instincts, repression, resistance—and agencies robbed the psychoanalytic exchange of its personal, intimate quality, as the analyst struggled to fight and to overcome a slew of driven psychic activities of which the analysand was totally unaware. As interpersonal relevance came to the fore, explanations were sought in the relational exchanges of new communications. When the ego and its functions were highlighted and the relevance of the self deemed of central import, then attention became focused on reapportioning ego functions, augmenting some, diminishing others, and fortifying "selves." Psychoanalysis, broad enough to encompass all of these aspects of intrapsychic and interpersonal relationships, could contain and satisfy all requirements. The method changed relatively little, while theories went all over the place. Psychoanalysis is intrinsically interpersonal, inherently new, providing a real space with infinite illusory potential, in which we are asked to lay bare not only all those layers of private experience which have made us who we are, but further, to examine this in the revealing context of unwitting repetition. And the only instrumentation is the symbolic medium of language.

The psychoanalytic situation consists of two individuals committed to the understanding of one, in which the other provides interpretive expertise and offers him- or herself as a new object for the purpose of understanding the other's contextual experience. The psychoanalyst will invite the analysand to talk, and only to talk. This injunction contains two provisos: to restrain oneself from action and to recount everything. The analytic requirement to talk is a request to adopt a semantic attitude and, in the semantic space thus engendered, words will take on formidable expressive tasks. As Freud recognized, language could take the place of action (1895), as it represents what it signifies. With this in mind we can better understand the polyvalence and heightened charge that words take on in the psychoanalytic situation. "Interpreting means finding a hidden sense to something" wrote Freud (1917a, p. 87), or it can be an act of empathy, of giving, permitting, seeing, affirming, connecting, feeding, holding, demanding, shaming, criticizing—any one or a mixture of many of these, according to the subjective frame and developmental requirements of the analysand who hears it. Loewald (1956) writes, "In analysis a mature object-relationship is maintained with a given patient if the analyst relates to the patient in tune with the shifting levels of development manifested by the patient at different times, but always from the viewpoint of potential growth, that is, from the viewpoint of the future" (p. 20). To abstain from action and "put it into words" is already a growth-inducing proposition, as language must subsume within a consensually shared symbolic exchange a multitude of impulses, feelings, experiences, and desires, otherwise often hidden defensively or impulsively acted out. Moreover, as a reliably constituted bridge, language becomes the analytic metaphor for engagement, belonging, attachment, care. Not only is it multidetermined, it is polyvalent.

Due to the way language is used in psychoanalysis, as a vehicle for expressing personal experience, it will also quickly become adopted instead, as a tool of substitution and vicarious gratification for all the actions which the analysand is wont to do when at liberty to do so. What is being done with language thus often becomes as important a focus of analytic scrutiny as what is being said. The analytic dyad, which has no history and no future other than the internalization of its current purpose, provides a real and an illusory interpersonal arena in which the analysand may express everything semantically, and find meaning in the experiences engendered therein. "It requires an objectivity and neutrality the essence of which is love and respect for the individual and for individual development," writes Loewald (1956, p. 20), to provide such an arena and to facilitate the potential for rediscovering early paths of development and the nature of primary relationships, in order to find new ways of relating and of being oneself. The analytic relationship threads through these multiple aspects and provides avenues of discourse for all developmental levels. "The objectivity of the analyst has reference to the patient's transference distortions," writes Loewald (1956); however, "In his interpretations, he implies aspects of undistorted reality which the patient begins to grasp step by step as transferences are interpreted" (p. 18; see also Arlow, 1979, 1987).

Gradually, by means of the analyst's comments, questions, interpretations, and most consistently by the persistent analytic insistence on the transformation of affects and impulsions, fleeting memories and ideas into linguistic form, there develops a semantic attitude of self-reflection, the observing ego. The observing ego will be called upon again and again to position itself where it can reflect an aspect of oneself to oneself—unlike expressing one's experience or identifying one's identity, this is an even more complex task. It requires an observational stance along multiple vectors and in multiple dimensions of personal experience—and it is in the *act of verbalizing these, identifying and experiencing these contextually,* in this act and this act alone, that new structuralization occurs in psychoanalysis. This new symbolizational dimension transcends self-consciousness to consciousness of selves that have been forgotten, hidden or buried in time, that have never been accepted or represented, and in this very process, enables the reconstruction of experiences which consolidate a new sense of oneself. The psychoanalytic narrative is one of rebirth, and corresponds to a mythic, Promethean descent into the underworld and transformational ascent in regeneration. It is precisely in these myths of transformation that the symbolic step bringing higher abstraction and new awareness is best depicted. The heroic journey always requires transcendence of self—a transformation of experience through a transformative ordeal. In the psychoanalytic requirement for the reification of self, we find a contemporary, parallel metaphor for the mythical feats of ancient heroes.

A linguistic situation in which the self appears as the only referent would be useless, other than for narcissistic purposes, were it not for the occurrence of an identificatory split which materializes out of the multiple reflective images which come to be mirrored in the course of the psychoanalytic process. How is this condition of reflexivity brought about? In 1934 Sterba wrote, "amongst all the experiences undergone by the ego during an analysis, there is one which seems to me so specific and so characteristic of the analytic situation that I feel justified in isolating it and presenting it to you as the 'fate' of the ego in analytic therapy . . . the fate that inevitably awaits the ego is that of dissociation" (pp. 117, 120). Freud (1933) asks: "How can this be done? The ego is the subject *par excellence*: how can it become the object? There is no doubt, however, that it can be done. The ego can take itself as object, it can treat itself like any other object, observe itself, criticize itself, do heaven knows what besides with itself" (p. 58, cited in Sterba [1934, p. 120]). The analyst provides the medium, is the catalyst if you will, of the symbolizing action which abstracts the self in its observation of current relevant realities within a contextual reflective examination of its history. This is the hall of mirrors of which I spoke earlier. As Sterba explained it, "the subject's consciousness shifts from the center of affective experience to that of intellectual contemplation" (pp. 121, 125). In conclusion, Sterba comments, perhaps "the therapeutic dissociation of the ego in analysis is merely an extension into new fields, of the self-contemplation which for all time has been regarded as the most essential trait of man in distinction to all other living things" (p. 125).

This distinguishing trait of humankind, to become aware, enabled by our capacity to abstract experience, is the function which, in my opinion, is stretched by the psychoanalytic process in ways in which it would otherwise never be stretched. We would rather act than sit in contemplation of our actions, move, than think about what moves us. One of the greatest joys in life is to be lost in the innocence of virtual experience; how much easier and more gratifying it is to just be and do than contemplate one's being and doing—an argument the existentialists have long held. Every symbolic step, as it strives to elaborate concepts out of experience, is effortful and must be taken autonomously; therefore, while the analyst is the catalyst or coconstructor in the process, the conclusive, insightful communication that joins past with present and reconciles fantasy with reality and puts affects into words must be formulated and uttered by the analysand him- or herself in a new, abstractive, integrative step. Working through, in this sense, is conceived as a metabolization of affects linked to ideational or mnemic triggers. By putting these into language, they are transformed and reconstituted at a higher level of representation and shaped into a new, analytic, narrational experience (Greimas, 1976).

As the analyst as a real new object becomes blurred by the subjective impositions of past interpersonal experiences, and the juxtaposition of multiple tensions testing the analysand's old narratives along vertical and horizontal dimensions strains communication, it is the anchoring of the investigative nature of the situation, and the analyst in it, that provides safe haven for continued trust in the demands for revelation and reflection. The psychoanalytic situation is itself a symbolic therapeutic device, as it consists of adopting a surface structure, language, for the understanding and interpretation of a deeper structure, unconscious meaning. It is unique in symbolic complexity as the analysand is brought into a contextual field in which what is felt and what is spoken, what is dreamt and what is done, what is experienced *now* as it is revealed to be what was experienced *then*, must all be conjointly sifted and sorted out through observation and understanding. This is an extraordinary symbolizational demand.

The analysand has come to psychotherapy, recall, with a knapsack still weighted with the past, desirous of alleviating the burden, of burying the ghosts, of taming the feelings, conscious of a need for change yet unaware of how to bring this about, and eager to experience love, integrity, fulfillment. The therapeutic process will require that the analysand withstand the extended tensions of moving between recollection and reenactment, silence and response, illusion and reality, the past and the present, between what is believed to be and what *is*, what was passionately wished for and what must be renounced, as the process reproduces the simultaneity in time which mirrors experience in the unconscious. Meaning is the distillate of all of this for "meaning always involves retrospection and reflexivity, a past, a history" (Turner, 1980, p. 152). There is no reality principle or secondary process, only men and women who organize their experience according to its valence and significance. "Meaning," is the only category which grasps the full relation of the part to the whole in life, for valence, being dominantly affective, belongs essentially to an experience in a conscious present" (Turner, 1980, p. 152). And the time in psychoanalysis is always the present; the relevance of a contextual present.

The past is carried into the present via repetition only as long as it remains unspoken and maintains is unlawful, amorphous, connotive strength, unrepresented in sequential time or narrative discourse. Discursive form situates those nebulous forms of earlier significance into a narrational past and transmutes their residual affective intensity into higher expressions of abstraction. The personal narrative, constructed out of multiple selected significances, changes shape in the very process of being reconstructed; its recounting, embarrassingly cognizant of possible alternate truths, can only find sufficient justification in one, subjective, forceful tale, which is transmuted as it is laid to rest. This is why the landscape of our inner world is littered with memories of things that never actually happened, and why the purpose is to find coherence, to make it all intelligible in a new way, and not to ascertain a truth. Memory carries its own truth, anyway, and yesterday's story will reflect today's viewpoint. As with all histories, explanations are always retrospective, contextual, circumstantial (Nietzsche, 1874; Spence, 1982).

"The problem of biographical memory, then," writes Langer (1972), "is the problem of how current experiences are relegated to memory in a more or less constant, automatic way, lose their feeling of present impact and emergence, and acquire the 'sense of pastness' in a normal and steady flow that is the subjective passage of time" (p. 343). Today, we would attribute to the ego the integrative skills for assembling events and metabolizing their potentially powerful affective accompaniments. Only a weak or weakened ego would allow itself to be assaulted by memories, thoughts, or feelings which it cannot effectively lay to rest. Yet people come every day, beleaguered by the incursions of the undigested past. Freud wrote that the pathogenic ideas, the "nodal points" in hysteria, surrounded by "abundant causal connections," functioned as *motive forces* for the "whole of the products of the neurosis" (1895, p. 299; emphasis added). He likened psychotherapeutic treatments to surgical operations, using the analogy of "the opening up of a cavity filled with pus, the scraping out of the carious region, etc." (p. 305), and affirmed, "it is only with the last word of the analysis that the whole clinical picture vanishes, just as happens with memories that are reproduced individually" (p. 299).

Due to its linearity and narrational propensity, discursive form organizes experience temporally and causally, in addition to transforming its sensory immediacy or deep structure into representational form. The curative effect occurs as "it brings to an end the operative force of the idea which was not abreacted in the first instance, by allowing its strangulated affect to find a way out through speech" (Breuer and Freud, 1895, p. 17). Making the unconscious conscious reinforced the ego—hence, where id was, there, through language, the ego appeared. Yet Freud was well aware that "being linked with word presentations is not the same as becoming conscious, but only makes it possible to become so" (1915b, pp. 202–203). Language alone did not suffice in bringing about the transformation into consciousness; a particular focus of attention, the additional prerequisite, an awareness of becoming aware, was required. This is the abstractive leap the psychoanalytic method makes use of, the reification of self which the technique and process require. It is a unique drawing of attention onto all aspects of oneself, of gathering up and objectifying the self of one's past, present, and contextual feelings and experiences of observing them and representing them to another; a particular phenomenon of attention in which one is beckoned to becoming simultaneously agent and narrator of one's life.

Schafer (1980) writes, "The competent analyst situated in the present . . . takes the talking also as a showing. . . . The analyst has only tellings and showings to interpret, that is, to retell along psychoanalytic lines" (p. 35). While noting that interpretively, the analyst is working in a temporal circle in order to comprehend, organize, define, and arrange an "analytically coherent and useful account of the present" (p. 48), Schafer concludes, "under the provisional and dubious assumption that past, present, and future are separable, each segment of time is used to set up series of questions about the others, and to answer the questions addressed to it by the others'' (p. 48)—accounts and constructions which will keep changing, along the course of the analytic dialogue. And so the tracing activity will end when all the threads have been absorbed into this context or have converged onto the occurrence of new events, or have disappeared entirely from the whole historical field, their impact and significance having been integrated into a sense of the pastness of the past.

The psychoanalytic situation sets up an illusory space within a real one, like the site of ritual or the stage in a theater. It provides a new sociocultural domain in which patterns and parts of patterns of behaviors are studied and harnessed as referents for understanding, reconstructing, and translating into the reflective analytic attitude of the semantic. It provides a timeless place within a time-conscious structure, a nonjudgmental cultural oasis within strict adherence to linguistic form, and offers the possibility of a new relationship within the context of reliving many old ones. Timeless, because affective relevance is always current; time-bound because the analytic hour is rooted in reality. The analysand will learn to move in and out of time, through it, integrating regressive experience with current exchange, daily occurrence with dream, identifying what was believed to be reality and what now comes to be real. Out of the disintegration and disequilibrium of transference and the assimilation of analytic communications emerges a new level of equilibrium, at once broader, more flexible, reflectively capable of acknowledging oneself more reliably and objectively, out of which evolves the construction of a new, analytically informed narrative (Ricoeur, 1980, 1984; Edel, 1984).

One thinks of the shaman's journey wherein, as Turner (1982) describes, ''the initiand is broken into pieces and then put together again as a being bridging visible and invisible worlds. Only in this way through destruction and reconstruction, that is, transformation, may authentic reordering come about. Actuality takes the sacrificial plunge into possibility and emerges as a different kind of actuality'' (p. 160). Were these words not taken to depict Eliade's (1951) analysis of the cogency of ritual, "a time and place lodged between all times and spaces" (Turner, 1980, p. 161), we might well take this ritual symbolism suspended in time, exemplifying an essential, irreversible transformative process, to be the psychoanalytic situation itself. Have we found in psychoanalysis a new psychic ritual for the developmental, individuating expression of humankind in the twentieth century? Are we observing the principles we have called Dionysian and Apollonian, those of disorder and order, unconsciousness and consciousness, here materialized in a modern, secular rite which voluntarily takes the self as its object of deconstruction and reconstruction? As with reference to postmodern trends, "Through all these signs," writes Habib Hassan (1982), "moves a vast will to unmaking, affecting the body politic, the body cognitive, the erotic body, the individual psyche—the entire realm of discourse in the West" (p. 269).

Gradually, through the coding and decoding of the stream of words, conceptual assumptions that held together old teleologic sequences dissolve as affects give way to reason, egocentrism to decentrism. Finding a balance between emotional, subjective, and creative impulse, the analysand will acquire the analytic capacity for the objectification of experience in contemplation, a stance which lends itself to delay, to the task of representing and integrating motives and actions. Out of this there crystallizes an autonomous will and a new narrative (Kermode, 1966).

In an 1896 letter to Fleiss, Freud writes, "I am working on the assumption that our psychical mechanism has come into being by a process of stratification, the material present in the form of memory-traces being subjected from time to time to a rearrangement in accordance with fresh circumstances—to a re-transcription" (Freud [1887–1902, p. 235], cited in Bellin [1984, p. 4]). The present context, in other words, brings new significances as it rearranges the past; the story changes in the very act of its reconstruction. Discursive form, because it has undergone a process of socialization and is interpersonally oriented, is enabled, through the bond established by language between thoughts and words, to represent both connotive and denotive aspects of experience. Nondiscursive form, just because it is individual, private, idiosyncratic, remains tied to imagery, to organic activity, even to organic movement. "The overall direction of the psychoanalytic investigation would seem to be not so much toward consciousness per se, but toward an optimal communication, an interpenetration and balance of the two forms of mental processes..." (Loewald, 1971, p. 98). The mere fact, then, of talking to another, of telling one's thoughts and expressing oneself to another rather than of keeping silent and knowing only within oneself, must be of enormous importance in the resulting structuring that these different mental activities bring about (Piaget, 1962).

The effects of this reflexivity and interpersonality are experienced by the analysand in the articulation of a new autonomy, that of an autonomous voice expressed as conscious will. The psychoanalytic endeavor yields autonomous thought, which, for its autonomy, must be rid of unwitting, organic intrusion; autonomous language, which in its independence is utilized as a symbolic vehicle rather than a signaling system; and an autonomous narrative, one which has been reconstructed in accordance with the instrumentation of autonomous thought and autonomous language. The task of unveiling oneself and understanding, not just one's experiences but what these have meant in the construction of one's personal narrative, will have come to an end when one can confront the opportunities of each fresh day; or, as Freud more pessimistically stated it, when pathological misery will have been transformed into common unhappiness.

The psychoanalytic process is one of transformation and integration—not of transformation in a magical sense, but in the implications of what it means to linguistically represent multiple, diversely structured layers of experience, along multiple vectors of signification. Freud postulated a tripartite model of mind in which divisions between systems and agencies were sharply demarcated by dynamically determined censorship and a repression barrier. The simile of concentric stratification, however, describing psychic strata, had appeared as early as 1895, in "Psycho-Therapy of Hysteria," and he frequently alluded to a continuity between id and ego (Breuer and Freud, 1895). Whether one visualizes concentric or hierarchic stratifications, what is important is to lay emphasis on the simultaneity which typifies psyche, in which multiple layers and levels of differently represented experience coexist as part of a whole, and find expression in diverse symbolic modes.

Every moment of experience recorded by perception or the senses simultaneously activates literal, allegorical, and fantastical forms of somatic, protosymbolic and symbolic representations pertaining to that moment, as well as many associated percepts, sensations, and concepts related to or resembling the experience of that moment; this, in my mind, corresponds to the essential "nature of the psychical." When theoretizing, it appears to be advantageous to conceive of mind in terms of enduring structural layers of experience, from which motives and meanings are derived, rather than to address contents, conflictual, mythological, or otherwise. Greater emphasis can thus be laid on the symbolic level in which any meaning or motive is represented, since it will be through the expressive features and modes in which such meanings are cast that developmental concerns will appear and to which attuned and effective interventions can be tailored.

Adopting this model, it would be possible to distinguish between pathological processes or vectors of experience, the etiology of which originates essentially in deficiencies or distortions of the symbolic process itself, from those which have arisen out of traumatogenic, affective experiences prior to the symbolic function, at protosymbolic stages. Theoretically, we must try to weave the psychological more skillfully with its biological correlate; nor can the symbolic–lexical aspects be divested of their urgent affective connections to primary physiological roots. It is the entire organism that undergoes developmental transformations, and all aspects of somatopsychic functioning will always reflect the entire person. We need more fruitful formulations than ids, egos, superegos, or even selves, to articulate the nature of human experience and grasp the developmental implications encased in the expressions of subjective meanings.

At the deepest level, biologically rooted patterns find partial expression in broad organic attitudes and defenses which later form representational ideation and, only with great difficulty, may become denoted in discursive form. Subsequent strata will find expression through protosymbolic sign and signaling phenomena and other nondiscursive symbolic forms and modes, until such experiences can, with considerable analytic work, become represented linguistically and be put into words.

A correlate model of therapeutic intervention might view the analyst as both a new object for internalization (and therefore reexperiencing) *and a* catalyst for expanding areas of awareness and articulation of symbolization; and, by way of the psychoanalytic situation itself and its intent, as a coconstructor in a dialectic which produces a new personal narrative and world view. In terms of interventions, far greater precision can be obtained in the fit between an interpretation and how it is received, when the analyst can identify to what degree material is symbolized or still in protosymbolic forms, these modes operating in both vertical and horizontal dimensions. Grounded in organismic premises, this model does not need to dichotomize soma and psyche, archaic and advanced mentation, or indeed, mind and brain, since these polarizations are absorbed in the linearity of a developmental paradigm of mind viewed as transformations of planes of experience. It frees the clinician from procrustean molds or forms of content, to better hear the nature of the analysand's subjective experience.

The model here proposed embodies and schematizes the hierarchic organization of symbolic structuralization, taking the activity of the symbolic process itself as the key to the meaning of unconscious and conscious aspects of all experience. Transformations brought about by this abstractive process alone account for the transition from unconsciousness to consciousness, without recourse to energic or economic analogies. It is of note, however, that any symbolic system can be viewed as an economic device, since it provides the means for representing in condensed form a deeper structure of multiple referents, often far richer and more complex, by comparison (Waelder, 1936). Moreover the translation from one representational mode to another is always very difficult and meets with considerable resistance, since it impinges on the very fabric of how knowledge is organized as it attempts to reshape this at a new level of conceptual abstraction. The difficulty apparent in the effort to translate what is in nondiscursive, protosymbolic forms and render it linguistically (making the unconscious conscious), I believe, has less to do with censorship (although morals and ideals will come to exploit defenses enabled by repressive activity) than with the fact that consciousness itself corresponds to modes of representation in the symbolizational process. While what has been suppressed voluntarily will eventually reveal itself, sometimes spontaneously, in a prolonged atmosphere of trust, unrepresented, early determining experiences and their encumbent defenses can, only with persistent scrutiny in the here-and-now and focused introspection through reconstruction, become transmuted into linguistic form.

This model has the added advantage of correlating with neurobiological theories. In a paper which studies consciousness through language pathology, the neurologist J. W. Brown (1976) offers a basic structural model wherein four levels of cognition, defined in their anatomical and physiological aspects, recapitulate a sequence of evolutionary plateaus. Each level is conceived as a closed system and represents what was once in our prehistory an endstage in cognitive evolution.

Providing a stable framework toward what he calls "an account of the microgenesis of consciousness" (p. 72) cognition is presented as evolving along a series of phylogenetic levels which further develop ontogenetically in both form and structure. "The evolutionary process has an emergent character, with new strata appearing as core differentiations within older, more diffusely organized zones" (Brown, 1976, p. 70). These levels should not be thought of as "separate brains," but as widely distributed systems that evolve seriatum out of one another, in a continuously unfolding pattern of transformations into successive states of increasing differentiation.

Brown notes that awareness moves developmentally from an original sensorimotor, undifferentiated state to different levels in a "unitary formative process . . . awareness is another aspect of the microgenesis of action, perception and language and differs according to the development of these components" (1976, p. 73). It makes better sense to think in terms of modes of presentation of conscious states, corresponding to phases in the unfolding of symbolization, than of any fundamental aspect of an underlying nature of consciousnss as a system, extrinsic to content. Brown's tracing of the phylogenetic and ontogenetic

A STRUCTURAL MODEL OF COGNITION

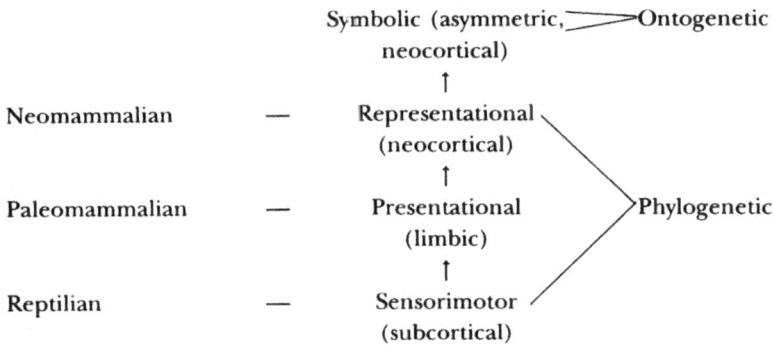

	Symbolic (asymmetric, ──►Ontogenetic	
	neocortical)	
	↑	
Neomammalian	— Representational	
	(neocortical)	
	↑	
Paleomammalian	— Presentational	Phylogenetic
	(limbic)	
	↑	
Reptilian	— Sensorimotor	
	(subcortical)	

[Brown, 1976, p. 68]

neuroanatomical base, and his state-specific approach to consciousness, is a correlate of the stages of symbolization presented in this work and, I believe, provides the neurophysiological substrate to corroborate this new paradigm.

Throughout, I have tried to emphasize the importance of understanding early development as an interdigitation of multiple developmental lines which influence and are influenced by each other. Mahler's separation–individuation theory, Greenspan's levels of learning, Piaget's developmental model of cognitive operations, are all closely interconnected in the intricate early construction of a world of feelings, things, and people. In this interwoven process, the dialectic of the object vis-à-vis subjective experience, is central. In this sense, Freud's calamities of childhood reflect and are parallel to the developmental stages of symbolization with their correlate internalizing capacities, and are still useful and evocative guiding points. Along the course of development processes of internalization will correspond to degrees of differentiation, or lack of it, and accordingly will reflect microgenetic steps in the stages of symbolization, viewed as intrinsically interrelated to every other aspect of development. The dialectic of self with other is thus implicitly part of any advance in symbolization, as shifts in representational levels are mediated through relationship. As I have repeatedly emphasized, connectedness and separateness are the soil in which the symbolic function takes hold; in both form and content symbolization is the transformational vehicle which keeps inner and outer, imagination and perception, self and other, in juxtaposed coordination.

The progressive struggle toward forming true symbols, to abstract and represent experience, is coterminous with an ongoing individuating process. The notion of directiveness toward knowing, "ego strength," and differentiation, go hand in hand throughout life. Brown suggests that microgenetically, the phases of mental evolution are recapitulated every moment, that structure must determine function. "The process which supports this cognitive form, the series of transformations from one level to the next, is inwardly inseparable from the cognitive form which it supports" (1976, p. 91; Grand, Freedman, Feiner, and Kiesky, 1988). In the absence of a reality principle, with its imposed objectivity, there are only planes of subjective constructions of world, always present, always real for the subject at each level of comprehension.

To the degree that something is acted out it cannot be apprehended—it is being enacted instead of being represented. In its representational function symbolization induces a separation, or a gap, between experience and its emotive immediacy. What is lost to the senses is transformed into mind; when it articulates awareness, language encases and transmutes experience.

Only when introspection and reflection take the place of action can a conceptual construction come about; and in assuming that concepts are never static constituents of knowledge and meaning, but constantly fluctuating aspects of current experience, it is in this fluid, conceptual, symbolic transformation through communicated language, that psychoanalysis presumes to eventuate change. Abstractive organization alters structure. Talking cures.

5.

Psychoanalysis Revisioned: Implications of a Revised Theory

> Earth, isn't this what you want: to arise within us,
> invisible? Isn't it your dream
> to be wholly invisible someday?—O Earth: invisible!
> What, if not transformation, is your urgent command?
> [Rainer Maria Rilke, 1922]

The model of developmental stages of symbolization presented in the previous chapter is designed to provide a scaffolding or framework in which to embed a new metatheory for psychoanalysis, one which begins to trace the ontogenesis of the laws that govern the development of symbolic systems; of the forms, processes, and states involved therein, and how this development impacts dynamically, behaviorally, and phenomenologically on the construction of reality and elaboration of meaning. My goal in this work is nothing less than to propose a new paradigm for a psychoanalytic, general model of mind which can provide "maximum internal coherence and the closest possible fit to nature" (Kuhn, 1962, p. 3). The main focus of this reformulation, with respect to Freud's metapsychological explanations, has been to reconceptualize the notion of instinctual energy and its convertibility, and the main feature of this revision has been to operationalize meaning. It is my belief that a developmental model of symbolization can change the very idiom in which we articulate the essential process of psychic transformation as effectuated in the course of psychoanalytic therapy. Perhaps it can do even more. It may open a gateway to a systematic approach to the study of the forms of symbolic systems and the variegated modes in which, intrapsychically and intersystemically, these forms become manifest in the individual and in the formation of cultural groups. It may even begin to guide research in the area of the interrelationship of these and the implications for communicative, interpersonal events.

The guiding revisionary aim behind this work is founded on the conviction that Freud devised a metapsychology for his findings, a temporary "scaffolding," as he called it, based on the biologistic orientation of his time, in line with the contemporary scientific ethos. But more essentially, that he did so because he did not have a symbolic model or a system of reference, much less a guiding developmental framework available to him. Moreover, a careful reading of Freud's writings reveals both his awareness of the shortcomings of metaphoric, physicalist analogies for psychological phenomena and, particularly at the end of his life, a recognition of the profound "obscurity" in which lay the "still shrouded secret of the nature of the psychical" (1940, p. 163). It is precisely the "nature of the psychical" that this chapter strives to make manifest.

It is my contention that the mind's abstracting process, or stages in the ontogenesis of symbolization, holds the key to a new way of understanding the transformations of psychic reality, as these occur in normal development and in the clinical situation. Specifically, that various organismic forms of meaning-organization acquiring increasingly symbolized representation constitutes the original and natural soil of psychoanalysis, both theoretical and clinical. To recontextualize the mind as a symbolizing process, and to locate meanings within operative stages of a microgenetic developmental sequence of symbolization effectively grounds our theory in a conceptual base which finds correspondence with our practice and methodology. From the outset, Freud's psychoanalysis emerged out of a treatment mode and research vehicle in which method and approach were the operational correlates of his theory of mind and of therapeutic action. "If we take method seriously," writes Richards (1990), "we are constrained to build theories anchored in the assumptions that method makes . . . the theory of mind on which the method is premised is the metatheoretical bedrock of psychoanalysis; any theory that lays claim to the appellation 'psychoanalytic' is obliged to take this bedrock as foundation (Bachrach, 1989; Rapaport, 1944; Shevrin, 1984)" (Richards, 1990, pp. 356–357). As Richards notes, Freud's hypotheses ended up producing a mixed theory, simultaneously encompassing a theory of intrapsychic and external reality, a motivational and a causal theory, a drive and an interpersonal psychology, the current version of which is "Freudian but not Freud's," having assimilated the diverse contributions of numerous generations of analysts. Freud achieved comprehensiveness at the expense of simplicity, a trend which has continued (Richards, 1990). While there has certainly been an awareness of the need and call for major revisions, a profusion of offshoot additions has encumbered the field with increased complexity "through the complementary use of models based on differing premises" (Gedo, 1991, p. 71). While many have been brisk to announce that Freud's metapsychology has outlived its conceptual value, most still use it, and very few have emerged willing to tackle the full implications of a radical paradigm shift, which can maintain Freud's psychoanalysis as Freud's by recasting it in fresh hypotheses.

In the current obfuscatory confusion produced by the plethora of existing mixed or semitheories, more and more is being written about things which have already been said, as less and less is being conceptualized that is really new. Big problems have been broken up into little pieces, and many partial theories have emerged which partly solve only some aspects of a whole theory (Hawking, 1988). The field has been in a long-standing 'crisis,' surviving only on artificial life support systems. The task appeared to be to detect the areas of maximum difficulty and find the simplest way of exploring the central questions, so as to approximate a theory that fit the facts. I took it as my responsibility to trace the course of the history of the ideas that had become the bedrock of our theories and, after considerable integration and synthesis, arrived at a relatively simple paradigm of symbolization stages. As Kuhn (1962) emphasized, assimilation of a radically new paradigm approach "requires the reconstruction of prior theory and the re-evaluation of prior fact," an intrinsically revolutionary process which is "seldom accomplished overnight or by a single person" (p. 7). The implications, applicability, and ramifications of the model here proposed are beyond the scope of this work which has, rather, been devoted to its presentation and explication.

Heeding the sharp message wielded by William of Occam's fourteenth-century philosophical razor, "thou shalt not multiply entities needlessly," the entire thrust of this work has been fueled by a desire for theoretical unity and simplicity; a need to synthesize and integrate, to distill and abstract until the emergent conceptual frame thus materialized may encompass all of the essential propositions strewn about in current pluralism. Viewing simplicity as an important criterion in the selection of a theory that approaches a "truth," or one which, at least, approximates a "right categorization" (p. 37), Goodman (1984) writes: "for simplification is systematization, and systematization is virtually the soul of science" (p. 43). Reexamining competing models of mind, Gedo and Goldberg (1973) concluded that no less than five different theoretical subsystems could be resorted to for the optimal explication of data elicited in the psychoanalytic situation, five models which, moreover, are "fully independent constructs" (Gedo, 1991, p. 72). Understandably, Gedo now calls for the "simplest possible clinical theory," one which will "add to existing theories of motivation and development only the concepts needed to explicate reasons for these shifts in modes of functioning" (p. 71).

This tendency for psychoanalytic theoretical pluralism originated in Freud, so that a full hundred years later, we are still attempting to find an appropriate scientific realm in which to place the entire field (Grünbaum, 1984; Spence, 1987). As Loewald (1971) criticizes, "To the extent to which Freud . . . places psychoanalysis in a continuum whose referent is not mind but living matter, he loses the subject of psychoanalysis" (p. 113). Yet unlike psychology and psychiatry, which are content to categorize behaviors nosologically, and find solace in descriptive diagnostics, methods which "stultify an appropriate approach and grasp of psychic life," psychoanalysis, according to Loewald (1971), adopts a method which is "derived from or devised for a different realm of reality" (p. 116). Where psychiatry must busy itself with the classification of pathologies and the differentials of their underlying neurochemical substrate, psychoanalysis has delineated its field of operation by focusing on psychic reality and its transformation, within a linguistic context dedicated to the exploration, understanding, and interpretation of meanings through their variegated expressions. Adopting the idea that language may be only one of numerous other ways of "knowing," and that we are dealing with one particular mode of symbolic articulation, opens the field to the vast new and unexplored, interdisciplinary terrain of human symbolic systems. Consequently, any genuine psychoanalytic model has to define the pivotal role of language in development and its therapeutic action. It must also reconsider the clinical phenomena of repetition, transference, resistance, and working through and encompass the unconscious and conscious dimensions of all experiences. All of these require new ways of conceptualizing and understanding the processes of memory and affects, and their relationship to the construction of meaning. I have attempted to open the door to this with my posited paradigm of symbolizational stages. In stating at the outset that a revised model must adopt both a fitting epistemology for issues of mind and a broad enough theoretical base to accommodate all the general principles, I believe I drew attention to the requirement for a redefinition of what a genuinely psychoanalytic model should encompass (Gedo, 1979, 1986).

And here we return to the central problem already delineated in chapter 1, namely that psychoanalysis is an interpretive science (Ricoeur, 1970), a science of human expressive systems, conceptualized in natural science terms. Ensuing repercussions from this internal incoherence have led to years of continuing divisive disputes regarding what is biological and what psychological, what is inside and what outside, what pushes or what pulls the motor, what is endogenous and what is acquired, what is body and what is mind, and centrally, what is actually occurring in the process of change as analysand and analyst talk. The central stumbling block preventing the unification of psychoanalytic clinical and theoretical models, as I see it, remains an epistemologically based incompatibility of methodological approaches and goals (Richards, 1990).

On the one hand, through its objective method and doctrine of replication, natural science sets up questions in terms of causal relationships and establishes confirmation in a rigid concept of prediction. On the other, and consonant with the idea of hermeneutics, the interpretive sciences ground their method in a collaborative dialogue in which a dialectical process of exploration and interpretation of experience coconstructs an understanding of meanings, currently referred to as meaning analysis or intersubjectivity; "human understanding," writes Steele (1979), "exists in the complex interaction of language, meaning, history and self-reflection" (p. 391). Having laid the foundations for a motivational theory of causal explanations, Freud precipitated psychoanalysis into an unresolvable predicament, because subjective experience does not result from causes but rather is the singular elaboration of an individual's subjective experience. The fundamental difference, succinctly stated by Home (1966), is the "difference between 'interpretation' and 'explanation' " (p. 43). Nevertheless (and this remains a theoretical blindspot for hermeneutists and hard scientists), this does not negate the fact that principles governing the construction of subjective experience may be understood and, in broad terms, used to provide a guiding framework for understanding the human mind.

Artfully discussing the illogical superimposition of a scientific metapsychology onto a humanistic discipline, Home (1966) emphasized the crucial methodological distinction to be made between categories of living and dead objects: "if they are seen as dead, their behavior has to be accounted for in terms of causes; if they are seen as alive, they have to be accounted for in terms of a spontaneous subject" (p. 44). Psychoanalysis is concerned with meanings, he states, and its discourse requires "an unscientific logical framework which maintains a clear distinction between behavior and meaning," and concludes, "until psychoanalytic theory is restated in these logical terms, it will necessarily stand outside the framework of universal knowledge" (p. 49). In commenting on the "slippage of Freudian terminology from the material to the psychological," revisiting the old debate whether psychoanalysis is an art or a science,

Steele (1979) affirms that it is both: it is "a systematic, interpretive method whose goal is the creation of understanding" (p. 407). My effort to recontextualize and operationalize meaning within a developmental framework represents an attempt to recast our theory in the logical terms Home emphasizes above, but also to provide principles and parameters for testability, in order to unify the scientific and humanistic, the conceptual and the methodological aspects of psychoanalytic practice and its model of mind.

In a detailed discussion of the semiological foundation of psychoanalysis, Edelson (1972) also tackled the implications of the epistemological problems inherent in seeking causal explanations versus coherence, or consensual understanding. Discussing the status of instigators of dream construction, he wrote, " 'Laws,' in symbolic functioning govern the relations between members of the symbolic system and construction of a symbolic form, rather than the relations between a stimulus and a response to it" (p. 243). One cannot explain or predict the dream from an examination of the instigator, he reasons. Further, he adds: "Many of Freud's statements seem to cry out for reformation as instructions specifying how to proceed" (p. 249), and the direction Edelson points to is the understanding of symbolic form: "To understand a symbolic form is to know how it is made. To comprehend how it is made is to understand the mind that made it. To discover mind through the analysis of the modes of construction of the symbolic structures made by man—his poetry and his science, his mathematics and his history, his religion and his symptoms . . ." (p. 250), is the essence of the psychoanalytic theory. And, Edelson concludes succinctly, "That which is signified is the meaning of a symbolic form" (p. 250).

Despite the fact that Freud "dealt always and almost exclusively with patterns of meaning," writes Holt (1976), "Meanings still have no recognized place in metapsychology; 'drive-derivative' and equivalent expressions are merely a back door by which they are smuggled in despite their lack of proper scientific credentials" (p. 168). Holt emphasizes the necessity to do away with the theory of instinctual drive itself, "this central part of psychoanalysis is so riddled with philosophical and factual errors and fallacies that nothing less than discarding the concept of drive or instinct will do" (p. 159). In an earlier paper, carefully seeking revisionary strategies and approaches to the theoretical problems of the primary process, Holt (1967) comments, "psychoanalysis is strangely silent about structures," despite the fact that "Freud gave a number of indications that he realized the need for structural concepts to account for irrational, magical, wishful and symbolic, as well as for realistic and adaptively effective forms of thought" (p. 352). In heeding Holt's concern for an urgent reconceptualization of the "economic point of view of metapsychology" (Rapaport, 1959), I also hope to have fulfilled his prediction that it would be possible "to develop structural concepts that would obviate . . . economic ones while retaining their desirable properties" (p. 397). With regard to the primary process, he emphasized the important point that when we discern functions, "we must logically assume structures of some kind that do the functioning" (p. 151), and underscored the many statements in Freud's opus which implied and called for "more differentiated structures than the general system within which the processes were taking place" (p. 352). Here too, with reference to my postulated three (there may be more) nondiscursive, prerepresentational stages, and the incumbent restructuralization of the primary process, I hope to have fulfilled Holt's revisionary intent.

Even as sophisticated an author and theoretician as Greenspan (1979), and one to whose work I refer extensively, is found puzzling as to how one can "account for the relationship between changing somatic experience and representational experience without using a concept such as transformation of energy?" (p. 334). The question for Greenspan remains: "How do we develop a unifying construct which can begin to take into account the data emerging from many sources and settings—from psychoanalytic, cognitive, and neurophysiological studies, from direct observational, naturalistic, laboratory, or controlled settings? Such an integration requires an organizing construct that is at a different level of abstraction, rather than a construct closely tied to a given content area" (p. 339). In full agreement with this requirement, it is my hope that the organizing construct presented in my stages of symbolization is a step toward such an integration.

It has been a misleading **axiom,** in my opinion, and one resulting from a natural science epistemology, to insist that a psychoanalytic model of mind be explained in terms of motivations; for motives are derived from meanings, and all human behaviors, actions, affects, or representations and depictions, as mediums which give shape to experience, are the expressions of these meanings. Where theory has been directing our focus onto energic vectors, internal motivational structures, and their primary biological sources, the process of cure has consistently pointed in another direction. Interpretation never directly seeks to disclose or "explain" motives; it strives instead, through a symbolic system, to promote the understanding of a person, particularly of the feelings and disavowed ideas of this person, and how these feelings have been engendered, and themselves engender, all manner of personal meanings. In other words, it recognizes or affirms the analysand via a denotive medium of communication. Interpretations seek to encourage further expansion and elaboration of these feelings in a shared context and in linguistic form. The therapeutic endeavor strives not for motivational change, but for symbolizational transformation, and these transformations of mind, which organize meanings, are what constitute the "nature of the psychical."

The mind works neither to discharge tension nor to achieve inactive pleasure states; it works by symbolizing experience. Each level of symbolization radically alters the meaning of what is currently represented for the subject, and therefore the nature of psychical experience. The psychic reality, or the meanings incumbent upon this structurally altered organization, bring about changes in the very nature of motives and the modes in which these will become expressed in behaviors, actions, or relationships. Our theory and practice are about degrees in a continuum of symbolizational development, and the diverse modes in which experience finds expression in the content of human symbolic systems.

The persistent emphasis on mental contents and a current descriptive nosological frenzy continue to obscure the clinical relevance of the relationships between form and content in human behavior. Conflict and compromise formation represent aspects of mental contents, in a mind reified as container of agencies pitched in dynamic tension; equally the zealous categorization of personality styles, defenses and characteristic attitudes addresses form. (See Shapiro [1965] for a masterful approach to this.) Both reflect a tendency toward descriptive models of behavior, but not a theory of mind. Yet repeatedly, in the consulting room, people emerge uniquely individual, with their armamentarium of richly diverse experiences to be told and withheld and repeatedly reenacted in the confluence of form and content, which, only within the vicissitudes of co-constructed understanding, will slowly become accessible as these are transformed and expressed in verbal, representational vehicles of communication. Expressivity is here understood as a means of communication, in which variously charged symbolic mediums gradually supplant the immediate signal function of sometimes displayed or disavowed, emotionally salient experiences.

With human expressiveness as a focal guiding concept rather than motivation, we are invited to understand manifestations of mind as expressive forms of meaning. Such meanings, in their beginnings, are conveyed through deeply rooted biological patterns finding partial expression in broad organic attitudes and defenses which later form iconic presentational ideation and only with difficulty become denoted in discursive form. Subsequent strata will find expression through protosymbolic sign and signaling phenomena and other nondiscursive symbolic forms. Such a view of mind leads us into the very heart of subjective meanings and provides diagnostic precision in the assessment of the degree to which an experience is still somatically embedded or on its microgenetic route to becoming symbolized and acquiring consciousness.

For years, however, the classical mold has resolved the problem of meanings by pegging these onto Freud's stages of psychosexual development, the operational correlate of "libido." In order to reconceptualize the bedrock of psychoanalytic principles, so as to genuinely reflect the clinical method and process of therapeutic action, and to bridge the seemingly insurmountable gap between a biological and a linguistic model, it has become imperative to recast our metatheory in terms of a new and different developmental paradigm.

The implications are considerable and may, initially, be uncomfortable. The model of psychosexual stages is skillfully woven into the vernacular of clinical cogitation, so that it has become second nature to identify and refer to such configurations of behavior and characteristically colored impulsions as oral, anal, phallic, oedipal. These evocative metaphors encompassing whole classes of behaviors and styles associated with correlate developmental concerns are so apt that they grasp our imagination and form a coherent descriptive framework within which to organize our clinical observations. Like the power of myths, Greek, psychoanalytic, or any other, they hold within them multiple levels of connotive appeal, subsuming many allusive implications. It nevertheless remains true that these descriptive analogies pertain and remain attached to a concept of instinctual "energy," drive, or libido which, however compelling, does not exist. And while infants certainly do perceive the world somatically, in terms of bodily experience, it is the whole sensorium which is involved and not a stage-progressive primacy of one or another organ. Somehow, and perhaps due to their ingenious correspondence with observed behavioral relevance, we have lost sight of the hypothetical nature of these descriptive analogies and come to refer to these psychosexual constructs as though they were real. Because they are tied to underlying energic implications, however, and because they tie up our clinical focus in a particular way, they detract from a view of mental functioning as planes of organization in a process of referencing.

While the characteristic constellations of impulsions and defenses encumbent upon psychosexual stages are vividly suggestive and have for years provided an explanatory picture for clinical material, a broader theoretical framework articulated above the level and outside the domain of descriptive analogy leads to the understanding of individual experience and behavior without foreclosing theoretical conclusions. Clinically, we are freed from the procrustean chains of myths or models within

which to try to mold our patients and our own experiences with
them, but rather, can attend to the relevant realities which will
unfold between us in the fluid fluctuations between telling and
hearing, past and present, understanding and reenacting.

In recasting the entire model in terms of stages of symbolic
organization, what we would observe clinically are different
forms, modes, and degrees of disparately symbolized expressions of experience moving hierarchically from: (1) unconscious grossly enactive prerepresentational somatic expressions
(implicating the autonomic nervous system and somatic manifestations inclusive of undifferentiated affects) through;
(2) presentational iconic forms (dreams, anecdotal narratives,
art, and presentational–psychosomatic manifestations, i.e.,
panic attacks which in analysis yield ideational content, etc.)
to; (3) preconscious, fully representational, symbolized material
articulated linguistically (memories, events, observations), and
ultimately; (4) consciously, the reflective abstraction of self-observation articulated as awareness in the psychoanalytic process.
Further subdivided these correspond to nondiscursive (figurative) and discursive (conceptual) symbolic form.

Much of the analytic work could thus be understood as
striving toward understanding sign and signaling messages of
prerepresentational stages, subsumed in metaphors and similes,
dreams, or unconscious behavioral attitudes, and facilitating
their verbalization through understanding; or, alternately, as
decoding the linguistic form and semantic garb in which defenses are often clothed, and deciphering and naming the nature of the experiences from which these arose, through
empathic reconstruction. This can often be assisted by attentive
focus on linguistic form and structure itself,[1] which reveals itself
in the here-and-now, contextually, transferentially, and stylisti-
cally, through characteristic patterns, projections, and responses. In this sense, it is not so much the persisting primacy
of unconscious infantile wishes that motivate behavior, but
rather that current motives, desires, and attitudes governed by
current goals and aspirations, find affective resonance with

---

[1]For a most sophisticated linguistic scheme organizing dynamic and defensive
operations as these find expression through pathways of language function, see Shapiro (1970).

strata of experience at earlier presymbolic levels; the new finds correspondence with these.

This formulation and approach is directly consonant with Schimek's (1975) observations and directives, paraphrased in the following; namely, the need to deal with linguistic problems; the requirement for a close analysis of the assumption and steps of the process of interpretation and nature of psychoanalytic interactions; less emphasis on contents and more on recurrent structures, modes, and configurations; and finally, greater interest in the diversity of the "manifest" and its specific context, including detailed descriptions and reconstructions of the experiential world of the patient, and less of a tendency to reduce all levels to "equivalent manifestations of an unconscious infantile wish" (Schimek, 1975, p. 186).

The model (Figure 5.1) I propose discerns and illustrates the workings of an abstractive process which structuralizes mind along a continuum, in which each new stage potentially alters the entire structure while maintaining all of its earlier features. It is believed that it is preferable to think of mind as a unified continuum of levels of symbolization which reveal themselves in content-specific expressions according to degrees and forms of abstraction, rather than to conceive of it as a sharply dichotomized duality or as polarized agencies and repressive forces. Here, planes of experience are organized within a unitary frame of similar rather than dissimilar processes. Meaning is thus effectively operationalized, as it is now understood as a correlate of and intrinsic to a particular level of subjective experience, the expressive form of which may manifest in as diverse modes of expressivity as a gesture, an illness, a phrase, a repetitive reenactment, a melody, a story. In its representational function, symbolization induces a separation or a gap between experience and its emotive quality of immediacy—what is lost to the senses is transformed into mind. When language is used in its full denotive sense, in truly symbolic fashion as a vehicle of expression and communication, it transmutes the nature of experience and therefore the nature of reality for the subject. Subjective experience, psychic reality, meanings, all highly interrelated terms currently used interchangeably, correspond to

Freud's "nature of the psychical," or the workings of the human mind.

In this sense constructivism, particularly the kind of "radical relativism with rigorous restraints" (p. 39) advocated by Goodman (1984), provides psychoanalysis not only with a sound philosophical orientation and epistemologically correct scientific base, but throws in a theory of cognition as well. This constructivist view of cognition, as the subjective making of reality, is ideally suited to the psychoanalytic version (one that is decidedly developmental) of what constitutes relevant data with regard to mental stability, and how the method adopted to attain it, works.

Let me also briefly state that I consider the psychoanalytic situation and its methodological tradition and approach, a frame of reference, if you will, a "special space and place," around which we have drawn a boundary and laid down certain contextual laws founded on certain philosophical, developmental, and theoretical premises. Our laws differ, in many respects, from those of the cultures in which we practice. In fact they extend backward and forward in a scope that would require another essay to adequately address. In so doing we have created a *therapeia*, a psychoanalytic reality (which we must still strive to bring to more accurate correspondence with more facts) upon which our "right discourse" depends. Since, recursively "right discourse is dependent on a reality that is dependent on discourse" (Goodman, 1984, p. 69) it is imperative to construct a viable psychoanalytic developmental framework for our theory of mind, within which to negotiate appropriate levels of interchange, ones which fit or correspond to and correlate with the levels of expressive exchange in which the analysand is currently primarily communicating. If this points to the need for an exquisitely fine attunement of our instrument of understanding, so be it. It does, however, provide us with a correct referential frame out of which to further refine clinical work. Because the psychoanalytic frame invites and initiates a special interpersonal context based on the semantic attitude, it organizes discourse according to a reality based on the integrative, maturational, and curative effect of the symbolic system inherent in linguistic exchange—again, it was baptized "the talking cure." Herein lies the clinical value of the proposed developmental model of symbolization presented here.

For some, who tend to think nonsequentially, also in pictures, as I do, the immediate visibility and ordering of ideas enabled by a schematic illustration can be a very useful device; in fact, as Goodman might view it, denotive in its clarity. For the sake of clarity I have designed a second diagram which, elaborated from the first, serves as an initial bridge from the more general structuralization outlined in the six stages to the more specific content-form inherent in the gradual progression of an ascending, increasingly abstract and discrete denotational and linguistic process. As mentioned earlier, typically, the transformational sequence observable during the course of psychoanalytic therapy moves from enactive repetitions, transference manifestations, and broad characterological traits and attitudes which are unconscious, to their gradual working through, wherein presentational iconic equivalents, with interpretive assistance, slowly give rise to conscious verbalization and concomitant evidence of behavioral change.

The observations Freud accounted for in his topographical and structural models in terms of energy and agencies have to do with psychic transformations. I believe that these transformations are due to the symbolizational process, an observable sequence in which linguistic denotive referencing—wherein the symbol is detached from its referent—brings about dynamic changes and intrapsychic shifts understood as transformations of psychic reality. The following diagram is designed to trace the ascending route of referencing in linguistic symbolization as this correlates with processes of change and becoming conscious during the clinical situation, and to sketch the means whereby characterological defenses which have become embedded in the confluence of behaviors and linguistic structure, may be better detected and understood. Again, I underscore the importance of giving attention to the interrelationship between form and content in clinical interactions.

While my descriptive commentary follows a developmental trajectory and must, perforce, be presented sequentially, it is essential in this model to conceptualize the different strata of psychic organization as patterning experience simultaneously, as would the various sounds of different instruments in an orchestra intone a unified sound when played together. Reflecting the whole personality, the entire functional structure is always involved; and in its developmental origins, it is through the juxtaposition of decentrism and increased objectivism along multiple vectors of experience, that symbolization (now defined as an abstractive device) increases the range of vague processes and experiences accessible to psychodynamic reorganization.

Because the method is embedded in linguistic exchange, all of these processes—sensorimotor schemata, constituent units of internalization, identifications, memory systems, affects, defenses, current and past experiences—will crystallize into symbolic vehicles and become channeled through language. In this sense, when used as a denotive representational means for expressing everything that "comes to mind," language is our particular system of referencing (I assume there are others) and provides us with a view of psyche as a symbolizing process which, in constructing our reality, also creates the meanings with which we imbue it.

Thus, as Goodman (1984) remarks "organization of discourse participates notably in the organization of a reality.... In the denotational hierarchy and in chains of reference lie parts of the structures of any worlds we have" (p. 68).

In clinical work, experience organized at the stage 1 level would correspond to very basic, broad somatopsychic cycles underlying broad patterns of interpersonal responses. The anlage for characterological defenses at this level, partly endogenously determined, would be cast at neurovegetative levels via the ebb and flow of proximity seeking and distancing maneuvers, management of physiological appetitive and satiety states, titration of affective intensity, frustration, fear, and so on, and the neuromuscular tonus of alertness and exchange with the environment. All of these will ultimately coalesce into broad outlines of basic attitudes and behavioral style.

The primal anxiety corresponding to the organization of these very early and very basic underlying strata may be conceptualized as the dissolution of the somatopsychic unity, or breakdown of internal cohesion or integrity of physical boundaries, and perceptual rupturing of the contours of external objects.

		Forms of Expressivity

6. The Reification of Self: The Psychoanalytic Process — Language used denotively, in dissociative observation, to objectify multiple somatic and connotive ideas, memories, feelings, and experiences. Expressions manifest in all modes can now become integrated and represented linguistically.

5. Secondary Symbolization — Language used principally as denotive vehicle and communicative bridge to express concepts, ideas, and feelings. Language available to mediate affects and behavior and integrate inner experience. Connotive expression of affective meanings can manifest through artistic creation. Linguistic structure can now reflect defenses and protosymbolic organization.

[WORKING THROUGH]

CS

Discursive Form

Symbolic representation

4. Primary Symbolization: Language — Denotive reference of words. More differentiated and specific use of language as vehicle for expressing ideas and feelings. Expression is revealed in linguistic structure as well as content.

Representational Form

3. The Symbolic Function: Single Word — Connotive reference of word meanings. Words express entire affective sense and global experience of "things" and groups of things. Expression is partly somatic-affective and partly represented in "naming" function.

PCS

CONCEPTUAL
— — — —
FIGURATIVE

Iconic (image)

Presentational Form

2. Primary or Archetypal Signs and Signals — More differentiated and specific affective responses in familiar patterns of interpersonal exchanges. Broad categories of contrasted experiences are somatically expressed. Affection and rage sharply divided, projective identification, etc.

UCS

Enactive (action)

Pre-representational Form

1. The Protosensory Anlage — Global, motor responses. Anlage for broad neurovegetative cycles and somatic patterns of interpersonal shaping.

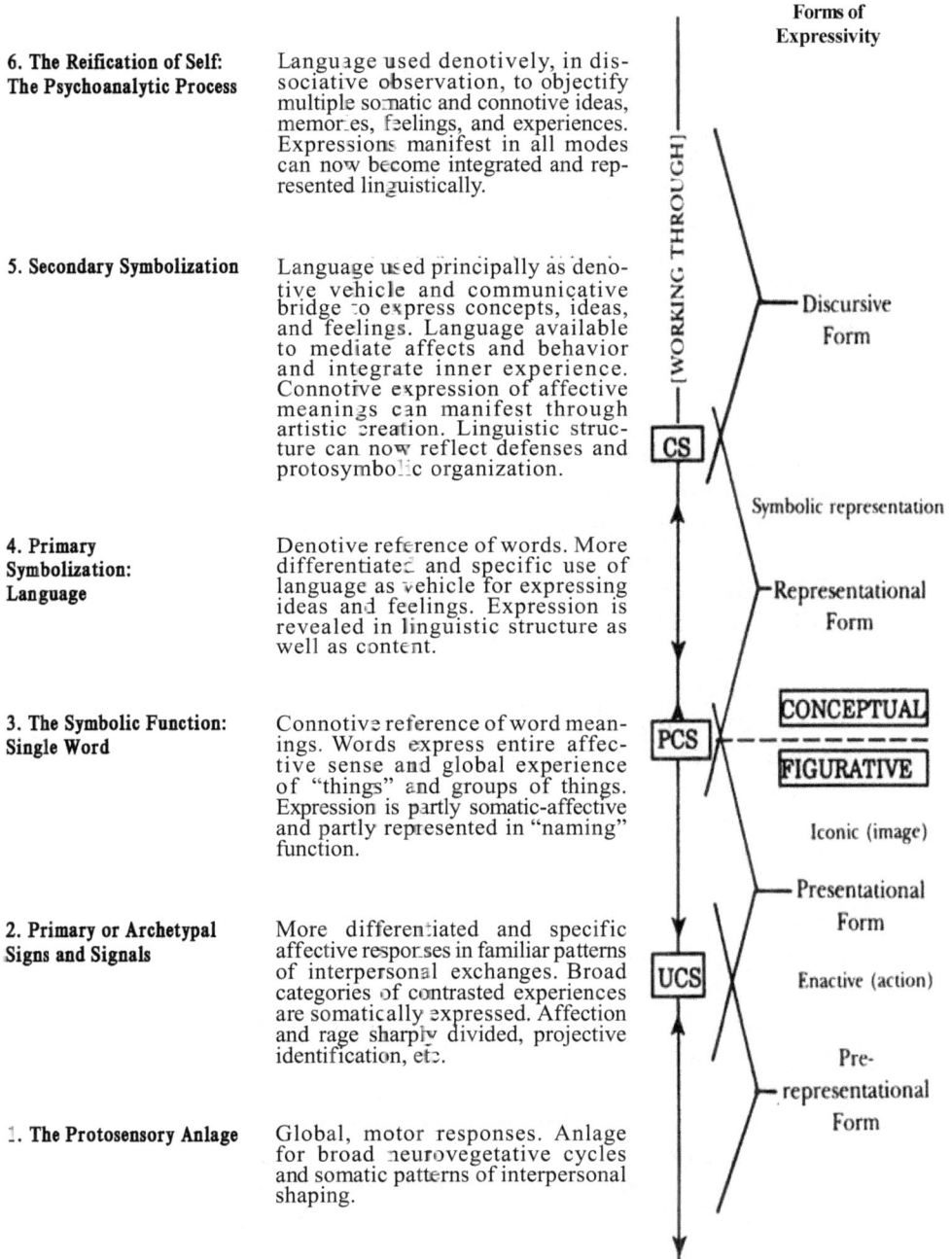

Figure 5.1 Ontogenesis of symbolization and correlated expressive modes

While the manifestations of this underlying level of organization are not readily discernible in overt ways or detectable within any particular constellation of material, they are evident in the underlying patterns of the forms taken by characteristic behaviors. The broad underlying shaping of physioaffective patterns adopted for coping become evident and clinically more tangible in the manifestations of crystallized behavioral forms, much like a sketch provides the underlying outline of which the painting will be the final result.

So, in the stratification of character, this primal level will have provided a basic anlage for psychophysical responses upon which later elaborations will build. Negotiated somatically, these levels continue to process and, for some, determine the processing of information and responses to it.

The second stage of organization begins to see the embryonic beginnings of psychic formation in the encoding of signs which indicate and signals which provide guidance and directives in the ordering of interpersonal communication. Because both initiate an orientation toward recognizing significance, they lay the rudimentary foundations for referencing and therefore the attribution of meaning. Internal cohesion is maintained by the interpersonally determined signifying and signaling functional use of affects and actions which now become more differentiated as they are responded to in specific and different ways by the environment. Pleasure (closely allied with safety at this level), the glue of interpersonal contact, serves as a powerful reinforcer both in the use of and response to signs and signals, at these nonverbal, intuitive levels. Powerful attachment patterns to benign or sadistic caregivers are lodged at such deep levels and are often reenacted transferentially involving just such physio–affectively organized interpersonal patterns. While verbal content provides often articulate distraction, resistively, underlying somatopsychic patterns are tenaciously repeated.

Communication through facial expression, eye contact, posture, gesture, touch, and sound now gauge the degree of involvement, or lack of it, with the environment. While affects, in fact all impressions and responses, have become more differentiated, sensoriaffective tone is still the primary determinant of experience. Familiarity (constancy) begins to serve a stabilizing function interpersonally and a cohesive purpose internally, in which attachment becomes a central organizing fulcrum. Clinically, when interpersonal experience is organized at this level the reliability of the analyst's presence, the invariant arrangement of time and place, the unchanging layout of the furniture, the attentive gesture (i.e., the proverbial Kleenex), and most importantly the tone and attitude of attunement of the analyst, are functionally most important. They satisfy developmental needs which organize experiences of continuity and psychic stability: far from gratifying sexualized wishes, they lay the foundations for the possibility of becoming related. Again, it is not an indulgence at this level to reflect and give verbal stature to the analysand's psychic achievements or notable progress. Akin to early mirroring, such affirmation provides internal referencing in place of often chaotic, affectively based experiences, and encourages self-referents based on linguistic exchange and the semantic attitude.

The typical anxiety at this strata of organization manifests in panic at separation from a primary person of attachment. The catastrophic response reflects the fear of a catastrophic experience of dissolution precipitated by the loss of the cohesive function procured by the presence of the person, at this stage. Thus, pleasure is dependent on safety and closely tied to constancy at this level, in which attachment and security begin to coalesce into what will become manifest as basic trust and a capacity for intimacy.

Conversely, premature losses, abrupt detachment, empathic failures, and separation, will undermine the formation of internal cohesion, disrupt the foundations of trust, and sever the threads of temporality which, in their organization, also facilitate or impede impulse control.

Broad affectively determined attitudes—quiescence and confidence, panic and rage, empathy and affection—will evolve into subjective experiences of lassitude and vigor, withdrawal and illness, or outgoingness and enthusiasm. Loving and hating, at this level dramatically segregated, appear clinically as splitting. The confusing term *projective identification* is better conceptualized at this undifferentiated level as the externalization of intolerable inner feelings, or the confusion between and rejection of what has been induced by the environment. Anxiety at this level is managed through dissociative maneuvers, primitive splitting and denial, and projective mechanisms. What cannot be contained or integrated is ejected or eliminated in one way or another, through primitive defenses or somatic–affective expressive means.

It is at this third stage, in which the inchoate is becoming more particular and the general grouped into categories, that the somatic acquires shaping through iconic–fictive images and imagos. In accordance with the egocentric phenomenalism governed by subjective states typical of this level, the fictive and the real, like the figurative and operative facets of encoding are still confused and merged. It is at this point that I posit the appearance of what will become archetypal images; the felt expression of significance and impression condensed into some outstanding feature of a class and displaced by overdetermination; for example, Father-tree (tall and imposing). This prototypical presentation crystallizes out of fragments of memories and, primarily affective, sensory impressions of interactions, significant people and events. The archetypal image thus formed will, later on, much like a metaphor, come to represent the prototype for a general class or an entire category of experience.

This is the stuff dreams are made of. It is also the stuff of hallucinations, nightmares, perhaps the affective component of paranoia, and the iconic exemplification of psychosomatic presentations—half soma/half psyche. Thus, awakened by a vivid dream and wandering into his parents' room, the little boy asks, "Mommy, are you all right? . . . I thought you were made of paper and I crumpled you up and threw you away. . . ."

In clinical work, behaviors, beliefs, and attitudes expressed through material organized at this nonverbal, unconscious, affectively charged level respond to and convey phenomena which directly indicate (signs) and alert (signals). Even though the ongoing clinical process is occurring at higher levels of verbal referencing, experiences are being processed, in parallel fashion, primarily in these nonlinguistic, protosymbolic experiential ways in which the concrete, such as availability or nonavailability of a constant mirroring presence, are what really count. Similarly, experiences are processed and incorporated in concrete ways, at the level of actions, tone, facial expression, which only gradually become accessible to representation and verbalization as words acquire greater denotive distance from their connotational underpinnings, the sequence being from somatic to fictive to real.

Out of initial, rudimentary codification established in the conditioning world of signs and signals, in development, there emerges the first true act of denotive reference—the single word and the symbolic function. Clinically, the appearance of this important transition from inchoate–enactive and iconic presentation to representation and denotation, indicates the beginnings of naming at a preconscious level. At this level words may easily become equivalents of their referents and be used only in literal ways as in schizophrenia. A single word, in such cases, may signify an entire range of experience. In clinical process a single word may represent, like a metaphor, an entire constellation of issues and memories which have not as yet been worked through. The metaphor or simile contains the whole affective world and will express this connotively, until it gives way to elaboration and further breakdown of constituent meanings. This leads to emotional working through and further preconscious awareness.

The verbal utterance, when it appears, indicates that there has been an internal effort to give shape, to symbolize, and bring to consciousness by representing internal experience through denotive articulation. And this despite the fact that, at this level, words straddle two worlds, one that is unconscious or connotively depictive, and another which is increasingly denotive and conscious. At this preconscious level words still participate of their affective equivalents or unconscious meanings and are only on the way to acquiring the greater denotive distance—of the symbol from its referent—which will gradually loosen them from their connotational underpinnings.

At stage 4, with the establishment of language as the primary symbolic vehicle of communication, and, in the clinical situation, of expressing awareness, the denotive, referential function of words serves as an important bridge between inner and outer and from affective-felt to referred to and observed. With increasing denotation, and its more specific and differentiated use as a symbolic instrument, language begins to subsume greater aspects of all experiences and assists in the articulation of abstract concepts.

Now, frequently, those affectively charged unconscious connotive aspects of word meanings become woven into locutions through language structure, tone, and slips of the tongue, which are context-bound and brought to relevance during analytic discourse. It is important to keep in mind that while I continue to be constrained by the sequential nature of explanation in the laying out of this symbolizational trajectory, once hierarchical dominance has been established, the stages are actually occurring all at the same time. Thus, in the flow of associations, material is characteristically uneven and disparately expressed. For example, content may exemplify a narrative similar to one which has recently been dreamt or is being reenacted in the here-and-now, but do so with further connections to memories and current affective experiences. Here the proto-symbolic aspects, or the unconscious connections, are becoming symbolized denotively and verbally integrated into consciousness via an examination of their past impact through current meanings.

As the analysand talks, communication is occurring simultaneously at all levels and is being expressed, to varying degrees, in all modes. One could conceptualize the presymbolic pathologies as being predominantly organized around and expressed through somatic and protosymbolic expressive channels, communications alerting to and indicating various internal states and conditions. The therapeutic task is then primarily focused on understanding the nature of these presymbolic expressions and their protosymbolic iconic presentations, and through interpretive naming, to give them denotive, symbolic status in linguistic form. Here, understanding has served an affirming, holding function, and naming, a denotive and symbolizing one.

At this stratum of the referential hierarchy, however, language begins to be harnessed to conceal rather than reveal; the flow of free associations far less free than might appear. Anxiety

now serves a swift signaling function triggering effective defenses which avoid affect flooding, and are woven into context
and discourse. In other words, at the level in which language is
becoming the predominant expressive–communicative medium
for interpersonal exchange, it promptly adopts all of the maneuvers and defenses designed to gauge interpersonal relatedness which had earlier been elaborated in somatic and
presymbolic modes. Now, all the unconscious, connotive–expressive features of word meanings become intertwined in the
form and structure as well as the content of this representational
system. Herein I emphasize the importance of viewing the person as a whole, a somatopsychic unity.

The flow of the linguistic production, in the confluence of
form and content, will now itself reflect, through ambiguity,
implication, exemplification, or obfuscation, the defensive maneuvers and interpersonal strategies, spoken and disavowed, of
the analysand. Thus, a frequent problem in the analytic context,
an apparent copious flow of verbosity, can be a major resistance
to the process itself.

At the fifth stage of symbolization, and within the theoretical and methodological parameters of psychoanalytic discourse,
language is not only the primary medium of interpersonal exchange but also a mediating instrument of the entire personality. Verbal symbols, having become quite distinct from their
referents, can be used as the principal tool of communication,
expressing inner experience, memories, feelings, and thoughts
which can now become integrated and articulated at various
distances in a denotational hierarchy. The mind equipped with
a fluid referencing ability is an adaptive, dexterous world which
can move in and out of metaphorical and literal forms, closeness
and separateness, the concrete and the abstract, and can manipulate inner experiences and concepts at will, increasing inner
cohesion.

The flexibility afforded by symbolization in language at this
level is like the assistance afforded by a trampoline for a high
dive—it provides buoyancy and ascent. For the mind which can
move fluidly between levels of abstraction, entering into any

level of a referencing chain or frame, can also harness experience organized at any or all of the stages, and depict these connotively or derive from them new and abstract ideas conveying an array of meanings and even creating new ones. Artistic creation and expression, utilizing any representational system or modality, can be conceptualized in such a way.

Psychologically and psychodynamically, at this level of organization, language is a powerful tool, infinitely dexterous, giving depth and mediating power which extends from one particular frame of reference to aspects of experience that are still inchoate, encased in affective, unconscious expression.

Stage 6. With language and linguistic exchange as reliable instrumentation, we are enabled, given a contextual facilitator, to segregate one referencing pole of experience and assign to this articulation the task of self-observation along multiple vectors of experience: from present to past, past to present, from here to there and vice versa, one person to another, from imagined to real, iconic to verbal, unconscious to conscious. Process, in psychoanalytic discourse, requires a pronounced use of this new lens.

The observing ego, an essential accompaniment to the therapeutic alliance, and the only reliable ally of reality during the disorienting reflections of distorting transferential mirrors, provides anchorage and stability between the multiple referential orbits which must be managed during analytic work. The mediating and cohesive function of symbolization, when utilized denotively within an interpersonal matrix, is best exemplified in the psychoanalytic situation at this sixth level, wherein language will come to represent and transform the motives, meanings, and modes of expression of a personality.

In a context independent from judgments of truth or falsity or rightness and wrongness, in which multiple narrative structures are revealed and coconstructed daily giving new light to old unchartered ways, the new pathway learned and trodden will continue to lead inward, giving rise to referential routes of further understanding.

One of the hallmarks of psyche is simultaneity; this model provides a theoretical key to the way in which multiple meanings are embedded in unconscious and conscious aspects of all experience, as well as the multiple levels and modes in which meanings are expressed. It places meaning within a functional–structural framework in which content finds correspondence with levels of symbolic organization according to the nature and degree to which experience is symbolized. Further, this model accounts for the central role and specific function of language along the unconscious–conscious dimension, within the psychoanalytic clinical situation, and with regard to a reorientation of primary and secondary processes, viewed as two different vectorial lines serving diverse functions and modes of processing and articulating experience.

Most importantly, it provides a truly psychoanalytic developmental paradigm in which the proper role of symbolization, its instrumentation, and subtle nuances in mental transformations are spelled out, and distinguishes between cognitive capacities and psychic activity, in which various manifestations of protosymbolic and symbolic expressions are substantiated. In providing a structural framework within which meanings find correspondence with developmental planes of symbolization and their concomitant modes of expression, this model points the way toward important questions regarding a correlate evolution of internalization processes. Pegging incorporative, introjective, identificatory, and other forms in the phenomenology of internalization to specific developmental levels of organization provides further guidelines for clinical understanding and appropriate interventions. By identifying a developmental course for the central organizing instrumentation of mind, this model articulates a theory of psychoanalytic principles at a high level of abstraction, above the level of content, agencies, or systems, and thereby obviates the need for reification. It is a paradigmatic model for health as well as for mental disorders.

In a seminal state-of-the-art paper, Richards (1990) drew attention to the timeliness of a reconsideration of theory. Noting the difficulty in making firm predictions about the future of psychoanalytic theory, Richards nevertheless advanced numerous important ideas pertaining to his own personal vision which find correspondence with the interdisciplinary approach adopted in this work.

The psychoanalytic theory which prevails will be one which best converges with data from other fields, neuroscience (Reiser, 1984) . . . and observational research . . . on infancy and childhood (Blum, 1989) in particular. For recognition of convergences is requisite in an epistemologically sophisticated understanding of the mind–body problem. It also requires an understanding of the relations between a theory of mind and theories of a biological or neurophysiological nature. Recent works from the standpoint of neuroscience (Hobson, 1988) and cognitive science (Colby and Stoller, 1988) pay no attention to this epistemological issue and end up giving short shrift to analysis as an autonomous theory of mind. . . [p. 358].

Richards continues, ". . . in the decades to come analysts will refine theory by assigning a more systematic place to biology. . . . But," he cautions, "we must be wary of regarding these issues as the exclusive province of medicine; medical background is hardly prerequisite for developing and employing a biologically inclusive theory of mind. The contributions of non-medical biological scientists in advancing psychoanalytic theory in this respect are to be welcomed as much as they are to be expected" (p. 359).

He believes that psychoanalytic theory will place biology within a "unitary conception of mental illness that does not equate biological imperatives with a reductionistic bias which holds that biological determinants will be established as the sufficient cause of all major mental illness. In fact, to situate illness within a broad biological framework is antithetical to ascribing the pathology to any single cause" (p. 360). He cites Maguire's (1982) argument that what distinguishes analysis is precisely its "ability to reconcile dialectically both poles of the Cartesian mind–body dichotomy" (p. 360).

Implicit in Richards' idea of theoretical refinement is the belief that advance can be made toward the selection of one "true" theory which, "consistent with the warrantable claim of psychoanalysis to be a science of mind . . . will be more rather than less consequential for clinical practice" (p. 361). Accordingly, viewing theory as crucially related to clinical technique,

Richards predicts that a "true" theory "will be anchored in the most comprehensive theory of mind available" (p. 357). He criticizes the current eclecticism—"a smorgasbord of theoretical options"—and, in disagreement with Wallerstein (1988) and Pine (1985, 1988), who both support their own versions of pluralism, believes that theoretical differences must "neither be minimized . . . nor submerged" but rather "accepted as the dialogic nexus out of which any eventual consensus will emerge" (p. 363). Further, Richards asserts that his vision of the psychoanalytic theory of tomorrow can be realized "only if we promote vigorous dialogue among proponents of the divergent theoretical viewpoints of today . . . [a dialogue that] must compare theories not on the basis of literal truth but of empirical adequacy . . . [which] must go beyond, or perhaps beneath, the issues of empirical adequacy to consider the basic issues of epistemology and methodology that underlie our theories" (p. 363).

Finally, in considering what can be done to encourage constructive dialogue, Richards turns to the essential prerequisite for a coherent training experience, one "that will produce analysts capable of evaluating rival theories" (p. 364). Implicitly, he voices Gedo's (1991) view that psychoanalysis "can survive only if the members of the psychoanalytic community feel themselves to be in the vanguard group of the highest social and intellectual calibre." Gedo (1979, 1986, 1988), a man of culture whose ideal encompasses the fusion of science and humanism, and whose works have consistently reflected a sophistication characteristic of the intelligentsia of days of yore, bemoans the deintellectualization of psychoanalysis in America, "virtually the deprofessionalization" of our discipline, in his opinion (1991).

Many of the requirements, speculations, and predictions quoted above identify and specify theoretical problems which urgently needed to be addressed. These and similar concerns form the themes and focus of this entire work, and, I believe, are successfully addressed in a model which effectively provides an alternate theoretical conceptualization and approach. The current pluralism in our field, in my opinion, reflects the breakdown of a paradigm and the concomitant attempts to account for many aspects of psychoanalysis which should rather, and can, be subsumed in a supraordinate model. The call for inter-disciplinarity is virtually unanimous, as is the need for synthesis and correlation of research data culled from diverse fields. The idea of a unified psychoanalytic theory of mind, one which will be grounded in the time-tested principles underlying our clinical method, is appealing only to those whose vision can encompass an entirely new way of thinking about mind and who can acknowledge a theory articulated above content areas, at a high level of abstraction.

Attempting to eradicate the misleading dichotomies and physicalist imagery with which our discussions of mind are still replete, and strictly informed by events of the psychoanalytic situation, the paradigm I have proposed pinpoints the transformational activity and process of mind. The developmental course I delineate correlates with the development of normal mental structuralization and is centrally concerned with language in its various functions and ability to simultaneously express diverse levels of disparately represented experiences. It provides a developmental framework which encompasses the conscious and unconscious dimensions of subjective experience, or psychic reality, and the multiple modes and configurations in which humans express meanings. It is a model of mind grounded nevertheless in the body, a holistic–organismic model, effectively bridging the illusory gap between biology and psychology as these interweave with each other; one which integrates findings from current child development research, neurophysiology, cognitive psychology, and psychoanalytic propositions, and operationalizes the central hermeneutic task of our clinical method, the interpretation of meaning.

By casting subjective experience in developmental stages which recapitulate phylogeny, the model proposed effectively substitutes developmental, structuralizing organization for functional agencies or economic systems, and in distilling from multiple theoretical propositions one focal transformational process, greatly simplifies and unifies our theory of mind. Moreover, the model proposed reconsiders Freud's central discovery in "the study of psychical qualities" (1940, p. 21), namely, the different functional laws of the primary and secondary processes, and reconceptualizes these as coexisting aspects or modes of organizing experience tied respectively to a connotive, expressive, inner-oriented focus and a denotive, communicative, outer-oriented mode, both of which contribute and participate in ongoing development throughout life. (Perhaps further developmental trajectories might be developed tracing the course of development and the features characterizing in each of these modes.).

The model proposed is broad enough to encompass the great diversity of manifest phenomena, while laying less emphasis on the reduction of all levels of experience to genetically derived contents originating in the infantile "wish"; emphatically, it is one that provides an organizing construct for specific and unique manifestations of personal meanings. Indeed all meanings and therefore motives, are understood as being intrinsically tied to individualized aspects of levels of symbolic organization. Such a perspective, in addition to uniting the implicit natural science and humanistic facets of our theoretical propositions, obviates the need in clinical work to cast expressions of personal experience in the reified terms of agencies, such as selves, or egos. Furthermore, it is a model which offers the possibility for a unified, psychoanalytic theory that integrates such illusive aspects of human expression and apprehension as creativity, intuition, and empathy. Many other epistemological and theoretical issues and themes raised, discussed, and recast in contemporary terms[2] thread through the fabric of this work—too many to reiterate. Suffice it to say that I have striven not for brevity but for the breadth and depth required for a comprehensive and thorough exploration of all the theoretical concerns under discussion and of the literature serving as a background for the theoretical revisions proposed.

In recontextualizing the central role of language and its therapeutic action in the psychoanalytic situation, and by identifying the transforming effect of symbolizational activity in the process of referencing, my model attempts to unify metatheoretical and clinical principles of method and cure, providing a

---

[2]Central among these are the relevance of affects, the primacy of instinctual attachment, a social propensity in humans, and a propulsion toward 'knowing' characteristic of our species, which assists a posited general "self-righting" tendency that seeks to integrate experiences through reflection (Lichtenberg, 1989).

unitary, simplified, general theory of mind which "can be applied to the history of civilization, to the science of religion and to mythology, no less than to the theory of the neuroses, without doing violence to its essential nature" (Freud, 1917a, p. 389).

There is a general consensus among analysts regarding the validity and efficacy of psychoanalysis as a treatment mode and model of mind. There is also, however, much dissention with regard to the possibility or even the desirability, of framing psychoanalysis within a scientific protocol. Those who do voice their allegiance to psychoanalysis as a science, often on the condition that metapsychology be discarded wholesale, emphasize the need to adopt a methodology which will permit the testing of its hypotheses. Others have pointed out, I believe correctly, that the method already exists—it is, and always has been, the clinical situation. Psychoanalysis has, as a result, been referred to as a science *"in potentia"* (Richards, 1990), awaiting the formulation of propositions which can be tested. A suitable theoretical model therefore had to be formulated which would yield testable propositions. "[M]ental contents and states exist in nature," writes Richards (1990), and "these contents and states can be apprehended through the psychoanalytic method . . ." (p. 361). As a science which attempts to grasp the function of the human mind, psychoanalysis should be able to generate principles and propositions according to the protocols of science, through its method, which can be objectively tested.

The principles underlying my developmental model of symbolization, correspond to a transformational sequence identified by Freedman (1985) (with Brucci) in their research on the therapeutic process. These observed sequential increments of change, moving toward symbolic articulation, were presented by Freedman (1985) as shifts in mental organization occurring around "an associative organizer" or "nonfluency," a pause. The phenomenon was termed "the transformational unit" and found to be triphasic; a prerepresentational, a symbol generating, and a symbol deployment phase (p. 333), and it is viewed as the essential process of psychic structure building. In broad terms this corresponds to my posited three early stages in the development of the symbolic function and recapitulates a microsequence in the course of which experiences become symbolized and transformed into concepts. At the very least, such a formulation posits a definite sequence of events which can provide hypotheses which can be tested according to the cannons of science.

The great astrophysicist Hawking (1988) writes that a good scientific theory has to satisfy two requirements: "It must accurately describe a large class of observations on the basis of a model that contains only a few arbitrary elements, and it must make definite predictions about the results of future observations" (p. 9). He continues, "Each time new experiments are observed to agree with the predictions the theory survives, and our confidence in it is increased; but if ever a new observation is found to disagree, we have to abandon or modify the theory" (p. 10). The propositions generated by my developmental model are testable according to the conditions of this protocol. Research based on the principles of symbolization can be structured around the process of becoming conscious, transformations in analytic therapy, linguistic flexibility in the use of metaphors versus literal word meanings, the mediating effect of language on affects and behavior, or any number of other key issues revealed in the psychoanalytic method. Moreover, because these developmental principles are observable in microsequences in normal development as well as in broad phases in therapy, they yield a theoretical model which lends itself to a variety of experimental and prediction outcome studies.

The process of psychoanalytic therapy brings about certain changes thus far ill-defined, "where id was there ego shall be," or more recently described as "Changes in mental organization," or "structural modification." No clear definition has been offered as to what this organization is or what these structural modifications exactly do. This work has been an attempt to fill this void, not with descriptive metaphors or analogical explanations, but by pinpointing the central process of mind and formulating a radically new way of thinking about our theory and method. The goals I spelled out at the outset, those of reformulating the concept of the convertibility of instinctual energy, operationalizing meaning and revising the theory of therapeutic action, have now come together in the context of a unifying template for a developmental–structuralist model of psychic transformation.

TRANSFORMATION-SUBLIMATION-TRANSFIGURATION

Of all the enigmas Freud was confronted with upon disclosing the presence of unconscious determinants in human activity perhaps the profoundest, and one that still perplexes today, is that regarding the nature of psychic transformations. For in the psychoanalytic enterprise are registered not merely changes in state, from unconscious to conscious, from unknown to spoken, but also shifts modulating motives and goals, transformations of purpose, of personality, and of the psychic pathways chosen as channels for the expressions of these. Indeed, were it only for its fluidity, flexible in both its energic and theoretical functions, the notion of libido provides a powerful analogy.

For Freedman (1985) a concern with transformation has become "the hard rock . . . the central issue deemed essential for understanding human nature" (p. 317). He focuses on the process by which transitions from one stage of mental organization to the next are brought about by a dialectic conflict engendered in the clinical dyad which leads to reorganization at higher levels. Invoking the centrality of a "disjunctive experience," he claims shifts occur only after a "state of disequilibrium has unleashed dynamic forces" (p. 323). Yet transformation can also occur silently, internally, without extrinsic disruption.

Transformation is a key concept in development and change, one which also plays a central part in the idea that humans may take a variety of courses for the expression and realization of their personal fulfillment and that, characteristically, when satisfaction cannot be found via one route, this purpose will be diverted from its original aim, and find an expressive channel through an alternate course. *Sublimation* is the term Freud designated for this important transformation of "lower" aims into higher "sublimated" activities (Hartmann, 1955).

While classical libido theory has, and continues to be, severely criticized with regard to its drive implications for object relations, very little emphasis has been placed on the way it resolves this crucial shift in the changing pathways of satisfaction and their transforming tendency. In fact, the question as to how what used to be viewed as "energy" becomes transformed or transmuted through a "diversion of aim," is given scant attention today. As Loewald (1988) highlights, attributing sublimation to the ego relegates it to a class of defense, hardly a worthy theoretical solution for a sophisticated understanding of the origin of some of humankind's highest and most sublime achievements.

In my conviction that mind, and therefore human purposes and activities, must function in similar rather than dissimilar ways, I find that symbolization may hold a key to the nature of this transformational process in other than energic or defensive terms, but quite simply in the roots of the abstractive, representational tendency observed throughout this work.

What follows is a preliminary attempt to formulate some ideas on sublimation as these evolve naturally, as extensions from the theoretical framework provided by the developmental paradigm of symbolization here proposed. In finding correspondence with the basic premises of this model, that differently represented experiences find expression through diverse modes and means and symbolic channels, these ideas begin to crystallize around a psychoanalytic theory of art.

The formulation I suggest, unlike that of Freud, premised on transformations of sexual energy, or that of Freedman (1985) premised on the "disjunctive experience," or indeed that of Loewald (1988) premised on relational "reconciliation," is premised rather on renunciation and symbolization, a principle isomorphic to that of the origin of the symbolic function itself; what is lost to the senses becomes mind. A diversion of "aim," is none other than a diversion of expressive means through one or another symbolic system. I am identifying a representational transformation rather than an energic one.

In his 1988 monograph *Sublimation*, Loewald presents several essays including a brief chapter on symbolism probing the problems of "theoretical psychoanalysis." Although, as he defines it, this is an "unfinished work . . . a fragment" (p. 82) and the six chapters have the quality of preliminary excursions rather than systematic revisions, Loewald offers a personal inquiry expressed with the sensitivity and insight which characterize his theoretical writings and style. "Short as it is," he writes, the book was written and reflects the evolution of his thinking over a period of several years. In it, Loewald addresses his central topic, sublimation, and questions an underlying premise of psychoanalysis which, "from the vantage point of instinctual–unconscious mentation, tends to regard more differentiated or further advanced modes of psychic life as embellishments of the elementary, true, psychic reality of instinctual-unconscious life" (p. 1). As he has in other works, Loewald continues to question the underlying premises of libido theory while striving to accommodate relational emphasis into its central ideas.

This work is of particular interest due to its searching, questioning quality. It is clear that Loewald is attempting to fit together some very important pieces of a theoretical puzzle. His interest in symbolism comes via earlier elaborations on sublimation, defenses, transitional objects and phenomena, separateness and union, internalization, differentiation, aim inhibition and repression, to name just a few of the various themes he touches upon. With regard to his chapter on symbolism, Loewald's stated indebtedness to Werner and Kaplan (1963) ground his ideas in similar roots to those that are represented in the research of Freedman (1985) and his associate, have flowered in the works of a handful of psychoanalytic authors mentioned earlier, and have been incorporated here in the systematized, revisionary model proposed in chapter 4. Although he acknowledges not having undergone an in-depth study of the "vast general literature" on symbolism, and that this work, aiming neither to be comprehensive nor systematic, should be viewed as an initial exploration of a series of reformulations, it is surprising not to find the seminal works of Langer (1942, 1972) in his bibliography. Without her crucial and determining definition of symbolization, like a great captain without a compass, Loewald lacks a fundamental instrument that could steer him through his revisionary forays, which, while rich and erudite, lack a central organizing thread to pull them together. I say this while in complete accord with his pungent critique of Jones' (1916) restrictive view of symbolism, indeed, with most of the content of his essay, and in particular with his recognition of symbolization as being "of universal range in human mentality . . ." an essential aspect of "what *mind* means"

(p. 52). Later he adds, "It is the capacity for symbolization that clinical psychoanalysis promotes" (p. 57). As central concepts of this entire work, both these ideas have been amply documented and theoretically integrated in earlier chapters of the present work.

Running as a superordinate theme throughout Loewald's investigations, and of central import to these, is his dissatisfaction with a basic psychoanalytic theoretical premise. This is the idea that the formation of "higher" psychic organization results from defensive mechanisms, a premise which, he writes "makes the ego, as an organization . . . in its very nature and purpose a defense structure posed against the id . . . a structure designed, as it were, to disguise or impede the true psychic reality represented by the id" (p. 4). This "comprehensive concept of defense," in Loewald's view does not attempt to discriminate between what is higher psychical organization and what are defenses, but rather "explains higher organization as a defense" (pp. 4, 5), an assumption premised on the existence of a "pleasure principle" and the inherent idea that the thrust of all instincts is toward inertia, both assumptions which Loewald finds questionable. Although he objects to the theoretical implications of drive theory and its assumptions that all motives are propelled by the energic transformation of instinctual satisfaction, however, he remains firmly rooted in its premises: "It will be useful to keep in mind that a distinction may be made between processes that dam up, countercathect, instinctual life and processes that channel and organize it" (p. 5). Yet the fundaments are now cast in object relations terms, by turning to the mother–infant matrix and focusing on this "undifferentiated phase of psychic development, as contrasted with the notion that the primary given is the id . . ." (p. 14). The shift is from an infrastructure to an interpersonal matrix, and emphasis is now given to the "essential part this emerging differentiation plays in sublimation" (p. 14).

Sublimation, as higher psychic organization, can thus be explained in terms that reconcile object relations theory with drive psychology as "a kind of reconciliation of the subject–object dichotomy . . .—an atonement for that polarization (the word *atone* derives from at-one) and a narrowing of the gulf between object libido and narcissistic libido, between object world and self" (p. 20). Contrasting his formulation with Hartmann's (1955), Loewald maintains that "both narcissism and the structure of the ego resulting from the organization of narcissistic libido are instinctual in origin and nature, that narcissistic libido is no less instinctual than object libido" (pp. 20, 21). Now, in response to his original question, "What is it that is being changed in the process called sublimation?" (p. 5) Loewald can respond with impunity that it is passion, "Sublimation is passion transformed" (p. 9). Still operating within the concept of psychic energy, he concludes, "it is neither the nature of this energy nor its source that marks the difference between the ego and the id, but, rather, the way in which and the level at which energy is organized" (p. 21). In the notion of level of energy organization, Loewald can satisfactorily reunite sexuality with spirituality and return passion to sublimation which, as he says, is "especially active and experienced in creative work, be it of a scientific, artistic, therapeutic or religious nature . . ." (p. 22). However, we are still firmly rooted in energic premises.

"Sublimation is not a form of defense—not even of 'successful' defense—against instinctual life, desire, passion, the unconscious: instead sublimation belongs in the area of ego development and of internalization as distinguished from defense," he writes, and concludes, "I conceptualize its dynamic quality broadly as *reconciliation*" (p. 33). Loewald goes even a step further in his restating in process terms, and suggests that the important psychoanalytic concept of aim inhibition, the delay of immediate instinctual discharge, is not *due to the ego's control*, but rather represents the formation of the ego itself, as it evolves out of the id; "this delay is the resultant of that organization of instinctual energy which we call by the name of ego" (p. 21). Here Loewald is describing structural levels of organization, but, in retaining the premise of "instinctual energy," and without reformulating the essential nature of the ego, his conceptualization obscures the old theory without really establishing a new one. One might, even correctly, surmise that this sort of gradual theoretical evolution by accretion is organically endemic to psychoanalysis, so typical has this propensity toward partial modification been in our history.

In Loewald's reformulation, "instinctual energy" is now restored to an original id–ego continuum, without the need to cast passion filled, higher aim expressions such as sublimation, in the light of defensive maneuvers. Yet, having blurred the boundaries between the differences that traditionally have distinguished the id from the ego, without providing a comprehensive new framework for this revision, and still tied to a dichotomous view of external and psychic reality, the concept of mastery (conceived as "coming to terms") receives flighty definition: "[I]t brings external and material reality within the compass of psychic reality, and psychic reality within the sweep of external reality. In its most developed form in creative work it culminates in celebration. This 'manic' element of sublimation is not denial, or not only that, but an affirmation of unity as well . . . , the organization of the ego itself, to the extent to which it is non-repressive, is such a celebration already" (p. 22).

If sublimation, in its dynamic quality, is conceived as a "reconciliation," it has little to distinguish it from other adaptive ego mechanisms, moreover, it has lost its particular "sublimatory" quality and no longer corresponds to Freud's more subdued characterization of the ego as a "precipitate of abandoned object-cathexis." There is, in this definition, an unmistakable awareness of loss in the transformation of id into ego; just as there is an unmistakable quality of renunciation in the diversion from common satisfactions to those characteristically associated with sublimation.

For Loewald, sublimation "brings together what had become separate" (p. 22); "in sublimation the experience of unity is restored, or at least evoked, in the form of symbolic linkage" (p. 45). And here is the point of great conceptual divergence between Loewald's understanding of symbol and my own. Quoting Winnicott (1953), he illustrates, ". . . 'symbol' means that the transitional object is an embodiment of that union . . . a separation that is not a separation but a form of union" (Winnicott, 1953, p. 369), cited in Loewald, p. 23). "In genuine sublimation . . . and at the point of the initiation of their state of separateness (Winnicott, 1953, p. 369) . . . this alienating differentiation is being reversed in such a way that a fresh unity is created by an act of unity" (p. 24). This idea is antithetical to my own, based on the notion of the symbol as a developmental achievement arising out of loss, indeed generated by and out of genuine differentiation, in which the only reward is a transformation of subjective experience, at once more objective and internally richer. The transitional object is by definition not yet a symbol, but as "an embodiment" of union is protosymbolic, akin to the amulet developmentally, substituting for the object, not yet a symbol of it. The symbol proper does not replace loss, it transcends it—this apparently small conceptual differentiation has monumental theoretical implications, reverberating at all levels of psychic organization and experience.

Loewald's rejection of the notion of the evolution of psychic structure as being contingent on defensive mechanisms is a welcomed revision, as are his ideas regarding the aim of the ego, the inherent passion in sublimation, his theoretical underpinnings in the undifferentiated matrix of the primary dyad, and his basic dissatisfaction with the commitment of psychoanalysis to "scientific materialism" in dealing with an "immaterial" subject matter (p. 2). Yet, none of these important ideas is sufficiently rerooted or thoroughly regrounded. Loewald modifies problematic facets of the theory but leaves the fundamentals that generate these problems intact.

Having sketched at the outset a few of the problems presented by sublimation, Loewald's exploration proceeds along disparate paths and vectors of thought, as he states, "unsystematically," discussing aspects of the subject from "various angles and perspectives and by adopting diverse modes and moods of discourse" (p. 8). Many of the themes and threads initiated are not spun into a coherent whole—perhaps this would have required a more comprehensive work and more radical reevaluations. For these, and many other reasons elaborated in the body of my thesis, I am unable to wholeheartedly embrace Loewald's recasting of the id and ego, his redefinition yet preservation of "instinctual energy," his reconciliatory concept of sublimation, and most essentially, the theoretical implication of his view and premise of the symbol. For if the symbol restores unity, our whole evolutionary thrust would have a regressive core, there would be no reason to or means for reflecting upon what is absent or yet to be—there would be substitution but not transmutation, satisfaction but not transcendence, restitution but not sublimation.

Spurred by Loewald's theoretical reevaluation of sublimation and in line with Freedman (1985), I turn now to a superordinate theme, one of central concern in psychoanalytic theory and of singular interest to me, in which many concepts discussed throughout this work and in the above converge—that of transformation. My focus in the following will be to identify what I perceive as an isomorphic pattern, a central principle consonant with my developmental paradigm, and to incorporate this into the theoretical framework of the model of mind I have proposed.

The ideas that follow will, of necessity, be presented in embryonic, preliminary, and only sketchy form. They may be viewed as pointers for future investigations to be carried out in areas that can and must further be elaborated upon in order to refine the paradigm and theory of mind here proposed. The following may serve as an index toward which further exploration and research might go.

> The intellect of man is forced to choose
> Perfection of the life, or of the work
> And if it take the second must refuse
> A heavenly mansion, raging in the dark
> [W. B. Yeats, "The Choice," 1932, p. 147].

> For somewhere reigns an old hostility
> between our living and the great work
> [Rainer Maria Rilke, *Requiem*, 1908].

Let me reiterate: I do not subscribe to the traditional psychoanalytic postulation of "psychic energy" (libido) and its transformations, but rather view mind as a symbolizing process, whereby stages of symbolization transform subjective experience and its modes of expression. Transformation, throughout, will refer to this process of mind and not an energic concept.

Ideas of transformation are not only part of quotidian subjective and objective experience from our first stirrings in the world, they are also universally woven through cultural themes and into ideologies and narratives the globe over. From their beginnings as magical transmutations, they evolve into heroic transformations, and finally ascend to the highest ecumenical and spiritual principles of beatification and transfiguration. In its narrational urge, the human mind is highly attuned to and preoccupied with notions of change and transformation, as though bound by some primeval concept that perceives things as having little fascination unless they are transformable into something else (Lundkvist, 1992). Events of change, temporal sequence and transformation are of course also used as primary markers for teleological and causative reasoning, organizations of thought which form the propositional structure of many of our beliefs and much of our narrative discourse (Propp, 1968; Greimas, 1976; Bettelheim, 1977; Calvino, 1980; Bruner, 1983).

In the first of these genres, the most primitive, the fairy tale, transmutation is little more than an instantaneous wish fulfillment wherein, as in dreams, change occurs miraculously as does enchantment, pursuant to some magical power in a realm of fantasy. Most stories pertaining to this primitive genre anthropomorphize and project feelings and fears onto the dramatis personae used as narrative devices with little complexity other than their immediate displacement value. Here broad categories of good and bad are prominent, and poetic justice permits only of happy endings. In myth, on the other hand, the second genre, heroes and heroines, are created by virtue of their valor, charged with enduring ordeals which occur in cause-and-effect circumstances wherein they become transformed and elevated due to their own superior moral or physical strength. Herein is an implicit internalization of and identification with the moral value of valor and endurance. The narrative form contains an implicit code of moral integrity based on internal, self-propelled controls which are, however, contextual and embedded in a social nexus. In the third, the religious realm of faith, illusion, mysticism, and spirituality, epitomized by the Christ story, the transformational process occurs in extremis, as the renunciation of a worldly life unfolds into a sublime transcendence, a resurrection in the transfiguration of life through death—perhaps the most profoundly archetypal of all concepts of transformation. Inherent, is the idea that relinquishing life on earth wins life eternal. In each of these, the precondition for transformation is the renunciation of a previous state.

Assuming that mind is a part of nature, it will follow that a mind which so profusely produces transformational stories must itself have some familiarity, even if inarticulate, with an underlying principle of transformation of which it is itself a part. Expressing a similar idea, Freud (1940) wrote, "we construct . . . a sequence of conscious events complementary to the unconscious psychical processes" (p. 159). Form, science teaches, determines function. If content and form are irrevocably tied together, then the mind that invokes transformational narratives must also be a transforming mind. This is the premise at the heart of my thesis, that mind is not an organ propelled by "energy," but rather, is itself a transformational process, an instrument of the entire organism, one that transforms subjective experience into concepts through symbolization and expresses these meanings through various symbolic modes and systems. As such, mind can only be conceptualized or apprehended via its modes of manifesting meaning. These, as we have seen, can alter according to the symbolic level in which experiences are represented and according to the chosen means for expressing these, which characteristically move from undifferentiated, unrepresented-somatic, through partially differentiated iconic-presentational (in nondiscursive symbolism), to fully differentiated representational forms which may be expressed in discursive or nondiscursive modes. In the latter case, when in the realm of art which can harness any stage and any one of many symbolic modes, the formal properties of the medium are utilized to attain the highest aesthetic ideal, as representational vehicles of expression. Here, the rich, evocative, emotive sentience of nondiscursive symbolic levels finds vehicular expression for its connotive feeling-depths in symbolic mediums, such as music, painting, and dance, and in discursive form through poetry and literature. These symbolic forms become the denotive means for the expression of connotive significance, just as occurs in language. There is nothing primary or "inferior," psychologically speaking, either in ideation or representational efficacy. On the contrary, these artistic forms often reach us more directly, more immediately, and more deeply. My model obviates the necessity to create fictitious dichotomies between so-called "lower" and "higher" mentation or processes, and clarifies rather than distorts the origins and sources of art and creativity within a greatly simplified theoretical framework.

While traditionally in psychoanalysis the term *sublimation* refers to a desexualized transformation of instincts, this model, rather, understands sublimation as a transformation of expressive means—the transformation of subjective experiences (sentient and emotive) as expressed through a different vehicle or a symbolic medium with an aesthetic form. Such a conceptualization of sublimation can leave "passion" intact, neither sexualized nor desexualized, since it addresses the vicissitudes of expressive manifestations, the transformation of planes and modes of symbolization, not the transformation of energy. My model additionally greatly clarifies the otherwise mysterious notion of conversion, somatization, and psychosomatic illness, as being the inverse of sublimation; "in both the clinical and psychoanalytic sense," writes Loewald (1988), "sublimation . . . denotes some sort of . . . transmutation from a lower to a higher, and presumably purer, state or plane of existence—be it the transmutation of a material substance or of an instinct and its object and aims. The psychoanalytic term *conversion*," he continues, "designates transformation in the opposite direction . . . from higher levels . . . to a lower level manifested only in somatic form . . . Conversion and other forms of somatization," he concludes, "appear to be the opposite of sublimation" (pp. 12–13)—and leaves it at that. Rather than polarized as opposites, these covert modes expressive of affects and connotational meanings or of self-expression, may be understood as the least represented when they are manifested somatically, and most represented when manifested purposively and aesthetically. If, in accordance with the model of symbolizational stages, we replace instincts and their aims with modes of symbolizing and their expressive means, then it becomes apparent that the least represented, undifferentiated manifestations of subjective meanings will be expressed organismically, through somatic channels, and the most represented manifestations will find vehicular expression through the articulation of sophisticated and

complex symbolic mediums and systems. In all cases and at all
levels, we are dealing with forms and modes of expressivity,
whether these are conscious or remain unconscious (see Figure
5.1, p. 345).

In order to manipulate information and achieve theoretical simplicity, physics pushes its principles to paradigmatic ideals,
where, at such high realms of abstraction, the few sparse concepts derived can be made to articulate an otherwise astonishing
array of mutually limiting elements. For the purpose of theorizing, I believe there is a valuable lesson to be learned from
this approach.

Were one to adopt this method in theoretical psychoanalysis, one such basic principle to distill, and central to the classical
theory of sublimation, would be the notion of aim inhibition
and its closely allied clinical tenet, abstention from acting out.
In the former, the metatheoretical premise lies in the assumption that instinctual energy, pressing for discharge, will redirect
its aim. In the latter, its clinically related parallel idea, the assumption is that by abstaining from action, the impulse will be
raised to a "higher organization" and will be "talked about" instead.

The underlying theoretical assumption in what appears to
be a basic psychoanalytic principle is that aim inhibition, or
abstention from impulsive action, and in the psychoanalytic situation itself the interpolation of a delay, will cause a "diversion
of aim," producing thought, and a new and higher psychic
structure. Without clouding this relatively straightforward idea
with obfuscatory discussions regarding the existence of pleasure
or unpleasure principles or the moral merits and fallacies of
what "lower" and "higher" aims are, we can identify a basic
principle of psyche characterized by a structural transformation
incumbent on deferment.

Stripped of "instinctual," or "energic," or "discharge" implications and coupled with its clinical sister concept of restraint
or abstention from action, the notion of "aim inhibition" theoretically comes to resemble a little dictum I have been using
throughout; what is lost to the senses is gained to the mind
(i.e., when deprived of one avenue of immediate expression,

organization pushes to another level of symbolization or another means for its symbolic expression). This comes to look very much like (1) Freedman's (1985) "non-fluency" pause, which initiated the symbolizational transformative unit; and which, I believe, finds its earliest origin in (2) the void left by separation, out of which the symbol is born; and is analogous to (3) the notion of increased differentiation and abstraction inherent in the hierarchic sequence of symbolizational stages; and (4) is central to Freud's (1923) concept of ego formation and functioning; "By interposing the processes of thinking, it secures a postponement of motor discharge and controls the access to motility . . ." (Freud, p. 55).

The notion of structural transformation incumbent upon deferment runs through my entire theoretical model as a basic paradigmatic proposition, just as shifts in libidinal energy represented the spine of classical metapsychology. Yet in my model explanation is found to reside in the mind's transformative symbolizational stages as these become expressed through different symbolic means, rather than in the transformation of energy and its redirected aims. Both formulations strive to conceptualize the formation of what has been called the "ego."

At the core of a linear isomorphism inherent in a simplified psychoanalytic theory is the notion of renunciation—the idea that psychic transformation occurs through reorganization of stages of symbolization during and as a part of the process of giving up a previous state of affairs or an earlier representational template. Indeed, the term *transform* inherently implies that the process and result are one.

Let us now return to Winnicott's "point of initiation of the state of separateness," a crucial juncture in human development through which, in one way or another, we have all had to pass. Loewald, concurring with Winnicott, would see this paradigmatic point of separation as engendering a "new unity," a symbolic connection for the purpose of reuniting; at its most evolved, "sublimated" level, Loewald refers to this as a "reconciliation." Yet the thrust of the theory, clinical and metatheoretical, points in another direction. And, in revisiting this crucial point of initiation of separateness, we find that the opposite must occur,

namely, that it is in the transcendence of separateness, the renunciation of a previous state of union, in the reflective void
left by absence, that the symbol is invoked. In its incipience, the
symbol emerges out of loss and differentiation (albeit gradual),
and what is lost to the senses, now an instrument of reflection,
is transformed into mind. Therefore frustration produces structure, id becomes ego, delay increases symbolization, and renunciation inheres in sublimation. Sublimation is isomorphic to
symbolization, it follows the same basic principle, and its premise lies in the transformation of vectors, or aspects, of subjective
experience into symbolic expression. This is a transfigurative
realization of expressivity through a new symbolic medium.

The lives of creative individuals are characteristically enveloped in contradictory images associated with the sublime transcendence of the creative spirit, visited by inspiration only after
long and exhausting travail, and ultimately overriding the
weighty tribulations of all manner of earthly difficulty. While it
is not always the case that suffering and creativity are inevitably
matched, as the illustrious lives of some of the most celebrated
people of all time attest to, yet, we suppose that transforming a
particular and unique way of knowing about the world into an
expressive vehicle, requires some outstanding or singular form
of concentration. From the great philosophers, scientists, and
poets to the great shapers of images, we are aware of a powerful
quality of "inwardness," by which we are drawn and enchanted,
to their "outward" expressiveness. Yet, the flip side of the jubi-
lant omnipotence inherent in creative work is the discomfort
of its lonely gestation, the burden of its compelling inner presence, and the arduous labor of its painful birth.

Moreover, for the creative individual whose products or
ideas are disseminated around the globe, neither the finality of
time nor the limitations of physical space, in which the paths
of natural life are confined, need exist since both are tran-
scended by the creative experience itself and overridden by the
continuing life of the creative product. The creations themselves attain immortality, transcending both the creator's isolation, inevitable decline, and death. In such a way, also, the
insubstantial, subjective sentience and feelings of the creator
find palpable manifestation in the physical world through a

product, the expressive qualities of which are objectified and abstracted symbolically. Here is a genuine transfiguration of the expressive essence of a life. Somewhere, deep in the premise of our understanding of creativity, lies the tacit knowledge of some ancient inimicality between the common satisfactions of life and "the great work." That inevitable tradeoff producing a mysterious alchemy of affect, talent and compelling, concentrated effort which transfigures what life denies into imagination and pushes it into creation; "Literature," Simon de Beauvoir is believed to have said, "is born when something in life goes slightly adrift." Or as Schiller so beautifully captures it, "What would live in song immortally, must in life first perish."

Goethe's abandonment of his beloved Friederike Brion is seen by his biographer, Nicholas Boyle (1991), as an action necessary for the survival of his art, in that "the poetic transformation of this relationship, as of others, became objective symbols of central truths about himself" (Schweitzer, 1991). According to Boyle, Goethe's opus can be divided into works of the first half of his life, subsumed under the rubric "The Poetry of Desire," and, once the poet had become aware of the requirements to live "a symbolical existence," one of Entsagung or "renunciation," works of the second half, subtitled "The Age of Renunciation, 1790–1832."

"Nowhere . . . will world be but within . . ." wrote Rilke, perhaps "more exclusively a poet than anyone before him or since" (Leppmann, 1987). This most sublime and archetypal of poets who, even at the threshold of death is found standing dispassionately outside his passionate inwardness, rendering unto life's expression his own ending:

> Oh life, Oh life: to be without such blaze
> But I am burning. No one knows my face.

A face, whose wrenching inner cry we can now feel echoing in these resounding lines which express all that a face might never convey. A man of intellectual genius as well as consummate poetics, Rilke depicted his aspiration in a 1908 poem, "Requiem," in which he mourns the death by suicide of a young poet. He speaks of "the ancient curse" of those poets who, like invalids, use language to exploit their distress, pointing at their hurts and pains, instead of "transforming themselves into words," like the "stone masons of a cathedral," who immerse themselves "into the stones' equanimity." And, in a blend of "hubris and humility" all his own, yet revealing the very distillate of the transformational redemption in creation, Rilke ventures the view that if the young man had learned this lesson, it might have been his salvation (Leppmann, 1987).

So, creativity demands a ransom, a certain sacrifice; when forced to choose, one "must refuse a heavenly mansion . . ." writes Yeats. The creative individual is one who suspends and captures some aspect, or many, of life experience and molds this subjective sentience, transforms it through a symbolic medium, into an expressive entity, in which others can participate. Or, as Rilke would have it, and as occurs in the dance, one who *becomes* the medium itself. The prototype for this, perhaps a more primitive version, is to be found in the collective fusion and enactive transformative participation of ritual. The spiritualist and shamanistic trances are also transformations of individuals into mediums, but these belong to a still more primitive realm of superstition and magical belief in which incantation is purposive, designed to perform some illusory function, rather than figurative or depictive, at the aesthetically higher and more purely expressive realm of art.

"*Sublimation*, in both the clinical and the psychoanalytic senses," writes Leowald, "denotes some sort of conversion or transmutation from a lower to a higher . . . plane of existence" (p. 12), a transmutation which entails renunciation and symbolization. This transformational process is isomorphic to that of the original birth of the symbol, emerging at the point of separation, out of the void left by absence. Like the symbol, a "higher state" is generated by and through increasing differentiation: the loss of union entailed therein, derives from this an instrument of reflection or transfiguration, not a restitutional substitute. Sublimation is the offspring of renunciation, not reconciliation.

A pervasive "renunciation" inheres in the abstractive process itself; this is apparent from stage to stage as experiences previously bound at undifferentiated levels are distilled into concepts and then are progressively decontextualized in more differentiated ways along the abstractive continuum. What is lost to the senses is transformed into mind. This simple principle whereby experiences are transformed into concepts through the process of symbolization, is itself isomorphic at all systemic levels. In its developmental stratification, it represents a model of mind as *transformative* process, one that gives form to its expression by shaping symbolic mediums. These become expressive vehicles when one avenue of enactment is, for whatever reason, renounced. Nowhere is this more dramatically visible than at the highest level of sublimatory expression in which life is transfigured into art. Emily Dickinson—who spent fifteen years in pristene, barren isolation, behind windows, away from the testy tribulations of the real world—writes inwardly, symbolically:

> At last, the lamps upon thy side
> The rest of Life to see!
>
> Ah, What Leagues there *were*
> Between our feet, and Day!

For Loewald, the psychoanalytic notion of sublimation "comes readily to mind" when explanation is sought for the presence or emergence of what are uniquely human functions, or the psychic structures related to these, "those which bespeak a complex level of mental functioning" (p. 7). "The term, regardless of how little it has been understood or elaborated, points to something exceedingly important to mankind. Without this something—tentatively conceived as a form of transformation from primitive to more advanced levels of mentation —without these transmuting processes and capacities, man would not be man" (p. 8).

At the risk of being redundant, my claim is that this "exceedingly important 'something' " to which Loewald alludes is the process of symbolization, out of which the plethora of elaborate and beauteous symbolic systems of humankind are generated. And here, the model of mind and theory I propose come together and find symmetry in the central principles of our uniquely human symbolizing tendency.

The hypothesis we have adopted of a psychical apparatus extended in space, expediently put together, developed by the exigencies of life, which gives rise to the phenomena of consciousness only at one particular point and under certain conditions—this hypothesis has put us in a position to establish psychology on foundations similar to those of any other science, such, for instance, as physics. In our science as in others the problem is the same: behind the attributes (qualities) of the object under examination, . . . we have to discover something else . . . which approximates more closely to what may be supposed to be the real state of affairs . . . [Freud, 1940, p. 196].

In 1915, during the process of laying down his seminal theoretical formulations for psychoanalysis, a psychology which now encompassed a newly discovered sphere of unconscious processes, Freud introduced various standpoints from which to view "the scheme of mental phenomena." "It will not be unreasonable to give a special name to this whole way of regarding our subject-matter, for it is the consummation of psycho-analytic research . . . ," and proposes that "when we have succeeded in describing a psychical process in its dynamic, topographic, and economic, we should speak of it as a *metapsychological* presentation" (1915b, p. 181). To these were added the genetic, the structural, and later also the adaptive points of view. In order for a theoretical formulation of any psychoanalytic hypothesis to be complete, and satisfy the criteria for a metapsychological examination, it must be inclusive therefore, and take each one of these perspectives into account.

Loewald (1988) recommends that the title *theoretical psycho-analysis* (as analogous to theoretical physics or theoretical biology) be adopted to replace the term *metapsychology* for encompassing the fundamental conceptual premises of our science. It is a good idea and one that might be taken up by the profession. However, due to the scope of my proposed revisions and to the fact that they refer to Freud's formulations, I take it as my responsibility to satisfy, as much as I am able, Freud's criteria for a *metapsychological* presentation. As Freud pointed out, while most scientific enterprises take as their objects of inquiry manifestations which appear as phenomena in the external world, psychoanalysis has the added difficulty of being a science which must take as its object of inquiry the very same mind which it is trying to conceptualize. Subject and object here are not merely intimately interconnected, they are virtually one. The difficulty is further compounded by the fact that theories exist only in our minds and provide models which in any case are only approximations of what we observe. Nevertheless, if we substitute the idea of structural relationships and manifestations of related symbolic processes and modes, which are themselves purely mental constructs, for agencies, systems, and the energic forces that move them, which are the operations of purely *physical* phenomena, we may be able to find alternative explanations to satisfy Freud's criteria, while providing answers which are framed in an entirely new and different way.

With this as my starting point, I turn to a dynamic perspective of mental processes, "the phenomenology of the subject" (Freud, 1940, p. 156). Specifically with respect to Freud's notion of the tension brought about by instinctual demands and the multiple, circuitous routes by which these find satisfaction in the relation among agencies, or, as he wrote, "in raising the passage [of events] in the id to a higher dynamic level (perhaps by transforming freely mobile energy into bound energy) . . ." (p. 199). While in the general concept of dynamics we understand a tension brought about by the juxtaposition of opposing forces, its application to psychoanalytic theories refers specifically to intrasystemic conflict and compromise formation, and to processes of cathexis, countercathexis, censorship, resistance, and the transition of impulses from unconscious expression to conscious status.

In viewing the entire organism as a dynamic, evolving process, a dynamic explanation for the process of symbolization invokes the notion of inherent difficulty in shifting the phenomenological experience of the subject. Insofar as experiences encoded at one developmental level of meaning represent "reality" to the subject, only with great difficulty will they yield to the decentering or objectifying transmutation essential for reconstituting it at another, more abstracted level of organization.

The dynamic tension here parallels Freud's life and death instincts, and is apparent between the striving to "know," to apperceive, or understand through the reflective act of conceptualization, and its polar opposite, to remain "unknowing," to resist the decentering transmutation and remain at the current level of apperception of reality. If I may be permitted to push a theoretical analogy to its furthest point (to an abstract realm where theory loses its practical application), we come quite close to Freud's polar forces, since advance in the stages of symbolization requires new "condensations" to form concepts or, in the terms of Eros, new "unities." And all resistance to the integrative effort in expanding our apperception and forming new concepts more consonant with current reality necessarily leaves experience in "unknown," disjoined, or unconscious condition. Where Eros, affiliated with the (ego's) tasks of knowing and understanding (mastering), strives for integration, not knowing or understanding works regressively, perpetuating schismatic or inchoate experience and repetition or stagnation.

Freud's topographical construct, later to be closely connected with his structural formulation, provided a descriptive framework within which to organize the relations between psychical qualities (the characteristics of being either Ucs, Pcs, or Cs) and the provinces or agencies of the psychical apparatus, the id, ego and superego of the 1923 structural model. Of this, in his final work, Freud (1940) wrote:

> But it should not be forgotten that in fact it is not a theory at all but a first stock-taking of the facts of our observations, that it keeps as close to those facts as possible and does not attempt to explain them. The complications which it reveals may bring into relief the peculiar difficulties with which our investigations have to contend. It may be suspected, however, that we shall come to a closer understanding of this theory itself if we trace out the relations between the psychical qualities and the provinces or agencies of the psychical apparatus which we have postulated...[p. 161].

From the perspective of topographical and structural conceptualizations, a symbolizational model provides very different solutions, first because its developmental–structuralist design subsumes Freud's mental mapping, and second, because a paradigm of planes of mental organization eschews all notions of localization or reified "agencies" in favor of developmental stages structuring experience. We have moved from systems and agencies to patterns and processes; the change is radical and epistemological. Structure is now understood in process terms as a level of organization rather than an agency. Configurations of experience along a hierarchic developmental continuum now inherently express a particular "psychical quality," according to level and mode of representations, and with respect to being unconscious, preconscious, or conscious. Like Freud's topographical theory, my model of symbolization provides psychoanalysis with a theory of reference. However, due to its developmental organization it goes a step further. It provides a framework for the dynamic processes of referencing wherein "the psychical qualities and the provinces . . . of the psychic apparatus . . ." (Freud 1940, p. 161), albeit without localization, can indeed be traced.

The new paradigm provides a broad framework for manifold expressions and configurations of subjective experience at different levels of symbolization; its explanatory value lies in its replacement of entities and locations with a structuralizing process organized at a higher level of abstraction, in a conceptual realm which fuses form and content.

Freud's mental apparatus, a mechanistic model, runs on energic premises; indeed, the internal coherence of his entire theory rests on the postulation of instinctual drives issuing from somatic sources as excitations provide quantities of motivational energy which, in the course of pursuing the quickest route to satisfaction, become highly malleable. The energy of Eros, operationalized as libido, "serves to neutralize the destructive tendencies . . ." of the death instinct (Freud, 1940, pp. 149, 150). These fluid, opposing energies, the former striving for "unities," the latter to "undo connections," are capable of changing their aim and replacing one another.

It is the *economic* point of view which attempts to trace or "follow out the fate of a given volume of excitation," and addresses the question of the "quantitative distribution of libido"

(Freud, 1940, p. 156). And it is of course this energically based economic premise, the bedrock of Freud's metapsychology, which this entire work radically revises.

In the context of recasting theoretical psychoanalysis in terms of a model of symbolizational development, in such a way as to unify its conceptual framework and practical application and bring these into correspondence, the new paradigm of mind substitutes a transformational process for notions of transformation of energic economy. True symbols, as we have seen, are personal creations which, in their condensation of various experiences and abstraction of these into new form, come to stand for, or represent them. The symbol is distinct from its referent—condensation and displacement are its constitution. Symbolization is the transformation of experience into concepts, an abstractive process, and as such can be viewed as an economic device in that a symbol originates from multiple and varied sources which are condensed into one vehicle of meaning. Yet symbolization is also a transforming process which produces structural reorganization, not a transformation or redistribution of energy. It is itself an economical instrumentation of mind for the purpose of "thinking about," for *re*presenting experience, and as emphasized earlier, the uniquely human, symbolizing mind finds extraordinary satisfaction in the act of making a narrative, either in self-contemplation or in understanding things of the world.

"Analytic experience has convinced us of the complete truth of the assertion so often to be heard that the child is psychologically father to the adult, and that the events of his first years are of paramount importance for his whole later life" (Freud, 1940, p. 187).

The genetic perspective refers to a causal belief in the determining effect of early life experience. Psychoanalysis holds, and "with a fair degree of certainty," that "The determining cause of all the forms taken by human mental life is, indeed, to be sought in the reciprocal action between innate disposition and accidental experience" (Freud, 1940, p. 183), and that the result of this interaction produces a most lasting impact during the period of early childhood (approximately to age 6) despite the fact that symptoms may become manifest only later on in life. Freud's model refers to the ego's compromise solutions resulting from the means of satisfying instinctual pressure, and emphasizes the impact of the infantile neurosis and its complete repression (infantile amnesia) which gives rise to the nature and disorders of the ego. In this, the "quantitative disharmonies" are thought to be etiologically determining: "The neuroses and psychoses are the states in which disturbances in the functioning of the apparatus come to expression" (Freud, 1940, p. 183).

With regard to a genetic viewpoint, the validity of which is not in question, a symbolizational model emphasizes rather the etiological significance of disturbances or regressions in the symbolic function itself; a process, not a state. What is stressed is the centrality and impact of the early differentiation–individuation process, upon which normal development of the symbolic function primarily depends, and of the early history of affect tolerance and management. The process of differentiation, or psychological birth, is intimately intertwined with protosymbolic stages and the formation of true symbols; hence the new model emphasizes the potentially disruptive effect of early traumata and intensely aroused or uncontained affects, with respect to primary caretakers, as these will affect the normal evolution of the symbolic function, predisposing to desymbolizing regressions, or ego and boundary dissolution (see Klein, 1930; Rodriguez, 1956; Rycroft, 1956; Segal, 1957; and principally Kubie, 1953; Searles, 1962; see chapter 3).

The symbol arises in the space left by separation—it is reflective, not restitutional. On this simple principle rests an explanatory window toward an entire spectrum of mental disorders. Early "ego" development, in this model, is virtually synonymous with the development of symbolization. A progression along the developmental stages of symbolization, in ever expanding spheres of experience, *is* the maturation of mind.

In order to satisfy the critera for a complete metapsychological presentation, there remains only one further perspective from which to address my model of symbolization, namely, the adaptive, reflecting the relation of a mental process to reality.

As we have seen, the expression par excellence of our symbolizing capacity is reflected in the outgrowth of its function and denotive intent—language. It would be both redundant and beyond the scope of this work to underscore the pivotal adaptive function of language both phylogenetically in the evolution of the species, and ontogenetically in the personal history of each one of us. Suffice it to say that in its denotive function (discursive–symbolic form) it provides arbitrary communicational vehicles which bring people together, not only to impart shared information, but principally by providing an important interpersonal bridge. This "symbolic" bridge, is an indispensable aspect of social interaction, and in addition, anchors the self in a relational matrix. Assuming that evolution has molded our species into social animals, then the communicative capacity and expressive value of "vehicles of meaning," is quite apparent. The relation of the symbolic process to reality is one of linking experiences with the environment to an inner pole of symbolic reference, and vice versa, as a communicational bridge connecting inner experience to outer reality and the people in it.

As the instrumentation of thought and concept-formation, symbolization is also the means by which adaptation to reality is enabled to take place. Symbolization is the vehicle of reflection—it is the tool of knowledge, understanding, communication, notation, integration, the wellspring of all our representational manifestations and the source of our efficient, versatile and sometimes sublime means of expression. The symbolic function has rightly been called the fundamental process of mind, the sine qua non of our uniquely human adaptation, that which distinguishes us from all other animals, and the single attribute which makes "animal symbolicum" (Cassirer, 1944) less contingent on the making of tools per se than on the capacity to conceive of them and their uses, through the mind's medium. For only a mind that can draw concepts from experience can give meaning to this in contemplation; and only a mind that can contemplate is able to articulate and understand things of the world.

In the closing lines of his *New Introductory Lectures in Psychoanalysis* (1933) Freud, somewhat disparagingly, referred to the "scientific" *Weltanschauung* of which he considered his psychoanalysis to be a branch. This scientific *Weltanschauung* which, he wrote, "scarcely deserves such a grandeloquent title (pp. 181–182), still in its infancy, limited, and incomplete, had been unable thus far to cope with or encompass many of the great questions. As a man of astonishing conviction and integrity, he had had to be willing to stand by his revolutionary observations and theories, ideas which, in having scandalized society and stretched the confines of the establishment, were met with considerable resistance and often used to ridicule or discredit him.

To serve his vision, Freud adopted the "intellectual scaffolding" of the prevailing scientific ethos of his day. He utilized its instrumentation as "an approximation" for formulating his propositions and conceptualizations of mind. But, as a man of great vision, he also "looked forward to their being modified, corrected and more precisely determined as further experience is accumulated and sifted" (1940, p. 159). While the predominant tone in our literature today is conservative, divisively dogmatic, and often pious, psychoanalysis was not born out of conservatism, nor was its great founder a tame spirit. Today's reverence has its regressive aspects, inhibiting progressive intent and holding the conceptual base "in a morass of reified concepts" (Home, 1966, p. 49).

It does not fault Freud's impeccable observations to recast these in contemporary garb, particularly with reference to the responsibility of our legacy, namely, to psychoanalysis as a psychology of conscious and *unconscious* processes. On the contrary, I believe it serves to realize his wish that psychoanalysis be redetermined in fresh hypotheses, in the logical terms of an epistemology which can provide a framework for a science of meaning, as a general theory of mind. "A theory of mind and any part of it must explain why someone is doing something and must explain it in terms of reasons," writes Home (1966). "To understand that mind is the meaning of behavior, is to give ourselves a touchstone for testing the meaningfulness of our theories" (p. 48). My thesis has been that "meaning" is a personal construction which is contingent upon and alters according to the level of symbolic organization in which experiences are represented.

We are living in an era of rapid movement and radical change, of global upheaval and reassessment and, in epistemology as some have called it, a paradigm revolution. Out of this shift have emerged new frontiers of thought and new forms of conceptualization, freeing ideas that were obscured by the obfuscatory terms in which they were cast. This paradigm shift enables psychoanalysis to review its much criticized metapsychology, to revise and recast its conceptual base so as to unify its theoretical and clinical aspects.

The goals I spelled out at the outset have been fulfilled in the context of proposing a new psychoanalytic model of mind which operationalizes meaning. This has been an effort in synthesis and integration; it is my hope that emerging from and as part of a new scientific *Weltanschauung,* the revisionary restating of the psychoanalytic theory of mind in these logical terms will enable psychoanalysis to be placed within the framework of universal knowledge.

References

Abend, S. (1988), Intra-psychic vs. inter-personal: The wrong dilemma. *Psychoanal. Inq.*, 8:497–504.

Abraham, K. (1924), A short study of the development of the libido viewed in the light of mental disorders. *Selected Papers on Psychoanalysis*, tr. D. Bryan & Strachey. New York: Basic Books, 1960, pp. 393–406.

Ackoff, R. L. (1975), *Redesigning the Future*. New York: John Wiley.

Adams, R. McC. (1968), Archeological research strategies: Past and present. *Science*, 163:1187–1192.

Alkon, L. D. (1989), Memory storage and neural systems. *Sci. Amer.*, 261:42–50.

Allport, G. (1961), *Patterns and Growth in Personality*. New York: Holt, Rinehart.

Ames, A., Jr. (1946–1947), *Nature and Origins of Perception: Preliminary Laboratory Manual for Use with Demonstration Disclosing Phenomena which Increase Our Understanding of the Nature of Perception*. Hanover, NH: Institutes for Associated Research, Mimeographed.

Ardrey, R. (1970), *The Social Contract*. New York: Atheneum.

Arieti, S. (1975), The cognitive transformation. In: *Interpretation of Schizophrenia*. New York: Basic Books, pp. 225–302.

Arlow, J. (1969a), Fantasy, memory and reality testing. *Psychoanal. Quart.*, 38:28–51.

——— (1969b), Unconscious fantasy and disturbances of conscious experience. *Psychoanal. Quart.*, 38:1–26.

——— (1979), Metaphor and the psychoanalytic situation. *Psychoanal. Quart.*, 48:363–385.

——— (1987), The dynamics of interpretation. *Psychoanal. Quart.*, 56:68–86.

Bachrach, H. M. (1989), On specifying the scientific methodology of psychoanalysis. *Psychoanal. Inq.*, 9:282–304.

Balint, M. (1960), The three areas of the mind: Theoretical considerations. *Internat. J. Psycho-Anal.*, 39:328–340.

———— (1968), *The Basic Fault*. New York: Brunner & Mazel.

Bandura, A. (1977), *Social Learning Theory*. Englewood Cliffs, NJ: Prentice-Hall.

Barratt, B. (1983), Preliminary notes on the epistemology of psychoanalytic transformation. *Psychoanal. & Contemp. Thought*, 6:483–508.

———— (1988), Why is psychoanalysis so controversial? Notes from left field. *Psychoanal. Inqu.*, 5:223–239.

Barten, S. (1980), How does the child know? Origins of the symbol in the theories of Piaget and Werner. *J. Amer. Acad. Psychoanal.*, 8:71–94.

Basch, M. F. (1973), Psychoanalysis and theory formation. *The Annual of Psychoanalysis*, 1:39–52. New York: International Universities Press.

———— (1977), Developmental psychology and explanatory theory in psychoanalysis. *The Annual of Psychoanalysis*, 5:229–261. New York: International Universities Press.

Bateson, G. (1972), *Steps to an Ecology of Mind*. New York: Ballantine.

———— (1979), *Mind and Nature: A Necessary Unity*. New York: Dutton.

Bellak, L. (1974), Contemporary character as crisis adaptation. *Amer. J. Psychotherapy*, 28:46–58.

Bellin, E. H. (1984), The psychoanalytic narrative: On the transformational axis between writing and speech. *Psychoanal. & Contemp. Thought*, 7:3–42.

Bemporad, J. R., ed. (1980), *Child Development in Normality and Psychopathology*. New York: Brunner/Mazel.

Beres, D. (1965), Structure and function in psychoanalysis. *Internat. J. Psycho-Anal.*, 46:53–63.

———— Joseph, D. E. (1970), The concept of mental representation in psycho-analysis. *Internat. J. Psycho-Anal.*, 51:1–9.

Bernard, C. (1957), *An Introduction to the Study of Experimental Medicine*. New York: Dover.

Bettleheim, B. (1977), *The Uses of Enchantment*. New York: Vintage Books.

Blakeslee, S. (1991), Brain yields new clues on its organization for language. *New York Times*, September 10:C1, 10.

Blos, P. (1962), *On Adolescence*. New York: Free Press.

Blum, H. P. (1978), Symbolic process and symbol formation. *Psychoanal. Quart.*, 49:356–359.

—— (1989), Value, use and abuse of infant developmental research. In: *The Significance of Infant Observational Research for Clinical Work with Children, Adolescents, and Adults.* Workshop series of the American Psychoanalytic Society, Mongr. 5, ed. S. Dowling & A. Rothstein. Madison, CT: International Universities Press, pp. 157–174.

Bonnaterre, P. J. (1800), Notice Historique sur le Sauvage de l'Aveyron et sur Quelques Autre Individus qu'on a Trouvé dans les Forêtes à Différentes Époque. Paris: Panckoucke.

Bowlby, J. (1969), *Attachment, Separation and Loss,* Vol. 1. New York: Basic Books.

—— (1973), *Attachment, Separation and Loss,* Vol. 2. New York: Basic Books.

—— (1980), *Attachment, Separation and Loss,* Vol. 3. New York: Basic Books.

Boyle, N. (1991), *Goethe: The Poet and the Age.* Oxford: Clarendon Press/Oxford University Press.

Brazelton, T. B. (1973), *Neonatal Behavioral Assessment Scale.* Philadelphia: Lippincott.

Breger, L. (1967), The function of dreams, Part 2. *J. Abnorm. Psychol.,* Monograph 72:1–28.

Breuer, J., & Freud, S. (1895), Studies on Hysteria. *Standard Edition,* 2. London: Hogarth Press, 1955.

Brown, J. A. C. (1961), *Freud and the Post-Freudians.* Harmondsworth, U.K.: Penguin Books.

Brown, J. W. (1976), Consciousness and pathology of language. In: *The Neuropsychology of Language: Essays in Memory of Eric Lennenberg,* ed. R. Reiber. New York: Plenum, pp. 67–93.

Brown, N. O. (1959), *Life Against Death: The Psychoanalytic Meaning of History.* Middletown, CT: Wesleyan University Press.

Bruner, J. S. (1964), The course of cognitive growth. *Amer. Psychol.,* 19:1–15.

—— (1973), The organization of early skilled action. *Child Develop.,* 44:1–11.

—— (1983), *Child's Talk.* New York: W. W. Norton.

—— Goodman, C. C. (1947), Value and need as organizing factors in perception. *J. Abnorm. Soc. Psychol.*, 42:33–44.

Calvino, I. (1980), *Italian Folk Tales.* New York: Pantheon Books.

Cannon, W. (1927), The James-Lange theory of emotions: A critical examination and an alternative theory. *Amer. J. Psychol.*, 39:106–124.

—— (1932), *The Wisdom of the Body.* New York: W. W. Norton.

Cassirer, E. (1874–1945), *Philosophy of Symbolic Forms,* tr. R. Manheim. New Haven, CT: Yale University Press, 1953–1957.

—— (1944), *An Essay on Man,* tr. R. Manheim. New Haven, CT: Yale University Press, 1957–57.

—— (1953–1957), *The Philosophy of Symbolic Forms,* tr. W. Hendel. New Haven, CT: Yale University Press.

Chomsky, N. (1957), *Syntactic Structure.* The Hague: Mouton.

—— (1965), *Aspects of the Theory of Syntax.* Cambridge, MA: M.I.T. Press.

Clark, E. V. (1983), Meanings and concepts. In: *Cognitive Development,* Vol. 3, ed. J. H. Flavell & E. M. Markman. New York: John Wiley.

Colapinto, J. (1979), The relative value of empirical evidence. *Fam. Proc.,* 18:427–442.

Colby, K. M., & Stoller, R. J. (1988), *Cognitive Science and Psychoanalysis.* Hillsdale, NJ: Analytic Press.

Darwin, C. (1859), *The Origin of Species.* London: John Murray.

—— (1872), *The Expression of the Emotions in Man and Animals.* Chicago: University of Chicago Press, 1970.

Davidson, J. R. (1980), Consciousness and information processing: A biocognitive perspective. In: *The Psychobiology of Consciousness,* ed. J. M. Davidson & J. R. Davidson. New York: Plenum Press.

Dell, P. F. (1982), Beyond homeostasis: Toward a concept of coherence. *Fam. Proc.,* 21:21–42.

Deri, S. (1978), Transitional phenomena: Vicissitudes of symbolization and creativity. In: *Between Reality and Fantasy (Transitional Objects and Phenomena),* ed. S. M.Grolaide & L. Barkin. New York: Jason Aronson.

—— (1981), Acting out and symbolization. In: *Object and Self: A Developmental Approach,* ed. S. Tuttman, C. Kaye, & M. Zimerman. New York: International Universities Press.

—— (1984), *Symbolization and Creativity*. New York: International Universities Press.

de Saussure, F. (1955), *Course in General Linguistics*. New York: Philosophical Library.

Deutsch, F. (1959), *On the Mysterious Leap from the Mind to the Body*. New York: International Universities Press.

Dewey, J. (1920), *Reconstruction in Philosophy*. Boston: Beacon Press.

Dilthy, W. (1924), *Gesammelte Schriften*, Vol. 6. Stuttgart: Teubner.

Dollard, J., & Miller, N. J. (1950), *Personality and Psychotherapy*. New York: McGraw-Hill.

Donadeo, J. (1974), Symbolism. In: *Trauma and Symbolism*, Series of the Kris Study Group, New York Psychoanalytic Institute, Monograph V. New York: International Universities Press, pp. 77–102.

Eagle, N. M. (1984), *Recent Developments in Psychoanalysis: A Critical Evaluation*. New York: McGraw-Hill.

Edel, A. (1985), Book review: *The Foundations of Psychoanalysis: A Philosophical Critique*, by Adolph Grünbaum. *Psychoanal. Psychol.*, 2:79–83.

Edel, L. (1984), *Writing Lives*. New York: W. W. Norton.

Edelson, J. (1983), Freud's use of metaphor. *The Psychoanalytic Study of the Child*, 38:17–59. New Haven, CT: Yale University Press.

Edelson, M. (1972), Language and dreams: The interpretation of dreams revisited. *The Psychoanalytic Study of the Child*, 27:203–282. Chicago: Quadrangle.

—— (1983), Is testing psychoanalytic hypotheses in the psychoanalytic situation really possible? *The Psychoanalytic Study of the Child*, 38:61–112. New Haven, CT: Yale University Press.

—— (1984), *Hypothesis and Evidence in Psychoanalysis*. Chicago/London: University of Chicago Press.

Eliade, M. (1951), *Shamanism: Archaic Techniques of Ecstacy*. New York: Bollingen Foundation, 1964.

Emde, R. (1983), The prerepresentational self and its affective core. *The Psychoanalytic Study of the Child*, 38:165–192. New Haven, CT: Yale University Press.

———— Kligman, D., Reich, J. H., & Wade, T. D. (1978), Emotional expression in infancy: I. Initial studies of social signaling and an emergent model. In *The Development of Affect,* ed. M. Lewis & L. Rosenblum. New York: Plenum, pp. 125–148.

———— Buchsbaum, H. K. (1980), Toward a psychoanalytic theory of affect II: Emotional development and signaling in infancy. In: *The Course of Life,* ed. S. Greenspan & G. H. Pollock. Madison, CT: International Universities Press, 1989.

Erikson, E. (1946), Ego development and historical change—Clinical notes. *The Psychoanalytic Study of the Child,* 2:359–396. New York: International Universities Press.

———— (1950), *Childhood and Society,* rev. ed. New York: W. W. Norton, 1963.

———— (1951), On the sense of inner identity. In: *Psychoanalytic Psychiatry and Psychology: Clinical and Theoretical Papers,* Vol. 1. Austen Riggs Center, ed. R. P. Knight & C. R. Friedman. New York: International Universities Press, 1954, pp. 351–364.

———— (1980), *Identity and the Life Cycle.* New York: W. W. Norton.

Escalona, S. (1953), Problems of infancy and childhood. In: *Transactions of the Sixth Conference, March 17 and 18, 1952, New York,* ed. J. E. M., Senn. New York: J. Macy Jr. Foundation.

———— (1962), The study of individual differences and the problem of state. *J. Amer. Acad. Child Psychiatry,* 1:11–37.

———— (1968), *The Roots of Individuality: Normal Patterns of Development in Infancy.* Chicago: Aldine.

Fairbairn, W. (1954), *An Object-Relations Theory of the Personality.* New York: Basic Books.

Fenichel, O. (1945), Character disorders. In: *The Psychoanalytic Theory of Neurosis.* New York: W. W. Norton, pp. 463–540.

Ferguson, M. (1988), The clinical situation and epistemological problems in psychoanalysis: A response to Grünbaum. *Psychoanal. & Contemp. Thought,* 11:535–561.

Fraiberg, S. (1969), Libidinal object constancy and mental representations. *The Psychoanalytic Study of the Child,* 24:9–47. New York: International Universities Press.

Franklin, G. (1990), An open-ended approach to psychoanalytic theories. *Contemp. Psychoanal.,* 26:518–539.

Freedman, N. (1985), The concept of transformation in psychoanalysis. *Psychoanal. Psychol.,* 4:317–339.

Freud, A. (1937), *The Ego and the Mechanisms of Defense.* New York: International Universities Press, 1946.

Freud, S. (1887–1902), *The Origins of Psychoanalysis—Letters to Wilhelm Fleiss, Drafts and Notes: 1887–1902.* New York: Basic Books, 1954.

——— (1887–1904), *The Complete Letters of Sigmund Freud to Wilhelm Fleiss,* tr. & ed. J. M. Masson. Cambridge, MA: Harvard University Press.

——— (1894), The neuro-psychosis of defense. *Standard Edition,* 3:327–355. London: Hogarth Press, 1962.

——— (1895), Project for a scientific psychology. *Standard Edition,* 1:283–387. London: Hogarth Press, 1966.

——— (1900), The Interpretation of Dreams. *Standard Edition,* 4 & 5. London: Hogarth Press, 1953.

——— (1901), The Psychopathology of Everyday Life. *Standard Edition,* 6. London: Hogarth Press, 1960.

——— (1905a), Jokes and Their Relation to the Unconscious, *Standard Edition,* 8. London: Hogarth Press, 1960.

——— (1905b), Three essays on the theory of sexuality. *Standard Edition,* 7:125–243. London: Hogarth Press, 1953.

——— (1908), Creative writers and daydreaming. *Standard Edition,* 9:141–153. London: Hogarth Press, 1959.

——— (1911), Formulations regarding the two principles of mental functioning. *Standard Edition,* 12:215–226. London: Hogarth Press, 1958.

——— (1913), A note on the unconscious. *Standard Edition,* 12:257–266. London: Hogarth Press, 1958.

——— (1915a), Instincts and their vicissitudes. *Standard Edition,* 14:111–140. London: Hogarth Press, 1957.

——— (1915b), The unconscious. *Standard Edition,* 14:161–215. London: Hogarth Press, 1957.

———— (1916), Metapsychological supplement to the theory of dreams. *Standard Edition,* 14:219–235. London: Hogarth Press, 1957.

———— (1917a), Introductory Lectures on Psychoanalysis. *Standard Edition,* 15 & 16. London: Hogarth Press, 1963.

———— (1917b), Mourning and melancholia. *Standard Edition,* 14:239–258. London: Hogarth Press, 1957.

———— (1920), Beyond the pleasure principle. *Standard Edition,* 18:3–64. London: Hogarth Press, 1955.

———— (1921), Group psychology and analysis of the ego. *Standard Edition,* 18:67–143. London: Hogarth Press, 1955.

———— (1923), The ego and the id. *Standard Edition,* 19:3–66. London: Hogarth Press, 1961.

———— (1924), The loss of reality in neurosis and psychosis. *Standard Edition,* 19:183–187. London: Hogarth Press, 1961.

———— (1926), The problem of anxiety. *Standard Edition,* 20:77–174. London: Hogarth Press, 1950.

———— (1927), The question of lay analysis. *Standard Edition,* 20:177–258. London: Hogarth Press, 1950.

———— (1933), New Introductory Lectures on Psycho-analysis. *Standard Edition,* 22:3–182. London: Hogarth Press, 1964.

———— (1937), Analysis, terminable and interminable. *Standard Edition,* 23:211–253. London: Hogarth Press, 1964.

———— (1940), An outline of psycho-Analysis. *Standard Edition,* 23:141–307. London: Hogarth Press, 1964.

Friedman, L. (1980), The barren prospect of a representational world. *Psychoanal. Quart.,* 49:215–233.

Fromm, E. (1947), *Man for Himself.* New York: Holt, Rinehart & Winston.

———— (1964), *The Heart of Man.* New York: Harper & Row, 1980.

———— (1980), *Greatness and Limitations in Freud's Thought.* New York: Harper & Row.

Furth, H. G. (1970), On language and knowing in Piaget's developmental theory. *Hum. Develop.,* 13:247–257.

Gardner, H. (1982), *Art, Mind and Brain.* New York: Basic Books.

Gay, P. (1988), *Freud: A Life for Our Time*. New York: W. W. Norton.

Gedo, J. E. (1979), *Beyond Interpretation, Towards a Revised Theory of Psychoanalysis*. New York: International Universities Press.

———— (1986), *Conceptual Issues in Psychoanalysis*. Hillsdale, NJ: Analytic Press.

———— (1988), *The Mind in Disorder*. Hillsdale, NJ: Analytic Press.

———— (1991), Between prolixity and reductionism: Psychoanalytic theory and Occam's razor. *J. Amer. Psychoanal. Assn.*, 39:71–86.

———— Goldberg, A. (1973), *Models of the Mind*. Chicago: University of Chicago Press.

Geertz, C. (1973), Thick descriptions: Toward an interpretive theory of culture. In: *The Interpretation of Cultures: Selected Essays*, ed. C. Geertz. New York: Basic Books.

Geschwind, W. (1972), Language and the brain. *Sci. Amer.*, 266:76–83.

Gill, M. (1967a), The primary process. In: *Motives and Thought*. New York: International Universities Press.

———— (1967b), Motives and Thought: Psychoanalytic Essays in Honor of David Rapaport, ed. R. R. Holt. *Psychological Issues,* Monogr. 18/19. New York: International Universities Press, pp. 260–298.

Gombrich, E. H. (1961), *Art and Illusion*. Princeton, NJ: Princeton University Press.

Goodman, N. (1984), *Of Mind and Other Matters*. Cambridge, MA: Harvard University Press.

Grand, S., Freedman, N., Feiner, K., & Kiesky, S. (1988), Notes on the progressive and regressive shifts in levels of integrative failure. *Psychoanal. & Contemp. Thought*, 2:705–739.

Greenberg, J. R. (1991), *Oedipus and Beyond: A Clinical Theory*. Cambridge, MA: Harvard University Press.

———— Mitchell, S. A. (1983), *Object Relations in Psychoanalytic Theory*. Cambridge, MA: Harvard University Press.

Greenspan, S. (1979), *Intelligence and Adaptation: An Integration of Psychoanalytic and Piagetian Developmental Psychology*. New York: International Universities Press.

——— (1982), Three levels of learning: A developmental approach to awareness in mind body relations. *Psychoanal. Inqu.*, 1:659–694.

——— (1989), *The Development of the Ego*. Madison, CT: International Universities Press.

Greimas, A. G. (1976), The cognitive dimension of narrative discourse. *New Literary History*, 7(3).

Groddeck, G. (1923), Das Buch Vom ES, Int. Psychoanalyst, *Verlag*, Wien, 1926.

Grotjahn, M. (1922), Der Symbolisierungszwang ("The urge to symbolize"). *Imago*, 8:67.

——— (1945), George Groddeck and his teachings about man's innate need for symbolization. (A contribution to the history of early psychoanalytic psychosomatic medicine). *Psychoanal. Rev.* 32:9–24.

Grünbaum, A. (1977), How scientific is psychoanalysis? In: *Science and Psychotherapy*, ed. R. Stern, L. S. Horowitz, & J. Lynes. New York: Haven Publishing.

——— (1980), Epistemological liabilities of the clinical appraisal of psychoanalytic theory. *Nous*, 14:307–385.

——— (1981), *Can Psychoanalysis be Cogently Tested on the Couch?* Pittsburgh Series on the Philosophy of the History of Science. Berkeley: University of California Press.

——— (1984), *The Foundations of Psychoanalysis. A Philosophical Critique*. Berkeley: University of California Press.

Guba, E. G. (1981), Criteria for assessing the trustworthiness of naturalistic inquiries. *Ed. Commun. & Technol. J.*, 29:75–92.

——— (1985), The context of emergent paradigm research. In: *Organizational Theory and Inquiry*, ed. Y. Lincoln. Beverly Hills, CA: Sage.

Guntrip, H. (1969), *Schizoid Phenomena, Object Relations and Self*. New York: International Universities Press.

——— (1971), *Psychoanalytic Theory, Therapy and the Self*. New York: Basic Books.

Habermas, J. (1971), *Knowledge and Human Interests*, tr. J. J. Shapiro. Boston: Beacon Press.

Harlow, H. F. (1959), Love in infant monkeys. *Sci. Amer.*, 200:68–74.

——— Harlow, N. K. (1961), A study of animal affection. *Nat. Hist.*, 70:48–55.

Hartmann, H. (1939), *Ego Psychology and the Problem of Adaptation.* New York: International Universities Press, 1958.

——— (1950), Comments on the psychoanalytic theory of the ego. *The Psychoanalytic Study of the Child,* 5:74–96. New York: International Universities Press.

——— (1951), Technical implications of ego psychology. *Psychoanal. Quart.,* 20:31–43.

——— (1955), Notes on the theory of sublimation. *The Psychoanalytic Study of the Child,* 10:9–29. New York: International Universities Press.

——— (1960), *Psychoanalysis and Human Values.* New York: International Universities Press.

——— (1964), *Essays on Ego Psychology.* New York: International Universities Press.

——— Kris, E., & Lowenstein, R. M. (1946a), Comments on the formation of psychic structure. *The Psychoanalytic Study of the Child,* 2:11–38. New York: International Universities Press.

——— ——— ——— (1946b), Papers on Psychoanalytic Psychology. *Psychological Issues,* Monogr. 14. New York: International Universities Press.

Hassan, H. I. (1982), *The Dismemberment of Orpheus: Toward a Post-Modern Literature,* 2nd ed. Madison, WI: University of Wisconsin Press.

Hawking, S. W. (1988), *A Brief History of Time.* New York: Bantam Books.

Hebb, D. O. (1949), *The Organization of Behavior: A Neuropsychological Theory.* New York: John Wiley.

——— (1955), Drives and the central nervous system. *Psycholog. Rev.,* 62:243–254.

——— (1957), Perception and perceptual learning. Address to the Eastern Psychological Association, New York, April.

——— (1958), *A Textbook of Psychology.* Philadelphia: Saunders.

Hegel, G. W. F. (1807), Introduction. *Lectures on the History of Philosophy,* tr. T. M. Knox & A. V. Miller. Oxford: Oxford University Press, 1987.

Helmholtz, H. von (1910), *Treatise on Physiological Optics,* Vol. 3, 3rd ed. Rochester, NY: Optical Society of America, 1924–1925.

Heron, J. (1981), Philosophical bases for a new paradigm. In: *Human Inquiry: A Source Book of New Paradigm Research,* ed. P. Reason & J. Rowan. New York: John Wiley.

Hess, E. H. (1958), "Imprinting" in animals. *Sci. Amer.,* 198:81–90.

———— (1962) Ethology: An approach toward the complete analysis of behavior. In: *New Directions in Psychology,* ed. T. N. Newcombe. New York: Holt, Rinehart & Winston.

———— (1972), "Imprinting" in a natural laboratory. *Sci. Amer.,* 227(2):24–31.

Hesse, N. (1980), *Revolutions and Reconstructions in the Philosophy of Science.* Bloomington: Indiana University Press.

Hilgard, E. (1951), The role of learning in perception. In: *Perception: An Approach to Personality,* ed. R. R. Blake & G. V. Ramsey. New York: Ronald, pp. 95–120.

———— (1962), Impulse versus realistic thinking. An examination of thought. *Psycholog. Bull.,* 59:477–488.

Hobson, J. A. (1988), *The Dreaming Brain.* New York: Basic Books.

Hoffer, A. (1985), Toward a definition of psychoanalytic neutrality. *J. Amer. Psychoanal. Assn.* 33:771–795.

Holt, R. (1965), A review of some of Freud's biological assumptions and their influence on his theories. In: *Psychoanalysis and Current Biological Thought,* ed. N. S. Greenfield & W. C. Lewis. Madison: University of Wisconsin Press, pp. 93–124.

———— (1967), Beyond vitalism and mechanism: Freud's concept of psychic energy. *Sci. & Psychoanal.,* 11:1–41.

———— (1976), Drive or wish? A reconsideration of the psychoanalytic theory of motivation. In: Psychology vs. Metapsychology. *Psychological Issues,* Monogr. 36. New York: International Universities Press, pp. 158–196.

———— (1985), The current state of psychoanalytic theory. *Psychoanal. Psychol.,* 2:289–365.

———— & Gill, M., eds. (1969), Motives and Thought: Psychoanalytic Essays in Honor of David Rapaport. *Psychological*

Issues, Monogr. 18/19. New York: International Universities Press, pp. 260–298.

Holton, G. (1973), *Thematic Origins of Scientific Thought. Keppler to Einstein.* Cambridge, MA: Harvard University Press.

Home, H. J. (1966), The concept of mind. *Internat. J. Psycho-Anal.,* 47:29–42

Horowitz, M. J. (1972), Unbidden images: Control and loss of control over image formation. In: *The Nature and Function of Imagery,* ed. P. Sheehan. New York: Academic Press.

Humboldt, W. von (1884), *Die Sprachphilosophischen Werke Wilhelm von Humboldt's,* ed. Steinhal. Berlin.

Hutten, E. (1981), Meaning and information in group process. In: *The Evolution of Group Analysis,* ed. M. Pines. London: Routledge, Kegan Paul.

Jackson, J. H. (1831), *Selected Writings of John Hughlings Jackson,* ed. J. Taylor. London: Hodder & Stoughton.

Jacobson, E. C. (1964), *The Self and the Object World.* New York: International Universities Press.

James, W. (1842–1910), *The Principles of Psychology,* Cambridge, MA: Harvard University Press.

——— (1884), *Psychology: Brief Course.* New York: Crowell-Collier, 1962.

Jaynes, J. (1976), *The Origin of Consciousness in the Breakdown of the Bicameral Mind.* Boston: Houghton-Mifflin.

Johnson, G. (1991), What Really Goes on in There? *New York Times Book Review* (November 10):1.

Jones, E. (1916), The theory of symbolism. In: *Papers on Psychoanalysis,* 5th ed. Baltimore: William & Wilkins, 1948.

Jung, C. G. (1958), *Psyche and Symbol,* ed. V. de Laszlo. Garden City, NY: Doubleday/Anchor Books.

——— (1959), *The Basic Writings of C. G. Jung.* New York: Modern Library/Random House.

——— (1964), *Man and His Symbols.* London: Alders Books/W. H. Allen.

Kagan, J. (1967), On the need for relativism. *Amer. Psychologist,* 22:131–142.

——— (1984), *The Nature of the Child.* New York: Basic Books.

Keeny, B. P. (1982), What is an epistemology of family therapy? *Fam. Proc.*, 21:153–167.

Keeney, V. P., & Sprenkle, D. H. (1982), Ecosystemic epistemology: Critical implications for the aesthetics and pragmatics of family therapy. *Fam. Proc.*, 21:1–19.

Kermode, F. (1966), *The Sense of an Ending: Studies in the Theory of Fiction.* New York: Oxford University Press.

Kernberg, O. (1982), Self, ego, affects and drives. *J. Amer. Psychoanal. Assn.*, 30:893–915.

——— (1984), *Object-Relations Theory and Clinical Psychoanalysis.* Northvale, NJ: Jason Aronson.

——— (1993), The current status of psychoanalysis. *J. Amer. Psychoanal. Assn.*, 41:45–62.

Kestenberg, J. S. (1975), *Children and Parents: Psychoanalytic Studies in Development.* New York: Jason Aronson.

Klein, G. (1970), *Perception, Motives and Personality.* New York: Alfred Knopf.

——— (1973), Two theories or one? Perspectives to changes in psychoanalytic theory. *Bull. Menninger Clinic,* 37:102–152.

——— (1976), *Psychoanalytic Theory: An Exploration of Essentials.* New York: International Universities Press.

Klein, M. (1930), The importance of symbol-formation in the development of the ego. *Internat. J. Psycho-Anal.*, 2:24–39.

——— (1945), *Contributions to Psychoanalysis 1921–1945.* London: Hogarth Press, 1948.

——— (1955), *New Directions in Psychoanalysis.* New York: Basic Books.

Knapp, P. H. (1969), Images, symbol and person, the strategy of psychological defense. *Arch. Gen. Psychiatry*, 21:392–406.

Kohut, H. (1971), *The Analysis of the Self.* New York: International Universities Press.

——— (1977), *The Restoration of the Self.* New York: International Universities Press.

——— (1984), *How Does Analysis Cure?* Chicago: University of Chicago Press.

Konner, M. (1982), *The Tangled Wing: Biological Constraints on the Human Spirit.* New York: Holt, Rinehart & Winston.

Kris, E. (1951), Ego psychology and interpretation in psychoanalytic theory. *Psychoanal. Quart.*, 20:15–30.

Krishner, L. A. (1991), The concept of the self in psychoanalytic theory, and its philosophical foundations. *J. Amer. Psychoanal. Assn.*, 39:157–182.

Kubie, L. (1953), The distortion of the symbolic process in neurosis and psychosis. In: Symbols and Neurosis, ed. H. J. Schlesinger. *Psychological Issues,* Monogr. 44. New York: International Universities Press.

Kuhn, S. T. (1962), *The Structure of Scientific Revolutions.* Chicago: University of Chicago Press.

Lacan, J. (1973), *The Four Fundamental Concepts of Psycho-Analysis,* ed. J. Miller, tr. A. Sheridan. New York: W. W. Norton, 1978.

Lane, H. (1976), *The Wild Boy of Aveyron.* Cambridge, MA: Harvard University Press.

Langer, S. K. (1942), *Philosophy in a New Key.* Cambridge, MA: Harvard University Press.

——— (1953), *Feeling and Form.* New York: Scribner.

——— (1957), *Problems of Art.* New York: Scribner.

——— (1962), *Philosophical Sketches.* Baltimore, MD: Johns Hopkins University Press.

——— (1967), *Mind: An Essay in Human Feeling,* Vol. 1. Baltimore, MD: Johns Hopkins University Press.

——— (1972), *Mind: An Essay in Human Feeling,* Vol. 2. Baltimore, MD: Johns Hopkins University Press.

Lashley, K. S. (1960), *The Neuropsychology of Lashley: Selected Papers,* ed. F. A. Beach et al. New York: McGraw-Hill.

Leichtman, M. (1990), Developmental psychology and psychoanalysis: The context for a revolution in psychoanalysis. *J. Amer. Psychoanal. Assn.*, 38:915–950.

Lenneberg, E. H. (1967), *Biological Foundations of Language.* New York: John Wiley.

——— (1973), The neurology of language. *Daedalus,* Summer:115–133.

Leppmann, W. (1987), *Rilke,* tr. M. Stockman & R. Exner. New York: Fromm International.

Leshner, A. I. (1978), *An Introduction to Behavioral Endocrinology. New York:* Oxford University Press.

Lévi-Strauss, C. (1958a), *Structural Anthropology*, tr. C. Jacobson & B. G. Schoepf. New York: Basic Books.

———— (1958b), The effectiveness of symbols. In: *Structural Anthropology*, tr. C. Jacoboson & B. G. Schoepf. New York: Basic Books.

———— (1983), *The View from Afar*, tr. J. Neugroschel & P. Hoss. Chicago: University of Chicago Press, 1992.

Levinson, E. (1983), *The Ambiguity of Change*. New York: Basic Books.

Lichtenberg, J. D. (1989), *Psychoanalysis and Motivation*. Hillsdale, NJ: Analytic Press.

Lincoln, Y., ed. (1985), *Organizational Theory and Inquiry: The Paradigm Revolution*. Beverly Hills, CA: Sage.

———— ed. (1985), The concept of the paradigm shift. In: *Organizational Theory and Inquiry. The Paradigm Revolution*, ed. I. S. Lincoln. Beverly Hills, CA: Sage.

———— Guba, E. (1985), *Naturalistic Inquiry*. Beverly Hills, CA: Sage.

Linnell, M. Z. (1990), What is mental representation? A study of its elements and how they lead to language. *J. Amer. Psychoanal. Assn.*, 38:131–165.

Lipps, T. (1897), Der Begriff des Unbewussten in der Psychologie. *Records of the Third International Congress of Psychoanalysis*. Munich.

Loch, W. (1977), Some comments on the subject of psychoanalysis and truth. In: *Thought Consciousness and Reality*, ed. J. H. Smith. New Haven, CT: Yale University Press, pp. 217–256.

Locke, J. (1690), *Essay Concerning the Human Understanding*, ed. A. O. Fraser. Oxford, U.K.: Clarendon Press, 1960.

Loewald, H. (1956), On the therapeutic action of psychoanalysis. *Internat. J. Psycho-Anal.*, 41:16–32.

———— (1971), On motivation and instinct theory. *The Psychoanalytic Study of the Child*, 26:91–128. Chicago: Quadrangle.

———— (1978), Instinct theory, object relations and psychic structure formation. In: *Papers on Psycho-Analysis*. New Haven, CT: Yale University Press, 1980.

———— (1988), *Sublimation*. New Haven, CT: Yale University Press.

Lomas, P. (1968), Psychoanalysis Freudian or existential. In: *Psychoanalysis Observed*, ed. C. Rycroft, G. Gorer, A. Storr, J. Wren-Lewis, & P. Lomas. Baltimore, MD: Penguin Books.

Lorenz, K. (1950), The comparative method in studying innate behavior patterns. In: *Psychological Mechanisms in Animal Behavior*, ed. J. F. Danielli & R. Brown. San Diego, CA: Academic Press, pp. 221–268.

——— (1952), *King Solomon's Ring*. New York: Crowell.

——— (1958), The evolution of behavior. *Sci. Amer.*, 199:67–78.

——— (1963), *On Aggression*. New York: Harcourt, Brace & World.

——— (1970), *Studies in Animal and Human Behavior*, Vol. 1. Cambridge, MA: Harvard University Press.

——— (1977), *Behind the Mirror: A Search for a Natural History of Human Knowledge*. London: Methuen.

Lundkvist, A. (1992), *Journeys in Dream and Imagination*, tr. A. B. Weissmann & A. Plack. New York: Four Walls Eight Windows.

Luria, A. (1966a), *Higher Cortical Functions in Man*. New York: Basic Books.

——— (1966b), The functional organization of the brain. *Sci. Amer.*, 207:66–78.

MacLean, P. D. (1949), Psychosomatic disease and the "visceral brain": Recent developments bearing on the Papez theory of emotion. *Psychosom. Med.*, 11:338–353.

——— (1973), *The Triune Concept of Brain and Behavior*. Toronto: University of Toronto.

Maguire, J. G. (1982), The concept of transference: Empathy knowledge and the approximate valence of transference content. *Psychoanal. & Contemp. Thought*, 5:575–604.

Mahler, M. (1979), *Selected Papers of Margaret S. Mahler*. New York: Jason Aronson.

——— Pine, F., & Bergman, A. (1975), *The Psychological Birth of the Human Infant*. New York: Basic Books.

Mandlebaum, M. (1971), *History, Man and Reason*. Baltimore, MD: Johns Hopkins University Press.

Marshack, A. (1972), *The Roots of Civilization*. New York: McGraw-Hill.

——— (1989), Evolution of human capacity: The symbolic evidence. *Yearbook of Physical Anthropology,* 32:1–34.

Maturana, H., & Varela, S. A. (1980), *Autopoiesis and Cognition: The Realization of the Living.* Dordrecht, Holland: D. Riedl.

McCulloch, W. (1965), *Embodiments of Mind.* Cambridge, MA: M.I.T. Press.

McDevitt, J. B. (1975), Separation-individuation and object constancy. *J. Amer. Psychoanal. Assn.,* 23:713–742.

McDougall, W. (1923), *Outline of Psychology.* New York: Scribner.

Mead, G. H. (1909), Social psychology as counterpart of physiological psychology. *Psycholog. Bull.,* 6:401–408.

Michels, R. (1988), One psychoanalysis or many? *Contemp. Psychoanal.,* 24:359–372.

Miller, N. E., & Dollard, J. (1941), *Social Learning and Imitation.* New Haven, CT: Yale University Press.

Milner, N. (1952), Aspects of symbolism in comprehension of the NOT-self. *Internat. J. Psycho-Anal.,* 33:181.

Mitchell, S. (1981), Twilight of the Idols. *Contemporary Psychoanalysis,* 17:374–398.

Mitchell, S. A. (1988), *Relational Concepts in Psychoanalysis. An Integration.* Cambridge, MA: Harvard University Press.

Mitchell, W. J. T., ed. (1980), *On Narrative.* Chicago: University of Chicago Press.

Modell, A. C. (1968), *Object Love and Reality. An Introduction to a Psychoanalytic Theory of Object Relations.* New York: International Universities Press.

——— (1981), Does metapsychology still exist? *Internat. J. Psycho-Anal.,* 62:391–401.

——— (1984), *Psychoanalysis in a New Context.* New York: International Universities Press.

Morgan, G. (1983), Part 1, Research as engagement: A personal view, pp. 11–18. Part 3, Exploring choice: Reframing the process of evaluation, pp. 392–404. In: *Beyond Method: Strategies of Social Research.* Beverly Hills, CA: Sage.

——— ed. (1983), *Strategies of Social Research.* Beverly Hills, CA: Sage.

Morris, C. W. (1938), *Foundations of the Theory of Signs.* Chicago: University of Chicago Press.

Nauta, W., & Domesick, V. B. (1980), Neural associations of the limbic system. In: *Neural Substrates of Behavior*, ed. A. Beckman. New York: Spectrum.

Nietzsche, F. W. (1872), *The Birth of Tragedy from the Spirit of Music*. Garden City, NY: Doubleday.

———— (1874), *The Use and Abuse of History*, rev. ed. Indianapolis: Bobbs-Merrill.

Neugarten, B. (1979), Time, age, and the life cycle. *Amer. J. Psychiatry*, 136:887–893.

Novey, S. (1958), The meaning of the concept of mental representations of objects. *Psychoanal. Quart.*, 27:57–79.

Noy, P. (1969), A revision of the psychoanalytic theory of the primary process. *Internat. J. Psycho-Anal.*, 50:155–178.

———— (1979), The psychoanalytic theory of cognitive development. *The Psychoanalytic Study of the Child*, 34:169–216. New Haven, CT: Yale University Press.

Nunberg, H. (1931), The synthetic function of the ego. In: *The Practice and Theory of Psychoanalysis*, 10:120–136. New York: International Universities Press, 1955.

Opatow, B. (1988), The self as desire. *Psychoanal. & Contemp. Thought*, 11:615–637.

Panel (1970), Language and psychoanalysis. Chairman: V. Rosen. *Internat. J. Psycho-Anal.*, 51:137–242.

———— (1978), Symbolic processes and symbol formation. Reporter: H. Blum. *Internat. J. Psycho-Anal.*, 59:455–471.

Papez, J. W. (1937), A proposed mechanism of emotion. *Arch. Neurol. Psychiatry*, 38:725–748.

Pavlov, I. P. (1927), *Conditioned Reflexes*, tr. G. V. Anrep. London: Oxford University Press.

Peterfreund, E. (1980), On information and systems models for psychoanalysis. *Internat. Rev. Psychoanal.*, 54:327–345.

Piaget, J. (1937), *The Construction of Reality in the Child*. London: Routledge & Kegan Paul.

———— (1950), *The Psychology of Intelligence*. New York: Harcourt, Brace, 1950.

———— (1952), *The Origins of Intelligence*. New York: International Universities Press.

———— (1962), *Play, Dreams and Imitation in Childhood*. New York: W. W. Norton.

——— (1970), *Genetic Epistemology*. New York: Columbia University Press.

——— Inhelder, B. (1969), *The Psychology of the Child*. New York: Basic Books.

Pine, F. (1985), *Developmental Theory and Clinical Process*. New Haven, CT: Yale University Press.

——— (1988), The four psychologies of psychoanalysis and their place in clinical work. *J. Amer. Psychoanal. Assn.*, 36:571–595.

——— (1990), *Drive, Ego, Object and Self. A Synthesis for Clinical Work*. New York: Basic Books.

Pines, M. (1981), The frame of reference of group psychotherapy. *Internat. J. Group Psychother.*, 31:275–284.

Pinker, S. (1994), *The Language Instinct*. New York: William Morrow.

Plutchik, R. (1980), *Emotions: A Psychoevolutionary Synthesis*. New York: Harper & Row.

——— (1984), Emotions: A general psychoevolutionary theory. In: *Approaches to Emotion*, eds. K. R. Scherer & P. Ekman. Hillsdale, NJ: Lawrence Erlbaum.

Polanyi, M. (1958), *Personal Knowledge*. London: Routledge & Kegan Paul.

——— (1966), *The Tacit Dimension*. Garden City, NY: Doubleday.

Pollock, G. (1977), Mourning processes and organizations. *J. Amer. Psychoanal. Assn.*, 25:3–34.

——— (1978), Process and affect-mourning and grief. *Internat. J. Psycho-Anal.*, 59:255–275.

Popper, K. (1968), *The Logic of Scientific Discovery*. London: Hutchinson.

Postman, L., & Bruner, J. (1952), Hypothesis and the principle of closure: The effect of frequency and regency. *J. Psychology*, 33:113–125.

Pribram, K. (1965), Freud's Project: An open biologically based model for psychoanalysis. In: *Psychoanalysis and Current Biological Thought*, ed. N. S. Greenfield & W. C. Lewis. Madison: University of Wisconsin Press, pp. 81–92.

——— (1969a), The neurophysiology of remembering. *Sci. Amer.*, 220:387–398.

——— (1969b), The neurophysiology of memory. *Sci. Amer.,* 220:387–398.

——— (1977), Hemispheric specialization. Evolution or revolution. *Ann. NY Acad. Sci.,* 299:18–22.

——— Nuwer, M., & Baron, R. (1974), The holographic hypothesis of memory structure in brain function and structure. In: *Contemporary Developments in Mathematical Psychology,* Vol. 2, ed. R. Atkinson, O. Krantz, R. Loce, & P. Suppes. San Francisco: Freeman.

Propp, V. (1968), *Morphology of the Folk Tale.* Austin, TX: University of Texas Press, 1968.

Protter, B. (1988), Ways of knowing in psychoanalysis. *Contemp. Psychoanal.,* 24:498–522.

Rapaport, D. (1944), The scientific methodology of psychoanalysis. In: *The Collected Papers of David Rapaport,* ed. M. M. Gill. New York: Basic Books, 1967, pp. 165–220.

——— ed. (1951), *Organization and Pathology of Thought.* New York: Columbia University Press.

——— (1957a), Cognitive structures. In: *Collected Papers.* New York: Basic Books, 1967, pp. 631–664.

——— (1957b), The theory of ego autonomy. A generalization. In: *Collected Papers.* New York: Basic Books, 1967, pp. 722–744.

——— (1959), The Structure of Psychoanalytic Theory: A Systematizing Attempt. *Psychological Issues,* Monogr. 6. New York: International Universities Press, 1960.

Reich, W. (1933), *Charakteranalyse. Selbtverlag des Verfassers.* Berlin.

Reiff, P. (1966), *The Triumph of the Therapeutic.* Chicago: University of Chicago Press.

Reinharz, S. (1979), *On Becoming a Social Scientist.* San Francisco: Jossey-Bass.

——— (1981), Implementing new paradigm research: A model for training and practice. In: *Human Inquiry,* ed P. Reason & J. Rowan. New York: John Wiley, pp. 415–435.

Reiser, M. F. (1984), *Mind, Brain, Body. Toward a Convergence of Psychoanalysis and Neurobiology.* New York: Basic Books.

Richards, A. (1990), The future of psychoanalysis: The past, present and future of psychoanalytic theory. *Psychoanal. Quart.,* 59:347–369.

Ricoeur, P. (1970), *Freud and Philosophy. An Essay on Interpretation.* New Haven, CT: Yale University Press.

————— (1977), The question of proof in psychoanalysis. *J. Amer. Psychoanal. Assn.,* 25:835–872.

————— (1980), Narrative time. In: *On Narrative,* ed. J. W. T. Mitchell. Chicago, London: University of Chicago Press.

————— (1984), *Time and Narrative.* Chicago: University of Chicago Press.

Ridley, B. K. (1976), *Time, Space and Things.* Harmondsworth, Middlesex, U.K.: Penguin.

Rilke, R. R. (1908), Requiem for Wolf Graf von Kalckreuth. In: *Rilke,* ed. W. Leppmann, tr. M. Stockman & R. Exner. New York: Fromm International, 1987.

————— (1922), The Sonnets to Orpheus II, 29. In: *Rilke,* ed. W. Leppman, tr. R. Exner. New York: Fromm International, 1987.

Ritchie, A. D. (1936), *The Natural History of the Mind.* London: Longman's Greene.

Rodriguez, E. (1956), Notes on symbolism. *Internat. J. Psycho-Anal.,* 27:147–157.

Roland, A. (1971), The context and unique function of dreams in psychoanalytic therapy. *Internat. J. Psycho-Anal.,* 52:431–439.

————— (1972), Imagery and symbolic expression in dreams and art. *Internat. J. Psycho-Anal.,* 53:531–539.

Rosen, V. (1969), Sign phenomena and their relationship to unconscious meaning. *Internat. J. Psycho-Anal.,* 50:197–207.

Rosenblatt, A., & Thickston, J. (1977), *Modern Psychoanalytic Concepts in General Psychology.* New York: International Universities Press.

Rycroft, C. (1956), Symbolism and its relationship to the primary and secondary processes. *Internat. J. Psycho-Anal.,* 27:137–157.

————— Gorer, G., Wren-Lewis, J., Storr, A., & Lomas, P. (1966), *Psychoanalysis Observed.* London: Pelican.

Sandler, J., & Rosenblatt, B. (1962), The concept of the representational world. *The Psychoanalytic Study of the Child,* 17:128–134. New York: International Universities Press.

Schafer, R. (1970), An overview of Heinz Hartmann's contributions to psychoanalysis. *Internat. J. Psycho-Anal.,* 51:445–446.

——— (1976), *A New Language for Psychoanalysis.* New Haven, CT: Yale University Press.

——— (1980), Narrative in the psychoanalytic dialogue. In: *On Narrative,* ed. J. W. T. Mitchell. Chicago: University of Chicago Press.

——— (1983), *The Analytic Attitude.* New York: Basic Books.

Schimek, J. (1975), A critical re-examination of Freud's concept of unconscious mental representations. *Internat. Rev. Psychoanal.,* 2:171–187.

Schwartz, P., & Ogilvy, E. G. (1979), The emergent paradigm: Changing patterns of thought and belief. *Analytic Report 7, Values on Lifestyles Program.* Merlo Park, CA: SRI International.

Schweitzer, C. (1991), The Man Who Invented Storm and Stress. *The New York Times Book Review.* July 28:3.

Searles, H. (1962), The differentiation between concrete and metaphorical thinking in the recovering schizophrenic patient. *J. Amer. Psychoanal. Assn.,* 10:22–42.

——— (1965), *Collected Papers on Schizophrenia and Related Subjects.* New York: International Universities Press.

Sechehaye, M. (1951), *Symbolic Realization.* New York: International Universities Press.

Segal, H. (1957), Notes on symbol formation. *Internat. J. Psycho-Anal.,* 38:391–397.

Shapiro, D. (1965), *Neurotic Styles.* New York: Basic Books.

Shapiro, T. (1970), Interpretation and naming. *J. Amer. Psychoanal. Assn.,* 28:399–421.

——— (1971), The symbolic process: A colloquium. *Amer. Imago,* 28:195–215.

——— Emde, R. N., eds. (1992), *Affect: Psychoanalytic Perspectives.* Madison, CT: International Universities Press.

Shevrin, H. (1984), The fate of the five metapsychological principles. *Psychoanal. Inqu.,* 4:33–58.

Silberer, H. (1905), On symbol formation. In: *Organization and Pathology of Thought,* ed. D. Rapaport. New York: Columbia University Press, 1951.

Skinner, B. P. (1938), *The Behavior of Organisms.* New York: Appleton-Century-Crofts.

Slavin, M., & Kriegman, D. (1990), Toward a new paradigm for psychoanalysis: An evolutionary biological perspective on the classical-relational dialectic. *Psychoanal. Psychol.,* 7:5–31.

Spence, D. (1982), *Narrative Truth and Historical Truth.* New York: W. W. Norton.

—— (1987), *The Freudian Metaphor Toward Paradigm Change in Psychoanalysis.* New York: W. W. Norton.

Spencer-Brown, G. (1969), *Laws of Form.* London: Allen & Unwin.

Spitz, R. (1965), *The First Year of Life.* New York: International Universities Press.

Spotnitz, H. (1957), The borderline schizophrenic in group psychotherapy. *Internat. J. Group Psychother.,* 7:155–174.

—— (1968), The management and mastery of resistance in group psychotherapy. *Group,* 1:5–20.

—— (1974), Group psychotherapy with schizophrenics. In: *Group Process Today. Evaluation and Perspective,* ed. D. S. Milman. Springfield, IL: Charles C Thomas.

Steele, R. (1979), Psychoanalysis and hermeneutics. *Internat. Rev. Psychoanal.,* 6:389–409.

—— Jacobsen, P. (1977), From present to past: The development of Freudian theory. *Internat. Rev. Psychoanal.,* 5:393–411.

Stekel, W. (1911), *Die Spraches des Traumes.* Wiesbaden.

Sterba, R. (1934), The fate of the ego in analytic therapy. *Internat. J. Psycho-Anal.,* 15:117–126.

—— (1968), *Introduction to the Psychoanalytic Theory of the Libido,* 3rd ed. New York: Robert Brunner.

Stern, D. (1985), *The Interpersonal World of the Infant.* New York: Basic Books.

Stone, L. (1961), *The Psychoanalytic Situation.* New York: International Universities Press.

Storr, A. (1989), *Freud.* New York: Oxford University Press.

Strachey, J. (1934), On the nature of the therapeutic action in psychoanalysis. *Internat. J. Psycho-Anal.,* 15:127–159.

Sullivan, H. S. (1953), *The Interpersonal Theory of Psychiatry*. New York: W. W. Norton.

Teeter, K. V. (1973), Linguistics and anthropology. *Daedalus*, Summer:87–111.

Thorndike, E. L. (1898), Animal intelligence: An experimental study of the associative processes in animals. *Psychological Review Monograph Supplements*, 2:1–109.

———— (1900), Instinct. *Biological Lectures from the Marine Biological Laboratory of Woods Hole*, 1899:57–67.

Tinbergen, N. (1951), *The Study of Instinct*. Oxford: Oxford University Press.

Titchener, E. B. (1904), *Lectures on the Experimental Psychology of the Thought Processes*. New York: Macmillan.

Tolman, E. C. (1932), *Purposive Behavior in Animals and Man*. New York: Century.

———— (1959), Principles of purposive behavior. In: *Psychology: A Study of Science*, Vol. 2, ed. S. Koch. New York: McGraw-Hill, pp. 92–157.

Tomkins, S. (1984), Affect theory. In: *Approaches to Emotion*, ed. K. R. Scherer & P. Ekman. Hillsdale, NJ: Lawrence Erlbaum.

Toulmin, S. (1953), *The Philosophy of Science*. New York: Harper & Row, 1960.

Turner, V. (1980), Social dramas and stories about them. In: *On Narrative*, ed. J. W. T. Mitchell. Chicago, London: University of Chicago Press, 1980.

———— (1982), *From Ritual to Theatre: The Human Seriousness of Play*. New York: Performing Arts Journal Publications.

Varela, F. (1979), *Principles of Biological Autonomy*. New York: North Holland.

Vignola, G. (1972), *Riti Magici di Ieri e di Oggi*. Milano: Giovanni de Vecchi, Editore.

von Bertalanffy, L. (1950), The theory of open systems. *Science*, 3:23–28.

———— (1952), *Problems of Life and Evaluation of Modern Biological Thought*. London: Watts.

———— (1966), General systems theory and psychiatry. In: *American Handbook of Psychiatry*, Vol. 3, ed. D. A. Herley & H. K. H. Brodie. New York: Basic Books, pp. 705–721.

——— (1968), *General Systems Theory.* New York: Braziller.

von Foerster, H. (1974), Notes for an epistemology of living things. In: *L'Unité de L'Homme,* ed. E. Morin & M. Piatelli. Paris: Seuil.

Vygotsky, L. S. (1962), *Thought and Language.* Cambridge, MA: M.I.T. Press.

Waelder, R. (1936), The principle of multiple function. *Psychoanal. Quart.,* 5:45–62.

Wallerstein, R. S. (1988), One psychoanalysis or many? *Internat. J. Psycho-Anal.,* 69:5–21.

——— (1989), Psychoanalysis: The common ground. Paper presented at the 36th International Psychoanalytic Association Congress, Rome.

Watson, J. B. (1925), *Behaviorism.* New York: People's Institute.

Weiner, N. (1948), *Cybernetics.* New York: John Wiley.

Weinrich, J. D. (1980), Toward a sociobiological theory of emotions. In: *Emotions: Theory, Research and Experience,* Vol. 2, ed. R. Plutchik & H. Kellerman. New York: Academic Press.

Wellek, R., & Warren, A. (1977), *Theory of Literature.* New York: Harcourt, Brace & Jovanovich.

Werner, H. (1940), *Comparative Psychology of Mental Development,* rev. ed. New York: International Universities Press, 1957.

——— Kaplan, B. (1963), *Symbol Formation.* New York: John Wiley, 1967.

Whitehead, A. N. (1927), *Symbolism.* New York: Macmillan.

Wilson, A., & Weinstein, L. (1992a), An investigation into some implications of a Vygotskian perspective on the origin of mind: Psychoanalysis and Vygotskian psychology, Part 1. *J. Amer. Psychoanal. Assn.,* 40:349–379.

——— ——— (1992b), Language and the psychoanalytic process: Psychoanalysis and Vygotskian psychology, Part 2. *J. Amer. Psychoanal. Assn.,* 40:725–759.

Winnicott, D. W. (1953), Transitional objects and transitional phenomena. *Internat. J. Psycho-Anal.,* 34:89–97.

——— (1958), *Collected Papers: Through Paediatrics to Psycho-Analysis.* New York: Basic Books.

——— (1965), *The Maturational Processes and the Facilitating Environment.* New York: International Universities Press.

———— (1971), *Playing and Reality*. New York: Basic Books.

Winson, J. (1986), *Brain and Psyche*. New York: Random House/Vintage.

———— (1990), The meaning of dreams. *Sci. Amer.*, 263:86–96.

Wittgenstein, L. (1953), *Philosophical Investigations*. Oxford: Blackwell.

Wordsworth, W. (1807), Ode. Intimations of immortality from recollections of early childhood. In: *Reading Poems. An Introduction to Critical Study*, 8th ed., ed. T. Wright & S. G. Brown. New York: Oxford University Press, 1941.

Yeats, W. B. (1932), The choice. In: *The Norton Anthology of Modern Poetry*, ed. R. Ellman & R. O'Clair. New York: W. W. Norton, 1973.

Author Index

Subject Index

Abstracting process, 330–331
Abstraction, 82–83, 297–298
  flexibility of, 351–352
  levels of, 371
  as perception of form, 162
  process of, 160
  root of, 158–159
  through symbolization, 309–310
Abstractive mechanism, 155
Abstractive organization, 328
Accommodation, 260
  assimilation and, 296–297
  strategies of, 35–36
Acting out, 305–306
Action language, 138–140
Adaptation, 309
  versus dual drive theory, 112–113
  symbolization and, 151–152
Adolescence, self-awareness and
      identity in, 300–310
Affect. *See also* Emotions
  categorical, 259–260
  grounded in physiological
      functions, 109–116
  monitoring of, 261
  in psychosexual development, 86
  relevance of, 357n
  tolerance of, 116
Affective assimilation, 200–201
Affectivity, organization around,
      268–269
Aggressiveness, instinctual, 104
Aim inhibition, 371–372
Amulet, 207, 274
Analysand, disclaimer locutions of,
      139–140
Analytical thinking, 33–34
Animistic attitude, 283–284
Anna O case, 311–313

Anxiety
  ego and, 135
  at second stage of symbolization,
      346–347
  signaling function of, 350–351
  at third stage of symbolization, 348
Apperceptive insufficiency, 172, 174
Archaeology, process-oriented,
      149–151
Archaic remnants, 167
Archetypal images, 348
Archetypal signs, 265–268
Archetypes, 165–166, 167
Artistic expression, 216–220. *See also*
      Creativity
Assimilation, 200–201, 260
  accommodation and, 296–297
  developmental principle of, 78–79
Associative memories, 248
Associative organizer, 222–223,
      358–359
Associative triggers, 250
Attachment, 105, 143
  constellation of, 105–106
  pleasure and, 347
Authoritarian tradition, 28–29
Autobiography of a Schizophrenic Girl
      (Sechehaye), 191–196
Awareness, expanding areas of,
      325–327

Behavior
  arousal of, 113
  directional gradients in, 106
  patterns of, 142–143
Biology, mental illness and, 354
Brain
  development of, 264
  emotions and, 110–111
  function of, 80
  functional differences in, 111

mnemic, 245–246, 313
multidetermination of, 172
nondiscursive, 244–245, 253, 254,
    338, 369–370
psychoanalytic, 204
reflective, 382
sexual, 165
signals and signs in continuum of,
    206–208
true, 197, 215, 278, 328
as vehicle of thought, 160–161
Syntax, 214
Synthesia, 250–252
Synthetic thinking, 34
Systems theory, 34–35, 37, 38

Taboos, 274
Tactilokinesthetic sensation, 267
Taking in, 121–123
Talking cure, 311–312, 342
Tension, reduction of, 93
Thalamus, 110–111
Thanatos, 56
Theoretical pluralism, 332–333
Theorocentrism, 213
Theory
    based on observations, 11
    subjectivity of, vii–viii
Therapeia, 342
Therapeutic intervention model,
    324–328
Thermodynamics, second law of, 36
Thing presentation, 237, 285
Thing-cathexis, 270–271, 280
Thought processes, 242–243. *See also*
    Primary process thinking;
    Secondary process thinking
Three Essays on the Theory of Sexuality
    (Freud), 68, 94n
Tonal communication, 269–270
Topographical model, 16, 129,
    379–380
    core of, 235
Totems, 274
Transfiguration, 373–374
Transformation, 235, 323, 360–361

concept of, 220–223
ideas of, 367–368
nature of, 360–385
structural, 372
sublimation as, 370–371
from unconscious to conscious,
    227–229
Transformational process, 222,
    318–328, 372, 381
    abstraction in, 330–331
    mystery of, 238
Transformational redemption,
    374–375
Transformational stories, 368–369
Transformational unit, 358–359
Transmutation, 368–385, 375–376
Transmuting internalizations, 123
Trust-mistrust crisis, 76–77
Trustworthiness, special criteria for,
    48
Truth, 26

Unconscious
    becoming conscious, 124–127
    core of, 243
    dream images and, 268–270
    Freudian vs. Jungian, 165–167
    phenomenology of, 236–237
    single, 29–30n
    types of, 252–253
Unconscious fantasy, 212
Unconscious knowledge, 253
Unconscious mental processes, 128
Unconscious mental representation,
    10
    ambiguity of, 117
Unconscious-conscious dimension,
    233, 235. *See also*
    Transformation;
    Transformational process
Understanding, hermeneutic task of,
    30–31
Undifferentiated sensorimotor
    experience, 121
Unified theory, x–xi
    lack of, 13–14

Were I to be writing this book today, I would have included the works of A.R. Damasio, J. LeDoux, G.E. Lakoff, M. Johnson, G.E. Edelman, and E.O. Wilson, all of whom have since made contributions that amplify our study of the many aspects of mind that psychoanalysis encompasses. I would also be indebted to the Biosemiotic interdisciplinary community for inspiring me to bring theoretical psychoanalysis into international academic circles, and especially to the ideas of Professor Marcello Barbieri in his comprehensive integration of body and mind, biology and semiosis, along evolutionary lines.

—A.A.

www.ingramcontent.com/pod-product-compliance
Lightning Source LLC
Chambersburg PA
CBHW072040020426
42334CB00017B/1343